A Firstbook of Old English

A FIRSTBOOK

OF OLD ENGLISH

Revised Edition

by Robert D. Stevick

Wipf and Stock Publishers
Eugene, Oregon

Wipf and Stock Publishers
199 West 8th Avenue, Suite 3
Eugene, OR 97401

A Firstbook of Old English
Revised Edition
By Robert D. Stevick

ISBN 1–59244–353–2

PREFACE

The text of this book is of my own making. Its coming to be, its make-up, its final form, and its publication owe a great deal to many others. It is fitting to express my thanks to them at the outset.

To Kenkyusha Publications, Ltd., and particularly to Mr. Yoshiaki Hamamatsu, who undertook publication of this book I am most grateful. In turn, I wish to express my deep gratitude to Professor Shoichi Oguro, who introduced the text to Kenkyusha; if he had not done so, it would in all likelihood still be a private set of instructional materials.

Members of the Humanities and Arts Computing Center (HACC), University of Washington (Seattle), offered help of many kinds, all of them important, some of them crucial: initially, Dr. Gerald Barnett brought about the essential transition from typewriter to computer format for the text, knowing how to do this and why it needed to be done; from outset to final text, Dr. Thomas B. Ridgeway, Director of HACC, knew what had to be done, whether in PC technology, font design, or book production, and provided the ample and essential help; Dr. Stacy Waters understood the process and solved assorted problems; Elizabeth Tachikawa quietly gave the right cues and suggestions that could come only from someone who knew Old English and the technology for presenting it. Dr. Eric Dahl and Dr. Ruth L. Harris most helpfully read, emended, and proofed portions of the text at various stages.

The make-up of the book—it almost goes without saying—relies heavily on the standard treatments of Old English. The major ones are cited separately at the end of Chapter 1, a number of others at various places in the book. The study of Old English has had exemplary development from the outset of Indo-European philology, but most recently in the production of a complete concordance, a comprehensive grammar, a lengthy syntax, not to mention editions of texts, examination of particular facets of the language, and study of literary sources.

Thanks finally are offered to those forces of fate which brought about my own interest in Old English, and specifically the teaching of it. Professor Frederic G. Cassidy was my first teacher of Old English. The rest of the history is too diffuse to try to record.

PREFACE TO REVISED EDITION

Because the original publisher, Kenkyusha Publications, Ltd., did not under-take distribution of this book in North America or the Commonwealth, a new publisher was needed if this textbook is to be readily available and appropriately priced outside Eastern Asia. With permission of the original publisher, Wipf and Stock Publishers are undertaking publication of this, a revised edition of the book published originally in 1992. While the text is generally the same as in the original edition, this new edition permits expansions, revisions, corrections where needed, and thorough re-writing of the Introduction and of the appendix describing grammatical number, gender, and case.

With this revision, it may be appropriate to recommend a sequence of lessons that will make best use of its second-language instruction potential.

I   The language and its speakers (Chapter 1);
      Phonology and graphemics of Old English (Chapter 2, Appendix A).

II   Pronouns, pronominals, designators (Chapter 3.1–2 and 3.4);
      also basic verbs (Chapter 6.1–2).

III Nouns and noun phrases (Chapter 5 and Appendix C);
      also more basic verbs (Chapter 6.3–4).

IV Quasi-pronominals, indefinites (Chapter 3.3 and 3.5).
      Reading: Ælfric's Sermon on the Nativity.

V   Adjectives and adverbs (Chapter 4).
      Reading: continue to Ælfric's Passion of St. Edmund.

VI Remaining Verbs (Chapter 6.5–8).
      Reading: conclude the two Ælfric texts.

—   Continue prose readings, beginning with The Legend of St. Andrew, and only then proceed to verse readings. Also, Appendix B.

CONTENTS

Part Two: Readings

Part One

GRAMMAR

INTRODUCTION

Ġenōh byð sōþlīċe þām leorning-cnihte þæt hē sȳ swylċe his lārēow.

Two purposes underlie beginning courses in Old English. One is to bring students along far enough in learning this ancestral form of English that they can read texts, literary and historical, from the times of King Alfred and Abbot Ælfric. The other is to introduce students to elements of Old English as they supply a crucial part of the history of English, standing at the beginning of the recorded history of the language. The purposes may be called 'literary' and 'philological' (or 'linguistic').

The books widely used for basic courses have their several merits, and it is noteworthy that through editions dating back more than a century, *Sweet's Anglo-Saxon Primer* continues to do good service. These books tend, though, to take the form of condensed grammar books, and to be organized according to grammarians' traditional categories. Some of them have graded readings along with the gobbets of grammar. The morphology marches through in the close formation of boldface paradigms: the 'strong' ranks lead, followed by the 'weak,' then the 'minor,' and lastly the 'anomalous.' The phonology appears in these books typically as a reflex of West Germanic, so that the sounds of the language are presented essentially as the results of centuries of sound changes. In this context it is easy then to claim that irregularities, say, in verb conjugation are not much more than lightly veiled regularities that become recognizable as soon as the pre-history of English sounds is mastered(!). Or, the phonology is laid out as a compact set of directions for assigning sounds to letters: '**g** often occurs between **i** and **e**, while **g**(**e**) may also replace **i**.' The syntax—dealt with in any detail only in the more recent textbooks—is also compactly summarized under grammarians' rubrics, not in the speaker's typical 'transformational' patterns.

The information as usually presented is valuable, and certainly it does enable students to learn the language. But the conventional presentations do not provide some other useful materials: specifically, they provide neither students nor instructors with the most effective materials for developing early and firmly the kinds of language skills which a speaker or reader normally makes use of in speaking or reading. A conventionalized mélange of philologists' formulations (with or without extended treatment of syntax), useful as it is for some historical and comparative and analytic purposes in language study, is less efficient for a beginner than what this book tries to provide: descriptions accompanied by practice lists that introduce normal constructions—phrases and sentences—as early as is practicable.

While the purposes of this book, too, are literary and philological, its aims and methods make it different in format and in some of its contents from the reference-manual (or even teach-yourself) types of book. It aims, first, to avoid conditioning a student merely to replace Old English texts piecemeal with Modern English lexical equivalents—word-for-word or even phrase-by-phrase. Instead, it is intended to help a student learn to read Old English texts in Old English. That is the reason for including the extensive practice lists.

To a large extent, translation is treated as only a heuristic device—a help along the way to reading the earliest English texts. Glossing in the descriptions and illustrations sometimes gives an equivalent for an entire phrase or sentence, or sometimes offers alternative translations for a single Old English word. There is no way in which a glossary can tell the correct meaning of þā (to take the simplest kind of example). Its meaning in a given context is not best arrived at by a process of elimination of glossary and paradigm items—looking through a list until a meaning is found that makes sense (and hoping to find no more than one that does); it must be recognized immediately by its position in relation to a following noun, in relation to clause onset, in relation to inferred degree of stress. **Wræc** may mean either 'exile' (noun) or 'uttered' (past tense of verb): the thing to be learned first and with complete confidence is to recognize **wræc** as verb or as noun—the meaning then can be looked up in a glossary or dictionary, if that is necessary. The adjacent glossing regularly included with the illustrations and readings is there only to assist a student in making direct linguistic response to a complete utterance that is best read and heard and analyzed in Old English.

A second aim is to serve the needs of historical study of English. That study customarily begins (in detail) with King Alfred's West Saxon English. Descriptions of Old English accordingly will be accommodated chiefly to the subsequent rather than to the antecedent history of language; the orientation of English among early Germanic languages is mostly left for later study.

The method of presenting Old English is that of supplying descriptions accompanied by illustrations plentiful enough to serve as drills. The descriptions are presented economically, the illustrations tend to be profuse. In this regard the method will also be quite unlike those methods specially worked out to have students trying to read certain set texts from the outset. Rather, the primary intention here is for the descriptions and illustrations to enable a student to comprehend Old English as both analytic knowledge and language habits—being able ultimately to reconstruct the 'rules' of the language from examples, or to supply examples to illustrate any rule. It is urged, therefore,

that the instructor's role be active in each part of the twofold plan, not only re-
peating, recasting, and supplementing the descriptions as students may require,
but implementing the drills (even extending them) with the sense of timing
and emphasis that experience has taught. For a student it is urged that the
illustrations and practice lists be read and studied enough that by reflection
and analysis the corresponding descriptions can be reformulated from the Old
English materials themselves.

The presentation of Old English in this book is therefore not at all compact.
While it is possible to distil the main facts about Old English phonology into
two or three pages (as in Appendix A), they are presented here in detail and
illustrated profusely through about forty pages (Chapter 2), because fluency in
interpreting the written forms is gained from practice, not from reading (and re-
reading) a compact description. The greater the fluency, the better a person can
proceed in learning the grammar of the language and ultimately in appreciating
its literature. There is another benefit to be gained from the copious illustrations
of the sounds and sound patterns of Old English. Because all the practice
words have Modern English glosses, the relations between the vocabularies of
Old and Modern English rapidly can be recognized: some words such as **henn**
'hen' and **finger** 'finger' persist, others such as **wange** 'cheek' and **giedd** 'song,
saying' do not; those with short vowels usually keep them, those with long
stem vowels systematically change in pronunciation, and so on. In morphology,
the forms of the pronouns and pronominals can be laid out in a page or two.
Fluency in recognizing the forms here again should be aided by the illustrations.
In addition, the *system* of inflections of nominal elements of the language is
introduced with a quite simple set of forms, rather than along with the initially
bewildering variety of noun inflections. A flowchart fitting easily on a single page
will 'capture' the distribution of **the** in Modern English but it will never teach a
person how to use the definite article (especially if that person's first language
is not European); the same point can be made about the related forms (**se,
sēo, þæt**) in Old English. Aspects of Old English syntax are presented through
examples, primarily, rather than through discursive description: patterns of
coordination, of concord, of ordering of principal elements, and the like are
provided with multiple illustrations throughout Chapters 3, 4, 5, 6.

Although the descriptions of grammatical matters are kept brief, they are
regularly keyed to three standard reference works, A. Campbell's *Old English
Grammar* (*OEG*), Bruce Mitchell's *Old English Syntax* (*OES*), and F. Th.
Visser's *An Historical Syntax of the English Language* (*HSEL*).

This book is also unusual in ordering its materials according to their frequency of occurrence and their potential for immediate utility. It is in just those

elements that are most frequent that English has undergone least change—the pronoun system, interrogative forms, the 'everyday' nouns, verbs, and adjectives. Within each of the chapters on morphology, therefore, the most frequently occurring forms are introduced earliest. Thus, the verbs are arranged in just the reverse of the traditional sequence: anomalous verbs come first, Weak verbs Class III precede Class II and Class I verbs, and Strong verbs follow Weak—the Old English forms of **be**, **do**, **have** are introduced before the ancestral forms of **teach**, **sing**, **write**, **swear**. Before the conjugations and declensions, still more fundamental elements are explained and illustrated fully; these include the stress-patterns in compounds, the clustering patterns of consonants, the distribution patterns of long and short vowels. For similar reasons, within the chapter on phonology vowels are introduced first (no word occurs without at least one), then stop and resonant consonants (/**p t k b d g m n l r**/) which have not changed significantly, and only then the spirants, which have changed considerably, so that at every stage whatever is learned subsequently can be learned without at the same time re-inforcing any wrong guesses about the sounds of Old English and how they were written. Even so, the larger organization by chapters, together with the appendices, stays with the formal categories of English grammar for other, equally valid pedagogical reasons. It is far easier to re-locate information about any item if the items are grouped by their affinities—class of sounds, part of speech, grammatical category of inflection. In addition, it is easier to learn about strong verbs, or the grammatical case system, and the like if the descriptions and illustrations for any of these topics are grouped together.

The extensive lists for illustration and practice have been selected and arranged with special care. They make up, in fact, a virtual workbook built into the various chapters and their parts. The typical layout of two columns for these lists puts Old English text on the left: that is the exercise—or problem—column. The Modern English equivalent on the right provides the answers, or solutions. To hide and to reveal the answers needs nothing more technologically advanced than movement of the reader's hand, either by itself, or augmented by a card or piece of paper.

In these practice and illustration lists, the chapter on phonology, for instance, introduces many Old English words cognate with Modern English words, to make apparent by example the ways they can be recognized. Many of them are words that occur frequently and are the kind that can be learned early. There are also examples chosen to illustrate phonemic contrasts and inflectional variants. In the chapters on morphology the paradigms and illustrative lists employ many words of high frequency of occurrence, and phrase and sentence examples are selected so that many of the lexical items are repeated. The prose readings have been chosen for their internal repetition of forms and constructions, as well as for their clarity in sustained, good Old English. The verse readings illustrate translations, paraphrases, and free composition in Old English, without duplicating most of the heavily edited texts that are readily available in grammars and popular anthologies. The established 'canon' may be better approached after learning the basic language, rather than as the medium for learning it.

No obvious division between Early West Saxon and Late West Saxon has been made in the selection of materials and readings. Differences between the English of Alfred and that of Ælfric, real as they are, do not need to be presented in detail during introductory study. The Schriftsprache established in the late tenth century builds on Alfred's earlier Wessex dialect and constitutes the 'classical' Old English of Ælfric, the poetic codices, and beyond. Whatever notice is given to differences between Early and Late West Saxon concerns phonology and spelling and any inflectional variants contingent upon phonological change. Where distinction is made, mainly in the paradigms, Early West Saxon is offered as providing the essential, basic data, for reasons paralleled generally in language history: later features may be derived from earlier ones, but features that do not persist in fact or in effect cannot be reconstructed.

Finally, the design of this textbook intentionally dispenses with a whole-book glossary, depending rather on a student's use of a dictionary. Glossaries belong to specific texts, not to sets of examples encompassing the conjugation of '(to) be,' the comparison of adjectives, passive verb constructions, and so on through the grammar of Old English. Glossings are implicit and inseparable in the lists for pronunciation practice. They are joined to some of the verse texts among the Readings, typically as line-by-line glosses on the facing pages. But for some prose texts in the Readings, as well as for illustrations throughout this textbook, a dictionary should be the normal, ready source of lexical information. Glossaries tend to say 'translate that word with this word,' while dictionaries say 'here is the range of meanings the word had in Old English.' A glossary can help in reading a particular text, but a dictionary can help in learning a language.

Witodlīċe sē þe þurhwunað oð ende, sē byþ hāl.

Chapter 1

THE LANGUAGE AND ITS SPEAKERS

In England now it is sometimes possible to stand at an excavation site where a new building is to be constructed and in a sense to see just where and when Old English was spoken. Along the main street of an old city, with a department store, a chemist's shop, a tourist information office, a hi-fi store, there may be a large hole in the ground and a team of archeologists with brushes, shovels, wheelbarrows carefully uncovering remains of earlier constructions. At the lowest level of excavation may be the stone paving of a Roman road; at a higher level the foundations of an Anglo-Saxon church; at a still higher level some artifacts dated to the fourteenth century, and so on, up to the present street level. The contours of the land have changed very little (though the vegetation may be altogether changed), and the same river runs through the lower end of town that ran through it in Anglo-Saxon times, Roman times, and times much earlier than these. Old English was spoken in this settlement, along this street, at a time a little 'above' Roman Britain but still well 'below' the present time.

This language began as dialectal speech of West Germanic peoples who migrated to the British Isles. The dialectal varieties were mutually intelligible among those who migrated, and for a long time with dialects of those who did not. The migration began with some uninvited settlers and with mercenary warriors hired to protect an outpost of the Roman empire left unprotected by withdrawal of Roman military forces. It continued when the mercenaries saw the fertility of the land and the possibility of taking of it what they wanted. Over several generations their linguistic and cultural relatives crossed the channel from the European continent to the main island to the northwest. Old English survived because enough of those who migrated after the mid fifth century moved as families and groups, with the result that they formed self-sufficient communities. Their children learned English first, any other language secondarily, and their native language remained either their sole or their principal language; their descendants kept to the same social pattern. A measure of the separateness of the Germanic peoples in Britain is the nearly complete absence of Roman and British words adopted into their language, and most notably those of place-names.

When the migration began—and for much of the subsequent history of Old English—these people spoke a minority language, and one without prestige; at the outset it was also a language without written records. It was only one of the languages spoken in Britain, along with Pictish, Irish, British, and Latin (and presumably others unrecorded). Only gradually did English come to be the majority language of the island.

The name of the language evolved during the early history of its speakers: **englisc** 'English' was formed from one of the national names, **Engle** 'the Angles,' similar to modern **Dane** : **Danish**, and the like. These peoples were only one of the three major nations of Germanic peoples who had migrated to Britain, and why their name became the basis for the generic name for the many Germanic dialects of the island is a question not yet resolved with likelihood of finality. Much of the reason a single language with a single name evolved, however, is very clear from the history of the time and place: the geographical confines of the island, its attacks from outside the island, the gradually developing sense of place among European peoples, and the adoption of a single, formalized religion (Christianity) by most of the inhabitants of the English language community.

Its now being called 'Old English' is the result of the development in modern times of an interest in knowing about the past. For the history of English, that interest began in issues of religious contention in England in the time of Elizabeth I, Shakespeare, Marlowe, the 'King James translation' of the Bible; developed fitfully in the next three hundred years; then with astonishing speed gave rise to a social science of about the most rigorous kind to survive its early development. Essentially, when the history of the English language became a genuine discipline of knowing, the earliest form of the language known through written records was given the name 'Old English.' The lexicon of comparative chronology dictated the rest: at the other end of the historical perspective was 'New' (or 'Modern') English, with a single term between, 'Middle English.'

Pacing off a thousand-year history of this language in only four giant and uneven strides shows changes like the those illustrated on the following page.

Language does not move in discrete stages from old to middle to modern, although understanding of its history is made easier when it is presented—or represented—that way. Rather, it changes continually. And so it is that the forms of the Old English language in the chapters following will not have the rigid consistency customary with modern, 'educated,' writing-based English. The earliest writers of English represented their language in an intelligent and untrammeled way: if the language differed among its dialects, if it differed from one half century to the next, most of them wrote the language as they knew it in speech. The only attempt to standardize the language seems to have been in the late tenth century, by the Benedictines, but this attempt was limited chiefly to a few lexical items.

And when they drew near to Jerusalem ... and Bethany, at the Mount of Olives, he sent two of his disciples, and said to them, Go into the village opposite you and as you enter it you will find a colt tied, on which no one has ever sat; untie it and bring it. If any one says to you, Why are you doing this? say, The Lord has need of it [and he will immediately send it here]. (Revised Standard, 1946. Present-day English)

And when they cam nye to Hierusalem ... and Bethani, be-sydes mount olivete, he sent forth two of his disciplies, And sayde vnto them, Goo youre wayes into the toune that is over agaynste you; and as sone as ye entre into it ye shall fynde a coolte bounde, where on never man sate; loose hym, and brynge hym hidder. And if eny man saye vnto you, Why do ye soo? saye, the Lorde hath neade of him, and streight waye he wyll sende hym hidder. (Tyndale, 1526. Very early Modern English)

And whanne Jhesus cam nyȝ to Jerusalem and to Betanye, to the mount of Olyues, he sendith tweyne of hise disciplis, and seith to hem, Go ȝe in to the castel that is aȝens ȝou; and anoon as ȝe entren there ȝe sculen fynde a colt tied, on which no man hath sete ȝit; vntie ȝe, and bringe hym. And if ony man seye ony thing to ȝou, What doen ȝe? seie ȝe, that he is nedeful to the lord, and anon he schal leeue hym hidir. (Wycliffe-Purvey, c. 1390. Very late Middle English)

Ða he ȝenealæhte Hierusalem and Bethania, to Oliuetes dune, he sende his tweȝen leorninȝ-cnihtas, And cwæþ to him, Faraþ to ðam castele ðe onȝen inc ys; and ȝyt ðar sona ȝemetaþ assan folan ȝetiȝedne, ofer ðæne nan man ȝyt ne sæt; untiȝeaþ hine and to me ȝelædaþ. And ȝyf hwa to inc hwæt cwyþ, secȝaþ, ðæt Dryhten hæfþ his neode, and he hine sona hider læt. (West Saxon translation, c. 1000. Late Old English)

When did Old English begin? It began with the migration, conquest, and settlement of Britain by speakers of dialects of West Germanic, but became distinct only when the speech of the Germanic peoples in Britain began to diverge from the speech of the West Germanic peoples elsewhere. These things occurred over the course of about five hundred years, starting in the fifth century in the chronology of the Christian calendar. Or about a thousand to fifteen hundred years ago. Or about forty to sixty generations ago, or about twenty to thirty grandparent-through-grandchild steps. Or about ninety percent of technology ago (as if that could be measured). Or maybe twenty percent of the chronological span of the Indo-European language family (a guess, perhaps several times too large).

When did it end? In a cultural sense, it has not ended, because English spoken today is that same language evolved by innumerable steps almost none of which its speakers ever noticed. Yet the form of the language now called 'Old English'—the earliest form of the language known through written records—ceased to be intelligible a few generations after it was spoken (it survived only in written form, of course). It was in the twelfth century, to use a crude demarcation, that Old English was succeeded by Middle English.

In its own time Old English had the characteristic features of the Germanic languages with little admixture. In common with its immediately cognate languages—that is, the other Germanic languages—English had in its structural basis five features that less cognate European languages did not have. One is the morphology of the verb system. Only two tenses were distinguished by inflectional variation (past and non-past), and the passive voice was phrasal, not inflectionally marked. Furthermore, there was a system of 'weak' verbs alongside another major system called 'strong' verbs. The 'strong' verbs mark contrasts of tense by alternate vowels in the word root, as *sing–sang* or *write–wrote* or *sit–sat*, and one of the participial forms is further also marked in this way—*sung, written, sat*—corresponding historically to patterns in other Indo-European languages. The distinctively Germanic 'weak' verbs mark these contrasts and forms by suffixes which contain a dental stop consonant, that is, either *d* or *t*, with a preceding vowel if the pronunciation system requires it. Old English *fylle–fylde* or *deme–demde* or *lufie–lufode* correspond to Modern English *fill–filled*, or *deem–deemed* or *love–loved*.

A second Germanic feature of English is the system of 'weak' adjectives alongside another system called 'strong' adjectives. Adjectives had grammatical inflections (in suffixes) for case, gender, and number, but there were separate sets of inflections, selected according to the presence or absence of a marker of definiteness within a noun phrase; for example, 'those good men' was expressed as **þas godan menn**, with weak adjective declension, while 'good men' was expressed as **gode menn** (see 4.1 Declension of Uncompared Adjectives).

A third characteristic is found in its lexicon—the stock of words of the language. For example, the English names of the cardinal directions, *north, south, west, east* are distinctively Germanic. So are topographical terms for *sea, sound, island, strand*, food terms such as *brew, broth, knead, dough, loaf*, titles such as *king* and *earl*, and the terms *book* and *write*.

Two other characteristics concern the speech sounds. Word accent was manifest as stress—loudness—of a particular syllable (as opposed, say, to pitch variation); and it was fixed on a given syllable in a word, whatever changes in syllable structure the word might have when grammatical inflections or derivational affixes were attached to it. In short, Germanic languages utilized a *fixed stress-accent* in the phonological structure of words.

Finally, consonant sounds of the Germanic languages included a set of stop and fricative units (shown in the box to the right) that had drifted systematically from the corresponding sounds in the non-Germanic Indo-European languages (shown in box to the left). (This drift is formulated in 'Grimm's Law.')

bh	$\longrightarrow$	b	$\longrightarrow$	p	$\longrightarrow$	f
dh	$\longrightarrow$	d	$\longrightarrow$	t	$\longrightarrow$	th
gh	$\longrightarrow$	g	$\longrightarrow$	k	$\longrightarrow$	h

First Germanic Consonant Shift ('Grimm's Law')

These distinctive features of the Germanic languages, from a common heritage, provide the explanation from historical development for the resemblance of English to German, Dutch, Frisian, and less directly to Swedish, Norwegian, Danish, Icelandic—in all respects other than in word-stock.

Most speakers of Old English could neither read nor write. As a result, the records of this language were made almost exclusively by and for small religious communities of Christians, the only people for whom reading and writing was essential. According to N. R. Ker, 'The extant literary manuscripts written entirely or mainly in OE before *c.* 1200 number less than 150, including fragments. If we add to that number the Latin-OE glossaries, the Latin texts which are furnished with a complete OE translation, ... and the mainly Latin manuscripts which contain a substantial amount of OE..., the total is still short of 200' (*Catalogue of Manuscripts Containing Anglo-Saxon*, xiv). Ker's Index to the Contents of the Manuscripts will show at a glance the nature of most of the writings that survive: homilies make the longest list, by far; the other main topics are laws and liturgies, grammar and computus, and poetry. These preserve a Schriftsprache—a non-casual, edited form of the language used for history, land-deeds, religious texts and translations—but they leave unrecorded the use of language for everyday conversation, threats and imprecations, children's play, and the like.

However else the speakers of Old English may be identified or known, they are a people who had their turn at learning, using, transmitting English. That was a millenium past and half that again. The language served all who spoke or understood it. They had neither the guidance nor the censureship of newspaper columnists or English teachers or government commissions or language planners or courts of law—no class or agency to tell them how to use their language. It was a language learned in its community, used for any and all social purposes, and transmitted unselfconsciously.

Some standard sources for the history of the Anglo-Saxons and of their language are the following.

David Hill, *An Atlas of Anglo-Saxon England*, contains a series of maps and commentaries representing many fundamental aspects of the culture of the speakers of Old English—settlement patterns, mining and agriculture, campaigns, and such. See also W. G. Hoskins, *The Making of the English Landscape* (1955), rev. (1988) with introduction and commentary by Christopher Taylor.

The *Historia Ecclesiastica Gentis Anglorum* by the Venerable Bede is the primary source of information about Anglo-Saxon England from the Germanic migrations to the early eighth century (when it was written); several English translations have been published.

Two general histories have become standard: Peter Hunter Blair, *An Introduction to Anglo-Saxon England* (1959), and F. M. Stenton, *Anglo-Saxon England* (1943). *The Origin of Anglo-Saxon Kingdoms*, ed. Steven Bassett (1989), studies a crucial social-political development early in Anglo-Saxon culture. Also, R. H. Hodgkin, *A History of the Anglo-Saxons*; D. J. V. Fisher, *The Anglo-Saxon Age* (1973); R. I. Page, *Life in Anglo-Saxon England* (1970); P. H. Sawyer, *From Roman Britain to Norman England* (2nd ed. 1998); J. Campbell, E. John, and P. Wormald, *The Anglo-Saxons* (1982); T. D. Kirby, *The Earliest English Kings* (1990).

J. N. L. Myres, *The English Settlements*, The Oxford History of England (1986), deals with the relation between the conditions in Roman Britain and the migration of the Germanic peoples in the period before the re-introduction of Christianity in Britain at the end of the sixth century. This was a period from which very little documentary evidence survives, so that topography, place-name evidence, and archeological finds are the principal sources of the history for this fundamental event in the evolution of Old English.

Virtually everything written in Old English to have survived has been published in edited form during the past century and a half, in one form or another. All the writings have been gathered for the preparation of *The Dictionary of Old English* whose first fascicles began appearing in microfiche in 1986. A complete concordance to the extant writings in Old English is available in two parts: R. L. Venezky and A. diPaolo Healey, comp., *A Microfiche Concordance to Old*

English, and R. L. Venezky and S. Butler, comp., *A Microfiche Concordance to Old English: The High Frequency Words* (1980 and 1985, respectively).

The principal dictionary (until *The Dictionary of Old English* is completed) is J. Bosworth and T. N. Toller, eds. *An Anglo-Saxon Dictionary* (1882–98); rpt. 1972. A shorter one (without citations and classified definitions) is J. R. Clark Hall, *A Concise Anglo-Saxon Dictionary*; 4th ed. with supplement by H. D. Meritt (1969). Also, C. W. M. Grein, *Sprachschatz der Angelsächsischen Dichter*, 2 Aufl. hg. J. J. Köhler (1912); Nachdruck (1974). Further, Charles T. Carr, *Nominal Compounds in Germanic* (1939), and Victor Strite, *Old English Semantic-Field Studies* (1984).

The standard reference grammar is A. Campbell, *Old English Grammar* (1959); rpt. 1977. Still serviceable is J. Wright and E. M. Wright, *Old English Grammar*, 3rd. ed. (1925); rpt. 1972. Using more recent linguistic theory is Richard M. Hogg, *A Grammar of Old English*, vol. 1: Phonology (1992). Of related interest, Willard James Rusch, *The Language of the East Midlands and the Development of Standard English* (York 1992).

Bruce Mitchell, *Old English Syntax*, 2 vols. (1985), is the most comprehensive of the treatments of syntax. Very useful for presenting Old English syntax within the history of the language is F. Th. Visser, *An Historical Syntax of the English Language*, 3 Parts (4 vols) (1963–1973).

A clear and practical description of the linguistic context of Old English is in Orrin W. Robinson, *English and Its Closest Relatives* (1992).

Three textbooks for beginning study of the language are especially to be recommended: Henry Sweet, *An Anglo-Saxon Primer*, 15th ed. rev. Dorothy Whitelock, as *Sweet's Anglo-Saxon Primer* (1967) with subsequent reprintings with corrections; S. Moore and T. Knott, *The Elements of Old English* (1925), with subsequent revision and reprintings; and R. Quirk and C. L. Wrenn, *An Old English Grammar*, 2nd ed. (1977), with later reprintings.

A review of the study of Old English and a consideration of 'the role of Anglo-Saxon studies in the postmodern age' is found in Allen J. Frantzen, *Desire for Origins: New Language, Old English, and Teaching the Tradition* (1990).

Two bibliographies provide important help. One is Stanley B. Greenfield and Fred C. Robinson, *A Bibliography of Publications on Old English Literature to the End of 1972* (1980). The other is Phillip Pulsiano, *An Annotated Bibliography of North American Doctoral Disserations on Old English Language and Literature* (1988). Both can be supplemented by annual bibliographic information published in the *Old English Newsletter*, in *Anglo-Saxon England*, or in *PMLA*.

All these sources are now extended and supplemented by various websites.

Chapter 2

THE SOUNDS OF OLD ENGLISH

2.0 How the Sounds Are Known

Evidence for what Old English speech sounded like is essentially the collection of writings that have survived from the Anglo-Saxon period of English history, all of them set down in an alphabetical system for recording linguistic messages.

An alphabetical system of writing represents only certain speech *sounds*, and only indirectly therefore can it record forms that have meanings (words, suffixes, and such), or sentence patterns, or meanings. Such a system serves to provide a graphic analog of the distinctive sounds in an utterance of any kind, as those sounds occur sequentially—a string of symbols ('letters') representing a succession of sounds. The purpose of the writing is to make a copy (of sorts) of what has been said which can be kept or carried, because it does not disappear as speech does as soon as the saying is done. The kinds of sounds to come along as it were in a row—one, then another, then another—are the so-called segmental units, that is, the vowels and consonants.

For this continuous component of Old English phonology evidence is more than ample. It requires interpretation, nonetheless, because the writing system was worked out by people who spoke Old English, not Modern English (or any other modern language), and because they were adapting a system that had been worked out for another language. As everyone knows who has learned another European language, the sounds of one language differ from those of another, on the one hand; and on the other, the roman alphabet—even with addition of umlaut, cedilla, circumflex, or other diacritical marks—represents sounds differently from one language to the next: *r* stands for quite different sounds in English, German, French, Spanish. Even so, adaptation of the same alphabet to the writing of many languages in the European past, and within the span of only a few centuries, has preserved a useful context for interpreting the evidence in Anglo-Saxon writings for the speech sounds they represented.

The most important part of this context is the fact that the roman system was the one used for writing Latin, the principal international language of western Europe in the Middle Ages. It was also a relatively stable language during this period, for being a language learned almost exclusively in schools, hence as a second language, and being usable only in communities (such as monasteries) where it was spoken only among persons for whom it was a second language; it was thus much less exposed to the social factors that cause language change than were the vernaculars. The nature of Christianity, which fostered and spread this system of writing, was another conservative factor, in that it included the requirement of keeping accurately the written texts on which its doctrines and traditions were based. Not least important is that Latin has been in use continuously down to the present day. All these factors make Latin a relatively fixed point of reference for interpreting the sounds underlying the early written records of the languages written in the same alphabet—and usually written by persons who learned their writing system with Latin. There are in fact a number of texts in Old English written by persons who were expert in Latin. Some manuscripts contain both Latin and English copied by the same person. There are even several copies of a grammar of Latin written in Old English.

Interpreting the written evidence is essentially a problem in understanding the 'fit' of the roman alphabet to the sound system of Old English. That fit was made very intelligently by the Anglo-Saxons, even if it is not perfect by any means. The simple letters they used for vowels (**a e i o u y**) were too few to represent the separate vowels of the language, and little was done to make up for this lack beyond adding **æ**. The most glaring deficiency was in the distinction between short and long vowels. The system worked well enough for those who knew the language, just as the modern system seems to work well enough despite the potential for confusion caused by such ambiguous spellings as *wind* and *wound* (nouns and verbs), *axes* and *fertile* (and there seems to be little interest in eliminating the multiplicity of ways to spell a single sound). Modern English has inherited a mixture of ways devised later to keep long and short vowels apart in writing, such as doubling vowel letters (but only *ee* and *oo* are still used) to represent long vowels, spelling a final *-e* after a single consonant (*fate, note, bite*) to signify length of the preceding vowel, or doubling following consonants to signify the preceding vowel is short (*letter–later, litter– liter, winner, simmer, silly*), but these were devised sometime later than the Old English period. Otherwise, the vowels of the language, along with the diphthongs, were spelled adequately with single symbols or double symbols (**ea, ie**, etc.).

The fit of the alphabet for the consonants was a bit better, with **p b t d m n l r h** transfering without problem. English sounds now spelled **th** (*ether, either, thigh, thy*) did not occur in Latin and new spellings had to be devised; that problem had more than one easy solution. Less successful was the use of **g** to represent three different sounds, **c** to represent two, and so on. It is

in the instances of letters standing for more than one sound that it becomes
important to add diacritical marks in grammars, dictionaries, and instructional
materials—distinguishing **a** from **ā**, **c** from **ċ**, and the like.

If the essential evidence for what the sounds were is the spelling of Old
English texts, then how is it we can know that some letters represented two
or even three different sounds, or that two letters sometimes represented one
distinctive unit rather than two? The answer lies in the wider context of the
written records. And the principal part of that context is the continuous record
of the writing of English from Anglo-Saxon times to the present. If **god** unques-
tionably means 'good' at one time, 'god' at another, if **æl** means 'awl' and also
'eel,' if **ham** means 'ham' except when it means 'home,' we have modern English
word-pairs differing only in the single vowel in each; and when the history of
English vowels is reconstructed, it becomes apparent that there must have been
pairs of words in Old English, too, that differed in pronunciation by only their
root vowel, even when they are spelled the same way. (A number of examples
occur in the illustrative lists to follow.) It is this kind of evidence multiplied
many times over that establishes the fact that there were two sounds spelled **a**,
two spelled **o**, and so on. In a still larger context, the continuous records of other
languages—especially the Germanic languages—confirm and refine the picture
of the sounds and spellings of the Anglo-Saxons. (A very thorough review of
the sound system is found in Richard M. Hogg, *A Grammar of Old English*,
Vol. 1: Phonology (1992).)

Even if alphabetic writing had been adapted to represent consistently and
completely the distinctive vowel and consonant sounds of a language, it would
not represent other aspects of the phonology of that language—word accent,
pitch variation, or whatever that language utilized. Additional symbols can
be combined with letters to record these other features—an accent mark for
stressed syllable, a question mark for rising pitch—but they belong to separate
systems of notation because these other elements of the sound system are separate from the segmental elements (the consonants and vowels). The fact is, of
course, that most linguistic messages can be decoded from an alphabetic record
alone; all that is lost is speed, occasionally clarity of structure, and of course
nuances conveyed by 'tone of voice.' At the time when the system of writing
Latin was adapted to the writing of English, 'punctuation' was not a regular
or consistent element of the graphic analog of speech acts. Whether a sentence
asked for a yes-or-no answer or made a matter-of-fact statement was not signaled by any marking at or near its end. The end of an introductory clause
was not distinguished from the end of a final clause. No markings showed that
an interruptive element—such as this one between dashes—was not an integral

part of the main sentence. Even the interruption of a string of contiguous letters by a blank space was not a regularized element of writing, as it now is, to separate words (as opposed, say, to marking only major pause points for colloquial effect, *Yer inna helluvamess*).

In sum, there is very good evidence for reconstructing the phonology of Old English segmental units (vowels and consonants), in terms not only of the letter-and-sound correspondences, but in terms of patterns in which they occurred in that language, as well. The elements of accent, pitch modulation, and timing are not as well documented, though some of their characteristics can be reconstructed. For these last elements there is no reason (at least at the outset) not to use accent, pitch, and timing of Modern English in reading aloud from the written records of Old English.

2.1 Vowels in Stressed Syllables

The descriptions to follow for the vowel and consonant systems of Old English use the terminology of articulatory phonetics. First, the vowels. The conventional chart to represent the way these sounds are made is this:

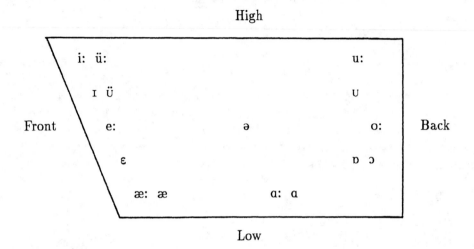

Pronunciation is represented in symbols of the International Phonetic Alphabet (see Appendix A).

The terms to be used are briefly glossed as follows:

Position of articulation is designated along two axes, **high – mid – low** and **front – center – back**.

Rounding refers to the shaping of the lips in articulation of the vowel, as either **round** or **unround**.

Length designates duration of a vowel articulation, which is binary—i.e., either **long** or **short** (not-long).

The term **phoneme** refers to a distinctive unit within the *system* of vowels and consonants of the language (not the incidental variants of sound that may result from stage of maturity, age, regional differences, illness, eccentricity, or whatever else).

A. The **simple vowels** in stressed syllables were distinguished by features of position, rounding, and length.

(1) The **back vowels** in stressed syllables constitute a set distinguished by threefold contrast of height and twofold contrast of length. Back vowels show no contrasts of rounding, a feature which they all share.

	High	Mid	Low
The phonemes:	/ū u	ō o	ā a/
Pronunciation:	[u: ʊ	o: ɒ	ɑ: ɑ, ɔ]

These vowels were normally represented in Anglo-Saxon orthography by **u, o, a.** In modern textbooks, grammars, and dictionaries, length is usually represented by a macron (-) over the vowel letter, thus: **ū, ō, ā.** The non-lengthened vowels are represented by the letters only. One-syllable words may be regarded here as having only stressed vowels.

/ū/ [u:]		/u/ [ʊ]	
ūs	us	**hund**	hundred; dog
mūs	mouse	**wund**	wound
hūs	house	**pund**	pound
lūs	louse	**stund**	period of time
fūs	eager	**sum**	a certain; some
ūf	owl	**sund**	sea; swimming
ūt	out	**wulf**	wolf
hū	how	**full**	full, entire
sū	sow	**munt**	hill
cū	cow	**mund**	hand
nū	now, now that	**wull**	wool
clūd	mass of stone	**turf**	turf
fūl	foul	**lust**	pleasure, desire
sūr	tart, sour	**rust**	rust
brū	eyebrow, eyelash	**dust**	dust
būr	bower	**dunn**	dun, dark-colored
mūr	wall	**burn**	brook, stream
ūp	up	**turl**	ladle
tūn	enclosure; village	**grund**	ground, bottom
mūl	mule	**dung**	dung

/ō/ [o:]

hōf	hoof
mōt	meeting, court
gōd	good
fōr	(he) went, fared
hōl	slander
glōf	glove
gōs	goose
tō	to; too
dō	(I) do
fōt	foot
mōd	mind; courage
stōd	(he) stood
stōl	stool, throne
mōr	moor, wasteland
flōr	floor

/o/ [ɒ]

hof	dwelling
mot	mote, atom
god	god
for	for, on account of
hol	hole, hollow
glof	cliff
word	word, statement
fox	fox
cosp	fetter
cost	choice
on	upon, among
of	from, out of
dol	foolish
dolg	wound, scar
folc	people, nation

/ā/ [ɑ:]

ā	ever
gā	(I) go; Go!
pād	covering
bād	(he) awaited
bān	bone
dā	doe
ān	one
wāc	weak
mā	more
wā	woe
mān	crime, evil deed
fām	foam
hām	home, region
swāt	sweat, toil
grāf	grove
gāst	ghost, spirit

/a/ [ɑ, ɔ]

ac	but, moreover
faran	(to) go, fare
fatu	vessels, cups
ham	ham
hwamm	corner, angle
camp	struggle
and*	and
ond	and
land	land
lond	land
man	man
mon	man
sand	sand
sond	sand
hand	hand
hond	hand

*Before a nasal consonant **a** and **o** spellings may alternate; see Appendix B.

(2) The **front vowels** in stressed position constitute an unbalanced set of
round and unround vocalic units. A threefold contrast of height distinguishes
unround front vowels; a twofold contrast of length distinguishes both round and
unround vowels.

	High	Mid	Low	High
The phonemes:	/ī i	ē e	ǣ æ	ȳ y/
Pronunciation:	[i: ɪ	e: ɛ	æ: æ	ü: ü]
	Unround		Round	

These vowels were normally represented by **i, e, æ, y** (æ is called 'ash'). The
macron in edited texts indicates length, **ī, ē, ǣ, ȳ**, with non-lengthened vowels
represented by the letters only.

/ī/ [i:]		/i/ [ɪ]	
wīn	wine	**hit**	it
pīn	anguish	**bist**	(thou) beest, art
sīn	his, her, etc.	**mid**	with
mīn	my, mine	**min**	small
līf	life	**milts**	mercy
sīd	vast	**in**	in, on, at
tīr	fame	**wind**	wind
tīd	time, occasion	**clif**	cliff
wīd	wide, vast	**bill**	battle-axe
līm	anything sticky	**lim**	limb, member
twīn	double thread	**twinn**	double
fīf	five	**swift**	swift
rīp	harvest	**ribb**	rib
rīm	number	**sibb**	peace
līn	flax, linen	**lid**	ship
slīm	slime	**sinc**	treasure
īs	ice	**lind**	lime-tree, linden
pīl	a pointed object	**dimm**	dark
hwīl	while, time	**blis**	joy, pleasure
swīn	wild boar	**swinn**	melody
wīf	woman	**flint**	flint
wīs	wise	**his**	his

/ē/ [e:]

wē	we
hē	he
mē	me
wēn	hope
cwēn	queen, woman
spēd	success
hēr	here
fēt	feet
bēn	request
mēd	meed, reward
gēs	geese

/e/ [ɛ]

menn	men
feld	open land
fenn	mud, fen
penn	pen, fold
nebb	beak, face
helm	protection
nest	nest
west	west(-ward)
bedd	bed
spell	story, history
nett	net

/ǣ/ [æ:]

ǣl	eel
ǣt	eatables
fǣt	metal plate
lǣst	least
mǣst	most
dǣl	portion
sǣd	seed
bǣl	fire, pyre
sǣl	time
bǣr	bed, litter
wǣd	garment
fǣr	sudden peril
wǣl	deep water
ǣ	law
gǣst	(thou) goest
ǣr	ere, before
blǣst	blast (of wind)
hwǣm	whom
glǣm	brilliant light
slǣp	sleep
stǣr	story, narrative

/æ/ [æ]

æl	awl
æt	at
fæt	vessel, cup
læst	fault
mæst	mast
dæl	dale
sæd	satiated
fæst	fast, firm
sæl	hall
bær	uncovered
wæd	shallow water
fær	journey
wæl	the slain
æppel	apple
æsp	aspen-tree
sæp	sap, juice
bæst	bast
bæc	back
græs	grass
bræs	brass
glæs	glass

/ȳ/ [ü:]

cȳ	cows
fȳr	fire
hȳd	hide, skin
hwȳ	why
hȳf	hive
hȳr	hire, wages
brȳd	betrothed woman
mȳs	mice
lȳt	few
ȳst	tempest
fȳst	fist

/y/ [ü]

wyrd	fate
wyrt	vegetable, herb
fyrn	former(ly)
fyrst	first
cynn	kin, race, type
mynd	memory
pyff	puff (of wind)
wyrm	serpent
lyft	air, sky
nytt	utility, duty
dynt	dint, stroke

B. Syllable nuclei other than simple vowels in stressed syllables consist of a progress of vocalic sounds, traditionally called **diphthongs**. They occur with gradation of articulation, and function in distinguishing morphemes in the same way that simple vowels do. In every instance the beginning of the diphthong is more heavily stressed, the second element less stressed (hence the nucleus being called a 'falling diphthong'). The second element probably varied [ɛ, ɑ, ɔ] with [ə], the neutral unstressed vowel sound. This second (the less-stressed) element apparently took the phonetic form of a glide. These diphthongs were spelled **ie, eo, ea**. Length is marked with a macron, as usual: **īe, ēo, ēa**.

The diphthongs:	/	īe	ie	ēo	eo	ēa	ea /
Pronunciation:	[	iːɛ	ɪɛ	eːɔ	ɛɔ	æːɑ	æɑ]
or:	[	iːə	ɪə	eːə	ɛə	æːə	æə]

/īe/ [iːɛ] or [iːə]

hīe	they
hīersum	obedient
sīere	sere, dry
stīeran	(to) steer, govern
nīed	necessity
tīen	ten
frīend	friends

/ie/ [ɪɛ] or [ɪə]

hierde	shepherd
fierd	army, campaign
siexta	sixth
wiell	well, foundation
dierne	secret, hidden
biernan	(to) burn
stiell	a jump, leap

/ēo/ [eːɔ] or [eːə]

wēop	(he) wept
bēo	be, am; bee
bēon	(to) be
bēor	strong drink
nēod	longing
sēoc	sick, ill
lēod	prince, man
fēond	adversary
fēol	file
dēop	deep
hēo	she
frēond	friend
lēof	beloved, desirable
dēor	animal; brave
mēos	moss

/eo/ [ɛɔ] or [ɛə]

eom	am
weorc	work
meolc	milk
feorr	far, distant
eorl	nobleman
deorc	dark, obscure
feorm	food, meal
beorn	man; noble
beorg	mountain; hill
deorc	dark, cheerless
heord	herd; custody
heorr	hinge
meox	filth; dung
reord	voice, speech
seolc	silk

/æa/ [æːɑ] or [æːə]

ēa	river, stream
ēad	riches, prosperity
wēa	misfortune, woe
ēam	uncle
lēan	reward, retribution
hēap	assembly, host
dēad	dead
stēap	deep, precipitous
stēam	steam
lēap	basket
lēas	without, free from
hēan	lowly
ēast	east(-ward)
grēat	great, massive
lēaf	leaf

/æa/ [æɑ] or [æə]

eart	art, are
eald	old
eall	all, everything
eard	dwelling place
earm	arm; poor
healp	(he) helped
bearn	offspring
beard	beard
weard	guardian
wearp	(he) threw
wearm	warm
wearn	reluctance
heals	neck
heald	custody
leax	salmon

2.2 Vowels in Unstressed Syllables

For the most part, the vowels in unstressed syllables are uniformly represented in any given word root and in the inflectional suffixes. (Diphthongal nuclei do not occur in unstressed syllables.) The fact that some variation does occur in spelling of the unstressed vowels (within single texts) together with the increasing frequency of this kind of spelling variation in the later texts indicate that the neutral vowel /ə/ was developing within the language as an alternative to any simple vowel. (The symbol ə is called 'schwa.') The subsequent history of English, of course, confirms this inference.

For the learning of Old English it is better to regard the vowels in unstressed syllables as identical phonetically to vowels with the same spelling in stressed syllables. They must have been virtually identical in the earlier period of West Saxon Old English, as the consistency of spelling them implies, and many of the texts of the tenth and early eleventh centuries were written under the conservative influence of the earlier models for the writing of English. But particularly, if the second syllable of **winde** and **winda** or of **gōde** and **gōda** (and countless others) are committed to one's audile memory as undifferentiated [ə], on the model of Modern English, it will be much more difficult to learn some fundamental inflectional distinctions that were in fact maintained throughout most of the period of Old English.

2.3 Individual Consonants

A. The **stop consonants** were distinguished in pairs by voice and in sets by position.

/p	t	k	Unvoiced	[p	t	k
b	d	g/	Voiced	b	d	g]

The **nasals** and **liquids**, not distinguished by voicing, form separate pairs.

/m	[m		/l	[l
n/	n, ŋ]		r/	r]

The spellings correspond closely to those of the descendant phones in Modern English: **p, t, c** (also **k** in later texts), **b, d, g; m, n; l, r.** The 'Insular g' used in writing Old English has the distinctive shape ᵹ; it is retained in both the Prose Readings and the Verse Readings.

The pair /p b/ was **bilabial**. Articulation of /t d/ was probably **dental** (rather than alveolar as it is in Modern English). The pair /k g/ was **velar**. The sound [ŋ] was an allophone of /n/, splitting off as a new phoneme only in Middle English; [ŋ] occurs only before /k/ and /g/, never in word-final position. (The contrast **win – wing** was not possible.) The liquid /r/ was probably trilled or tapped.

Reduplication in spelling indicates lengthening (i.e., increased duration) of the articulation of a consonant: **næddre** 'adder,' **blæddre** 'bladder.' Contrast of normal and lengthened consonants at the end of a word(-root) did not distinguish morphemes in Old English. Consonants were never lengthened initially in words. But medially, lengthened and non-lengthened consonants did contrast: **swellan** '(to) swell,' *vs.* **swelan** '(to) burn,' **racca** 'part of a ship's rigging' *vs.* **raca** 'rake.'

Adaptation of the roman alphabet to write English was new and without accumulated errors or mismatches of spelling and sounds resulting from language change. *A letter was not written unless there was a sound (or feature) it represented.* For learning this language, therefore, every spelled consonant should be restored with a spoken consonant (or distinctive feature of one).

In the illustrative lists for the consonants, primary accent is on the first syllable in all the examples.

/p/	pæll	silk robe	hēap	crowd, band	pīpe	pipe, tube
	pǣl	javelin	dēop	deep	uppan	on, upon
	palm	palm	grāp	(he) attacked	grīpan	(to) attack
	plot	plot of ground	nāp	(it) darkened	nīpan	(to) darken
	port	port, harbor	wearp	(he) cast	weorpan	(to) cast
	prēost	priest	healp	(he) helped	helpan	(to) help
	prīm	the first hour	lēap	basket	open	open, evident
	pund	pound	ūp	up	pāpa	pope
	penn	pen, fold	sæp	sap, juice	dyppan	(to) dip
	pening	penny, coin	top	top	lippa	lip
	pinn	pin, peg	rāp	rope	pipor	pepper

/b/	bæc	back	lamb	lamb	stybb	stump
	bǣl	fire, pyre	web	web	libban	(to) live
	bān	bone	neb(b)	beak, face	cribbe	stall, crib
	bāt	boat	clamb	(he) climbed	hæbbe	(I) have
	blǣd	glory; success	wamb	belly	nebb	beak, face
	blēo	color	camb	comb; crest	sibb	peace
	brēost	breast, mind	dumb	dumb, silent	ebba	ebb, low tide
	brim	surf, sea	ymb	by, about	lybb	drug, poison
	belt	belt, girdle	rib	rib	ribbe	rib-wort
	binn	bin, basket			hebban	(to) raise
	bār	boar			abbod	abbot

/t/	tūn	enclosure, town	hit	it	swēte	sweet, pure
	tam	tame, mild	wit	we-two	winter	winter
	tō	to; too	belt	belt, girdle	settan	(to) set
	twā	two; twice	munt	mountain	sittan	(to) sit
	twelf	twelve	sealt	salt	heorte	heart,
	tīd	time, while	sweart	swarthy; evil		spirit
	trum	secure, strong	heorot	hart, stag	mete	food
	tīr	fame, glory	hāt	heat; hot	wæter	water
	tīen	ten	strǣt	street	smitte	smudge
	tempel	temple	gāt	goat	setl	seat
	tappere	tapster	gǣt	goats	otor	otter

/d/	**dūn**	hill, 'down'	**dēad**	dead	**landes**	land (*infl.*)
	dæl	portion, part	**wyrd**	fate	**wurdon**	became
	drēam	joy	**word**	word, state-	**wordes**	word, state-
	dōm	judgment,		ment		ment (*infl.*)
		authority	**sweard**	hide, rind	**bedd**	bed, couch
	draca	dragon, sea-	**hold**	faithful,	**wedd**	pledge, agree-
		monster		loyal		ment
	dimm	dim, obscure	**mid**	with	**fōda**	food
	dēor	animal	**hād**	rank; form	**medu**	mead (drink)
	duru	door	**snōd**	head-dress	**ende**	end

/k/	**cribb**	stall, 'crib'	**dranc**	(he) drank	**drincan**	(to) drink
	cēne	bold	**swanc**	(he) labored,	**swincan**	(to) labor,
	cyrtel	kirtle		toiled		toil
	cyning	king	**folc**	folk, people	**folces**	folk (*infl.*)
	cēol	ship	**weorc**	work, deed	**weorces**	work (*infl.*)
	clamb	(he) climbed	**ēac**	also	**ēacen**	increased
	cēpan	(to) keep	**ac**	but	**locc**	lock of hair
	cwic	alive	**bōc**	book	**rocc**	over-garment
	cnīf	knife	**sēoc**	sick	**sticca**	stick, peg
	cnoll	knoll	**meolc**	milk	**lūcan**	(to) lock,
	cnyttan	(to) fasten,	**blæc**	black		enclose
		knit	**blāc**	bright,	**wōc**	(he) awoke
	cnēo	knee		shining	**hnecca**	neck
	cnæpp	summit	**āc**	oak	**tācen**	sign

/g/	**gār**	spear	**sprang**	(he) sprang	**springan**	(to) spring
	gēs	geese	**sang**	(he) sang	**singan**	(to) sing
	gōs	goose	**streng**	string, rope	**engel**	angel
	gāst	spirit, ghost	**strang**	strong, bold	**angel**	fish-hook
	glæd	bright, joyous	**fēng**	(he) seized	**hungor**	hunger
	grēne	green	**lang**	long, tall	**finger**	finger
	grund	bottom	**leng**	longer	**lengest**	longest
	gnæt	gnat, midge	**dung**	dung	**lagu**	law

/l/	lār	lore, learning	hāl	whole, sound	willan	(to) wish,
	lāf	remnant	eall	all, everything		be willing
	lāc	play; gift	weall	wall, rampart	ellen	zeal, courage
	lȳtel	little	til	good	weallan	(to) well,
	lind	linden, lime-	dol	foolish		bubble
		tree	ādl	sickness	swelan	(to) burn
	libban	(to) live	strǣl	arrow	swellan	(to) swell
	lyft	sky, air	stōl	stool, seat	feallan	(to) fall
	lang	long	stæl	place, spot	spillan	(to) waste
	leng	longer	sæl	room, hall	syll	sill, base

/r/	rād	(he) rode	ǣr	before	word	word
	rest	rest, quiet	lār	lore, learning	feorr	far, distant
	rinc	man, warrior	for	for	faran	(to) travel
	rēod	red, ruddy	tūr	tower, fortress	ord	point, spear
	rāp	rope	ēar	ear of corn	ēare	ear
	rǣd	advice, plan	timber	building	timbrian	(to) construct
	rǣs	onrush		material	māra	more
	rōd	rood	hār	hoary, gray	ōra	ore
	rēad	red	bær	bare	bora	ruler
	rēc	smoke	bǣr	bier	mere	sea, ocean

/m/	mā	more	eom	(I) am	fruma	origin
	mǣd	pasture	ēam	uncle	tīma	space of
	mīn	my, mine	holm	wave, ocean		time
	mē	me	wyrm	worm, dragon	nama	name
	mid	with	earm	arm; poor	samod	together
	mētan	(to) meet	rūm	spacious	lēoma	beam, radiance
	mīl	mile	nam	(he) took	niman	(to) take
	mete	food	rīm	number	rima	rim, border
	mōd	heart, mind	healm	stalk, stubble	hama	covering
	milts	mercy	ōm	rust	hāma	cricket

/n/	**nā**	not, no	**ān**	one	**wynn**	joy, delight
	ne	not, neither, nor	**in**	in, on, at	**dunn**	dun, dark-colored
			dōn	(to) do		
	nū	now	**on**	upon, among	**inn**	lodging
	næs	= ne wæs wasn't	**earn**	eagle	**bana**	slayer
			torn	anger, misery	**ancor**	anchor
	nǣre	= ne wǣre weren't	**rūn**	mystery	**sōna**	at once
			nān	none, not one	**bēna**	petitioner
	nolde	= ne wolde wouldn't	**stān**	stone	**bune**	cup
			wan	lacking	**wana**	lack
	nāt	= ne wāt know not	**gān**	(to) go, move	**cyning**	king
			bēn	request	**panne**	pan
	nǣdl	needle	**lān**	loan, gift	**denn**	den, lair

B. The **glide** /w/ [w] was spelled either **u**, **uu**, or **p** (*p* is called 'wen' or 'wynn'); it is usually replaced with **w** in modern editions.

/w/	**wē**	we	**swā**	so, as	**hrēaw***	raw
	wæs	(he) was	**swān**	swain	**snāw**	snow
	wǣron	(we) were	**swan**	swan	**sāwol**	soul
	willan	(to) wish, be willing	**twelf**	twelve	**āwa**	always, ever
			twinn	double		
	wolde	(he) wished	**hwǣr***	where	**hāwung**	observation
	wītan	(to) depart	**hwā**	who	**hīw**	appearance
	witan	(to) know	**hwæs**	whose	**hlǣw***	mound
	wāt	(he) knows	**hwǣm**	whom	**nīwe**	new, fresh
	writen	written	**hwone**	whom	**ēow**	you
	wrist	wrist	**dwolma**	chaos	**ēower**	your
	wlips	lisping	**dwīnan**	(to) waste away	**grōwan**	(to) grow
	wlanc	splendid, proud			**īw**	yew(-tree)
			cwic	quick, living	**ǣwe**	married
	wrǣstlere	wrestler	**cwēn**	queen, woman	**mǣw**	mew, sea-gull

*See note on *hw*-, *hr*-, and *hl*- spellings, next.

The **glottal spirant** /h/ was [h]; it was spelled **h**. Except in prehistoric Old English it occurred only in initial position.

/h/			
hē	he	**hlædder***	ladder
his	his	**hlāf**	loaf
him	him	**hlanc**	lank, thin
hine	him	**hlēo**	covering, protector
hit	it	**hlūd**	loud, sonorous
hēo	she	**hlid**	covering, lid, door
hī, hīe	they; them	**hnitu**	louse-egg, nit
him	them	**hnutu**	nut
hiera	their(s)	**hring**	ring
hengest	horse	**hwæt**	what
hors	horse	**hwelp**	whelp
horn	horn	**hwæl**	whale
hæbbe	(I) have	**hwēol**	wheel
hār	hoar, gray	**hrōf**	roof, ceiling
hell	hell	**hwisprian**	(to) whisper
hēr	here	**hwistle**	pipe, whistle
hāt	hot	**hwistlere**	piper, whistler
henn	hen	**hnappian**	(to) nap, slumber

Prehistoric OE		Historic OE
***wrēohan**	>	**wrēon** (to) cover
***sleahan**	>	**slēan** (to) strike, slay
***seohan**	>	**sēon** (to) see

*The *hl*-, *hr*-, *hn*-, *hw*- spellings have been analyzed alternatively as employing an *h*-spelling as a diacritic to mark voiceless [l̥, r̥, n̥, w̥], which could then be classed as allophones of /l r n w/. But in view of contrasting pairs such as **hlāf** 'loaf' **lāf** 'remnant,' it seems almost certain that the spellings do represent consonant clusters with *h*.

Another consonant /ġ/ was also spelled **g**. It is represented here as **ġ**. Variant spellings of a number of words indicate that it was evolving from a voiced **palatal spirant** [ǥ] into a **glide** [j]. Its reflex in Middle English is usually /y/, as in *yes, ye, yeer,͡ yaf, yong,* etc.

/ġ/							
	ġēa	yea, yes	læġde	(he) laid	læġ	(he) lay
	ġē	ye, you (pl.)	sæġde	(he) said	wǣġ	wave
	ġēar	year	dīeġlan	(to) conceal	weġ	way
	ġeaf	(he) gave	seġl	sail	hāliġ	holy
	ġierwan	(to) prepare	næġl	nail	weriġ	weary
	ġeong	young	reġn	rain	wiġ	battle
	ġeolo	yellow	bræġen	brain	dæġ	day
	ġeard	yard	tweġen	two, twain	mǣġ	kinsman
	ġeond	throughout	bēġen	both	mæġ	(he) is able
	ġēoc	help	eġe	fear	huniġ	honey
	ġeoc	yoke	sleġe	slaying	hīeġ	hay
	ġeorn	eager	tæġl	tail	grǣġ	grey
	ġiellan	(to) yell, shout	stæġer	stair(-case)	ǣġ	egg
	ġīet	yet, hitherto	fæġer	fair, lovely	cæġ	key
	ġeāra	of yore, formerly	wæġn	wagon, wain	clǣġ	clay

C. Two **palatal affricates** (articulated in same position as /ġ/) were distinguished by voice:

/č   [č], alternate notation [tʃ]
ǰ/   [ǰ], alternate notation [dʒ].

These phonemes, resulting from a split of /k/ and /g/ in English a little earlier than the earliest records, were spelled most often with letters also used to represent /k/ and /g/, but in some instances with letter combinations in which the second letter served as a diacritic for the first. Because only historical knowledge of pre-Old English can determine which phoneme is represented by **c** in many instances, modern editions commonly mark the *c* spelling of /č/ as **ċ**; it is so marked here. The spelling **cg** commonly represents /ǰ/; when **g** alone is the spelling of this sound, will be marked **ĝ** in this Grammar (but left unmarked as ȝ in the Readings.) Sometimes *e* was placed following *g* apparently as a diacritic to indicate /ǰ/. The phoneme /ǰ/ does not occur in word-initial position.

/č/	čēn	torch	ič	I	miċel	great, much
	ċild	child	drenč	drink	rīċe	kingdom
	ċeaster	castle, town	piċ	pitch	mēċe	sword
	ċēosan	(to) choose	swilċ	such (as)	drenċan	(to) give drink
	ċēapman	trader	hwilċ	which	biċċe	bitch
	ċēas	(he) chose	ælċ	each	swilċe	such (a one)
	ċeaf	chaff	stenċ	odor, scent	sēċan	(to) seek
	ċinn	chin	līċ	body	lǣċe	physician
	ċiriċe	church	beorċ	birch	tǣċan	(to) teach
	ċēace	cheek, jaw	finċ	finch	streċċan	(to) stretch
	ċealc	chalk, lime	sprǣċ	speech	wæċċan	(to) watch
	ċīecen	chicken	cryċċ	crutch,	styċċe	piece, bit
	ċeorl	layman,		staff	ġiċċan	(to) itch
		freeman			tiċċen	kid
	ċȳse	cheese			ynċe	inch
	ċīdan	(to) chide			lǣċċan	(to) grasp
	ċīdere	a chider			cyċene	kitchen
	ċīerran	(to) turn			wiċċa	sorcerer
	ċeosel	gravel			wiċċe	sorceress

/ǰ/		hecg	hedge	swenġan	(to) strike
		secg	man	senġan	(to) singe
		wecg	wedge	menġan	(to) mix
		ecg	edge, sword	twenġan	(to) pinch
		slecg	hammer		
		brycg	bridge		
		mycg	midge		
		wicg	steed		
		licgan	(to) lie		
		lecgan	(to) lay		
		secgan	(to) say		
		secga	sayer		
		hycgan	(to) think		
		hrycg	back, spine		
		cycgel	cudgel		

D. The **spirant** /s/ had two allophones—unvoiced [s] and voiced [z]. It is usually spelled **s**. Occasionally it is also represented when the cluster /ks/ is spelled **x**, as in **weaxan** '(to) grow, wax,' and when the cluster /ts/ is represented by **z** (rarely, and typically in Biblical names), as in **Nazareth**.

Pronunciation of this spirant is voiced [z] within a morphic sequence of voiced sounds—either vowel or voiced consonant—when it follows a syllable that carries word-stress; otherwise it is unvoiced [s]. To put it another way, there were no distinctions among words in Old English made on the basis of the voicing or non-voicing of this spirant as [z] or [s], as there are in Modern English **zinc–sink, eyes–ice**. The lengthened spirant, spelled -ss-, is unvoiced.

Three additional spirants form a set in which each is distinguished by position of articulation; as with /s/, voice is non-distinctive and both voiced and unvoiced allophones occur, distributed in a way parallel to [s] and [z] for /s/. (It is not possible in Old English to have contrasts such as **vat–fat, save–safe, either–ether**.)

/f/	pronounced	as	[f]	or	[v]
/þ/	"	"	[θ]	or	[ð]
/x/	"	"	[x]	or	[ɣ]

Labio-dental /f/ was regularly spelled **f**. **Dental** /þ/ was spelled **ð** ('eth') or **þ** ('thorn'). *These two symbols were interchangeable.* The lack of a symbol for this sound in the roman alphabet was made up for by marking a **d** with a stroke through its upper extension, to give **ð** (hence its also being called 'crossed *d*'). Another solution to representing this sound was to borrow the symbol **þ** from the runic alphabet. Yet another (which was abandoned early) was to write **th** for the sound in initial position.

The unvoiced allophone of **velar** /x/ was often spelled **h**, but also **g**; it did not occur initially, where /h/ is also spelt **h**. The voiced allophone of /x/ is normally spelled **g**. Both this last **g** and the **g** alternating with **h** for /x/ are not distinguished here by diacritical marking. The allophones are not easily distinguished in reading until their distribution in paradigms is observed (as they may be in listings of noun and verb inflections in subsequent chapters); a typical example is **dragan : drōh** , with [ɣ] and [x], respectively, '(to) draw : (I) drew.'

	Unvoiced [s]			Voiced [z]	
/s-/		**/-s/**		**/V́sV/**	
sǣ	sea	wæs	(he) was	wesan	(to) be
sǣd	seed	čēas	(he) chose	čēosan	(to) choose
samod	together	græs	grass	rōsen	made of
swā	so, as	gærs	grass		rose; rosy
slǣp	sleep	hūs	house	hūsa	houses'
smæl	thin, narrow	frēas	(it) froze	frēosan	(to) freeze
snotor	discerning			pise	pea
/-ss- -s(s)/		**/V̆s(V)/**		nēosan	(to) seek
wisse	(he) knew	éġesa	awe, peril	hūsel	housel
lǣssa	less	éġeslič	terrible	hosa	hose
næss	headland	Témese	Thames		
bliss	merriment	stānes	stone's		
cyssan	(to) kiss	stānas	stones		
/Vst/		**/Vts/**		**/V́sd/**	
bist	(thou) beest	bletsian	(to) bless	rǣsde	(he) rushed
wiste	(he) knew	blētsung	blessing,	līesde	(he) set free
mist	mist, dimness		favor		
lǣst	least	Lazarus	Lazarus		
west	west(-ward)			**/V́sl/**	
westan	from the west			hūsles	housel's
/Vsp/		**/Vps/**		**/V́sm/**	
æspe	aspen-tree	wæps	wasp	bosm	bosom
		hæpse	hasp		
/Vsk/*		**/Vks/**			
fisc	fish	oxa	ox		
disc	dish, bowl	tux	tusk		
/sk-/*		**/Vfs/**			
scīr	shire	drīfst	thou drivest		
scip	ship				
scop	poet, reciter	miscian	(to) mix		

*/sk/ was [ʃ]: scip 'ship,' wascan '(to) wash,' fersc 'fresh'; see 2.4 B.

Unvoiced [f]			Voiced [v]	
/f-/		**/-f/**	**/V́fV/**	
for	for, on account of	**stæf** staff	**stafas**	staves
		hōf hoof	**hōfas**	hooves
fæder	father	**wīf** woman	**wīfum**	women (*infl.*)
fær	peril	**wulf** wolf	**ofer**	over
fæt	vat, cup	**lāf** remnant	**ofen**	oven
fela	many, much	**ġeaf** (he) gave	**ġēafon**	(they) gave
firen	sin, outrage	**līf** life	**eofor**	(wild) boar
flān	arrow, dart	**fīf** five	**ǣfen**	evening
flōt	deep water	**twelf** twelve	**hēafod**	head
folc	nation	**dealf** (he) delved	**lifer**	liver
foran	before	**græf** grave,	**fefer**	fever
fram	from; forth	trench	**dēofol**	devil, demon
frēo	free, noble	**grāf** grove	**hlāford**	lord
full	full, entire	**cnīf** knife	**seofon**	seven
fūl	foul	**ċeaf** chaff	**beafer**	beaver
fnǣst	blowing	**stīf** rigid	**hefiġ**	serious
fnæd	fringe	**rōf** renowned	**ufan**	from above
flint	flint	**of** from	**Sæfern**	Severn
flīes	fleece	**healf** half	**/V́fdV/**	
			hæfde	(he) had
			lifde	(he) lived
/-f(f)/			**/V́lfV/**	
pyffan	(to) blow	**pyff** puff	**twelfe**	twelve (*infl.*)
		(of wind)	**delfan**	(to) dig
			delfere	digger
/Vfs/		Voiced [v]	**wulfas**	wolves
drīfst	thou drivest /	**-V́fn/**	**seolfer**	silver
		swefn dream	**/V́rfV/**	
/Vft/		**stefn** voice	**hærfest**	autumn
æfter	after	**hræfn** raven	**ċeorfan**	(to) carve
cræft	strength,	**/-V́fl/**	**hweorfan**	(to) turn
	cunning	**scofl** shovel		
scrift	penalty	**snofl** phlegm		
sceaft	origin			

	Unvoiced [θ]			Voiced	[ð]
/þ-/		**/-þ/**		**/V́þV/**	
þorn	thorn	āð	oath	āðas	oaths
þā	those; the	clāð	cloth	clāðas	cloths,
þā	then, when	cwæð	(he) said		clothes
þær	there, where	nīð	strife, evil	nīðas	strifes
þonne	then; while	sīþ	journey;	sīþas	journeys;
þū	thou		time		occasions
þīn	thy, thine	hæþ	heath	hæðen	heathen
þē	thee	bæð	bath	baðian	(to) bathe
þis	this	fylþ	(he) fills	swīðe	exceedingly,
þes	this	fȳlþ	filth		very
þēos	this	heorð	hearth	ēaðe	agreeable,
þanc	thought	morð	destruction		easy
þorp	thorp	wearþ	(it) became	brōðor	brother
þencan	(to) think	mūþ	mouth	āþum	son-in-law
þrīe	three	sūð	south(-ward)	māðum	treasure
þrines	trinity	norð	north(-ward)	ēþel	native country
þrēat	troop;	þrȳþ	strength	sūðan	from the south
	oppression	dēað	death	sūðerne	southern
þunor	thunder	hælþ	health	neoþan	from below
þūma	thumb	ȳð	wave	ȳðas	waves
þrotu	throat	tōþ	tooth	fiðele	fiddle
		brōð	broth		
		smið	craftsman		

/-þþ-/		**/V̆þ(V)/**			
oððe	or, either	seofoþa	seventh		
moððe	moth	nigoþa	ninth	**/V́rþV/**	
oþþæt	because	hæleþe	man (infl.)	eorðe	earth, land
		ealeþe	ale (infl.)	furðor	further
		mōnaþe,	month (infl.)	furðum	already
		mōnþe		weorþan	(to) become
/-þs-/		faroþe	current, sea	norðan	from the north
cwiþst	(thou) sayest		(infl.)	norðerne	northern
				byrðen	burden

	Unvoiced [x]			Voiced	[ɣ]
/V́xC/		**/-x/**		**/V́xV/**	
uht	dusk	**dāh, dāg**	dough	**dāgas**	doughs
eahta	eight	**drōg,**	(he) drew	**dragan**	(to) draw
riht	right, rule	**drōh**		**drōgon**	(they) drew
niht	night	**sāh**	(it) sank	**sīgan**	(to) sink
wiht	creature	**dweorg**	dwarf		
miht,	might,	**mearh**	horse		
meaht	strength	**scōh**	shoe		
dohtor	daughter	**þurh**	through		
dryht	multitude	**hēah**	high		
dryhten	lord	**nēah**	near		
hleahtor	laughter	**þēah**	although		
nīehsta	next	**holh**	hole, hollow		
hyht	hope	**lēah**	lea, meadow		
		eolh	elk		
		pleoh	peril, risk		
		þrūh	trough		
		wōh	twisted, perverse		

				/V́rxV/	and **/V́lxV/**
		beorg	hill	**beorgas**	hills
		bearg,	(I)	**beorgan**	(to) protect
/-xx-/		**bearh**	protected	**burgon**	(we) protected
pohha	bag	**swealg,**	(I)	**swelgan**	(to) swallow
hliehhan	(to) laugh	**swealh**	swallowed	**swulgon**	(we) swallowed

2.4 Consonant Clusters

The clustering patterns of Old English consonants correspond to those of Modern English consonants in so many ways as to make the historical identity of OE and MnE particularly apparent. By **consonant cluster** is meant a sequence of consonant phonemes within one syllable. There are some differences, nevertheless, as may be expected from the differences in the inventories of phonemes for the two stages of English, the differences in the incidence of allophones, and the differences in structural relations of the consonants within the two systems. See Richard M. Hogg, *A Grammar of Old English* (1992), vol. 1: Phonology, section 2.83.

A. In initial position no more than three consonants occur in sequence: /spr- str- skr-/. The cluster /sk-/, both by itself and in /skr-/, involved a palatal allophone of /k/ and had apparently come by the time of King Alfred to be pronounced [š] (equivalent to [ʃ]) as in Modern English *shoe, shred*; yet it continued in distribution to resemble clusters with /s-/ until early Middle English, when new [sk- skr-] clusters, in words borrowed first from Anglo-Danish and later from French, redefined the distribution of [š] and it in fact became a new phoneme /š/. In Old English it is regularly spelled **sc**. Thus -sc- is [š] in **huscword** 'scornful speech' (a compound of **husc** 'scorn' + **word**), but it represents [s] + [k] when the consonants occur in separate morphemes, as in **hūscarl**, i.e., a compound **hūs-carl** 'member of king's bodyguard.'

/spr-/		/str-/		/skr-/	
spræċ	language	**strǣt**	street,	**scrīn**	chest, coffer
springan	(to) leap		highroad	**scrincan**	(to) shrink
sprang	(he) leapt	**strand**	seashore	**scranc**	(it) shrank
sprungon	(we) leapt	**strang**	strong	**scruncon**	(they) shrank
sprenĝan	(to) strew	**strēam**	stream	**scrīc**	shrike
sprota	sprout, twig	**strēaw**	straw	**scrēad**	shred, scrap
spryttan	(to) sprout	**strīdan**	(to) stride	**scrift**	penance
sprecan	(to) speak	**strād**	(he) strode	**scrīfan**	(to) shrive,
spricð	(he) speaks	**strǣl**	arrow		prescribe
spræc	(he) spoke	**strangian**	(to)	**scrūd**	clothing
sprǣcon	(we) spoke		strengthen	**scrȳdan**	(to) clothe
sprǣdan	(to) spread	**strīð**	strife	**screpan**	(to) scrape
sprecol	talkative	**streċċan**	(to) stretch	**scrēpan**	(to) become dry

B. Two-member initial clusters are displayed below. They are arranged so as to represent some of the principles of initial clustering; no single two-dimensional arrangement can imply all those principles. Only a few illustrations are given. Others can be supplied from the preceding lists.

/sp-/ spell		/st-/		/sk-/ scyrt
sped				
/pr-/		/tr-/		/kr-/
/br-/		/dr-/		/gr-/
/pl-/				/kl-/
/bl-/				/gl-/
/sl-/	/sm-/		/sn-/	/sw-/
/hl-/	/hr-/		/hn-/	/hw-/
/fl-/	/fr-/		/fn-/	
	/þr-/		/þw-/	
	/tw-/			
				/dw-/
			/kn-/	/kw-/
			/gn-/ gnæt gnīdan gnidel	
/wl-/	/wr-/			

C. Clustering patterns of consonants in final positions in syllables or words are fewer and simpler than in Modern English. They pose no problem in the learning of Old English, and are not illustrated here.

Any medial cluster will begin with the largest possible sequence permitted for an initial cluster.

2.5 Distribution of Long and Short Vowels

Some characteristics of their distribution within words also distinguish long vowels and short vowels.

A. In any **unstressed syllable** a vowel is short. The words listed next have two syllables, the first taking full word-stress, the second being unstressed. The final syllable is part of the word-root, not a grammatical inflection.

fela	many	**fēower**	four
guma	man	**seofon**	seven
ofer	over, beyond	**ōðer**	other, second
miċel	much	**ēage**	eye
hine	him	**mōnað**	month
sele	hall, dwelling	**þūsend**	thousand
fæder	father	**nama**	name
ġearu	ready	**ðūma**	thumb

A practical corollary of this characteristic is that any vowel in a grammatical inflection is short, because inflectional syllables are always unstressed. The paradigm for /**storm-**/ 'storm' will illustrate. (The first form listed—and the fourth, too—lack overt inflection (are said to have 'zero-inflection').)

storm	**stormas**
stormes	**storma**
storme	**stormum**
storm	**stormas**

B. In either a **root morpheme** or a **derivational morpheme**, no more than one long vowel (or diphthong) will occur. Thus, for example, **rūmmōd** 'liberal, kind' can be only a compound, made up of **rūm** + **mōd** 'large-spirited.' Informally, a morpheme can be defined as a minimal element of an utterance that has a meaning. (A morpheme need not contain a long vowel, of course.) Illustration does not prove the absence of a distributional pattern. But here are some examples of words made up with one root morpheme and one derivational morpheme—'derivatives'—and with two root morphemes—'compounds.'

Derivatives		Compounds	
ā-drīfan	(to) drive out	**wīf-hād**	womanhood
tō-clēofan	(to) cleave asunder	**āc-lēaf**	oakleaf
hām-lēas	homeless	**blōd-rēow**	bloodthirsty
nēod-līċe	diligently	**blōd-rēad**	blood-red

C. When a vowel (or diphthong) occurs at the end of a word, in a syllable that is stressed, it is always long. In Old English there is a word /ā/ 'ever, always,' but there is no word */a/; /sǣ/ 'sea' is a word, but */sæ/ is not. The forms listed next are all separate words, and there is no corresponding OE word with a short vowel or diphthong.

ǣ	law, custom	**ēa**	water, stream
bā	both	**hēo**	she
bēo	be (indicative)	**sīe**	be (subjunctive)
blēo(h)	appearance	**hū**	how
brū	(eye)brow	**hwȳ**	why
bū	dwelling	**mā**	more
cnēo	knee	**frēa**	ruler, lord
cū	cow	**sū**	sow
dā	doe	**dō**	(I) do
flā	arrow	**tā**	toe
flēa	flea	**wā**	woe
twā	two	**rā**	roe, roebuck
swā	so; as	**þȳ**	the (*infl.*)

D. A few one-syllable words end in a vowel but ordinarily do not carry word-stress, hence the vowel need not be long. These are 'grammatical' words, rather than 'content' words.

One is a coordinating conjunction /ġe/ (in contrast to pronoun /ġē/ 'ye'): **be þisse ondweardan tīde, ġe ēac be þǣre tōweardan** 'concerning this present time, and also concerning the future (one).' **Hē bebȳt ġe windum ġe sǣ** 'He commands both the winds and the sea'; **ġe on lande, ġe on ōþrum þingum, ġe on ōþrum ġestrēonum** 'in land, in other things, and in other riches.'

The negative particle **ne** is another; it precedes the verb it negates (whereas Modern English **not** follows the auxiliary verb it negates). Before a finite verb: **Ne sleh ðū. Ne synga ðū. Ne stel ðū.** 'Thou shalt not kill. Thou shalt not sin (adulterously). Thou shalt not steal.' This form can also be used correlatively: **Ne iċ ne dyde, ne iċ ne dō** 'Neither did I, nor do I' (double negation, as in either of these clauses, is normal).

The relative particle **þe** (see 3.4 B) is yet another form that ordinarily lacks phrasal stress: **Sē ðe ēaran hæbbe tō ġehȳranne, ġehȳre!** 'He who has ears for hearing, (let him) hear!'

Alternation of stressed and unstressed forms of prepositions may occasionally be reflected in spelling differences. The spelling *big*, representing /biġ/, identifies a stressed form of this preposition, while the spelling *be* identifies an unstressed form: **Þās tācno … þe iċ nū biġ sæġde be þisse worlde earfoþnessum** 'These signs … which I just now spoke-about concerning the tribulations of the world' (and see **be þisse ondweardan tīde** etc., above). The usual spelling is *bi*, rendered ordinarily in edited texts as **bī**.

Pronouns are also believed to have had long final vowels when they had stress in sentence context, short vowels when they did not; they are listed in the grammars therefore as **wē, þē, mē, þū** , etc. The pronominals **sē** and **hwā** are similar (see 3.4 A and 3.2 A).

E. Any vowel (or diphthong) that is stressed and is non-final in a word may, of course, be either long or short: **gōd** 'good,' **god** 'god' (many similar pairs occur in the illustrative lists for the separate vowels).

2.6 Syllable Division

Syllable division is independent of the principles outlined just above. While it is true that exact description of points of onset and termination of syllables is not yet finally settled for Modern English and that we can never have samples of Anglo-Saxon speech for analysis, what evidence there is points to a general congruity of syllabication for both Old English and Modern English. Within syllables—which are phonologically defined—the distribution features of vowels are unlike those within morpheme structure (described in the preceding section); chiefly, a vowel carrying stress in a syllable may be final and yet be short. Apart from evidence provided by trends in historical development of English (evidence too complex to be more than mentioned here), there is evidence of syllabication in the writing of some Anglo-Saxon scribes. The scribal evidence has not been fully attended to, but a sample will indicate the nature of that evidence and the principles of syllabication recognized by some native speakers of Old English. The scribe who copied the first three-fifths of *Beowulf*, for example, wrote the following words with spacing in the positions indicated here by hyphens or spaces (or both). While his practice is not always to leave space between syllables of a particular word, he is fully consistent in respect to phonologically definable positions at which spacing has been left; the spacing corresponds to syllable boundaries that are also found in Modern English principles of pronunciation.

fre-me-don	ġe- fre-me-de
freme-don	ġe freme-de
ġe- frem-man-ne	ġe- freme-de
ġe- frem-me-de	ġe- fremed
ġe- fre-mede	fremeð
ġe- freme-de	ġe- freme-de
ġe- freme-de	ġe fremed
ġe- freme-don	ġe- fremede

Other written forms in the same context also show spacing contrary to morphemic principles; it seems interpretable only as syllable division. As the examples given next illustrate, division was commonly made so that any non-initial syllable begins with a consonant (or consonant cluster) regardless of the length of the preceding or succeeding vowel. The same scribe wrote one-syllable **bearn** 'son' with ligatured **ea**, but two-syllable **bearn** 'ran (into)' (past tense of **be-irnan**) with a slight space between **e** and **a**.

Manuscript spacing	Morpheme boundary
ġēa-fon (they) gave	ġeaf-on
(sele-) rǣ-den-ne -counselors	(sele-) rǣd-enne
scyl-ding Danes	scyld-ing
seal-de (he) gave	seal-d-e
hrē-þiġ triumphant	hrēþ-iġ
fyre-ne crime	fyren-e
scrī-það move, glide	scrīþ-að
ear-dode (he) dwelled	eard-od-e
man-na cyn-nes of the race of men	man(n)-a cyn(n)-es

Use of blank space between strings of letters was also an aspect of the writing of Old English that was being worked out, and it is different in some ways from the writing of Modern English. One problem was, What elements are to be separated with space—words, word-roots (as in a compound), syllables, phrases? Another was, Is spacing to be binary, or can it be variable? And ultimately, What in the utterance does it symbolize? The quite separate problem of capitalization was also solved only in subsequent stages of the writing of English.

Two pairs of terms relevant to syllable structure are standard. First, closed and open syllables. A **closed syllable** is one that terminates with one or more consonants, such as **dæġ** 'day,' **pæþ** 'path,' **hēold** 'held,' **forst** 'frost.' An **open syllable** is one that terminates in a vowel, such as **wā** 'woe, misery,' **tō** 'to,' or the first syllable of **æcer** 'field, acre,' **grǣdiġ** 'hungry, covetous.'

Next, long and short syllables. A **long syllable** is one that contains a long vowel (or diphthong) or terminates in two or more consonants, such as **sǣ** 'sea,' **lȳt** 'little,' **wyrm** 'serpent,' or the first syllable of **sōfte** 'softly.' A **short syllable** is one that contains a short vowel (or diphthong) without two or more consonants following it, such as **æt** 'at,' **sæt** 'sat,' **fæt** 'vat, vessel,' or the first syllable in **ufan** 'from above,' **fæder** 'father,' **fæġer** 'fair, beautiful,' **fæste** 'fast,' **guma** 'man,' **sunu** 'son.'

2.7 Word-accent

With the few exceptions that have been noted, words in illustrative lists in the preceding sections have been either monosyllables—taking full stress as citation forms—or simple polysyllabic words in which the initial syllable takes heavier stress than any succeeding syllable. Placement of principal stress has been indicated, and it will be apparent that word-accent in Old English is systemically congruent with that of Modern English: it is the word root that consistently carries principal stress, and it is the initial syllable of the root that is stressed if the root consists of more than one syllable.

A. Word-accent in Old English was also similar to that of Modern English for derivative and compound words. Principal stress remains in the word root in derivational constructions employing suffixes:

sǽd	seed, fruit	**mōd**	the inner being, spirit, mind
sǽdere	sower, 'seeder'		
sǽdian	(to) sow	**mōdiġ**	brave, noble-minded
sǽdlīċ	belonging to	**mōdigian**	(to) be proud, exult
	seed, seminal	**mōd-lēas**	spiritless, dull

B. In both compound adjectives and compound nouns, heavier stress is carried by the first root morpheme:

sǽd-bèrende	seed-bearing	**mōd-sòrh**	sorrow of soul or mind
sǽd-cynn	type of seed	**mōd-blind**	undiscerning
sǽd-lēap	sower's basket	**mōd-ċearu**	care of heart, grief
sǽd-tīma	seed-time	**mōd-sēoc**	sick at heart, distressed
wǽd-sǽd	woad-seed	**ófer-mōd**	pride
līn-sǽd	linseed	**glǽd-mōd**	of good cheer, pleasant

C. Verbs derived from compound nouns have the same accentual pattern, as **ánd-swàrian** '(to) answer,' but they are few. Quasi-compound verbs with prepositional adverbs preceding verb roots keep accent on the first element: **ín-gān** '(to) enter,' **bī-stàndan** '(to) stand by'; these are learned only from extensive experience in reading Old English. Most verbs formed as compounds with an

initial prepositional adverb—the most common type—have principal stress on
the original verb root: **for-béodan** '(to) forbid,' **ofer-cúman** '(to) overcome,' **tō-drĩfan** '(to) drive away, scatter,' **ymb-þénċan** '(to) consider,' **ġeond-scĩnan** '(to) shine upon, illuminate.' The initial root usually appears in the unaccented form of the morpheme if it differs from the accented form: **ǽ-wielm** 'fountain,' but **ā-wéallan** '(to) well up'; **bĩ-genga** 'inhabitant,' but **be-gãn** '(to) occupy.'

góld-hòrd	treasure	**ġèond-séon**	(to) examine
lǽċe-cræft	leachcraft	**ġeond-ðenċan**	(to) reflect upon
glæd-mōd	pleasant	**wið-stondan**	(to) stand against
mōd-cræft	intelligence	**wið-sacan**	(to) refuse
ān-mōd	unanimous	**for-rĩdan**	(to) intercept
un-mōd	depression	**for-scrĩfan**	(to) decree, proscribe
stĩð-mōd	brave, resolute	**un-bindan**	(to) unbind, loosen
wiþer-saca	adversary	**be-healdan**	(to) have, observe
and-swaru	answer	**ā-rĩsan**	(to) arise
and-swarian	(to) answer	**ā-cwellan**	(to) kill
tō-weard	facing	**be-sittan**	(to) besiege
in-gangan	(to) go in	**be-drĩfan**	(to) pursue
god-spell	gospel	**be-heonan**	on this side of
bĩ-spell	example, story	**of-tēon**	(to) deprive (of)

D. The prefix **ġe-** is always unstressed.

ġe-bed	prayer	**ġe-winn**	strife, hostility
ġe-biddan	(to) pray	**ġe-winnan**	(to) fight, contend
ġe-dāl	division	**ġe-hwæ̆r**	everywhere, always
ġe-dǽlan	(to) divide	**ġe-hwā**	each (one), anyone

Consonant clusters within any morpheme that precedes a root morpheme in the same word conform to the same patterns as found in simple words (shown earlier), whether the morpheme that precedes a root is derivational or, in the case of a compound, another root. This characteristic is presumably related to placement of stress in words.

Similarly, distribution of allophones of /n/ and of spirants /s f þ x/ within any morpheme that precedes a root morpheme in the same word is like that in simple words, whether the morpheme that precedes is derivational or another root. The verb **ingān** is made up from **ín** + **gān**, and has [n], not [ŋ], manifesting the first /n/. **Ðonne ġē ingān on þæt hūs** 'When ye enter into that house;' **Ðā hē inēode** 'When he (had) entered.' The noun **ingang** 'entrance, ingress' is formed similarly, as **in(n)** + **gang**: **ingang** and **ūtgang** 'ingress and egress.' While [v] manifests /f/ in **hærfest** 'harvest, autumn,' it is [f] in **ārfæst** 'honorable, virtuous,' an adjective compound of **ār** + **fæst**. Or, **þenian** '(to) stretch' is combined with **a-** 'out' in **aþénian** '(to) stretch out, extend,' with the spirant manifest as unvoiced [θ] rather than voiced [ð]. See Richard M. Hogg, *A Grammar of Old English*, Vol. 1: Phonology (1992), sections 2.84–2.91.

corn	grain	**æppel**	(any kind of) fruit
corn-hūs	granary	**æppel-hūs**	fruit storehouse
corn-berende	grain-bearing	**æppel-cynn**	kind of apple
corn-tēoðung	tithe of corn	**æppel-berende**	apple-bearing
corn-sǣd	a grain of corn	**æppel-trēow**	appletree
		æppel-ðorn	crab-apple tree
pipor-corn	a peppercorn	**æppel-wīn**	cider
sand-corn	grain of sand	**æppel-scrēada**	apple parings
		æppel-fæt	vessel for apples
bān	bone, tusk	**eorþ-æppel**	cucumber
bān-hūs	body, chest	**fīc-æppel**	fig(-fruit)
bān-hring	vertebra, joint	**finger-æppel**	finger-fruit, date
bān-sealf	salve for pain in bones		
		bæð	bath
bān-ġebrec	fracture of a bone	**bæð-hūs**	bathing place
bān-wærċ	pain in the bones	**bæð-sealf**	bathing-salve
		bæð-stede	bathing place
palm	palm (tree)	**bæð-stōw**	bathing place
palm-æppel	date	**bæð-fæt**	bathing tub
palm-dæġ	Palm Sunday		
palm-trēow	palm tree	**bōc-hūs**	library
palm-twig	palm twig, branch	**bōc-cræft**	learning, science
hand-bōc	handbook, manual	**hand-weorc**	handiwork
hand-cræft	manual skill	**hand-clāð**	handcloth, towel

tōð	tooth	brēmel-brǣr	bramble-briar
tōð-ece	toothache	brēmel-lēaf	bramble-leaf
tōð-gār	toothpick	brēmel-rind	bramble-bark
tōð-lēas	toothless	brēmel-æppel	blackberry
tōð-sealf	tooth salve		
tōð-sticca	toothpick	candel	lamp, candle
tōð-wærċ	toothache	candel-mæsse	Candlemas
tōð-wyrm	worm in the teeth	candelmæsse-æfen	Candlemas eve
tōð-rima	a gum	candel-stæf	candlestick
		candel-sticca	candlestick
mynster	minster, nunnery, monastery	candel-trēow	candelabrum
		candel-wēoce	candle-wick, torch
mynster-bōc	minster-book	candel-lēoht	candlelight
mynster-clūse	monastic close		
mynster-fæder	abbot		
mynster-hām	monastery	bisceop	bishop, high priest
mynster-land	land owned by a monastery	bisceop-hādung	episcopal ordination
		bisceop-hām	bishop's estates
mynster-līċ	monastic	bisceop-scīr	diocese
mynster-līf	monastic life	bisceop-rōd	bishop's cross
mynster-prēost	priest of a monastery	bisceop-land	diocesan land
		bisceop-dōm	bishopric, episcopate
mynster-munuc	monk who lives in monastery	bisceop-hād	office of bishop

sæ-ǣl	sea-eal	sæ-flōd	tide	sæ-rinc	seaman
sæ-bāt	sea-boat	sæ-lāc	sea-spoil	sæ-scell	seashell
sæ-beorg	cliff by sea	sæ-lād	sea-voyage	sæ-sīþ	sea-voyage
sæ-burg	seaport town	sæ-lāf	jetsam	sæ-snægl	sea-snail
sæ-ċeaster	seaport town	sæ-land	coast	sæ-steorra	guiding star
sæ-ċeosel	sea-sand	sæ-lēoð	rowers' song	sæ-strand	foreshore
sæ-clif	sea-cliff	sæ-mann	seaman	sæ-wæter	sea-water
sæ-col	jet	sæ-mearh	'sea-horse,' ship	sæ-weard	coastguard
sæ-cyning	sea-king			sæ-weġ	sea path
sæ-earm	arm of sea	sæ-net	fishing net	sæ-weall	sea-wall
sæ-fisc	sea-fish	sæ-ostre	sea-oyster	sæ-wiht	sea-animal

2.8 Exercises

A. Sets of Common Words

Most of the following words, when read aloud in sets, will not require dictionary look-up. A few sets appear with Latin equivalents—of which the Old English forms were originally glosses—when the Latin form, or a subsequent borrowing of the Latin (or related) form into English, should be familiar.

1.

ān	- - - - -	- - - - -
twā, tweġen	- - - - -	- - - - -
þrȳ, þrēo	þrēotȳne	þrittiġ
fēower	fēowertȳne	fēowertiġ
fīf	fīftȳne	fīftiġ
six	syxtȳne	syxtiġ
seofon	seofontȳne	hundseofontiġ
eahta	eahtatȳne	hundeahtatiġ
nigon	nigontȳne	hundnigontiġ
tȳn	twēntiġ	hundtēontiġ
endleofan	ān ond twēntiġ	- - - - -
twelf	(ond swā forð)	þūsend

2.

se forma	- - - - -	ānfeald
se ōðer	- - - - -	twȳfeald
se þridda	se þrēotēoða	ðrȳfeald
se fēowerða	se fēowertēoða	fēowerfeald
se fīfta	se fīftēoða	fīffeald
se sixta	se syxtēoða	syxfeald
se seofoða	se seofontēoða	seofonfeald
se eahteoða	se eahtatēoða	eahtafeald
se nigoða	se nigontēoða	nigonfeald
se tēoða	- - - - -	tȳnfeald
se endleofta	- - - - -	- - - - -
se twelfta	(ond swā forð)	twēntiġfeald

rīm 'number; counting'   **rīman** '(to) count'
rīm-cræft 'arithmetic'   **rīm-bōc** 'calendar'

Half of an element in counting is expressed in terms of the counting element in which the half occurs, rather than the counting element after which it occurs: **þridde healf** 'two and a half'; **fēowerþe healf hund** 'three hundred fifty'.

3. ġēarlīċ   *annuus* 'yearly'   for twām ġēarum,   *biennium*
    twȳwintre   *biennis*   tweġra ġēara fyrst
    þrȳwintre   *triennis*   þrēora ġēara fyrst   *triennium*
    fēowerwintre   *quadriennis*   fēower ġēara fyrst   *quadrennium*
    fīfwintre   *quinquennis*

4. twȳfēte   *bipes*
    þrȳfēte   *tripes*
    fyþerfēte,
       fēowerfēte*   *quadrupes*

5. Sunnandæġ   Mōnandæġ   Tīwesdæġ   Wōdnesdæġ
    Sunnanæfen**   Mōnanæfen   Tīwesniht   Wōdnesniht
    Sunnanniht**   Mōnanniht

    Ðunresdæġ   Frīġedæġ   Saterdæġ
    Ðunresniht   Frīġeniht   Sæterniht

6. fæder   *pater*   sunu   *filius*
    mōdor   *mater*   dohtor   *filia*
    ealda fæder   *auus*   brōðor   *frater*
    þridda fæder   *abauus*   sweoster   *soror*

    stēopfæder   stēopsunu
    stēopmōdor   stēopdohtor
    fōstorfæder   fōstorċild
    fōstormōdor   fōstorsweoster
    fōstorland   fōstorling

Siblinge *affinis vel consanguineus*

---

*Also, Lōc-hwæt hæbbe tȳn fēt *decempes* 'Whatever may have ten feet.'

**Sunnanæfen 'Saturday evening,' Sunnanniht 'Saturday night.'   Also, Sunnanūhta 'dawn of Sunday morning,' Sunnanmerġen 'Sunday morning.'

7.

lim	*membrum*	brēost	*pectus*
hēafod	*caput*	heorte	*cor*
bræġen	*cerebrum*	maga	*stomachus*
hnecca	*ceruix*	blōd	*sanguis*
foreweard		flæsc	*caro*
hēafod	*frons*	hȳd	*cutis*
nosu	*nasus vel*	sculdra	*scapula*
	naris	hrycg	*dorsum*
hǣr	*capillus*	earm	*brachium*
ēare	*auris*	elboga	*ulna*
ansȳn	*facies*	hand	*manus*
ēage	*oculus*	finger	*digitus*
mūð	*os*	næġel	*unguis*
weler	*labium*	ðūma	*pollex*
tōð	*dens*	sīde	*latus*
tunge	*lingua*	ribb	*costa*
gōma	*palatum*	þēoh	*femur*
þrotu	*guttur*	hype	*clunis*
ċinn	*mentum*	cnēow	*genu*
beard	*barba*	scinbān	*tibia*

8.

þunor	*tonitruum*	dæġ	*dies*
līġet	*fulgor*	niht	*nox*
rēn, reġn	*pluuia*	meriġen	*mane*
snāw	*nix*	æfen	*uesperum*
hagol	*grando*	wucu	*ebdomada*
forst	*gelu*	mōnað	*mensis*
īs	*glacies*	lencten	*uer*
lyft	*aer*	sumor	*aestas*
wind	*uentus*	hærfest	*autumnus*
weder	*aura*	winter	*hiems*
scūr	*nimbus*	tōdæġ	*hodie*
storm	*procella*	ġyrstandæġ	*heri*
rēnboga	*yris vel arcus*	wic-dæġ	'weekday'
		tō-morġen	'tomorrow'

B. Patterns and Contrasts of Sounds

1. Vowel Contrasts. (a) Practice pronouncing the following pairs of forms. (b) Consult a dictionary of Old English to learn the difference of meaning for forms in each pair; the difference in meaning matched to difference in pronunciation establishes the phonemic distinction of the vowels.

mūs	mȳs	tæċen	tæċen	metan	mētan
lūs	lȳs	mōt	mot	broc	brōc
bū	bȳ	tǣl	tæl	wær	wǣr
fōt	fēt	wītan	witan	brod	brōd
cū	cȳ	fūl	ful	bær	bǣr
gōs	gēs	pīċ	piċ	scop	scōp
lāf	līf	mān	man	swan	swān
ǣr	ār	ǣl	æl	blæd	blǣd
āc	ac	gōd	god	byre	bȳre
sǣd	sæd	ġēoc	ġeoc	grut	grūt

2. Consonant Contrasts. (a) Practice pronouncing the following sets of forms. (b) With the help of a dictionary of Old English, find still further examples of pairs or sets of forms that contrast in one consonant only.

swelan	swellan	raca	racca
stelan	stellan	tredan	treddan
scīd	scīp	scīr	scīn
scear	sceard	scearn	scearp
fā	fāg	fāh	fām
earm	earg	eard	earn
lēad	lēat	lēap	lēac
lēas	lēaf	lēah	lēan
heald	healt	healp	heals
healf	healh	healm	heall

3. Practice pronouncing the following variant forms; variations of these kinds are common in the writing of Old English.

herġe	herie	heriġe	'(I) praise'
āxode	ācsode	āhsode	'(I) asked'
wyrsa	wirsa	wiersa	'worse'
þeġen	þeġn	þēn	'thane, servant'

ġierd	ierd	'rod, staff'
ġeard	eard	'yard, dwelling'
ġerusalem	ierusalem	'Jerusalem'
þanciġende	þanciende	'thanking'
bearu	bearwes	'grove, wood' (uninflected and inflected)
āxian	āxiġean	'(to) ask'

C. Readings

1. In his Grammar of Latin, Ælfric writes (in Old English) of **stafas** 'letters'; the letter-names will conform to the principles of long and short vowel distribution in syllables. To say that *f*, for example, 'begins on the "letter" *e* and ends in itself' implies that its name is /ef/. On the other hand, the name of the letter *e* would have to be /ē/.

Littera is 'stæf' on englisc .
... Sōðlīċe on lēden-spræċe
synd þrēo ond twentiġ stafa:
. a . b . c . d . e . f . g .
h . i . k . l . m . n . o . p .
q . r . s . t . u . x . y . z .
Of þām syndon fīf *uocales*, þæt
synd 'clypiġendlīċe,' a . e .
i . o . u . Ðās fīf stafas æt-
ēowiað heora naman þurh hī
silfe; ond būton þām stafum
ne mæġ nān word bēon āwriten .
. . . Tō þisum is ġe·numen se
grēcisca . y . for intinga
grēciscra namena; ond se ylca
. y . is on engliscum ġewrytum

Littera is 'letter' in English.
... Truly, in Latin there are
twenty-three letters:
a, b, c, d, e, f, g,
h, i, k, l, m, n, o, p,
q, r, s, t, u, x, y, z.
Of those five are *uocales*, which
are vocal(-sounds), *a, e,*
i, o, u. These five letters
indicate their names by themselves; and without those letters
no word can be written.
... To these is added the
Greek *y* for the sake of
Greek names; and the same
y is in English writings

swīþe ġewunelīċ . Ealle þā ōðre
stafas syndon ġehātene *consonantes*
þæt is 'samod-swēġende,' for-þan-
þe hī swēgað mid þām fīf
clypiġendlīcum. Þonne bēoð ġyt
of þām samod-swēġendum sume
semi-uocales, þæt synd 'healf-
clypiġende'; sume syndon mutę,
þæt synd 'dumbe.' *Semi-uocales*
syndon seofon: . f . l . m . n .
r . s . x . Þās syndon healf-
clypiġende ġecīġede, for-þan-þe
hī nabbað fulle clypunge swā swā
þā *quinque uocales*, ond þā six
onginnað of þām stæfe . e . ond
ġe·endiað on him sylfum; . x .
āna onginð on þām stæfe . i .
. . . Þā ōþre nigon *consonantes*
synd ġecwedene mutę, þæt synd
'dumbe'; hī ne sind nā mid ealle
dumbe, ac hī habbað lȳtle clipunge:
þā synd . b . c . d . g . h .
k . p . q . t . Þās onginnað
of him sylfum ond ġe·endiað on
ðām clipiġendlīcum stafum:
b . c . d . g . p . t . ġe-
endiað on . e; . h . ond . k .
ġe·endiað on . a . æfter rihte.
. q . ġe·endað on . u ; . z .
ēac, se grēcisca stæf, ġe·endað
on . a . [ond swā forð].

extremely common. All the other
letters are called *consonantes*,
that is 'with-sounding,' because
they sound with the five vocal
sounds [i.e., vowels]. Then
there are yet of those consonants
certain semivowels, which are
'half-vowels'; some are mutę,
which are 'mute.' There are seven
semivowels: *f, l, m, n,
r, s, x.* These are called semivowels because they don't have
a full (vocal) sound as the
five vowels do, and the six
begin from the letter *e*, and
end on themselves; *x* alone
begins on the letter *i*.
... The other nine consonants
are called mutę, which are
'silent'; they are not altogether
mute, but they have little sound.
Those are *b, c, d, g, h,
k, p, q, t.* These begin
from themselves and end on
the vowel letters:
b, c, d, g, p, t end
on *e* ; *h* and *k*
end on *a*, rightly.
q ends on *u* ; *z*, in addition,
the Greek letter, ends
on *a* [and so forth].

2. A twelfth century manuscript lists the alphabet as follows. For several letter names, such as 'B be uel bei,' the latter spelling apparently represents a diphthongization with an off-glide similar to that in Modern English for words such as **day**, **say**, which was not present in the main period of Old English. ('Uel' is Latin for 'or.')

A a B be uel bei C ce uel cei D de uel dei E e F f ef G ge uel gei H hah uel hake I i K ka L l el M m em N n en O o Q quu R r er S s es T te V u X x ix Y y fix Z zede ... Anglicę litterę Ᵽ wen Ð ðet Þ þorn 7 and.

3. Some explanations of nature.

Rēnas cumað of ðǣre lyfte.... Sēo lyft liccað ond ātȳhð ðone wǣtan of ealre eorðan ond of ðǣre sǣ, ond ġegaderað tō scūrum; ond þonne hēo māre āberan ne mæġ, þonne fealð hit adūne tō rēne ālȳsed.

Rains come from the sky.... The sky licks and draws up the moisture from all the earth and from the sea, and gathers (it) into showers; and when it can't carry more, then it falls downward dissolved in rain.

Hagol cymð of ðām rēndropum þonne hī bēoð ġefrorene upp on þǣre lyfte ond swā siððan feallað.

Hail comes from the raindrops when they are frozen aloft in the air and thus afterwards fall.

Snāw cymð of ðām þynnan wǣtan þe byð upp ātogen mid þǣre lyfte ond byð ġefroren ǣr-þan hē tō dropum ġe-urnen sȳ, ond swā sæmtincges fylð.

Snow comes from the thin moisture that is drawn up with the air and is frozen before it is combined into drops, and so it falls continually.

Ðunor cymð of hætan ond of wǣtan. Sēo lyft tȳhð ðone wǣtan tō hire neoðan and ðā hǣtan ufon; ond ðonne hī ġegaderode bēoð—sēo hǣte ond se wǣta—binnan þǣre lyfte, þonne winnað hī him betwȳnan mid eġeslīcum sweġe, ond þæt fȳr āberst ūt ðurh līġette.... Swā hāttre sumor, swā māre ðunor ond līġet on ġēare.

Thunder comes from heat and moisture. The sky draws the moisture to it from below and the heat from above; and when they are gathered—the heat and the moisture—within the cloud (sky), then they contest between themselves, with an awful noise, and fire bursts out through lightning.... The hotter the summer, the more thunder and lightning (there is) in the year.

4. *Paternoster* and creed

Dū ūre fæder þe eart on heofonum, sȳ þīn nama ġe·hālgod; ġe·cume þīn
rīċe; sȳ þīn willa swā swā on heofonum swā ēac on eorðan. Syle ūs tō-dæġ ūrne
dæġ-hwamlīcan hlāf. Ond for-ġyf ūs ūre gyltas, swā swā wē for-ġyfað þām þe
wið ūs āgyltað. Ond ne læd þū nā ūs on costnunge, ac ālȳs ūs fram yfele. Sȳ
hit swā.

Iċ ġe·lȳfe on god fæder ælmihtiġne, scippend heofenan ond eorðan, ond iċ
ġe·lȳfe on hælend crist his āncennedan sunu ūrne drihten. Sē wæs ġe·ēacnod
of þām hālgan gāste, ond ācenned of marian þām mædene, ġe·þrowod under
þām pontiscan pīlate, on rōde āhangen. Hē wæs dēad, ond bebyrġed, ond hē
nyðer āstāh tō helle, ond ārās of dēaðe on þām þriddan dæġe. Ond hē āstāh
ūp tō heofonum, and sitt nū æt swīðran godes ælmihtiġes fæder, þanon hē wile
cuman tō dēmenne æġðer ġe þām cucum ġe þām dēadum. Ond iċ ġe·lȳfe on
þone hālgan gāst, ond ðā hālgan ġe·laðunge, ond hālgena ġe·mænnysse, and
synna for-gifennysse, ond flæsces ærist, ond þæt ēċe līf. Sȳ hit swā.

Remedy for snake-bite

Wið ealle wunda ond wið næddran slitas, ġenim þysse wyrte sēaw þe man
personaciam ond ōðrum naman *bōete* nemneð. Syle drincan on ealdon wīne.
Ealle nædran slitas hyt wundurlīċe ġehæleð.

'Against all wounds and for bites of snake, take the juice of this wort which
one names *personaca*, and by another name *boete* (beet). Give to drink (or, give
it to be drunk) in old wine. It wonderfully heals all bites of snake.'

D. How Speech Sounds are Made

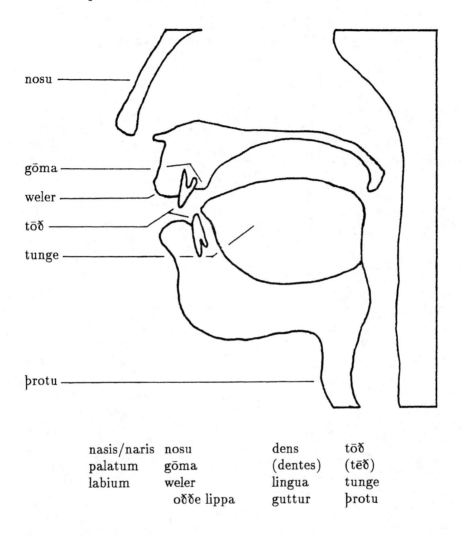

nasis/naris	nosu	dens	tōð
palatum	gōma	(dentes)	(tēð)
labium	weler	lingua	tunge
	oððe lippa	guttur	þrotu

Ǣlċ stemn byð ġeworden of ðæs mūðes clypunge ond of ðǣre lyfte cnys-
sunge. Se mūð drīfð ūt þā clypunge, ond sēo lyft byð ġeslagen mid ðǣre clypunge
ond ġewyrð tō stemne.

'Each [speech-] sound comes to be from the mouth's articulation and from
the beating of the air. The mouth drives out that articulation, and the air is
struck with that articulation and turns into sound.'

Chapter 3

PRONOUNS AND PRONOMINALS

Pronouns and pronominals are among the most frequently occurring words in Old English, being on the same order for Old English as **he, her, it, they, the, that, these, who, what,** etc. are for Modern English. They are also among the easiest forms to learn.

3.1 Personal Pronouns

A. The most common personal pronouns can be gathered into the following paradigms. (*OEG* 701–703)

Speaker(s)

	Singular	Plural
Nominative	**iċ** 'I'	**wē** 'we'
Genitive	**mīn** 'my, mine'	**ūre** 'our(s)'
Dative	**mē** 'me'	**ūs** 'us'
Accusative	**mec, mē** 'me'	**ūsiċ, ūs** 'us'

Addressee(s)

	Singular	Plural
Nominative	**þū** 'thou'	**ġē** 'ye'
Genitive	**þīn** 'thy, thine'	**ēower** 'your(s)'
Dative	**þē** 'thee'	**ēow** 'you'
Accusative	**þec, þē** 'thee'	**ēowiċ, ēow** 'you'

Other(s)

	Masculine	Feminine	Neuter	(General)
Nominative	**hē** 'he'	**hēo** 'she'	**hit** 'it'	**hīe** 'they'
Genitive	**his** 'his'	**hiere** 'her(s)'	**his** 'its'	**hiera** 'their(s)'
Dative	**him** 'him'	**hiere** 'her'	**him** 'it'	**him** 'them'
Accusative	**hine** 'him'	**hīe** 'her'	**hit** 'it'	**hīe** 'them'

Spelling variants such as **hīe hī hiġ** 'they' **hiera hira hyra** 'their(s)' are common, as will be evident in the illustrative citations.

The 'Speaker' (1st person) and the 'Addressee' (2nd person) forms are parallel in lacking gender-specification, in having a shared pattern of morphemes for case-inflection, and in both pronoun bases and inflections being distinguished as singular vs. plural (or nonsingular). The 'Other' (3rd person) forms are related by their common initial element **h–**; number distinction occurs only as a concomitant of their (final) case-inflection morphemes. Only the singular 'Other' inflections specify gender: masculine vs. feminine if sex-distinguished, vs. neuter if non-sex-distinguished. For these pronouns sex distinction of referent is the principal basis for gender selection, when the thing referred to is a person. When the referent of the pronoun is not a person, gender of the pronoun is the grammatical gender of the noun it replaces (see Chapter 4). (*OES* 243–256)

Pronouns have four categories of case inflections, as do the pronominals and the adjectives (Chapter 4) and nouns (Chapter 5). These cases are *morphological* categories—classes of grammatical inflections—and cannot be assigned notional definitions of much worth. What they do is to mark syntactical relations: the way a noun is related to a verb (its subject, its object), or to a preposition, and the like. (See Appendix C.)   The conventional case names are those carried over from Latin grammar.

Nū wylle wē ongynnan *pronomen.*	Now we will begin pronouns.
Iċ eom Apollōnius.	I am Apollonius.
Iċ eom Angin.	I am the Beginning.
Mīn se lēofesta fæder.	My most beloved (*lit.*, mine the most beloved) father.
Seġe mē þīnne naman.	Tell me thy name.
Iċ hit eom.	It is I (*lit.*, I it am).
Eom iċ hit?	Is it I?
Ġemiltsa mē.	Pity me.
Apollōni*us*, þū eart ūre.	Apollonius, thou art ours.
Iċ secge þē.	I say to you.
Iċ bidde þē þæt þū ġife him swā hwæt swā ðū wille.	I bid you that you give him whatever you wish.
Hwæt wylt ðū þæt iċ þē dō?	What do you wish that I do for you? (What wilt thou that I (for) thee do?)
Ne ġelǣd ðū ūs on costnunge.	Lead us not into temptation.
Þā cwæð hē tō Apollōnius.	Then he said to Apollonius.
Þā cwæð hēo tō Apollōni*us*.	Then she said to Apollonius.
Hē cwæð þā tō him.	He said then to him.
Se man him andswerode.	The man answered him.
Hē ne mihte hine þār findan.	He wasn't able to find him there.
Þā hēo becōm tō Apollōni*us*, þā ġewænde hēo onġēan tō hire fæder.	When she came to Apollonius, then she went back to her father.
Apollōnius hire þæs þancode.	Apollonius thanked her for that.
Ġif ðū āxsast æfter mīnum naman, iċ secge þē—iċ hine forlēas.	If you ask concerning my name, I say to you—I (have) lost it.
Hit bið his pleoh, nā mīn.	It is his risk, not mine.
Ġif ġē ða lufiað ðe ēow lufiað....	If ye love those who love you....
Wē willaþ ðæt ðū dō swā hwæt swā wē biddaþ.	We desire that you do whatsoever we ask.
Swā wē ǣr cwǣdon.	As we said earlier.

Onfōh mīn word mid þīnum ēarum. | Receive my words with thine ears.

Swā swā hē ēow ǣr foresǣde. | As he earlier foretold (to) you.

Ēalā, þū gōda cyngc, ġif ðū mē
ġelīfst, iċ secge þæt iċ on-
ġite þæt sōðlīċe þīn dohtor
ġefēol on sweġcræft, ac hēo
næfð [= ne hæfð] hine nā wel
ġeleornod.

O thou good king, if you will
believe me, I say that I perceive that truly your daughter
lacks (has fallen short) in
musicianship, (but) she has not
learned it (at all) well.

Se Hǣlend him ondswarode:
'Ġif iċ wuldriġe mē sylfne nis
[= ne is] mīn wuldor nāht.
Mīn Fæder is, þe mē wuldrað,
be þām ġē cweðaþ þæt hē sȳ
ūre god; and ġē ne cūðon hine.
Iċ hyne cann, ond ġif iċ secge
þæt iċ hine ne cunne, iċ bēo
lēas ond ēow ġelīċ. Ac iċ
hyne cann ond iċ healde his
sprǣċe.'

The Saviour answered them:
'If I glorify myself my glory is
nothing. It is my Father who
glorifies me, [Him] concerning
whom you say that He is our
God; and you do not know Him.
I know Him, and if I say that
I do not know Him, I would be
false and like you. But I
know Him and I keep His
saying.'

Hī āxsodon hine ond þus cwǣdon,
'Hwæt eart þū?' Ond hē ...
cwæð, 'Ne eom iċ nā Crist.'
Ond hiġ āxsodon hine and þus
cwǣdon, 'Eart ðū Elias?' Ond
hē cwæð. 'Ne eom iċ hit.'
Ðā cwǣdon hī, 'Eart ðū wītega?'
Ond hē andwyrde ond cwæð, 'Niċ
[= ne iċ].' Hiġ cwǣdon tō him,
'Hwæt eart þū, þæt wē andwyrde
bringon þām ðe ūs tō þē sendon:
hwæt seġst þū be þē sylfum?'
Hē cwæð, 'Iċ eom clypiendes
stefn on wēstene . . . .'

They asked him and said thus:
'What are you?' And he ...
said, 'I am not Christ.'
And they asked him and thus
said, 'Are you Elias?' And
he said, 'I am not (that one).'
Then they said, 'Are you the
prophet?' And he answered and
said, 'Not I.' They said to him,
'What are you, that we can bring
an answer to those who sent us to
you: what do you say of yourself?'
He said, 'I am the voice of (one)
crying out in the wilderness ....'

B. Another set of pronoun forms was used occasionally; it was lost entirely from the language in early Middle English. The referents are exactly two in number, hence the forms are labeled **dual pronouns.** Only Speaker and Addressee forms occur and, like the singular and plural Speaker and Addressee forms, they do not specify sex of referents. Their morphological relation to plural forms will be apparent. The nominative forms occur regularly in concord with plural verb inflections. (*OEG* 703, *OES* 257–259)

	Speaker	Addressee
Nominative	**wit** 'we-two'	**ġit** 'you-two'
Genitive	**uncer**	**incer**
Dative	**unc**	**inc**
Accusative	**uncit, unc**	**incit, inc**

'Hwæt wylle ġyt þæt iċ inc dō?'
Đā cwædon hiġ, 'Drihten, þæt
uncre ēagan sīn ġe-openede.'

Þā fyliġdun hym tweġyn blinde.
... Sōðliċe þā hē hām cōm, þā
blindan ġenēalæhton tō him ond
se Hǣlend cwæð tō him, 'Ġelȳfe
ġyt þæt iċ inc mæġ ġehǣlan?'
Hiġ cwædon tō hym, 'Witodlīċe,
Drihten.' Đā æt-hrān hē hyra
ēagena cweðynde, 'Sȳ inc æftyr
incrun ġelēafan.'

Đā cwæþ his mōdor tō him, 'Sunu,
hwī dydest þū unc ðus? Þīn
fæder and iċ sāriġende þē sōhton.'
Đā cwæð hē tō him, '... Nyste
ġyt þæt mē ġebyrað tō bēonne
on þām ðingum ðe mīnes fæder
synt?'

Hē sende his twēġen leorning-
cnihtas and cwæð tō him,
'Faraþ tō þām castele þe ongēan
inc ys, and ġyt þār sōna
ġemētað assan folan ġetīġedne.

'What do you-two wish that I do for
you-two?' Then they said, 'Lord,
that our eyes be opened.'

Then two blind (men) followed him....
Truly, when he came home the blind
(ones) approached him and the
Saviour said to them, 'Do you be-
lieve that I am able to heal you?'
They said to him, 'Indeed, Lord.'
Then he touched their eyes saying,
'Be it with respect to you-two
according to your faith.'

Then his mother said to him, 'Son,
why didst thou thus with us? Thy
father and I have sought thee
sorrowing.' Then he said to them,
'... Knew ye-two not that it behoves me to be about those matters
that are my father's?'

He sent his two disciples
and said to them,
'Go to the village that is opposite
you-two, and you-two straightway
will encounter there an ass's colt tied.

... Untīgeað hine and tō mē ġelædað. And ġyf hwā tō inc hwæt cwyð, secgað þæt drihten hæfð his nēode.'

And hiġ cwædon him betwȳnan, 'Næs uncer heorte byrnende þā hē on weġe wið unc spæc, and unc haliġe ġewritu ontȳnde?'

... Untie it and lead (it) to me. And if anyone says anything to you-two, say that the lord hath need of it.'

And they said one to another, 'Wasn't our heart burning when he talked with us on the way, and (when he) opened to us the holy writings?'

Remedy for nosebleed

Ġif men blōd ūt of nosum yrne tō swȳþe, syle him drincan fīflēafan on wīne, and smyre þæt hēafud mid þām. Ðonne oðstandeþ se blōdgyte sōna.

'If for a person blood runs out of his nose too much, give him fiveleaf to drink in wine, and smear the head with it. Then the blood gout will stanch at once.'

3.2 Indefinite Pronominals

The single form **man** is an indefinite pronominal that occurs only as subject of a clause, specifically to represent the indefinite (personal) agent of the action expressed by the verb. The form was replaced in later English by **one, they, you, people**, etc., or the agentive reference was shifted out of the subject position by replacing an active construction with a passive one. It always occurs with a singular verb. A subsequent pronoun referring to **man** is masculine unless (not very commonly) it is plural. (*OES* 363–377)

Ġif man ōþerne mid fyste in naso slæhð, iii scillingas.

If anyone strikes another on the nose with his fist, three shillings [in compensation].

Man brōhte his hēafod on ānum disce and sealde þām mǣdene.

His head was brought on a dish and given to the maiden.

Tō middyre nihte man hrȳmde.

At midnight there was a cry made (someone cried out).

Hit ġedēfe bið þæt mon his wine-dryhten wordum herġe.

It is fitting that one should praise his lord with words.

... þā hine mon in ġefeohte slōg, þā ġelomp þætte him mon āhēow þā hond mid þȳ earme of þǣm līċhoman.... Brōhte hēo man in þā cynelecan burg, þe mon nemnað Bebbanburg.

... when he was slain in battle, then it happened that his hand with the arm was cut off from the body.... They were brought into the royal city which is called Bamborough.

Đonne mon mā fæst ðonne hē ðyrfe.

When a person fasts more than he need.

Wudewanhād is, þæt man wuniġe on clǣnnysse ... æfter his ġemacan, ... ǣġðer ġe weras ġe wīf.

Widowhood is, that one should live after his mate in chastity, ... both men and women.

Hū mæġ man bēon eft ācenned þonne hē bið eald? Mæġ hē eft cuman on his mōdor innoð ond bēon eft ācenned?

How can one be born again when he is old? Can he enter once again into his mother's womb and be born again?

Nis nā ġenōh þat man his nēxtan gōd dō, būton hē hine lufiġe swā swā hine sylfne.

It is not enough that one do good for his neighbor, unless he love him even as himself.

The other indefinite pronominals correspond to 3rd person personal pronouns. They are similar to their Modern English reflexes except that, like the other pronouns, they are inflected for four (or five) cases. (*OEG* 716–717) It will be convenient to represent this set of forms collectively as **HW–**.

HW–	Personal		Nonpersonal
Nominative	**hwā** 'who'		**hwæt** 'what'
Genitive	**hwæs** (etc.)		**hwæs** (etc.)
Dative	**hwǣm**		**hwǣm**
Accusative	**hwone**		**hwæt**
(Instrumental)		**(hwȳ)**	

These indefinite forms show fewer distinctions than do pronouns and other pronominals. They do not show number (singular-plural) distinction. Further, the **HW–** forms do not show sex-gender contrasts; they show only personal *vs.* nonpersonal contrast. To use Jespersen's terms, **hwā** is 'a two-sex word,' **hwæt** is a 'no-sex word.'

The indefinite pronominals are used in interrogative constructions. In these, the utterances call for specification, in a responding utterance, of that which the forms designate as (at the time) unspecified. **Hwā dyde þis?** 'Who did this?' **Hwā lǣrde þē?** 'Who taught thee?' **Hwæt sæġst þū?** 'What sayest thou?' It should be noted that they nevertheless are not pronouns, in the sense in which the term is appropriate to the 'personal' pronouns; 'pronominals' is the term for them adopted here. (*OES* 348–354)

The indefinite pronominals are also used in noninterrogative constructions. In those subordinate constructions which are transformationally related to interrogative sentences—in 'dependent questions'—the forms signal the personal or nonpersonal nature of the referent that stands unspecified. **Swā wæs ... ġemearcod ... hwām þæt sweord ġeworht ... wǣre** 'Thus was marked for whom the sword was wrought.' **Hiġ nyston hwæt hē spræc tō him** 'They didn't know what he said to them.' In utterances that do not call for specification in a responding utterance, the forms designate that from which designation or specification may be made—with **hwā** 'any, anyone,' or in a generalized sense, 'every, everyone,' having a referent expressible by a nominal; or with **hwæt** 'anything.' **Ġif hwā ēaran hæbbe, ġehlyste mē** 'If anyone has ears, (let him) listen to me'; **Ġif hē næbbe hwæt hē selle ...** 'If he hasn't anything he can give.' **Ġif hwā is Gode ġecoren, and his willan wyrċð, þone hē ġehȳrð** 'If anyone is chosen by God, and works his will, that one he heareth.'

Although **hwȳ** is usually classified as the instrumental case form of **HW–**, both its origin and use are different from the other **HW–** forms.

Derivative forms **ǣġhwā**, **ġehwā** 'everyone' do not initiate interrogative constructions. The form **nāthwā** 'someone, anyone,' collapsed from the phrase **(iċ) ne wāt hwā** 'I do not know who,' is a special case.

The phrasal construction **swā hwā swā** 'whoever,' **swā hwæt swā** 'whatever' will be illustrated with other **hw-** forms later.

When a personal pronoun **H–** occurs in a following clause and refers to a personal indefinite **HW–** form, it is always a 'masculine' form: **Ġif hwā mē lufað, hē hylt mīne spræċe** 'If anyone loves me, he will keep my word.' The same convention of gender concord operates with **Þ–** forms (to be described in 3.4): **Sē ðe mē ne lufað, ne hylt hē mīne spræċe** 'That one who does not love me, he does not keep my word.'

Sum 'a certain, one (of many), part (of a whole)' is a different sort of indefinite pronominal, being quantitative. It may occur alone as **Sume hī bēoton, sume hī ofslōgon** 'Some they beat, some they killed,' or commonly it occurs with (partitive) genitive of a noun or pronoun referring to all members of the class it names, as **Wæs iċ þāra manna sum** 'I was one of those men,' **Wæs hira Matheus sum** 'Matthew was one of them,' **[Hē] ġewāt twelfa sum** 'He departed, one of (the) twelve.'

HW— – Verb – Subject in independent (positive) questions

Hwæt hātte Noes wīf?	What was Noah's wife called?
Hwā is manna þæt līfes wilniġe?	Who is (there) of men who desires life?
Tō hwām gā wē?	To whom shall we go?
On hwām mæġ man ġesēon mannes dēað?	By what can one foresee a man's death?
Hwæne sēċe ġē?	Whom seek ye? (*Quem quæritis?*)
Hwā is on worulde þæt ne wundriġe fulles mōnan?	Who is (there) in the world that does not wonder at a full moon?
Hwā is on worulde þæt ne wafiġe, būton þā āne þe hit ær wisson?	Who is (there) in the world that is not astonished, except the ones who knew it previously?
Hwā is moncynnes þæt ne wundrie ymb þās wlitegan tungl?	Who is (there) of mankind that does not wonder at the beautiful heavenly-bodies?
Hwæt eom iċ þæt iċ gā tō Pharaone ond ūt-ālædende sȳ Israhela bearn?	What am I that I should go to Pharaoh and be leading out the children of Isræl?
Đā cwæð Isaac, 'Hwæt eart þū?' Hē andwyrde, 'Iċ eom Esau.' Đā cwæð Isaac, 'Hwæt wæs sē ðe mē ær brōhte of huntoðe?'	Then Isaac said, 'Who are you?' He answered, 'I am Esau.' Then Isaac said, 'What was the one who earlier brought me [game] from hunting?'
'Saga mē, hwæt is God?' 'Iċ ðē secge, ðæt is God ðe ealle ðing on his ġewealdum hafað.'	'Tell me, what is God?' 'I say to thee, that is God which has all things in its governance.'
Þā þe teohhiað þæt hī scylen hī sylfe weorðian mid īdelre spræċe, hȳ cweðað, 'Hwī ne synt wē mūðfrēo? Hū ne mōton wē sprecan þæt wē wyllað? Hwæt ondræde wē hwylċ hlāford mæġ ūs forbēodan ūrne willan?'	Those who intend that they shall honor themselves with vain speech, they say, 'Why are we not free to speak? How are we not allowed to speak what we wish? What should we fear that any lord may forbid us our desire?'

... HW— – Subject – Verb in dependent clauses (interrogative or indefinite)

Hī ... smēadon hwæt þæt wǣre.	They ... pondered what that might be.
Iċ secgan wylle hwæt mē ġemǣtte tō midre nihte.	I will tell you what I dreamed at midnight.
Hī ... hlotu wurpon hwæt ġehwā name.	They ... cast lots what each-one should take.
[Hēo] þōhte hwæt sēo grēting wǣre.	[She] thought about what the greeting might be.
Ðā bīcnodon hī tō hys fæder hwæt hē wolde hine ġenemnedne bēon.	Then they signified to his father what he would have him named.
Hē nyste hwæt þæs sōþes wæs.	He didn't know what the truth of it was.
[Hīe] hogodon ġeorne hwā þǣr ... ǣrost mihte on fæġean men feorh ġewinnan.	They strove eagerly who there ... first might win the life of a fated man.
Men ne cunnon secgan hwā þǣm hlæste onfēng.	Men were not able to say who received that load.
Saga hwæt iċ hātte.	Say what I am called.
Iċ nāt [= ne wāt], ne ne can hwæt þū seġst.	I don't know nor (do I) understand what you say.
'Drihten, hwā eardað on þīnum temple, oððe hwā mōt hine ġe-restan on þǣm hālgan munte?' Þā andswarode Drihten ..., 'Iċ wāt, þēah iċ āhsiġe, hwā þǣr eardað.'	'Lord, who shall dwell in thy tabernacle, or who may lodge on the holy hill?' Then the Lord answered ..., 'I know, though I ask, who shall dwell there.'

Indefinite or generalized HW— 'any(one), every, anything' (*OES* 417–418)

Iċ næbbe hwæt iċ him tōforan lecge.	I haven't anything I can lay before him.
[Hī] næfdon hwæt hī æton.	They hadn't anything they could eat.
Ġif hwā wyle mē fyliġean	If anyone will follow me ....
Ġif hwā sȳ þæt hē nū ġyt ne cunne, hē hit leorniġe.	If there is anyone who still does not know, he may learn it.
Sōð iċ þē secge, būton hwā bēo edniwan ġecenned, ne mæġ hē ġesēon Godes riċe.	Truth I tell you, unless one be born anew, he will not see the kingdom of God.
Ġif hwā þeniġe mē, fyliġe mē .... Ġif mē hwā þēnað, mīn fæder hine wurðað.	If anyone will serve me, let him follow me .... If anyone serves me, my father will honor him.
And ġyf hwā tō inc hwæt cwyð, secgað þæt Drihten hæfð his nēode.	And if anyone says anything to you-two, say that the Lord has need of it.
Ġif ġē hwæt mē biddaþ on mīnum naman, þæt iċ dō.	If you ask (of) me anything in my name, I will do that.
Moyses sæde, ġif hwā dēad syġ and bearn næbbe, þæt his brōðor nyme hys wīf.	Moses said, if a man die and (he) hasn't children, that his brother should take his wife.
Ġif hwæs brōðor byð dēad ond wif hæbbe....	If a man's brother is dead and (if he) have a wife ....
... hwæt hwā ōðrum tō wō ġedō.	... what anyone may do wrongfully to another.
Sōþlīċe iċ secge ēow, ne winne ġē ongēn þā ðe ēow yfel dōð, ac ġif hwā þē slēa on þīn swȳþre wenge, ġeġearwa him þæt ōðer.	Truly I say to you, don't contend against those who do evil to you, but if anyone strike you on your right cheek, make ready for him the other.
Ġehȳre, ġif hwā ēaran hæbbe tō ġehȳranne!	If anyone has ears to hear, (let him) hear!
Nū bidde iċ ... ġif hwā þās bōc āwrītan wylle, þæt hē hī ġeornlīċe ġerihte.	Now I ask ... if anyone intends to copy this book, that he diligently correct it.

3.3 Some Related Forms

Certain forms are not inflected for case or number or gender but do have syntactic characteristics much like those of indefinite pronominals. The long-standing tradition of classifying these forms as adverbs had its beginning in Latin grammar, as an illustrative text later will show. (*OEG* 677–679, *OES* 1121, 1147–1150) Their characteristics within English, however, associate them with the pronominals. While none of these forms is inflected, the forms do make up sets of another kind, as will be apparent in the listing of the principal ones that follows:

hēr 'here'	**þǣr** 'there'	**hwǣr** 'where'
hider 'hither'	**þider** 'thither'	**hwider** 'whither'
heonan 'hence'	**þonan** 'thence'	**hwonan** 'whence'
[**nū** 'now']	**þonne** 'then'	**hwanne** 'when'
		hū 'how'
		hwȳ 'why'

The **hw–** forms in this set are very similar in distribution to the **HW—** pronominals. **Hiġ cwǣdon tō him, 'Hwār eardast ðū?' Hē cwæþ tō him, 'Cumað ond ġesēoþ.' Hiġ cōmon and ġesāwon hwār hē wunode.** 'They said to him, "Where are you dwelling?" He said to them, "Come and see." They came and saw where he dwelt.' **Iċ næbbe hwyder iċ mīne wǣstmas gadriġe** 'I don't have anywhere (that) I may store my crops.' **Hī nabbað hwanun hiġ hit þē for-ġyldon** 'They haven't anything with which they can repay it to you.'

The **h–** and **þ–** forms do not signal interrogative constructions in the way **hw–** forms may. **Nis hē hēr** 'He isn't here.' **'Hwǣr eart þū?'** ... **'Hēr!'** 'Where art thou?' ... 'Here!' **Wæs Hǣstēn þǣr cumen mid his here** 'Hǣsten was come (*or* had arrived) there with his army.' **Ġyf þǣr man ān bān findeð unforbærned...** 'If one finds there one bone not burned up....'

Unlike Modern English cognate forms, the **þ–** forms are used correlatively in Old English:

Þǣr ðīn gold is, þǣr is ðīn heorte.	Where thy gold is, there is thine heart.
Þār ēower goldhord is, þār byð ēower heorte.	Where your treasure is, there is your heart.
Ne hopa ðū tō swīðe tō þām ðe ðē	Do not trust too much in that which

man ġehāte: ðǣr lȳt ġehāta bið, ðǣr bið lȳt lygena.

is promised to you: where are few promises, there are few lies.

Ðǣr lȳtel ġehāten bið, þǣr bið lȳtel ālogen.

Where little is promised, there little is left unfulfilled.

Ðonne ðū ealle ġedǣlde hæfst, ðonne bist ðū self wǣdla.

When you have dispensed everything, then you yourself will be poor.

They are parallel but not correlative, however, in **Ðā cōm þǣr rēn and þǣr blēowon windas** 'Then came there rain and there blew winds.'

The þ- forms also occur 'with relative force' a bit like *wh*-forms in Modern English: **On ðǣre byriġ þǣr se cyning ofslæġen læġ** 'In that fortress where the king lay slain.' **Ġē ne magon cuman þyder iċ fare** 'Ye cannot come where I shall go.' **Far þǣr ðū frēonda wēne** 'Go where you may expect friends.' The use of these þ- forms is like that of **þæt**: **Hēr þū hæfst þæt þīn ys** 'Here you have what (*or* that which) is thine.' Iterative use of **þǣr** is also fairly common: ... **þæt iċ ne āslīde þǣr þǣr iċ stæppan scyle** '... that I shall not slide there (i.e., in that place) where I shall step.' Occasionally þ- forms occur with **ðe**, as do pronouns and pronominals (see 3.4 B): **Far nū þider þe þū wille** 'Go now wherever you wish.' **Ðider ðe Stephanus forestōp, ... ðider folgode Paulus** 'Where Stephen went before, ... there Paul followed.'

HW— – Verb – Subject in independent (positive) questions

Hū mæġ iċ sēċan þæt gāstlīċe
leoht þe iċ ġeseon ne mæġ,
oþþe hwanan sceal mē cūþ
bēon þæt iċ mid līċhomlicum
ēagum ġeseon ne mæġ?

How am I to seek that spiritual
light which I am unable to see,
or whence shall be known to me
that which with (my) bodily eyes
I am unable to see?

Hwyder ġewiton þā welan and
þā glengas? ... Oþþe hwyder
ġewiton þā mycclan weorod þe
him ymb ferdon and stōdan?
And hwær syndon þā þe hīe
heredan? ... And hwær cōm seo
frætwodnes heora hūsa? ...
Oþþe hwær cōm heora snyttro?
... Ealle þā syndon nū from
heora ēagum ġewitene, and ...
næfre ... hider eft ne cumaþ.

Whither have gone the wealth and
the ornaments? ... Or whither
have gone the great throngs who
encompassed and surrounded them?
And where are those who praised
them? ... And where has gone the
adornments of their houses? ...
Or where has gone their wisdom?
... All those are now gone from
their eyes, and ... never ...
shall come hither again.

Hwær syndon þā rīcran cāseras
and cynegas, þā ðe ġeo ġefyrn
wæron?

Where are the mighty rulers and
kings, the ones who once were
[i.e., living] long ago?

Hū sculon wit nū libban?

How are we-two to live now?

Hū ne synt ġē sēlran þonne hiġ?

How are you not better than they?

Hwī didest þū þæt?

Why didst thou that?

Hwanon cōmon ġē?

Where did you come from?

Hwanon eart þū?

What is your origin?

Hwȳ wolde hē hīe læran?

Why did he wish to teach them?

Hwænne beoð þās þing?

When will those things be?

Hwenne ġewyrð þæt?

When will that happen?

Hwær eart þū nū, ġefera?

Where art thou now, comrade?

HW— – Subject – Verb in Noun-clauses (interrogative and indefinite)

Nāt iċ hwæt hē is ne hwanon hē is.	I don't know what he is or whence he is.
Þū nāst hwanon hē cymþ ne hwyder hē gǣþ.	You don't know whence he comes nor whither he goes.
Iċ wāt hwanon iċ cōm and hwyder iċ gā; ġē nyton hwanon iċ cōm ne hwyder iċ gā.	I know whence I came and whither I go; you know not whence I came nor whither I go.
Iċ wāt ġe hwæt þū eart ġe for-hwon þū gnornast.	I know both what you are and why you grieve.
Wē ġehīrdon hū ġē ofslōgon twēgen cynegas.	We have heard how you destroyed the two kings.
Ne bēo ġē embe-þenċynde hū oððe hwæt ġē specon oððe ondswarian.	Be (ye) not considering how or what ye shall say or answer.
Wē nyton hū-mete hē nū ġesyhþ ne hwā his ēagan untynde.	We don't know by what means he sees nor who opened his eyes.
[Hī] behēoldon hwār hē ġelēd wǣre.	They beheld where he was laid.
Hē of-āxode hwæt his suna him dydon.	He found out what his sons had done to him.
Fræġn hē ēac mē tō-hwon iċ þider cōm and hwæt iċ þǣr wolde.	He also asked me why I came thither and what I wanted there.
[Hēo] ne mihte findan hwǣr hēo hire fōt āsette.	It [the dove] could not find where it might place its foot.
Abraham ... ġeseah hū þā ysla upp flugon.	Abraham ... beheld how the embers went up.
Uton ... witan hwæt hē sȳ tō sōðe, and hwanon hē cume, and hwæt hē dō on þām ġerīme, oððe hwȳ hē sȳ swā ġehāten, oððe hwā hine ġemētte.	Let us ... know what it really is, and what is its origin, and what it may do in computus, or why it may be so named, or who discovered it.

Designative-adverbial uses of þ— forms

And iċ þā þanon fōr and eft
ðyder cōm.

And then I went thence and
afterwards came thither.

Hē fōr þanon.

He set forth from that place.

Ðā fērde hē ðyder.

Then he traveled thither.

[Ðā] þe hine þyder lǣddon.

Those who had brought him thither.

Iċ ðǣr furðum cwōm tō ðām
hringsele Hrōðgār grētan.

I had just come there to the ring-
hall to seek out Hrothgar.

Sē þe þǣr ġehǣled wæs nyste hwā
hit wæs.

The one who had been healed there
didn't know who it was.

Hē wæs āna þǣr.

He was alone there.

Sēo lyft ðonne hēo āstyred bið is
wind; se wind hæfð mislīċe
naman on bōcum; ðanon ðe hē
blǣwð, him bið nama ġesett.

The air when it is stirred up is
wind; the wind has various
names in books; that place from
which it blows, to it is the
name assigned.

Ðæt flōd ys þanon tōdǣled on
fēower ēan.

From that point the stream runs
in four separate channels.

Fræġn hē ēac mē tō-hwon iċ þider
cōm and hwæt iċ þǣr wolde.

He inquired also of me why I came
thither and what I wished there.

God wunaþ on ðǣre ċeastre his
ānfealdnesse; ðonan hē dǣlþ
manega ġemetgunga eallum his
ġesceaftum, and þonan hē welt
ealra.

God dwells in the city of his
onefoldness; from there he dispenses
many (fit) measures to all his
creatures, and from there he rules
all.

Ðā ferede hine Godes hand þider
þǣr hine men siððan āredon.

Then the hand of God carried him
thither where men afterwards
found him.

Þonne ġē þanon ūt-gāð, āsceacað
þæt dust of ēowrum fōtum.

When you depart from there, shake
the dust from your feet.

Conjunctive-adverbial uses of þ— forms

Ēadiġe synt ġē þonne hī wyriað ēow.

Blessed are ye when they curse you.

Hwā sceal tō his rīċe fōn þonne
hē brōðer næfð, ne hē bearn
ne belǣfþ?

Who will succeed him (lit., take
his kingdom) when he hasn't a
brother nor leaves offspring?

Bēo ġelīċe þām mannum þe hyra
hlāfordes ābīdað, hwænne hē sȳ
fram ġyftum ġeċyrred, þæt
hiġ him sōna ontȳnon þonne
hē cymð and cnucað. Ēadiġe
synt þā þēowas þe se hlāford
wæċċende ġemēt þonne hē cymð.

Be like those men who wait for
their master, when he will be
returned from the marriage-feast,
so that they may open to him immediately when he comes and knocks.
Blessed are those servants whom the
master finds waking when he comes.

Nellen ġē goldhordian ēow
goldhordas on eorþan þǣr
ōm ond moððe hit fornimð and
þǣr ðēofas hit delfað and
forstelaþ; goldhordiað ēow
sōþlīċe goldhordas on heofenan
þǣr nāðor ōm ne moþðe hit ne
fornimð ond ðār þēofas hit ne
delfað ne ne forstelaþ.

Don't lay-up-treasures for yourself
on earth where rust and moth
will consume it and where thieves
will dig it out and steal it;
lay up treasures in heaven
where neither rust nor moth will
destroy it and where thieves
will not dig it up nor steal it.

Tō þām lande þǣr þē lust myneð
tō ġesēċanne.

To that region where desire directs
thee to go.

Iċ ġeċyrre on mīn hūs þanon iċ
ūt-ēode.

I will return to my house from
which I came.

... on ðā rīcu þonon þe hē ǣr
sended wæs.

... into the kingdoms where he
had been sent.

Hē ġewāt on Hibernia, ðonan hē
ǣr cōm.

He departed to Hibernia, from
which he had come.

swā hw— swā 'whoever, whatever,'
swā hw— swā 'wherever, whence(-so-)ever,' etc.

Eall swā hwæt swā hē findan mihte, ... hē dǣlde.	Everything he was able to find he dealt out.
'Wē wyllað þæt þū ūs dō swā hwæt swā wē biddað.' Þā cwæð hē, 'Hwæt wylle ġyt þæt iċ inc dō?'	'We desire that you do for us whatever we ask.' Then he said, 'What do you-two wish that I do for you?'
[Hē] ġelȳfð swā hwæt swā hē cwyð, ġewurðe þis.	He believes (that) whatever he says, this will come to pass.
Swā hwā swā ytt of ðyson hlāfe, hē leofað on ēċnysse.... Sē þe ytt þysne hlāf, hē leofað on ēċnysse.	Whoever eats of this bread, he will live eternally.... He who eats this bread, he will live forever.
Hweþer hī maġen ābiddan eall swā hwæt swā hēo biddað, and beġytan eall þæt hī ġewilniað.	Whether they are able to obtain everything she asks, and get all that they desire.
Swā hwār swā se līċhama bið, þyder bēoð earnas ġegaderud.	Wherever the body is, thither will be the eagles gathered.
Iċ fyliġe þē swā hwyder swā þū fǣrst.	I will follow you wherever you go.
Swā hū swā hit ġewurde.	However it may have happened.
Hī habbaþ æt Gode swā hū swā hī ġe-earniaþ.	They will have from God how(-so-) ever they merit.
Far nū swā hwider swā þū wille.	Go now wherever you wish.
Hī þæt mǣste yfel worhton swā hwār swā hī fērdon.	They wrought the greatest evil wherever they went.

Both indefinite pronominals and **hw–** quasi-pronominals also occur in fixed phrases with a preceding **lōc** or **lōca: lōca hwā** 'whoever,' **lōca hwǣr** 'wherever,' **lōca hwonne** 'whenever,' **lōc hwæþer** 'whichever (of two),' etc.

Lōc hwæþer þæra ġebrōþra.	Whichever of the (two) brothers.
Bide mē lōce hwæs þū wille.	Ask me for whatever you will.
Lōca hwylċ ēower sī synlēas, wurþe ǣrest stān on hī.	Whichever of you may be sinless, (let him) cast first a stone at her.
Lōca hwylċe hiġ bēoð.	Whichever they may be.
Lōca hwǣr bēo se mōna nīwe.	Wherever the moon is new.
Hī fērdon lōc hū hī woldon.	They went however they liked.
Swā þæt lōc whenne þæt flōd byþ ealra hēhst.	So that whenever the water is highest of all.
Lōca hwā þǣre mihte āge, hē mōt ġehæftne man ālȳsan.	Whoever has the power, he may release the captive man.

Quasi-pronominal **h–** forms

Þā iċ hēr ǣrest cōm.	When I first came here.
Ne mæġ iċ hēr leng wesan.	I am not able to remain here longer.
Hēr on þyssum lǣnum līfe.	Here in this transitory life.
Hēr endaþ sēo ǣreste bōc.	Here endeth the first book.
Ðæt scip ... bið drifen hider and ðider.	The ship ... is driven hither and thither.
Hī irnaþ hider and ðider dwoliġende.	They run hither and thither wandering.
Þā men secgaþ, þā þe þyder fērdon and eft hider cōmon, þæt....	Those men say, those who traveled thither and came back hither, that....
Iċ mæġ heonan ġeseōn.	I can see from here.
And ... betwux ūs and ēow is myċel dwolma ġetrymed. Þā ðe willað heonon tō ēow faran ne magon, ne þanun faran hidere.	And ... between us and you there is a great gulf fixed. Those who would travel from here to you cannot, nor from thence fare hither.

3.4 Designators

A. Two sets of pronominals have designative functions partially parallel to those of the Modern English forms **that–those** and **this–these**. One set, whose citation forms are **se sēo þæt**, will be called here 'determiners' (**Þ**—). The other set, whose citation forms are **þes þēos þis**, will be called 'specifiers' (**Þ**—s-). (*OEG* 708–711, *OES* 315–345)

Any form from either set may occur as a constituent of a noun phrase— **þā menn** 'the men' or 'those men,' **þās menn** 'these men,' much as in Modern English. Unlike Modern English, though, any of these forms may also occur as a pronominal: **Hēr synd þā** 'Here are those' or 'Here they are'; **þās cōmon tō þām hūse** 'These (ones) came to the house.'

Like third-person pronouns, these forms are inflected for grammatical case and gender, as well as for number. The extent to which the paradigms for these forms parallel those of third-person pronouns (**H**—) will appear in the side-by-side listing below. The arrangement follows the order used in 3.1 for paradigms of the personal pronouns. The fifth case forms are called 'instrumental.'

Singular

H—	Þ—	Þ—s-	H—	Þ—	Þ—s-	H—	Þ—	Þ—s-
hē	se	þes	hēo	sēo	þēos	hit	þæt	þis
his	þæs	þisses	hiere	þære	þisse(re)	his	þæs	þisses
him	þæm	þissum	hiere	þære	þisse(re)	him	þæm	þissum
hine	þone	þisne	hīe	þā	þās	hit	þæt	þis
	þȳ	þȳs		þære	þisse(re)		þȳ	þȳs

Plural

H—	Þ—	Þ—s-
hīe	þā	þās
hiera	þāra	þissa (þissera)
him	þæm	þissum
hīe	þā	þās
	þæm	þissum

Choice of singular or plural form was dependent on grammatical number of the following noun form when the form occurred within a noun phrase (*grammatical concord of number*); it was dependent on the number of items constituting the referent with pronominal uses of the forms.

Choice among the gender-distinguished forms was governed for the most part by the noun (or name) with which the form most directly structured, either within a noun phrase or in a referential relation in pronominal function (*grammatical concord of gender*). Grammatical gender (which will be explained for nouns more fully in Chapter 5) operated independently of 'natural' gender. While **þes** is selected to refer to a male person in the construction **þes ys of þām** 'This one [male] is (one) of them,' when such a form occurs linked to a noun, the choice of a gender-distinguished form by syntactic rule is automatic. Simply stated, certain classes of nouns occur with **se** or **þes** forms, others with **sēo** or **þēos** forms, still others with **þæt** or **þis** forms, and the patterns of co-occurrence are both constant and mutually exclusive (*grammatical government of gender*). Grammatical gender of nouns is defined in large part by these patterns of co-occurrence. See Appendix C.

Choice among case-distinguished forms was governed solely by the syntax of the clause in which the form occurs (*grammatical government of case*). See Appendix C. The clearest example is the specifier or determiner always showing the same case inflection as the noun it precedes within a noun phrase. As a pronominal, its case inflection reflects its function within its immediate clause.

The designative functions of these forms differ in a fundamental way from Modern English forms that occur in the same position within noun phrases. Because these pronominals form a closed set, the designative function of a given form is fully defined by its relation to the other forms in the same set. Old English has *two* of these designators þ— and þ—s- related historically to *three* forms in Modern English, **the, this–these, that–those.** Furthermore, *Old English did not have an 'indefinite article' to correspond to MnE* **a/an.** The entire system of expressing or marking *definiteness* in Old English thus will be unlike that of the system in Modern English.

Occurrence of either a determiner þ— or specifier þ—s- form in a noun phrase represents an option in discourse—roughly, þ— designates one, or a subgroup, of a general group that is apparent within the context, while deictic þ—s- specifies a particular member or subgoup of a (context-) designated group: **Ðæt folc þis wundor ġeseah** 'The people saw this wonder.' Satan, when cast into Hell, says: **Is þes ænga styde unġelīċ swīðe þām ōðrum [hām] þe wē ǣr cūðon!** 'This narrow place is exceedingly unlike that (*or* the) other [home] which we knew formerly!' **On þysum ġēare fōr se micla here** 'In this year went forth the (*or* that) large army.' **Þis ys sē be þām þe ġecweden ys þurh Esaiam ðone witegan . . . .** 'This is the one concerning whom is spoken by the prophet Esaias. . . .' **Drihten rīxað on ēcnesse on þisse worulde ġe on þǣre tōweardan** 'The Lord rules eternally in this world and in the one to come.'

Two examples will illustrate these matters. **Sōðlíce sum Pharisēisc man wæs ġenemned Nichodēmus. Sē wæs Iūdēa ealdor. Ðes cōm tō him on niht.** 'Verily a certain Pharisee-ish man was named Nichodemus. He was a leader of the Jews. This (man) came to him at night.' **Fenix—swā hātte ān fugel on Arabiscre þēode. Sē leofað fīf hund ġēara, ond æfter dēaðe eft ārīst ġe-edcucod; ond se fugel ġetācnað ūrne ǣrist on þām ende-nēhstan dæġe.** 'Phoenix—thus is called a bird in Arabic nations. It lives five hundred years, and after death arises again requickened; and the bird signifies our rising-up on the final day.'

Finally and importantly, the determiner-pronominals occur commonly in relative pronominal function: **Ġemetegung, mid þǣre sceal sēo sāwol ealle þing ġemǣtigian** 'Moderation, with which the soul shall measure all things.'

Determiner þ—

Hē behēold þā sǣ.	He looked at the sea.
Hē behēold þæt gold ond þæt seolfor ... ond ðā bēodas.	He beheld the gold and the silver ... and the tables.
Se cyning ond þā rīcostan men drincað meolc.	The king and the richest men drink milk.
Hēo cwæð tō þām mannum	She said to the men ....
Ðā cwæð hē tō ðām cynge	Then he said to the king ....
Gā intō ðāre ċeastre.	Go into the city.
Þā ġeseah hē sumne fiscere gān, tō þām hē beseah.	Then he saw a certain fisherman walking, to whom he looked up.
Þrȳ ġelǣrede weras ... þā ġirndon þæs cyninges dohtor.	Three educated men ... who desired the king's daughter.
Sēo sāwul, oððe þæt līf, oððe sēo edwist synd ġecwædene tō hyre sylfra.	The soul, or the life, or the substance are considered by themselves separately.
Þæt ġemynd, oððe þæt andġit, oððe sēo wylla bēoð ġecwædene tō sumum þinga.	The memory, or the understanding, or the will, are considered relatively to other (certain) things.
Sēo sāwul ... is þæs līċhoman līf and þǣre sāwle līf is God. Ġif sēo sāwul forlǣt þone līċhoman þonne swælt se līċhoma; and ġif God forlǣt þā sāwle þonne swælt hēo.	The soul ... is the life of the body and the life of the soul is God. If the soul forsake the body then the body dies; and if God forsake the soul then it dies.
Sēo sunne þe onlīht ealne mid-eard is Godes ġesceaft, and wē magon understandan þæt hyre lēoht is of hyre, nā hēo of þām lēohte; and sēo hætu gæð of þǣre sunnan, and of hire lēohte ġelīċe.	The sun which lights up the whole earth is God's creature, and we can understand that her light is from herself and not she from the light; and the heat proceeds equally from the sun and from her light.

native plurals

werewolf
man !!

Specifier **þ**—**s**-

Þis lēoht wē habbaþ wiþ nȳtenu
  ġemǣne, ac þæt lēoht wē
  sceolan sēċan, þæt wē mōtan
  habban mid englum ġemǣne.

Eal þes middanġeard, ond
  þās windas, ond þās reġnas.

Mid þisse sealfe and mid þȳs
  drenċe ...

On þissere nihte.

On þissum dæġe.

On þyssum fēowertigum nihte.

Be þisse tīde.

On þissere worulde.

Æfter þissum wordum.

Mid þissere andsware.

Þes ys smiþes sunu.

Nys þes Iōsepes sunu?

Ðes is sōþ wītega.

Ðes is, be þām þe āwriten is....

Hwanon is þysum þes wīsdōm?

Se Hǣlend cwæþ, þis ġehȳrende....

Nimaþ ðās þing.

Ðās gōdnysse wē sceolan lufian,
  ac þissere gōdnysse lufu ne
  mæġ bēon būtan on þǣre sāwle.

Hwæt ys þis? Hwæt is þēos nīwe
  lār?

Solomon on eallum hys wuldre næs
  ġescrȳdd swā þissa ān.

This light we have in common
  with animals, but that light
  we are to seek that we may
  have in common with angels.

All this earth, and these winds,
  and these rains.

With this salve and with this
  draught ....

On this night.

On this day.

In this forty night period.

Concerning this time.

In this world.

After these words.

With this answer.

This is the carpenter's son.

Isn't this Joseph's son?

This is a true prophet.

This one it is, concerning whom
  is written....

Whence is this wisdom in this (man)?

The Saviour spoke, hearing this....

Take these things.

This goodness we should love,
  but there may not be love
  of this goodness except in
  the soul.

What (thing) is this? What is
  this new teaching?

Solomon in all his glory wasn't
  arrayed as one of these.

On ðisum līfe wē behofiað hlāfes,
and lāre, and husel-ganges. On
þām tōwearden līfe wē ne behofiað
nānes eorðlīċes biġ-leofan. . . .
Hēr wē behofiað lāre and wīsdōmes.
On ðām heofonlīcan līfe bēoð ealle
full wīse, and on gāstlīcre lāre
full ġerāde, þā ðe nū, þurh wīsra
manna lāre, bēoð Godes bebodum
under-þēodde. And hēr wē behofiað
ðæs husles-ðyġene for ūre beterunge,
sōðlīċe on ðære heofonlīcan wununge
wē habbað mid ūs Cristes līċhaman,
mid þām hē rīxað on ēċnysse.

On þyssere worulde wē biddað ūre
synna forġyfenysse, and nā on þære
tō-weardan. Se man ðe nele his
synna behrēowsian on his līfe, ne
beġȳt hē nāne forġyfenysse on ðām
tō-weardan. And on ðisum līfe wē
biddað þæt God ūs ġescylde wið
dēofles costnunga, and ūs ālȳse
fram yfele. On ðam ēċan līfe ne
bið nān dēofol ne nān yfel mann,
ðe ūs mæġe dreċċan oððe derian.

B. A single form **ðe** functions as **pronominal marker**. Although **ðe** distinguishes formally neither case nor number nor sex- or grammatical-gender, being a set consisting of one form only, it is not ambiguous: it has a fixed and simple reference function, essentially serving to mark the place of potential recurrence of the pronoun or pronominal or determined noun most closely preceding it.

Besides its formal differences from pronouns and pronominals, **ðe** is distinguished from these other forms by its restriction to relative clauses, of which it is regularly the head; it does not occur in the position of a noun or nominal construction in principal clauses (or independent sentences). It is further defined distributionally in relation to pronouns and pronominals. Most commonly it occurs following a determiner or specifier pronominal or personal pronoun alone, or following a phrasal construction containing a noun marked by a preceding determiner or specifier form: **Se iunga man þe þū æfter āxsodest** 'The young man whom you inquired after'; **Ić hit eom þe wið þē sprece** 'It is I who speak with thee'; **Ðās þing þe mē sēo cwēn forġeaf** 'These things which the woman gave me'; ... **and on eorðan sibb mannum, þām ðe bēoð gōdes willan** 'and on earth peace to men, those who are of good will'; **Sē þe understandan ne mæġ, hē hit sceal ġelȳfan** 'That one who cannot understand [this], he must believe it.' It follows as well and refers to a construction defined by a determinative (genitive-case) pronoun: **Ić funde mīnne scylling þe ić forlēas** 'I have found my coin which I had lost.' It also may follow and refer to such quantifying forms as **ælċ** 'each,' and **ān** 'one, a/an,' **eall** 'all,' **fēawa**, 'few,' **sum** 'a certain,' when they are pronominal or designative, and a few others which are also definers (e.g., **þider, þǣr, þonan**, see 3.3 or **hwilċ**, see 3.5). All these precedent forms are deictic—words which point out their referent within the field represented in a general way by a noun.

Pronominal marker **ðe** is semantically replaceable by a directly referential word—either a noun or a pronoun or a pronominal: in a sense, it is a noun substitute twice removed. (*OES* 2145–2362)

In respect to syntax (as opposed to reference) **ðe** has functions like those of relative pronouns in later English, acting as a substantive in its own clause, referring to another substantive in another clause (its 'antecedent'), and signaling the downgrading—the subordination—of its clause to the other one. Put another way, **ðe** occurs only in a clause that is a (constituent) modifier in a syntactical noun-phrase; its clause follows the head noun (or pronoun) which it modifies, and it occurs at the beginning of that clause, whatever its syntactic role may be within its clause (subject, object, etc.).

Þ— ðe, Þ—s- ðe

Sē þe nys mid mē, hē is ongēn mē.

He who is not with me is against me.

Sē þe nis āgēn ēow, sē is for ēow.

That one who is not against you, he (that one) is for you.

Sē þe be him sylfum sprycð sēcþ his āgen wuldor; sē þe sēcþ þæs wuldor þe hyne sende, sē is sōþfæst.

The one who speaks on his own (authority) seeks his own glory; the one who seeks the glory of the one who sent him is true.

Sē ðe ġelȳfð on mē, hē wyrcð þā weorc þe iċ wyrċe.

The one who believes in me, he does those works that I do.

Sē ðe ne āwurðaþ þone sunu ne āwurþaþ hē þone fæder þe hine sende.

He who does not honor the son does not honor the father who sent him.

Þām bið ġeseald þe hæfð, ond þām ðe næfð [= ne hæfð], ēac þæt hē hæfð him bið æt-broden.

To that one is given who has, and for the one who has not, even that which he has from him will be taken.

Ūre ieldran, þā ðe þās stōwa ǣr hīoldon.

Our ancestors, (those) who formerly inhabited these regions.

Hwæt is þes þe hēr sprycþ woffunga?

What is this one who here speaks blasphemy?

Hwæt is sē ðe hyt biġ seġð? ... Hwæt ys hē?

What is that one he says it of? ... What is he?

Sē singð mid gāste, sē ðe clypað þā word mid mūðe and ne understænt þæs andġites ġetācnunge; and sē singð mid mōde, sē ðe þæs andġites ġetācnunge understænt.

He sings with spirit who utters the words with his mouth and does not understand the signification of the meaning; and he sings with the mind who understands its tokening.

Þæt is sōþ wȳsdōm þæt man ġewylniġe þæt sōðe līf on þām þe hē ǣfre lybban mæġ mid Gōde on wuldre ġif hē hit on þyssere worulde ġe·earnað.

That is true wisdom, that a man desire the true life wherein he may live forever with God in glory, if he merit it in this world.

Sē þe hæfð twā tunecan, sylle þām þe næfð; ond þām ġelīċe dō sē þe mettas hæfð.

He who has two coats, (let him) give to that one who has not; and let him do likewise who has food.

Sē þe hæbbe ēaran tō ġehȳrenne, ġehȳre.	Who hath ears to hear, (let him) hear.
Sē ðe ēaran hæbbe tō ġehȳranne, ġehȳre.	
Ġehȳre sē ðe ēaran hæbbe.	
Ġehȳre sē ðe ēaran hæbbe tō ġehȳranne.	
Dæt þe ācenned is of flǣsce, þæt is flǣsc; and þæt þe of gāste is ācenned, þæt is gāst.	That which is born of flesh is flesh, and that which is born of spirit is spirit.

Þis with **eall** follows the same pattern:

Iċ myngie ēow ... þæt ġē ġeorne þis eall understanden þe iċ ēow ġesǣd hæbbe.	I exhort you ... that you carefully understand all this (understand this fully?) which I have said to you.

Occasionally, the deixis usually carried by **se**, **þes**, **mīn**, and the like is provided by semantic characteristics of certain nouns; thus, in a homily on the Christian creed, **englas** is uniquely defined in and of itself, hence:

[Se scyppend] geworhte ealle ðing of nāhte, ... heofonas and englas þe on heofonum wuniað.	[The Creator] wrought all things from nothing, ... heavens, and angels which dwell in the heavens.

A rare construction uses a 'headless **þe**,' that is, **þe** without an overt referent preceding it:

Sōðlīċe þā Herōdes wæs forðfaren. ... Drihtnes engel ætȳwde Iōsepe on Egiptum and þus cwæð: 'Ārīs and nim þæt ċild and his mōdor, and far on Israhela land. Nū synd forðfarene þe ðæs ċildes sāwle sōhton.' Hē ārās ðā. . . .	Truly, then Herod was departed. ... The Lord's angel appeared to Joseph in Egypt and said thus: 'Arise and take the child and his mother, and go into the land of Israel. Now are dead who sought the child's soul.' He arose then. . . .

þ— – Noun (Name) – ðe
þ—s- – Noun (Name) – ðe

Se iunga man þe þū æfter
āxsodest is forliden man.

The young man whom you inquired
after is a shipwrecked man.

Se forlidena man is cumen þe ðū
æfter sændest.

The shipwrecked man whom you sent
for is come.

Næs þæt nā se Gōdric þe ðā gūðe
forbeah.

That was not at all the Godric
who turned from the battle.

Herōdes cwæð, 'Se Iōhannes þe iċ
behēafdode, sē ārās of dēaðe.'

Herod said, 'The John whom I beheaded, he arose from death.'

Eart þū se Bēowulf, sē þe wið
Brecan wunne?

Are you that Beowulf, the one who
contested with Breca?

Hwæt is þes iunga man ðe sit mid
sārlicum andwlitan?

What is this young man who sits
with sorrowful countenance?

Bið hē þām men ġelīċ þe ārærþ
sume hēage hlæddre.

He is like the man who raises up
a high ladder.

Iċ wyrċe þæs willan ðe mē sende.

I work the will of the one who
sent me.

Sēo sāwul is ġesæliġ ðe þone
scyppend lufað þe hī ġescēop.

That soul is blessed that loveth
the creator who created it.

Nimað þās þing mid ēow þe mē
sēo cwēn forġeaf, and gān wē
sēċan ūre ġesthūs.

Take these things with you which
the woman gave me, and let us
go seek our guest-house.

Hē hine ūp āhōf and lædde hine
mid him tō his hūse and ðā
ēstas him beforan leġde ðe
hē him tō bēodenne hæfde.

He raised him up and led him with
him to his house, and laid
before him the delicacies that
he had to offer to him.

De participio. Ðes dæl hæfð
þā ylcan tīda þe ðā word
habbað þe hē of cymð.

Concerning participles. This part
(of speech) has the same tenses
which the verbs have which it
comes from.

Se kok ðe wē ær ymb spræcon,
ær-ðæm-ðe hē crāwan wille,
hefð ūp his fiðru.

The cock which we spoke about
earlier, before it will crow,
raises up its wings.

Pronoun (...) ðe

Determinative (Possessive) Pronoun – Noun – ðe

Name ðe

Ðū ðe þār andweard wǣre.	You who were present there.
Fæder ūre, þū þe eart on heofonum.	Our Father, (thou) who art in the heavens (i.e., heaven).
Ealle ... ġē þe mȳne anlīcnysse habbað, cumað tō mē.	All ... ye who have my likeness, come to me.
Ġewītað fram mē, ġē þe worhton unrihtwȳsnesse.	Depart from me, you who wrought unrighteousness.
Iċ eom ēower God þe ēow lǣdde of Egypta lande.	I am your God who led you from the land of the Egyptians.
Iċ hit eom þe wið þē sprece.	It is I who speaks with thee.
Þū þe þyrstende wǣre monnes blōdes .xxx. wintra, drync nū þīne fylle.	You who have been thirsting for man's blood thirty years, drink now your fill.
Onġytað nū, kyningas, ond leorniað, ġē dōmeras þe ofer eorðan dēmað.	Consider now, kings, and be instructed, you judges who judge the world.
Wā ēow þe nū hlihaþ, for-þon ġē eft wēpað.	Woe (be) to you who now exult, for afterwards you shall weep.
Hēr ys þīn pund þe iċ hæfde on swāt-līn ālēd.	Here is your pound which I had placed in a handkerchief.
... his þēowas þe hē þæt feoh selde.	... his servants to whom he had given the money.
Syle mē mīnne dǣl minre ǣhte þe mē tō ġebyreð.	Give me my share of my possessions which belongs to me.
Iċ ġewende eft tō mīnum hūse þe iċ of ēode.	I will return to my house which I came from.
Hwǣr is þīn God þe þū tō hopast?	Where is your God that you trust in?
... betwuh him and his fēondum þe nāne ǣ Godes ne hēoldon.	... between him and his enemies who kept no law of God.
Þā cwæð Iudas þe hyne belǣwde.	Then said Judas who betrayed him.

Ǣlċ (...) ðe

Ǣlċ þe hine up-āhefð bið ġe-
nyðerud, ond sē ðe hine
nyðera, sē bið up-āhafen.

Anyone who raises himself up will
be put down, and the one who
humbles himself, he will be
raised up.

Ǣlċ þe yrsað hys brēþer byð
dōme scyldiġ.

Anyone who is angry with his brother
shall be in danger of the judgment.

Swā is ǣlċ of ēow þe ne wiðsæcð eallum þingum þe hē āh.

So is each of you who does not
renounce all things which he owns.

And ǣlċ mann þe þisne sealm
singð, hē hine singð be his
sylfe frōfre.

And each one who sings this psalm
sings it for his own consolation.

Ǣlċ īdel word þe men sprecað....

Every vain word that men speak....

Ǣlċ trēow þe ne bryncð gōdne
wæstm bið forcorfen ond on
fȳr āworpen.

Each tree that does not bring
forth good fruit will be cut down
and thrown into fire.

Se hǣlend ... cwæð tō him:
'Ǣlċ rīċe þe byð twyrǣde on
him sylfum byþ tōworpen, ond
ǣlċ ċeaster oððe hūs þe byð
wiþer-weard onġēn hyt sylf,
hit ne stent.'

The Saviour ... said to them:
'Each kingdom that is disagreeing
within itself will be cast down,
and each city or house that is
divided against itself, it will
not stand.'

Ǣlċ ðāra þe yfele dēð hata þæt
lēoht, ond hē ne cymþ tō
lēohte.

Each one who does evil hates the
light, and he will not come to
the light.

Ne gǣð ǣlċ þæra on heofona rīċe
þe cwyþ tō mē, 'Dryhten,
Dryhten'; ac sē þe wyrcð
mīnes fæder willan þe on
heofenum is, sē gǣð on
heofena rīċe.

Everyone does not go into the kingdom of the heavens who says to me,
'Lord, Lord'; but the one who does
my father's will who is in the heavens,
he goes into the kingdom of the
heavens.

Eall (...) **ðe**
Sum (...) **ðe**
Ān (...) **ðe**, and Others

Ealle þing þe æfre wæron.	All things that ever were.
Cumað tō mē ealle þe swincað ond ġesȳmede synt.	Come to me all who labor and are burdened.
Sume þe þār stōdon þus sædon him.	Some who stood there said thus to him.
Sume wīf þe wæron ġehælede of āwyrġdum gāstum.	Certain women who were healed of evil spirits.
Hē ġeseah ān fīctrēow þe lēaf hæfde.	He saw a fig tree that had leaf (i.e., was in leaf).
Ēower ān þe mid mē ytt ġesylð mē.	One of you who is eating with me will betray me.
Ān sāwul is ... þe þās ðrēo þing hæfð on hire.	There is one soul ... which has three things in it.
Ān circul is, þe ūðwitan hātað zodiacus oððe horoscopus.	There is a circle which scholars call the zodiac or horoscope.
Nis nān þe his hūs forlæt ... þe hundfeald ne onfō. [nān = ne ān]	There is none who has left his house ... who will not receive a hundredfold.
Ġif ðū ne finde nænne þe þē ġemiltsian wille....	If you find none who will pity you....
Þes iunga man ne æfestigað on nānum ðingum ðe hē hēr ġesihð.	This young man is not envious for anything which he sees here.
Fēawa synt þe synt ġehælede.	There are few who are saved.
Fēawa synt þe þone weġ findon.	There are few who may find the way.
Tweġen weras þe mid him stōdun.	Two men who stood with him.
Maneġa ōðre þe him of hyra spēdum þēnedon.	Many others who provided for them out of their abundance.
Fæla þe iċ hæfde tō mē ġewȳld.	Many whom I had subdued.
Hit (þæt is, senepes sæd) is ealra sæda læst þe on eorðan synt.	It (that is, a grain of mustard) is smallest of all seeds on earth.

3.5 Other Indefinite Pronominals

Two indefinite pronominals with initial **hw**– share distributional characteristics of the **HW**— pronominals. The principal ones are **hwæðer** 'which (of two)' and **hwylċ** 'which.' Another form **hūlīċ** 'of what sort' is encountered much less frequently. They have morphological characteristics similar to those of 'strong' adjectives (see Chapter 4), being inflected for grammatical gender, case, and number. Their inflectional endings closely parallel those of the determiners and specifiers (and therefore the personal pronouns).

		Singular	
	Masculine	Feminine	Neuter
Nominative	hwilċ	hwilċ	hwilċ
Genitive	hwilċes	hwilċere	hwilċes
Dative	hwilcum	hwilċere	hwilcum
Accusative	hwilċne	hwilċe	hwilċ

		Plural	
	Masculine	Feminine	Neuter
Nominative	hwilċe	hwilċe, -a	hwilċ
Genitive	hwilcra	hwilcra	hwilcra
Dative	hwilcum	hwilcum	hwilcum
Accusative	hwilċe	hwilċe, -a	hwilċ

Like **HW**— pronominals, these forms occur in interrogative sentence constructions: **Hwæðer wēnst þū nū?** 'Which (of the two) do you think now?' **Hwilċ is se cyning?** 'Which (one) is the king?' They are also used in subordinate clauses transformationally related to interrogative sentences: **hēt sēċan hwilċ ðære ġeogoþe glēawost wǣre** 'bade seek which of the youth was most skilled.' They occur as well in constructions that are noninterrogative, with a generalized meaning: **Ġif him þinċe ðæt hē on hwylċere fæġerre stōwe sī** 'If it seems to him that he is in some fair place....' And they too occur in fixed phrases with **swā**: **Ðæs cyninges þegnas ðider urnon, swā hwelċ swā ðonne ġearo wærþ** 'The king's thanes ran thither, whichever (of them) was then ready.'

When declined like **hwilċ**, the form **swilċ** also occurs as a pronominal, though its range of functions is not as wide as that of **hw**– forms and other pronominals. **Ne bið swylċ earges sīð** 'Such is not a venture of the cowardly.' **Swylċra siþfæt** 'The journey of such ones (those just mentioned).' Its adjectival function, in addition, will be apparent in these examples: **Hē ǣr ne sið**

ōðre swylċe lāre ġehȳrde 'Before nor since had he heard other such teaching.'
Manegum swylcum biġspellum hē spræc tō him 'With many such parables he
spoke to them.' The form also occurs, without inflection, as adverbial conjunction. (*OEG* 718–720, 725, *OES* 420–422, 435, 503–505, 2049 ff., and see Index
of Words and Phrases)

Dā cōm lēoht swilċ swā hī ǣr ne ġesāwon.	Then came such light as they had never seen before.
Swylċera is heofona rīċe.	Of such is the kingdom of heaven.
Ǣlċ byð fulfremed ġif hē (se leorning-cniht) is swylċe hys lārēow.	Each one is perfect if he (the disciple) is such (a one) as his teacher (is).
Blæc oþþe won oþþe swilċes hwæt.	Pale or livid or something of that kind.
Hē cwæþ tō him, 'Hwār magon wē findan swilċne man, þe mid Godes ġyfe sȳ swā āfylled?'	He said to them, 'Where may we find such a man, one who with God's gift may be so filled?'

In independent questions with hwilċ and hwæðer, sentence order is like that
for HW— interrogative sentences: hw— Verb – (Subject). With dependent
(embedded, or indirect) questions, usual sentence order is like that of HW—
constructions of the same kind: hw— (Subject) – Verb. On hwylcum anwealde
dēst þū ðās þing? ... Iċ secge ēow þonne on hwylcum anwealde iċ þis dō.
'On whose authority do you do these things? ... I will tell you then on whose
authority I do this.'

Seġe ūs, on hwylcum anwalde
wyrċst þū ðās þing oððe hwæt
ys sē ðe þē þisne anwald
sealde?

Tell us, on what authority do
you perform these things or
what is that one who gave you
this power?

Hwylċ man is þæt mæġ ārīman ealle
þā sār?

What man is there that can count
up all those sufferings?

Hwylċ man is of ēow þe hæfð hund
scēapa?

What man is there of you who has
a hundred sheep?

Tweġen gafol-ġyldon wǣron sumum
lǣnende. Ān sceolde fīf hund
penega and ōðer fīftiġ.
Ðā hiġ næfdon hwanon hī hyt
āguldon, hē hit him bām forġef.
Hwæþer lufode hyne swȳðor?

There were two debtors owing to a
certain man. One owed five
hundred pence and the other
fifty. When they hadn't where-
withal (that) they might repay
it, he forgave it to them both.
Which of the two loved him more?

Hwæþerne wylle ġē þæt iċ forġyfe
ēow of þisum twām?

Which do you desire that I give
you from these two?

Hwylċ þāra þrēora þynċð þē þæt
sȳ þæs mæġ þe on ðā sceaðan
befēoll?

Which of those three does it seem
to you may be compatriot of the
one who fell among thieves?

Hwæðer is ēðre tō secgenne tō
þām laman: 'Þē synd synna
forġyfene,' hwæðer-þe cweðan,
'Ārīs, nim ðīn bed and gā'?

Which is easier to say to the
crippled: 'For thee are (thy)
sins forgiven,' or to say,
'Arise, take thy bed and walk'?

Se cyngc ne mihte findan hwilċ
heora forliden wǣre.

The king was not able to find out
which of them was shipwrecked.

... þæt hēo sylf ġecēose hwilcne
ēowerne hēo wille.

... that she herself may choose
which one of you she wishes.

... ðæt þū miht ... ġecȳðan
hwilcne heora þū wille.

... that you ... can make known
which one of them you desire.

þæt iċ silf mōste ċeosan
hwilcne wer iċ wolde.

... that I myself should choose
which(-ever) man I wished.

Seġe ūs hwilċ tācn sī þīnes
tōcymys.

Tell us what sign there will be
of your coming.

[Hē] āhsode hwæt Alexander se
cyning dyde and hūlīċ mon hē

He asked what Alexander the king
did and what sort of man he might

wǣre ond in hwylċere yldo.

Cwæð hwæðer þē sēlre þinċe, swā
þrittiġ siðon twelf, swā
.xii.elf siðon .xxx.

be and of what age.

Say [i.e., calculate] whichever (way)
seems better to you—as 30 x 12,
(or) as 12 x 30.

Ġyt syndon sume naman, þe wǣron
unrihtlīċe ġetealde betwux
naman speliġendum [þæt is
pronomina] for-þan-þe naman
speliġend ne mæġ habban þā ġe-
tācnunga þe hī habbað. Ān
þǣra is *qualis* ond *quale*
'hwilċ,' þæt ġetācnað þrēo
þingc: *interrogationem* (þæt
is 'āxunge') and *infinitione*
('endelēasnysse') ond
relationem ('edlesunge').
Ġif iċ cweþe *qualis est rex*
'hwilċ is se cyngc,' þonne
bið hē *interrogatiuum* (þæt
is āxiendlīċ). Ġif iċ cweðe
nescio qualis est rex 'nāt iċ
hwilċ se cyngc is,' þonne bið
se *qualis infinitiuum* (þæt is
un-ġe-endiġendlīċ). Ġif iċ
cweðe *tu scis bene qualis
est* 'þū wāst wel hwilċ hē is,'
þonne bið hit *relatiuum* (þæt
is edlesendlīċ).

There are yet some forms that
were incorrectly accounted
among noun substitutes (that is,
pronouns), because pronouns
are not able to have the
signification that they have.
One of them is *qualis* and *quale*
'which,' that signifies three
things: *interrogationem* (that
is 'asking') and *infinitione*
('endlessness' [infinity]) and
relationem ('relation').
If I say *qualis est rex*
'which is the king,' then
it is *interrogatiuum* (that is
asking-like). If I say *nescio
qualis est rex* 'I don't know
which the king is,' then will be
that *qualis infinitiuum* (that is
unending-like). If I say
tu scis bene qualis est
'thou knowest well which he is,'
then it will be *relatiuum* (that
is relative).

Talis ond *tale* andwyrt þām
ōðrum: Ðū cwypst *qualis est
ille* 'hwilċ is hē'; iċ cweðe
talis est 'swilċ hē is.'

Talis and *tale* correspond to the
others: Thus sayest *qualis est
ille* 'which is he'; I say
talis est 'such is he.'

Indefinite or generalized **hwilċ** 'some, any, someone, anyone'

Ne hiġ ne ġelȳfað þēah hwylċ of dēaðe ārīse.	They will not believe even though someone should arise from death.
Ġif hwylċ cynincg wyle faran....	If any king will set forth....
Ġyf hwylċe ðær bēoþ ðāra ðe hwæt æbylhþa wið ōðre habbaþ....	If any of those are there who have any grudge against another....
Wē ġesāwon oft in ċyrċean æġðer ġe corn ġe hīg ġe hwylċe worold-līcu þing bēon ġehealdene.	We have often seen in churches grain and hay and any kind of secular things kept.
Swā hwylċne swā iċ cysse, hē hit is.	Whichever one I kiss, it is he.
Swā hwylċ swā sylþ ānne drinc....	Whosoever shall give a drink to one (of those)....
Swā hwylċe swā ġē ġebindað .ofer eorðan.... Swā hwylċe swā ġē ofer eorðan unbindað....	Whatsoever you shall bind on earth. ... Whatsoever you shall unbind on earth....
Swā hwylcum manna swā him ġemet ðūhte.	To whichever of the men as seemed to him fitting.
Swā hwylċne heora swā him se tān ætȳwde.	On whichever of them the lot should fall.
Swā hwylċ hūs swā ġē in-gāð, wuniað þār oð þæt ġē ūt-gān.	What house soever you enter, remain there until you depart.
Swā hwæðer swā hit sȳ.	Whichever (of two) it may be.
Heora ēaþmētto ne mihton nāuht forstandan ne hūru heora ofermētta dydon, swā hwæþer swā hȳ dydon.	Their humility availed naught nor indeed did their pride, whichever (course) they followed.
An fēo oþþe an āðe, swā hwæðer swā him lēofre sīe.	With goods or with oath, whichever is preferable to him.

Chapter 4

ADJECTIVES AND ADVERBS

For adjective inflections the categories of number, gender, and case are the same as those for personal pronouns and for nouns. But Old English, like the other Germanic languages, had a twofold inflectional system for adjectives. One system has already been represented in the paradigm for **hwilċ**. That form—together with **hwæðer**—has only the one set of inflections; for this reason it was described separately from adjectives. That system is here labeled 'Nondetermined'; it is also called variously the 'Strong' or 'Indefinite' declension. The other part of the twofold system, which is labeled here 'Determined,' is also variously called the 'Weak' or 'Definite' declension.

4.1 Declension of Uncompared Adjectives

With uncompared ('positive degree') adjective forms, a member of the 'determined' set is selected if a 'determinative' form also occurs within the same noun phrase; a determinative form always precedes an adjective if both occur. A determinative form, for this purpose, is any form from the **se sēo þæt** and the **þes þēos þis** paradigms or any of the genitive-case ('possessive') pronouns **mīn, ūre, his**, etc. Without an accompanying (preceding) determinative form, adjective inflection is selected from the 'nondetermined' pattern of inflections. Thus, for example, determined forms occur in **se gōda willa** 'that good will,' **Hē hæfde ðone gōdan willan** 'He had good intention,' **Iċ lufiġe þone forlidenan man** 'I love the shipwrecked man.' Nondetermined forms of these adjectives occur in **Hwæt is gōd willa?** 'What is good will?' **Þurh gōde dæda** 'Through good deeds,' **Ġemildsa mē, nacodum, forlidenum** 'Pity me, naked, shipwrecked.' Further illustrations: **Unicornus 'ānhyrne dēor': þæt dēor hæfð ænne horn bufan ðām twām ēagum swā strangne and swā scearpne, þæt hē fyht wið ðone mycclan ylp and hine oft ġewundað on ðære wambe oð dēað. Hē hātte ēac rinoceron and monoceron.** '*Unicornus*, "animal with one horn": that animal has one horn above the two eyes so strong and so sharp, that he fights with the great elephant and repeatedly wounds it in the belly until death. It is also called *rinoceron* and *monoceron*.' **Ac bēo þū hāliġ, Drihten, wið þā hālgan, and unsceðfull wið þā unsceðfullan** ... 'With the holy, Lord, be thou holy, and unharming toward the innocent....' **Ælċ man sylþ æryst gōd wīn.... Đū ġeheōlde þæt gōde wīn oð ðis** 'Each one serves first good wine.... You withheld the good wine until this (i.e., until now).'

Paradigms of uncompared ('positive degree') **gōd** 'good' and **dol** 'foolish' are as follows.

Nondetermined ('Strong')

Singular	'Masculine'		'Feminine'		'Neuter'	
Nominative	gōd	dol	gōd	dolu	gōd	dol
Genitive	gōdes	doles	gōdre	dolre	gōdes	doles
Dative	gōdum	dolum	gōdre	dolre	gōdum	dolum
Accusative	gōdne	dolne	gōde	dole	gōd	dol

Plural						
Nominative	gōde	dole	gōde, -a	dole, -a	gōd(e)	dolu
Genitive	gōdra	dolra	gōdra	dolra	gōdra	dolra
Dative	gōdum	dolum	gōdum	dolum	gōdum	dolum
Accusative	gōde	dole	gōde, -a	dole, -a	gōd(e)	dolu

Determined ('Weak')

Singular	'Masculine'		'Feminine'		'Neuter'	
Nominative	gōda	dola	gōde	dole	gōde	dole
Genitive	gōdan	dolan	gōdan	dolan	gōdan	dolan
Dative	gōdan	dolan	gōdan	dolan	gōdan	dolan
Accusative	gōdan	dolan	gōdan	dolan	gōde	dole

Plural						
Nominative	gōdan	dolan	gōdan	dolan	gōdan	dolan
Genitive	gōdra, -ena	dolra, -ena	gōdra, -ena	dolra, -ena	gōdra, -ena	dolra, -ena
Dative	gōdum	dolum	gōdum	dolum	gōdum	dolum
Accusative	gōdan	dolan	gōdan	dolan	gōdan	dolan

The **-u** inflection within the paradigms for non-determined adjectives occurs only with short-stem forms (see 2.6).

Ǣlċ gōd trēow byrð gōde wæstmas
ond ǣlċ yfel trēow byrþ yfele
wæstmas. Ne mæġ þæt gōde trēow
beran yfle wæstmas, ne þæt
yfele trēow gōde wæstmas. Ǣlċ
trēow þe ne byrð gōdne wæstm,
sȳ hyt forcorfen ond on fȳr
āworpen.

Each good tree bears good fruit
and each corrupt tree bears evil
fruit. A good tree cannot bear
evil fruit, and a corrupt tree
cannot bear good fruit. Each
tree that does not bear good fruit,
let it be cut down and cast into
the fire.

Gōd mann sōþlīċe of gōdum
goldhorde bringþ gōd forð.
Yfel mann of yfelum goldhorde
bringð yfel forð.

Truly a good man out of his good
treasure brings forth good.
An evil man from his evil treasure
brings evil forth.

Hē bið þām gōdum glædmōd on
ġesihðe.... Hē bið þām yflum
eġeslīċ tō ġesēonne.

To the good he is joyous in their
sight.... To the evil he is
fearsome to see.

Wyrd, ... þēah hit ūs maniġ-
fealdlīċ ðinċe, sum gōd, sum
yfel, hit is þēah him ānfeald
gōd, for-þām hē hit eall tō
gōdum ende bringþ.

Wyrd, ... though it seem to us
manifold, part good, part evil,
it is nonetheless to him onefold
good, because he brings it all
to a good end.

Þæs gōdan gōdnes biþ his āgen
gōd.

The goodness of the good is its
(or his) own good.

Iċ eom gōd hyrde: se gōda hyrde
sylð his āgen līf for his
scēapum.... Gōd hyrde wæs
Petrus, and gōd wæs Paulus,
and gōde wǣron ðā apostoli.

I am the good shepherd: the good
shepherd giveth his own life for
his sheep.... A good shepherd
was Peter, and good was Paul,
and good were the apostles.

Þā men hīe ġeflīemdon and hire
gōdne dǣl ofslōgon.

The men put them to flight and
slew a good part of them.

Hī gōdne friþ hēoldon.

They kept a good peace.

Ðǣr wearð Hēahmund bisceop
ofslæġen ond fela gōdra manna.

There Bishop Heahmund was slain
and many good men.

Spica is gōdes stenċes.

Spikenard is of good fragrance.

Mid ðǣm nosum wē tōscēadað gōde
stenċas and yfele.

With the nose we distinguish good
scents from bad.

Þā gōdan bīoþ simle wealdende
ond þā yfelan nabbaþ nǣnne

The good are continually holding
sway and the evil have no power.

anweald.

Dol biÐ sē Ðe gǣÐ on dēop wæter— sē Ðe sund nafaÐ, ne ġeseġled scip, ne fugles flyht, ne hē mid fōtum ne mæġ grund ġerǣċan.	Foolish is the one who goes in deep water—the one who doesn't have skill in swimming, or sail- equipped ship, or fowl's flight, or isn't able to reach the bottom with his feet.
Dol biþ sē þe his dryhten nāt.	Foolish is he who knows not his lord.
Tō dol wǣre, þā Ðū wēndest Ðæt þīnra feohġestrēona ende ne wurde.	It would be too foolish when you imagine that the end of your riches should not come about.

With the merest handful of exceptions, any adjective stem—in uncompared (or 'positive degree') form—may occur with inflection from either inflectional system. **Fela** 'many' is not declined; **ġewuna**, **bewuna** 'accustomed, wont' and **wona** 'lacking' usually are not declined. **Ōþer** 'second, other' has inflection from the nondetermined set only, and in some ways belongs in a subclass by itself. Possessive pronouns in adjectival function are also exceptional and will be illustrated separately. Determined forms of **eall** 'all,' **moniġ** 'many,' **genōg** 'enough' and a few others seldom occur. Adjective **sum** 'some, (a) certain' does not occur as a determined form. **Ilca** 'same' occurs only as a determined form. (*OEG* 638–656, *OES* 102–125, 132–135, 136–141)

Participles whose stems are formed with -**ende** may be inflected according to either pattern when they are adjectival: **Hwænne ġesāwe wē Ðē hingriendne and wē Ðē fēddon? þyrstendne and wē Ðē drinc sealdon?** 'When did we see thee hungering and fed thee? thirsting and we gave thee drink?' But they are often verbal, particularly in phrases with **bēon/wesan** or **weorÐan**: the language was undergoing a fundamental change in this respect. (*OES* 972–989)

Þæt hāliġe godspell.

The holy gospel.

Þis hāliġe godspell.

This sacred gospel.

Þæt hāliġe ġewrit.

Holy Writ.

Se hālga gāst is angin.

The holy spirit is the beginning.

Sēo hāliġe þrynnes.

The holy trinity.

Sēo stōw ys hāliġ eorðe.

That place is consecrated ground.

... ācenned wæs of þǣm hālgan mǣdene.

... was born of the holy maiden.

Be þǣre hālgan þrynnysse.

Concerning the holy trinity.

Mid þām hālgan fæder.

With the holy father.

Mid þām hālgan gāste.

With the holy spirit.

Tō þīnum hālgan altare.

To thy holy altar.

Hāliġe bēċ.

Holy books.

Ealle þā hālgan bēċ.

All the holy books.

Hāliġ sealt.

Holy salt.

On hālgum beorge.

At the holy mountain.

On hāliġre stōwe.

In the holy place.

On þā hālgan ċeastre.

Into the holy city.

Of his þām hēan hālgan setle.

From his (the) high holy place.

Hāliġ, hāliġ, hāliġ, Drihten God Allmæhtiġ.

Holy, holy, holy, Lord God Almighty.

Þurh þīn hāliġe word.

Through thy holy word.

Hāliġ is heofonrīċes weard.

Holy is the keeper of the heavenly-kingdom.

Hē wiste þæt hē wæs rihtwīs and hāliġ.

He knew that he was (a) righteous and holy (man).

... þæs hālgan gāstes bysmur-spræċ ne byð forġyfen.

... blasphemy against the holy spirit will not be forgiven.

Þāra hāligra martyra ēagan.

The eyes of the holy martyrs.

Ēac wē sculon beran ōðre hāliġe reliquias, þæt syndon hāliġra manna lāfe, ... and mid þām hāliġnessum eallum, wē sculon ēaðmōdlīċe gangan ymb ūre land on þissum hālgum dagum.

Also, we are to carry other holy relics, which are remnants of holy men, ... and with those relics all, we are humbly to go about our land in these holy days.

Hē is angin ealra þinga.	He is the beginning of all things.
Ān scyppend ealra ġesceafta.	One creator of all created things.
Ealle þā hālgan bēċ.	All the holy books.
Hē wāt ealle þing.	He knows all things.
Mid eallum līċhoman.	With the whole body.
Ealle līċhamlīċe þing lybbað....	All corporeal things live....
Sēo sunne, þe onlīht ealne mid-eard.	The sun, which lights all the earth.
Ġemetegung is eallra mæġena mōdor.	Moderation is the mother of all virtues.
Sēo sāwul oferstīhð ealle līċhamlīċe ġesceafta.	The soul excels all corporeal creatures.
Arcestrates, ealre þāre þēode cyningc.	Arcestrates, king of the entire nation.
Apollonius sæt and ealle þingc behēold.	Apollonius sat and beheld all the things.
Đā ongunnon ealle þā men hī herian.	Then all the men began to praise her.
Hī ðā ealle þrȳ ... grētton þone cyngc.	Then they all three ... greeted the king.
Basilius ... eallne þone wȳsdōm wundorlīċe āsmēade, þe grēcisc lārēowas him lǣran cūðon.	Basil ... wondrously drew out all the wisdom which Greek teachers were able to teach him.
Be eallum yfelum þe Herodes dyde.	For all the evils that Herod did.
Ofer ealle ġesceafte.	Over all creatures.
On ealre þīnre heortan and on ealre þīnre sāwle and on eallum þīnum mōde.	In all thy heart and in all thy soul and in all thy mind.
Iċ eom for-ealdod betwēoh eallum mīnum fēondum.	I am grown old amongst all mine enemies.
Eallra cyninga cyning.	King of all kings.
[Hīe] wunodon þǣr ealne þone winter.	They remained there all that winter.
Wālā! þæt wæs hrēowlīċ sīð and hearmlīċ eallre þissere þēode.	Woe! that was a wretched and grievous time for all this people.

Þis dēade līf.

This dead life.

Sceal yrfe ġedǣled dēades monnes.

The inheritance of a dead man shall be divided.

Mid ðām dēadan fellum.

With the skins of the dead.

[Hīe] forlēton hine swā licgan for dēadne.

They abandoned him for dead to lie thus.

Hī lǣddon him ǣnne dēafne ond dumbne ond hine bǣdon þæt hē his hand him on sette.

They brought to him a (person) deaf and dumb and urged him that he set his hand on him.

And hē dyde þæt dēafe ġehȳrdon ond dumbe sprǣcon.

And he brought it about that the deaf heard and the dumb spoke.

Ðā wæs him brōht ān dēofolsēoc man; sē wæs blind ond dumb.

Then a person possessed by devils was brought to him; that one was blind and dumb.

Hī brōhton him þā ǣnne blindne ond hine bǣdon þæt hē hine æthrīne; ond þā æthrān hē þæs blindan hand ond lǣdde hine būtan þā wīc.

They brought to him then a blind person and asked that he touch him; and then he touched the hand of the blind one and led him outside the village.

Manegum blindum hē ġesihþe forġeaf.

To many blind ones he gave sight.

Hiġ synt blinde, and blindra lāttēowas; se blinda, ġyf hē blindne lǣt, hiġ feallað bēgen on ǣnne pytt.

They are blind, and leaders of the blind; the blind, if he lead the blind, they both will fall into a pit.

... þæt þū grāpie on midne dæġ, swā se blinda dēð on þīstrum.

... that you grope at midday, as the blind one does in darkness.

Ġebrōhton hī hine binnan ðām blindan cwearterne.

They brought him into the dark prison.

Ac þænne þū ġebēorscype dō, clypa þearfan ond wanhāle ond healte ond blinde.

So when you have a feast, call the poor and the infirm and the lame and the blind.

Blinde ġesēoð ond healte gāþ, hrēoflan synt ġehǣlede dēafe ġehȳrað, dēade ārīsaþ, þearfan bodiað.

The blind see and the lame walk, lepers are healed, the deaf hear, the dead arise, to the poor [the gospel] is preached.

4.2 'Possessive Adjectives'

Genitive-case pronouns function as designators; they can occur in any position
that can also be filled by a determiner (**sē sēo þæt**) or specifier (**þes þēos þis**).
In this function, genitive-case pronoun forms for 'Speaker' and 'Addressee' (1st
and 2nd person) **mīn, ūre, incer**, etc. are declined as nondetermined adjectives
only. The remaining 'Other' possessive pronoun forms **his, hiere** do not take
adjective inflections.

Nellen ġē ... ne wurpen ēowre mere-
grotu tōforan ēowrum swȳnon.

Do not ... cast your pearls before
your swine.

Ġyf ġē ... ne forġyfað mannum, ne
ēower fæder ne forġyfð ēow
ēowre synna.

If you ... do not forgive men,
your Father will not forgive you
your sins.

Þæt hī ġesēon ēowre gōdan weorc
and wuldrian ēowerne fæder.

That they may see your good works
and glorify your father.

Eft iċ ēow ġesēo and ðonne blissiað
ēowre heortan, and ēowerne ġefēan
ēow nān mon æt ne ġenimð.

I shall see you again and your
hearts will rejoice, and no man
shall take from you your joy.

Ne bēo ġē ymbehydiġe ēowre sāwle
hwæt ġē etan ne ēowrum līċhaman
hwæt ġē scrȳdun.

Be not anxious about your soul,
what you shall eat nor what
you will clothe your body with.

Ālȳs mē mid þīnre handa and mid
þīne mæġene.

Free me with thy hand and with
thy strength.

Tō-hwī ġesihst þū þæt mot on þīnes
brōþor ēgan [sic] and þū ne
ġesyhst þone bēam on þīnum
āgenum ēagan?

For what reason dost thou behold
the mote in thy brother's eye and
thou beholdest not the beam in
thine own eye?

... on ealre þīnre heortan and on
ealre þīnre sāwle and on eallum
þīnum mōde.

... in all thine heart and in all
thy soul and in all thy mind.

Drihten, onfōh mīn word mid þīnum
ēarum; and onġyt mīne stemne and
mīn ġehrōp; and ðenċ þāra worda
mīnra ġebeda.

Lord, receive my words with thine
ears, and perceive my voice and
my cry, and remember the words
of my prayers.

Āra ðīnum fæder and ðīnre mēder.

Honor thy father and thy mother.

An additional 'possessive pronoun' sīn occurs occasionally, mostly in poetry; it is a single, non-gender-distinguishing form used exclusively with third-
person referents, whether masculine or feminine or plural. [**Hē**] **þā andswarode
... dryhtne sīnum** 'He then answered ... his lord'; **Mid sunum sīnum** 'with his
sons.' **Mid sīne līchoma** 'with his body'; **Hē ... anlīcnesse engla sīnra ġeseh**
'He ... saw the likeness of his angels.' **Þā** [**hē**] **sīne nihtreste ofġeaf** 'then he
left his couch.' **Ġeseh hē þā on grēote ġingran sīne** 'Then he saw on the seashore his followers.' **Him Hrōðgār ġewāt tō hofe sīnum** 'Hrothgar departed
to his dwelling.' **Bær ... sēo brimwylf ... hringa þengel tō hofe sīnum** 'The
she-monster-of-the-waters bore ... the prince of rings to her dwelling.' (*OES*
290–293)

As the examples illustrate, sīn commonly follows the noun it modifies,
unlike **his** and the other possessive forms, which normally precede the noun
that they accompany.

Remedy for soreness or looseness of teeth

Wið tōþa sāre ond ġif hȳ wagegan, ġenim þās ylcan wyrte (hydele). Hēo of
sumre wundurlīcre mihte helpeð. Hyre wōse ond hyre dūst ys tō ġehealdenne
on wintre for-ðām-þe hē ælcon tīman ne ātȳweð. Hyre wōs þū scealt on rammes
horne ġehealdan. Drīġe ēac þæt dūst ond ġeheald. Witodlīċe ēac hyt scearplīċe
fremað tō þām sylfan bryce mid wīne onbyrġed.

'For soreness of teeth, and if they wag, take the same wort (hydele). Out
of some wondrous power it will help. Its ooze and its dust is to be preserved in
winter because it does not appear in every season. Its ooze you must store in a
ram's horn. Also dry the dust and keep (it). Truly, it also effectually performs
the same benefit tasted with wine.'

4.3. Comparison of Adjectives

Besides occurring with obligatory inflections to signal case, number, and gender, adjective roots may also occur with bound forms for comparison. These comparative morphemes should be classified as postbase forms; they precede the syntax-signaling inflections (symbolized below as **I**), occurring immediately following the adjective root to produce the following invariable sequence:

Adjective Root + Postbase of Degree + Inflection.

Comparative degree is expressed regularly by /-r-/, superlative degree by /-ost-/ or /-est-/ (symbolized as /-Vst/). The noncompared ('positive') degree is not marked with an overt form; it can be represented as -ø- after the stem. Stress remains in the root morpheme. (*OEG* 657, *OES* 181–188) For example:

Noncompared	Comparative	Superlative
root -ø- I	root -r- I	root -Vst- I
ǽðel(e)-ø-e, etc.	**ǽðel-r-a**, etc.	**ǽðel-est-an**, etc.

Se eorl wæs æðele.	The earl was noble.
Ðǣre æðelan cwēne.	To the noble lady.
Æðelum cempan.	To the noble warrior.
Wuldriaþ æðelne ordfruman.	[They] glorify the noble origin.
On mōde æðelra þonne on ġebyrdum.	In mind more noble than in birth.
Ealle þā æðelestan bearn.	All the noblest men.
For ðām æðelestum weorcum.	For the noblest deeds.

Old English used only the patterns of comparison just described, regardless of syllable structure of the root or stem. Phrasal comparison—as in Modern English **more honorable, most unusual**—was not used: **Sēo wæstmberendeste eorþe** 'The fruit-bearingest (i.e., most fertile) earth,' **Sē is betra þonne ðū, æhtspēdigra feohġestrēona** 'He is better than you, more-wealthy-of-possessions of money-treasures (i.e., richer in treasures).'

Adjective stems with comparative degree morphemes regularly have case-number-gender inflection of the determined set. Adjective stems with superlative degree morphemes have either determined or nondetermined noncompared stems; that they usually have inflection of the determined set is a concomitant of their usual occurrence in constructions including determinative forms.

Earm biþ sē þe his frȳnd ġeswīcaþ.	Miserable is he whom his friends betray.
Iċ earm tō þē cleopie.	Wretched, I call to thee.
Đā cōm ān earm wuduwe.	Then came a poor widow.
Ġē syndon earme ofer ealle menn.	You are wretched above all men.
Sē wæs ordfruma earmre lāfe.	That one was chief of the poor remnant.
Nō iċ ġefræġn ... earmran mannon.	I have not heard of ... a more miserable man.
Forþām hī sint earmran ond dysigran ond unġesǣligran þonne iċ hit ārecan mæġe.	Because they are more wretched and more foolish and more unfortunate than I am able to relate.
... þǣm earmestum mannum.	... to the most miserable men.
Iċ wolde cweðan ðæt hī wǣron earmoste.	I should say that they were most miserable.
Bēo blīþe, þū gōda þēow.	Be joyful, thou good servant.
Wæs se blīþa gǣst fūs on forðweġ.	The blithe spirit was eager for departure.
Hē bæd hine blīðne bēon æt bēorþeġe.	He bade him be joyful at the beer-drinking.
Hȳ þā se æðeling grētte blīþum wordum.	The nobleman then greeted her with pleasant words.
Cyning wæs ðȳ blīðra.	The king was the more joyful.
Hiġ blīðust wǣron.	They were most joyful.
Iċ eom ... ġeong ond hwæt.	I am ... young and valiant.
Nis ... mon ofer eorþan ... tō ðæs hwæt ... þæt hē ā his sǣfore sorge næbbe.	There isn't ... a man on earth ... so bold ... that he hasn't always anxiety for his sea-journey.
Hȳ bēoð heortum þȳ hwætran.	They are in hearts the braver.
Đā Gotan ... cōmon of ðǣm hwatestan monnum Germanie.	The Goths ... come from the bravest men of Germania.
Osfrīþ, ...se hwatesta fyrd-esne.	Osfrith, ... the bravest warrior.

4.4 'Irregular' Comparison of Adjectives

Comparison of adjectives, like declension of nouns and of verbs, shows complexities ('irregularities') for a few forms, most of which are common words learned early. Thirteen of the one hundred most frequent morphs in Old English verse, for instance, occur as adjectives; of these **eall** 'all' and **ān** 'one,' the two most frequent, have a quantitative reference that is not gradable. The same is true of **ēċe** 'eternal.' In contrast, **miċel** 'great' and **gōd** 'good' belong to comparative sets utilizing more than one root. (*OEG* 659)

miċel	māra	mǣst
gōd	bettra,	bet(e)st,
	sēlra	sēlest

(The other eight of the thirteen most frequently occurring adjectives are **hāliġ** 'holy,' **sōð** 'true,' **hēah** 'high,' **lēof** 'dear,' **swīþ** 'strong,' **æðele** 'noble,' **fæst** 'firm,' and **wīd** 'vast.') Two others—**yfel** 'evil, bad' and **lȳtel** 'little'—are also in suppletive sets, having a root for comparative and superlative forms different from the uncompared forms. (*OEG* 659)

yfel	wiersa	wierrest, wyrst
lȳtel	lǣssa	lǣst

God ġeworhte twā miċele lēoht: ðæt māre lēoht tō ðæs dæġes līhtinge, and ðæt lǣsse lēoht tō ðǣre nihte līhtinge.

God made two great lights: the greater light for illumination of the day, and the lesser light for lighting of the night.

Þū hine ġedēst lȳtle lǣsse þonne englas.

Thou hast made him a little lower than the angels.

Sīo mycle burh þæs myclan cyninges.

The mighty stronghold of the great king.

Sēo ilca burg Babylonia, sēo ðe mǣst wæs and ǣrost ealra burga, sēo is nū lǣst and wēstast.

That same city of Babylonia, which was greatest and first of all cities, is now least and most desolate.

Forþām iċ secge ēow þæt ġē ne sīn ymbhȳdiġe ēowre sāwle hwæt ġē eton, ne ēowrum līċhaman mid hwām ġē sȳn ymbscrȳdde: hū nys sēo sāwl sēlre þonne mete ond ēower līċhama betera þonne þæt

So I say to you that you should not be anxious for your soul (or life), what you will eat, nor for your body with what you will be clothed: Isn't the soul better than food and your body better

rēaf? — than the raiment?

Sēlre mē wæs and sēftre, þæt þū mē ... ġehnæġdest. — It was better for me and gentler, that you humbled me.

Ofest is sēlost. — Haste is best.

Nū is ofost betost, ðæt wē þēodcyning ðǣr scēawian. — Now is speed best, that we may see there the great king.

Hū ne synt ġē sēlran þonne hiġ? — How are you not better than they?

Is hit miċlre sēlre ðæt wē hine ālȳsan. — It is much better that we should release him.

Hwæt sēlost wǣre tō ġefremmanne. — What may be best to do.

Hwonne his horse bett wurde. — Until his horse should be better.

Dæt hȳ wǣron beteran þeġnas. — That they were better thanes.

Scipio, se betsta Rōmana witena. — Scipio, the best of the Roman senators.

Dæt se hwǣte mæġe ðȳ bet weaxan. — That the wheat may grow the better.

Dis is manna se wyrresta. — This is the worst of men.

On ðone wyrrestan dēað. — To the most cruel death.

Hī for nānum ermþum ne bȳoð nō ðȳ betran, ac ðȳ wyrsan. — For no calamities are they the better, but the worse.

Sēo frecednes dæġhwamlīċe wæs wyrse and wyrse. — The peril daily was worse and worse.

Hē þæt betere ġeċēas, ... and ðām wyrsan wiðsōc. — He chose the better ... and rejected the worse.

Ne wearð ... nān wærsa dǣd ġedōn þonne þēos wæs. — There was ... no worse deed done than this one was.

Hī nǣfre wyrsan handplegan on Angelcynne ne ġemitton. — They never met with harder fighting in England.

A common morphophonemic variation of the adjective root reflects an earlier sound change of **a** to **æ** in certain contexts: for example, **hwæt–hwatost** 'brave–bravest,' beside unvaried **blīðe–blīðost** 'joyous–most joyous.' Some additional variations in adjective-root vowels, resulting from the operation of '*i*-umlaut' in comparative and superlative forms, are represented here as well; analogy sometimes removes the variation. See Appendix B. (*OEG* 658)

eald 'old'	**ieldra**	**ieldest**
ġeong 'young'	**ġingra**	**ġingest**
lang 'long'	**lengra**	**lengest**
strang 'strong'	**strengra**	**strengest**
hēah 'high'	**hīerra**	**hīehst**
nēah 'near'	**nēarra**	**nīehst**

Þū eart mæġenes strang.

You are strong of might.

Hwæt synd þā strangan? Ðā bēoð strange and trume ðe þurh ġelēafan wel þēonde bēoþ.

What are the strong? Those are strong and sound who through faith are fully excelling.

Hū mæġ man ingān on stranges hūs ond hys fata hyne berēafian būton hē ġebinde ǣrest þone strangan ond þonne hys hūs berēafiġe?

How can a person enter a strong man's house and steal from him his valuable-ornaments unless first he shall bind the strong one and then plunder his house?

Hē ys strengra þonne iċ.

He is stronger than I.

Ġit libbað mīne fȳnd, and synt strengran þonne iċ.

Mine enemies still live, and are stronger than I.

Þū ġenerest þone earman of þæs strengran anwealde.

You deliver the poor from the rule of the more mighty.

Se strangesta cyning Æþelfriþ.

The mightiest king Æthelfrith.

Cōm se stranga winter mid forste and mid snāwe and mid eallon unġewederon, þæt næs nān man þā on līue, þæt mihte ġemunan swā strangne winter swa sē wæs.

There came a severe winter with frost and snow and with all (kinds of) bad weather, (such) that there was no one then alive who was able to remember so severe a winter as that one was.

4.5 Adverbs

*Aduerbium est pars orationis
indeclinabilis. Aduerbium*
is ān dǣl leden-sprǣċe
undeclīniġendlīċ, *cuius
significatio uerbis adicitur*
and his ġetācnung biþ tō
wordum ġeþēod. *Aduerbium*
mæġ bēon ġecweden wordes
ġefēra, for-þan-þe hē biþ ǣfre
tō wordum ġeþēod, and næfþ
full andġit būton hē mid
worde bēo. *Sapienter*
is aduerbium. Iċ cweþe nū
swutelicor: *sapienter loquor*
'wīslīċe iċ sprece,' *feliciter
facis* 'ġesǣlīċe þū dēst,'
humiliter precatur 'ēadmōdlīċe
hē bit.'

*Adverbium est pars orationis
indeclinabilis.* 'Adverb'
is an undeclinable part of speech
(in Latin) ['undeclining-like'],
. . . .
and its signification is
connected to verbs. An adverb
can be termed a verb's
companion, because it is always
associated with verbs, and
doesn't have full sense unless
it is with a verb. *Sapienter*
is an adverb. I will say now
more clearly: . . . .
'wisely I speak,' . . . .
'happily thou doest,'
. . . . 'humbly he
beseecheth.'

A. In Old English adverbs are also separate forms that are not declined (or conjugated)—that is, they are stems that are not varied by attachment of grammatical morphemes. An adverb is 'a verb's companion' in the general sense of having no variety of syntactic functions in relation to the verb that might require distinguishing with morphemes like those that make up case and number inflections for adjectives and nouns, or the inflectional categories associated with verbs. They show morphological variation only for comparison: mostly, adverbs derived from adjectives are marked for comparative and superlative degree by -**or** and -**ost**. (*OEG* 670–676)

Noncompared	Comparative	Superlative
ġeorne 'eagerly'	**ġearnor**	**ġeornost**
ġearwe 'readily'	**ġearwor**	**ġearwost**
holdlīċe 'graciously'	**holdlicor**	**holdlicost**
heardlīċe 'with difficulty'	**heardlicor**	**heardlicost**

'Irregular' comparison follows patterns similar to those of related adjectives (see 4.4 and Appendix B), e.g.,

lange 'long'	leng	lengest
sōfte 'softly'	sēfte	sōftost.

The term 'a verb's companion,' even so, obscures the wide variety of functions which adverbs may have. Commonly an adverb may modify a verb: **Hū mæġ þis þus ġeweorðan?** 'How can this thus come to be?' **Hit wæs þā swā ġedōn** 'It was then done in that manner.' ... **þā þā hē on his gōdspelle swutolīċe þus cwæð** '... when he clearly spoke thus in his gospel';
or it may modify an adverb: **Đā ðū swā lustlīċe ġehērdest mīne lāre** 'When you so gladly listened to my instruction'; **swȳðe neah** 'exceedingly near,' **swȳðe hraðe** 'very quickly';
or it may modify an adjective: **þus maniġe men** 'thus many men,' **swȳðe rihtwȳs wer** 'an exceedingly righteous man'; **Ne ġemētte iċ swā miċelne ġelēafan** 'I have not found so great faith';
or it may specifically modify a numeral: **Þār wǣron nēah fīf þūsenda wera** 'There were nearly five thousand men'; similarly **ful nēah ǣlċ man þæs tiolað** 'nearly each person strives for that,' **Næfð hē full nēah nān andġyt nānes gōdes** 'He has nearly no understanding of any good.'

Occasionally an adverb modifies a noun, or a pronoun, or a prepositional phrase, or a conjunction (or clause), or is used predicatively. (*OES* 1100)

It is very common to list one use of adverbs as modifiers of a sentence, as **Sōþlīċe þū eart godes sunu** 'Truly thou art son of God.' It is probably better to analyze an ostensibly modified sentence as two sentences, a 'higher' sentence and a 'lower' or embedded sentence, the higher one being a 'performative' sentence from which everything has been deleted in the surface structure (the actual utterance) except for the adverb modifying the performative verb. Thus, **Sōðlīċe, þus wæs Cristes cnēores** should probably be understood to be derived from an underlying form in which **sōðlīċe** is a simple modifier of a verb: (**Iċ secge**) **sōðlīċe, þus wæs Cristes cnēores** 'I say truly, in such manner was the birth of Christ.'

The inventory of Old English adverbs is also quite varied in its make-up. (*OES* 591–593, 1100–1150) One group of adverbs consists of small sets of morphologically simple words such as

nū 'now,'   þonne 'then,'
hēr 'here,'   þǣr 'there' (see 3.3),
ful 'fully, completely,'   wel 'well, fully, properly,'
feor 'far,'   nēah 'near,'
swā 'so, thus,'   þus 'thus.'
ǣr 'before'   siþþan 'since, afterwards'.

'Direction' words occur as adverbs.

sūþ 'southwards'   sūþan 'from, in the south'
norð 'northwards'   norðan 'from, in the north'
west 'westwards'   westan 'from, in the west'
ēast 'eastwards'   ēastan 'from, in the east'
sūþanēastan 'in, from, to the southeast'
ūte 'out, outside'   ūtan '(from) outside'
inne 'inside, within'   innan 'on the inside'
up(p) 'up, upwards'   uppe 'above, aloft'

And so do forms such as **hwǣr-hwider, þǣr-þider** (see 3.3).

The adverbs of negation, as they are called traditionally (*OES* 1128–31, 1599–1625), are **ne, nā/nō,** and their transparent contractions **nǣfre** 'never,' **nealles** 'not, by no means,' **nāht/nōht/nāwiht** 'not, not at all.' Ne is better thought of as simply a negative particle, especially when it precedes a finite verb to negate the proposition of a sentence (see 2.5 D and 6.1). **Nǣfre** and **nealles,** which are contractions of **ni** with common adverbs, belong more clearly in the adverb word-class: **Ealle þās goldsmiðas secgað þæt hī nǣfre ǣr swā clǣne gold ... ne ġesāwon** 'All those goldsmiths say that they never before saw such pure gold.' In between, it seems, are **nā** and **nāht.** They very commonly occur in a clause containing **ne** + verb: **Þæt fȳr ne derede nāht þām ðrim cnihtum** 'The fire harmed not at all the three young men'; **Hē ne forhtode nā** 'He did not fear at all.'

B. The largest group of adverbs is an open set formed by processes of word derivation that involve addition of one of a small number of suffixes, such as **ġeorne** 'eagerly' derived from adjective **ġeorn** 'eager, desirous,' **heardlīċe** 'with difficulty' derived from **heard** 'hard, difficult,' **cynelīċe** 'royally' derived from **cynelīċ** 'royal,' **dearnunga** 'secretly' derived from **dyrne** 'secret, covert.' (*OEG* 661–666)

From	**hlūd** 'loud'	is derived	**hlūde** 'loudly'
	wrāþ 'angry'		**wrāþe** 'angrily'
	blīþe 'joyous, gracious'		**blīþe** 'joyously, agreeably'
	frēcne 'dangerous, daring'		**frēcne** 'dangerously, boldly'
	breme 'famous'		**breme** 'famously'
	þicce 'thick, solid'		**þicce** 'thickly, closely'
	nearu 'constricted, severe'		**nearwe** 'narrowly, strictly'
	hrædlīċ 'quick, sudden'		**hrædlīċe** 'quickly, suddenly'
	cræftlīċ 'skilful'		**cræftlīċe** 'skilfully'
	hetelīċ 'hostile, violent'		**hetelīċe** 'violently'
	dollīċ 'foolhardy, rash'		**dollīċe** 'foolishly, rashly'
	eornost 'earnestness, zeal'		**eornostlīċe** 'earnestly'
	hold 'gracious, loyal'		**holdlīċe** 'graciously'
	ān 'one'		**ǣnunga, ǣninga** 'entirely'
	eall 'all'		**eallunga** 'altogether'

Some had been derived by processes no longer productive in Old English:

sōna 'immediately, at once'		
ġēara 'formerly'	corresponds to	**ġēar** 'year'
twīwa, tūwa 'twice'	corresponds to	**twā** 'two'
ðrīwa 'thrice'	corresponds to	**ðrēo** 'three'
tela 'well'	corresponds to	**til** 'good'

Smēagan '(to) examine, consider,' **smēalīċ** 'searching, penetrating,' **smēalīċe** 'acutely, searchingly (of reasoning or inquiry),' **smēa-þancol, smēa-þancollīċ** 'acute, subtle,' **smēa-þancollīċe** 'thoroughly, searchingly.' **Hī smēadon swīðe smēaþancollīċe ymbe ðæt ēċe līf** 'They inquired most searchingly concerning eternal life.'

C. A third composite group is made up of a largely conventionalized set of inflected nouns and adjectives that have been shifted into adverbial function without change of form, such as **dæġes** 'daily, by day,' **nihtes** 'by night,' **hwīlum** 'at times, sometimes,' **nēdes** 'by need, necessarily.' (*OEG* 668–669, *OES* 1380–1427).

ealne weġ 'always'
samen 'together'
tela 'well, fittingly'
sūþweard 'southward'
norðweard 'northward'

āwiht 'at all, by any means'
fyrn 'formerly'
ġenōh, ġenōg 'sufficiently'
ūpweard 'upward'
tōweard 'toward'

þances 'gladly, willingly'
unþances 'unwillingly'
orþances 'heedlessly, thoughtlessly'
norðweardes 'northwards'
niðerweardes 'downwards'
sōþes 'in truth, truly'
ælċes þinges 'in every respect'
þæs ilcan ġēares 'in the same year'

ealles 'altogether'
nealles 'not at all'
endemes 'equally'
tō-weardes 'towards'
tōġēanes 'opposite, against'
rīmes 'in number'
sumera þinga 'somewhat'
singales 'continually, always'

stundum 'from time to time'
þrymmum 'mightily, powerfully'
micclum 'very much'
dropmǣlum 'drop by drop'
stundmǣlum 'gradually'

tīdum 'at times, occasionally'
searwum 'skilfully'
wundrum 'wonderfully'
fōtmǣlum 'step by step'
sundormǣlum 'singly'

Sume þās habbað þrȳfealde ġetācnunge. *Quando uenisti* 'hwænne cōm ðū?' is *interrogatiuum*, þæt is āxiġendlīċ. *Quando eram iuuenis* 'þā þā iċ wæs ġeong' is *relatiuum*, þæt is edlesendlīċ. *Quando ero doctus* 'hwænne bēo iċ ġelæred?' is *infinitiuum*, þæt is unġe-endiġendlīċ. *Quandoque* 'On sumne sæl.'

Some [adverbs] have threefold indication. 'When did you come?' is interrogative. '[At a time] when I was young' is relative. 'When will I be learned?' is infinitive, which is 'un-ending-like.' 'At some time.'

Sometimes ġēa 'yea, yes' and **nese** 'no' are classified as adverbs, sometimes as interjections. What they do is assert polarity of a proposition (its being positive or negative) separately from the expression of that proposition: this is more a matter of syntax than of word class, hence the difficulty of assigning them to the category of either 'adverb' or 'interjection.'

Đā andwyrde sum ōðer dēofol
and cwæð: 'Nese. Iċ wāt
ealle hyre weorc, and iċ wæs
dæġes and nihtes mid hyre and
hī bewiste, and hēo ā ful
ġeorne hlyste mīnre lāre
and ġeorne fyliġde.'

Then a certain other devil
answered and said: 'No. I
know all her deeds, and I was
with her day and night and
guided her, and she always
very eagerly listened to my
instruction and eagerly
followed (it).'

Nese, nis hit nā yfel; þæt is
þæt hēhste good [sic!].

No, it isn't evil at all; that
is the highest good.

Đā cwæð iċ, 'Nese, ne forġite iċ
hit nō.'

Then I said, 'No, I will not
forget it at all.'

Sume cwædon, 'Hē is gōd,' ōðre
cwædon, 'Nese, ac hē beswīcð
þis folc.'

Some said, 'He is a good [man],'
others said, 'No, but he
deceives this people.'

Sume cwædon, 'Hē hyt is,' sume
cwædon, 'Nese, ac is him ġelīċ.'

Certain ones said, 'It is he,' others
said, 'No, but [he] is like him.

Đā andswarode his mōdor, 'Nese,
sōþes, ac hē byð Iōhannes
ġenemned.'

Then his mother answered, 'No,
in truth, but he is named John.'

Ġēa, hē is.

Yeah, he is.

Æt ðū tōdæġ? Ġēa, iċ dyde.

Did you eat today? Yes, I did.

Seġe mē, beċeapode ġē þus miċel
landes? Hēo andwyrde, 'Ġēa,
lēof, swā miċel.'

Tell me, did you sell the land
for thus much? She answered,
'Yea, friend, for so much.'

Đā andwyrde þā ċypemen and him
tōcwædon, 'Nese, nese. Lēofa man,
ne miht þū ūs nā swā bepǣċean
mid þīnan smēðan wordan.'

Then the merchants answered and
said to him, 'No, No. Dear
sir, you can't deceive us thus
with your smooth words.'

Đā cwæð iċ, nese, lā nese.
Ne mæġ þæt nā ġewurðan.

Then I said, no, Oh no,
that can never come to pass.

Chapter 5

NOUNS

5.1 Names and Nouns

Although edited texts use capitalization for names to distinguish them from nouns, Old English manuscripts do not distinguish names and nouns by this graphemic device. Anyone who has read *1066 and All That* will remember the following spoof which turns on whether the form completing the construction **Hengest and Horsa** is to be construed as a name or a noun. 'Memorable among the Saxon warriors were Hengist and his wife (?or horse), Horsa. Hengist made himself King in the South. Thus Hengist was the first English King and his wife (or horse), Horsa, the first English Queen (or horse)' (p. 6). Even in *Beowulf*, (**Mod-**)**þryðo** is problematic, and **Hondscio** was for a time construed as 'glove, *lit.*, hand-shoe,' rather than the name of Beowulf's companion who was devoured by Grendel. Editorial decision has removed doubt about nearly every problem of this kind, signifying proper names by initial capitalization.

The distinction between nouns and names belongs more to reference and syntax than it does morphology in Old English. Nouns are selected for the paradigms, but names also appear in the illustrative lists.

Certain differences in the conventions of using forms that may translate as **the** with both nouns and names may be mentioned here, since they may strike a speaker of Modern English as odd, even occasionally confusing. Old English, like Modern English, omits a determiner (article) before **god** 'God,' but differs from Modern English by omitting it also before **dryhten** when that form refers to 'the Lord,' which in Christian, monotheistic terms, is fully defined for its reference: **tō drihtne þīnum gode** 'to the Lord thy God'; the determiner is usually omitted before **deofol** when the reference is clearly 'the Devil,' **Deofol is se stranga þe ūre drihten embe spræc** 'The Devil is the powerful one whom our Lord spoke about'; and it is also omitted before any other name or noun whose referent is already definite from either meaning or context. Neither Old English nor Modern English uses **the** or **that** (or their ancestral forms) before a proper noun except in constructions where it is not a unique name, or where there is a question whether the name applies to another person, as in 'Are you *that* Beowulf, the one who ...' or **Eart þū se Bēowulf, sē þe ....**

5.2 The Classes of Nouns

Nouns (and names) in Old English may be grouped in any of several ways. Traditional classification, embodied in grammars, handbooks, and dictionaries, reflects comparative and historical interests, in which stem-classes are of prime importance. The number of nouns belonging to respective stem-classes and 'genders' provides another basis of classification which is often combined with the first-mentioned type; the ranking or ordering of classes usually is based on this criterion. Number of members of a stem-type is another, hence such divisions as 'common,' 'minor,' 'irregular,' and the like. All three take their departure from historical-comparative classification. (*OES* 54–71)

Related structural patterns is the first principle of division for the groupings in which nouns will be presented here. The three major classes, traditionally called 'masculine,' 'feminine,' and 'neuter,' are set up on the basis of the sets of determiners, specifiers, adjective inflections, pronouns and pronominals with which they regularly co-occur. In order to distinguish these strictly grammatical classes of nouns from sex-distinguished pronoun classes, they will be called here simply **se**-nouns, **sēo**-nouns, and **þæt**-nouns. These terms exactly correspond respectively to the traditional gender-names. **Se**-nouns ('masculine') form the largest group, and many of the most frequently recurring nouns are of this type. **Sēo**-nouns ('feminine') and **þæt**-nouns ('neuter') together make up just over half the nouns commonly encountered. Each of these gender-based classes contains several sub-classes that are distinguished by their inflectional morpheme sets; the principal ones are the 'strong' and 'weak' patterns of declension.

The paradigms that follow are selected to serve three purposes: to illustrate the sub-classes of each of the 'gender' classes of nouns (and names); to introduce nouns that occur frequently; and to demonstrate typical alternations in the phonemic shape of noun roots. The subclasses, as they are traditionally designated on the basis of comparative-historical study, are identified in notes following the paradigms. *A Grouped Frequency Word-List of Anglo-Saxon Poetry*, by John F. Madden and Francis P. Magoun, Jr., has influenced selection of noun roots for illustration; it lists **(se) cyning**, for example, separately and also in derivational and compound words as occurring 591 times in the approximately 30,000 lines of extant Old English verse; some frequencies listed in the same source for other words given below are **(se) man** 1030, **dæġ** 502, **sīþ** 834, **engel** 305; **(þæt) weorc** 538; **(sēo) þēod** 460, **sāwol** 273. Variation in shape of the word root in combination with various inflectional suffixes is called *morphophonemic alternation*. Modern English has a few instances of this, e.g., **wife–wives, staff–staves, house–houses, wreath–wreathes**, which can be accounted for historically, stemming as they do from a time when [f] and [v] were allophones of /f/, [s] and [z] allophones of /s/, and [θ] and [ð] allophones of /þ/. While Old English morphophonemic alternations can also be accounted for historically, only brief annotation will be given.

The categories of noun inflections exactly parallel those of the classes of forms already described—the other forms that are constituents of or constitute noun-phrase constructions in sentences—except that no 'instrumental' case forms can be distinguished in Old English noun inflections; where instrumental case is indicated either by meaning or by an instrumental-case determiner or specifier with the noun, the inflection of the noun is not distinguished from the dative inflection.

A single inflection serves simultaneously to represent number and case directly and gender indirectly; only a few are unambiguous in representing case, number, and gender together.

Because nouns, like adjectives, constitute an open set of forms, and because all their inflectional categories have already been illustrated with pronominals and adjectives, they need less extensive illustration. Much of the illustration will concentrate on variations among the subclasses of noun inflections and in stem-shape of nouns.

From Ælfric's Grammar of Latin, 'Concerning Gender'

De Generibus. Æfter ġecynde syndon
twā cynn on naman, *masculinum*,
and *femininum*, þæt is 'werlīċ,'
and 'wīflīċ.' Werlīċ kynn
bi\ð *hic uir* 'þes wer';
wīflīċ *hec femina* 'þis wīf.'
Þās twā cynn synd ġecyndelīċe on
mannum and on nȳtenum.

According with nature there are two
genders [types] in nouns, masculine
and feminine, that is, 'man-like,'
and 'woman-like.' Masculine
gender is *hic uir* 'this man';
feminine *hec femina* 'this woman.'
These two genders are natural in
humans and in animals.

Nū is ġecweden æfter cræfte
'ġemǣne cynn,' þæt is ǣġþer ġe
werlīċ ġe wīflīċ, *hic et hec
diues* 'þes and þēos welega';
ǣġþer bi\ð weliġ, ġe wer, ġe
wīf ....

Now it is said according to knowledge
[of grammar] 'common gender,' that
is both masculine and feminine,
this [**þes**] and this [**þēos**] prosperous one; each is prosperous, both
man and woman ....

Neutrum is nāþor cynn, ne werlīċes
ne wīflīċes, on cræft sprǣċe,
ac hit bi\ð swā-þēah
oft on andġite, swā swā is ...
hoc animal 'þis nȳten'; ælċ nȳten
bi\ð o\ð\ðe hē o\ð\ðe hēo, ac swā-þēah
þis cynn ġebyra\ð oftost tō nāþrum
cynne, swā swā is *hoc uerbum*
'þis word,' *hoc lumen* 'þis lēoht.'

Neuter is neither type, neither
masculine nor feminine, in study of
language, but it is nevertheless
often in sense, as is ... *hoc animal*
'this animal'; each animal is
either he or she, but nevertheless
this type pertains most often to
neither gender, as is *hoc verbum*
'this word,' *hoc lumen* 'this light.'

Is ēac tō witenne þæt hī bēo\ð
oft ōþres cynnes on lēden ond
ō\ðres cynnes on englisc. Wē
cwe\ða\ð on lēden *hic liber*
and on englisc 'þēos bōc';
eft on lēden *hec mulier*
[feminine] and on englisc 'þis
wīf,' nā 'þēos' ....

It is also to be known that they are
often of one gender in Latin and
of another gender in English. We
say in Latin *hic liber* [masculine]
and in English 'this [feminine]
book'; again in Latin *hec mulier*
[feminine] and in English 'this
woman' [neuter] ....

5.3 Se-nouns ('Masculine')

A. The following **'strong' nouns** have uniform inflections. The base form /kyning-/ 'king' has no variants; the other paradigms illustrate the range of stem variations for nouns inflected according to this dominant system within the 'strong' noun class: **dæġ** 'day,' **engel** 'angel,' **þēow** 'servant,' **here** 'army,' **ende** 'end,' **mearh** 'horse.'

	Singular		Plural
se	cyning	þā	cyningas
ðæs	cyninges	þāra	cyninga
ðǣm	cyninge	þǣm	cyningum
ðone	cyning	þā	cyningas

se	dæġ	ðā	dagas	se	engel	ðā	englas
ðæs	dæġes	ðāra	daga	ðæs	engles	ðāra	engla
ðǣm	dæġe	ðǣm	dagum	ðǣm	engle	ðǣm	englum
ðone	dæġ	ðā	dagas	ðone	engel	ðā	englas

se	ende	ðā	endas	se	here	þā	hergas
þæs	endes	ðāra	enda	þæs	herġes	ðāra	herga
þǣm	ende	ðǣm	endum	þǣm	herġe	þǣm	hergum
þone	ende	ðā	endas	þone	here	þā	hergas

se	þēo(w)	þā	þeowas	se	mearh	þā	mēaras
þæs	þeowes	þāra	þeowa	ðæs	mēares	þāra	mēara
þǣm	þeowe	þǣm	þeowum	ðǣm	mēare	þǣm	mēarum
þone	þēo(w)	þā	þeowas	ðone	mearh	þā	mēaras

All inflectional sets of **se-**nouns just listed illustrate '**a-**stem nouns,' a collective designation of three historically different 'strong' noun classes. (*OEG* 570–584)

1. '**Pure a-**stems,' one of these three classes, are represented by **cyning, dæġ, engel,** and **mearh.**

(a) There are no stem variations for **cyning,** or for long monosyllabic stems such as **stān** 'stone,' **dōm** 'judgment,' **sīþ** 'journey,' **weard** 'guard,' **helm** 'protection, helmet,' or for short monosyllabic stems such as **wer** 'man,' **weġ** 'way' (see 2.6).

(b) The alternation of **dæġ-** and **dag-** results from a very early, pre-historic phonological change in which **a** was replaced by **æ** when not followed by a nasal consonant and when in a closed syllable, when followed by **h**, or when the vowel in the following syllable was a front vowel **i** or **e**; alternation of the stem-vowel is preserved in the modern reflexes of **stæf-**, **staf-** in *staff–staves*. (See Appendix B.)

(c) In disyllabic nouns such as **engel** the vowel in the second (and un-stressed) syllable is usually deleted, 'by syncope,' when an inflectional syllable follows, as in **englas**; when the first of the two syllables in any disyllabic stem is long (see 2.6), the unstressed second vowel is usually deleted, so also **dēofol**, **dēoflum** 'devil,' **dryhten**, **dryhtnes** 'lord.' Although for different historical reasons, in another group of nouns the second (unstressed) vowel is also usually deleted before a following inflectional syllable, as in **fugol**, **fuglas** 'bird,' **heofon**, **heofnum** 'heaven'; in such forms as **fæðm**, **fæðme** 'embrace,' the second stem vowel ordinarily does not appear at all in the written forms.

(d) The variations in **mearh**, **mēares**, etc. result from one of the last phonological changes in the pre-history of Old English, by which **h** was lost between a voiced consonant **r** or **l** and a following vowel; the preceding vowel was given 'compensatory lengthening' (see Appendix B). **Feorh**, **fēores** 'life' is another example. A similar variation occurs when **h** follows a vowel in the root form, as in **eoh**, **ēos**, etc. 'horse.'

2. Nouns such as **ende** and **here** represent a second class, 'ja-stems.' In words such as **ende**, the final -**e** in the stem is a remnant of a stem-formative element -*i*-, a form attached to the end of a noun root and preceding its inflec-tions; it does not remain in the forms with overt inflections, hence **endes**, **enda** (not *__ende-es__, *__ende-a__), etc. Nouns formed with an agentive suffix -**ere** have the same pattern of declension, as **bæcere** 'baker,' **bōcere** 'scribe,' **leornere** 'learner,' **wrītere** 'writer'; they are derived from **bac-an** '(to) bake,' **bōc** 'book, writing,' **leorn-ian** '(to) learn,' **wrīt-an** '(to) write.' The remnant of the stem-formant -*i*- appears usually spelled as **g** in forms with overt inflections when a short noun stem ends with **r**, hence **herġes**, etc.

3. A third class, called 'wa-stems,' is represented above by **þēo(w)**. In these, the earlier -*u*- stem-formative following a vowel or diphthong usually appears as **w**, as in **snāw** 'snow,' **lāreow** 'teacher,' **þēaw** 'custom'; in **bearu**, **bearwes**, etc. 'grove,' the postconsonantal -*u̯*- appears as vocalic **u** when final, and as consonantal **w** when preceding an overt inflection.

Ealra cyninga cyning.	King of all kings.
Se ofermōda cyning [Satanas].	The haughty king [Satan].
On þys ġēare wæs Æþelrēd tō cininge ġehālgod æt Cinges tūne.	In this year Æthelred was consecrated king at Kingston.
Þām æðelestan eorðcyninga.	For the noblest of earthly kings.
Ān woruldcyning hæfð fela þeġna.	An earthly king has many thanes.
Þǣr bēoð þearfan and þēodcyningas.	There will be paupers and monarchs.
Fīfe folccyningas.	Five kings of nations.
Siððan wit ǣrende gāstcyninge āġifen habbað.	After we-two have performed the errand to the king of spirits.
Þæt wæs hildesetl hēahcyninges.	That was the war-seat [saddle] of the great king [Hrothgar].
Iċ eom hēahengel heofoncyninges.	I am an archangel of the king of heaven.
[Hēo] Gode þancode, wuldorcyninge.	[She] thanked God, king of glory.
Ānes stānes wyrp.	A stone's throw.
Cweð þæt þās stānas tō hlāfe ġewurðon.	Command that these stones become bread.
Fram dæġe tō dæġe.	From day to day.
Se dæġ seġð þām ōðrum dæġe Godes wundru.	Day says to day the wonders of God.
Þrȳ dagas wǣron ǣr þām dæġe būtan sunnan and mōnan.	There were three days before that day without sun and moon.
Wē hātað ǣnne dæġ fram sunnan ūpgange oð ǣfen.	We call (it) one day, from the rising of the sun until evening.
Ġē nyton ne þone dæġ ne þā tīde.	Ye know neither the day nor the hour.

B. Guma 'man' represents **'weak'** (or *n*-stem) **se-nouns**, a large class.

se	guma	þā	guman
ðæs	guman	þāra	gumena
ðǣm	guman	þǣm	gumum
ðone	guman	þā	guman

Some of the common nouns of this class are **nama** 'name,' **mōna** 'moon,' **steorra** 'star,' **hunta** 'hunter,' **bana** 'slayer,' **cnapa** 'boy,' **nefa** 'nephew,' **wītega** 'prophet,' **loca** 'enclosure,' **cofa** 'chamber,' **spearwa** 'sparrow,' **frogga** 'frog,' **līchoma** 'body.' (*OEG* 615–619)

Grētte þā guma ōþerne.

Then one man saluted the other.

Gumena bearn.

The children of men.

Weċċað of dēaðe dryhtgumena bearn, eall monna cynn.

The sons of men, all mankind, shall wake from death.

[Dā] dryhtguman dōþ swā iċ bidde.

The retainers do as I bid.

Sē ðe brýde hæfð, sē is brýdguma. Sē þe is þæs brýdguman frēond ... mid ġefēan hē ġeblissað for þæs brýdguman stefne.

The one who has a bride is a bridegroom. The one who is the bridegroom's friend ... exults with joy because of the bridegroom's voice.

Ǣlċ libbende nýten, swā swā Adam hit ġecīġde, swā ys hys nama.

Whatever Adam called every living animal, that is its name.

Þǣr wǣron āwritene ealra þāra rīċestena monna noman.

There were written down the names of all the most powerful men.

Mann ... þæs nama wæs Iōhannes.

A man ... whose name was John.

Hē nemð his āgene scēap be naman.

He calls his own sheep by name.

Iċ wille wyrċan mē naman.

I will make a name for myself.

Ðone beorhtan steorran ðe wē hātaþ morgensteorra.

That bright star which we call morning star.

Hē cwæð tō ðām wanhālan,...
'Bēo þū hāl, cnapa, and stand on þīnum fōtum ætforan ūs ġesund.' Þā āras se cnapa and uprihte ēode.

He said to the infirm one,...
'Be thou whole, boy, and stand on thy feet before us in health.' Then the boy arose and went forth upright.

C. Other inflectional patterns for **se**-nouns are used with only small groups of words; most of the words in these statistically minor classes, on the other hand, are 'everyday' nouns, or names. The classes are represented by **mann** 'man,' **frēond** 'friend,' **fæder** 'father,' **sunu** 'son,' **wine** 'friend, protector'; national names **Dene** 'Danes,' **Engle** 'the English,' etc. occur only as plural forms. (*OEG* 620–634 passim)

se	mann	þā	menn	se	frēond	þā	frīend
ðæs	mannes	þāra	manna	ðæs	frēondes	þāra	frēonda
ðǣm	menn	þǣm	mannum	ðǣm	frīend	þǣm	frēondum
ðone	mann	þā	menn	ðone	frēond	þā	frīend

se	fæder	þā	fæderas	se	sunu	þā	suna
ðæs	fæder, -eres	þāra	fædera	ðæs	suna	þāra	suna
ðǣm	fæder	þǣm	fæderum	ðǣm	suna	þǣm	sunum
ðone	fæder	þā	fæderas	ðone	sunu	þā	suna

se	wine	þā	wine, -as			þā	Dene
ðæs	wines	þāra	wina, -i(ġe)a			þāra	Dena, -iġa
ðǣm	wine	þǣm	winum			þǣm	Denum
ðone	wine	þā	wine, -as			þā	Dene

The historical-comparative classifications of these additional 'strong' declension nouns are as follows:

Mann represents 'athematic nouns,' a group which also include **fōt** 'foot,' **tōþ** 'tooth.' Historically, there was no stem-formative element preceding inflectional suffixes with these nouns. The variation in root vowel results from operation of a sound change called '*i*-umlaut' with some of the inflections but not with others (see Appendix B).

Frēond represents '-*nd*-nouns,' including **fēond** 'enemy'; also **hettend** 'enemy,' **hǣlend** 'saviour,' **wīġend** 'warrior' (cf. **hete** 'hate, malice,' **hǣlan** 'to heal,' **wīġ** 'strife, battle'). Some alternate forms are **ðǣm frēonde** and **þā frēondas**.

Fæder represents a small group of 'relationship nouns,' including **brōðor** 'brother,' and **sēo**-nouns **mōdor** 'mother,' **dohtor** 'daughter.'

Sunu represents '*u*-nouns,' which also include **wudu** 'wood,' **bregu** 'prince,' **feld** 'field.'

Wine represents '*i*-nouns,' which include **mere** 'lake,' **stede** 'place,' and compounds with **-scipe** such as **frēondscipe** 'friendship'; also **bēorscipe** 'feast,' **ent** 'giant,' **wyrm** 'worm, dragon.'

Dene represents '*i*-nouns' in national names.

Se fēond ond se frēond.	The enemy and the friend.
Fēond on frēondes anlīcnesse.	An enemy in the likeness of a friend.
Se hlāford ne scrīfð ... frēonde ne fēonde.	The lord regards not ... friend nor foe.
Tōcnāwan þīne frīnd and þīne fȳnd.	To distinguish thy friends and thine enemies.
Ġē synt mīne frȳnd ġif ġē dōð þā þing þe iċ ēow bebēode.	You are my friends if you do those things that I command you.
Æġhwylcum men biþ lēofre swā hē hæbbe holdra frēonda mā.	For every man it is more desirable as he may have more loyal friends.
Selle hē his wæpn his frēondum tō ġehealdanne.	Let him give his weapon to his friends for holding.
Ne frīend ne fīend.	Neither friends nor foes.
Ðæt man friþ and frēondscipe rihtlīċe healde.	That one should rightly (lawfully) keep peace and friendship.
Sē ġefēhþ fela folca tōsomne mid frēondscipe.	He joins many people together with friendship.
Hē ongan winas manian, frȳnd and ġefēran.	He began to exhort comrades, friends and companions.
Meaht ðū, mīn wine, mēċe ġecnāwan?	Can you, my friend, recognize the sword?
Uton wirċean man tō ūre anlīcnesse.	Let us create man in our likeness.
Englas hē worhte, ðā sind gāstas, and nabbaþ nænne līċhaman. Menn hē ġescēop mid gāste and mid līċhaman.	He wrought angels, which are spirits, and have no body. He created men with spirit and with body.

5.4 Sēo-nouns ('Feminine')

A. The following **'strong' nouns** have uniform inflections. Final -*u* in singular nominative forms of words such as **lufu** 'love' occurs when the noun stem is short, alternating with -ø (absence of final -*u*) when the stem is long in words such as **lār** 'lore, learning' (see 2.6). Other sēo-nouns illustrated here are **sāwol** 'soul,' **langung** 'longing,' **ȳð** 'wave,' **dǣd** 'deed,' **beadu** 'battle,' and in plural forms only, **frætwe** 'ornament.'

sēo	lufu	þā	lufa, -e	sēo	lār	þā	lāra, -e
þǣre	lufe	þāra	lufa, -ena	þǣre	lāre	þāra	lāra
þǣre	lufe	þǣm	lufum	þǣre	lāre	þǣm	lārum
þā	lufe	þā	lufa, -e	þā	lāre	þā	lāra, -e
sēo	sāwol	þā	sāwla, -e	sēo	langung	ðā	langunga, -e
ðǣre	sāwle	þāra	sāwla	þǣre	langunge	ðāra	langunga
ðǣre	sāwle	þǣm	sāwlum	þǣre	langunge	ðǣm	langungum
ðā	sāwle	þā	sāwla, -e	þā	langunge	ðā	langunga, -e
sēo	ȳð	þā	ȳþa, -e	sēo	dǣd	þā	dǣda, -e
þǣre	ȳðe	þāra	ȳþa	ðǣre	dǣde	þāra	dǣda
þǣre	ȳðe	þǣm	ȳþum	ðǣre	dǣde	þǣm	dǣdum
þā	ȳðe	þā	ȳþa, -e	ðā	dǣde	þā	dǣda, -e
sēo	beadu	þā	beadwa, -e			þā	frætwa, -e
þǣre	beadwe	þāra	beadwa			þāra	frætwa
þǣre	beadwe	þǣm	beadwum			þǣm	frætwum
þā	beadwe	þā	beadwa, -e			þā	frætwa, -e

Most of the sēo-nouns just listed illustrate 'o-stem nouns,' a collective designation of three historically different 'strong' noun declensions. (*OEG* 585–598)

1. 'Pure o-stems' are **lufu**, **lār**, and **sāwol**; declined in the same pattern are abstract nouns formed with derivational suffixes -**ung**, -**ing**, illustrated above by **langung**.

2. The 'jo-stems' are illustrated by **ȳð**; abstract nouns such as **þrȳness** 'three-ness, trinity' formed with the common derivational suffix -**ness**, as well as several others, are declined like **ȳð**.

3. The 'wo-stems' are illustrated by **beadu** and **frætwe**.

Another historically distinguished class, the '*i*-stems,' is represented by **dǣd**; nearly all nouns in Old English of this type have long stems: **tīd** '(space of) time,' **wēn** 'expectation,' **wyrd** 'fate,' etc.

On bōclicum lārum.	In literary studies.
On wordsnotorlicum lārum.	In philosophical doctrines.
Hē sceal habban lāre þæt hē maġe [þæt] folc mid wīsdōme lǣran.	He must have learning so that he may be able to instruct the people with wisdom.
[His] dæġweorc biþ ... lār oððe leornung.	His daily work shall be ... teaching or learning.
Ne sceolan þā lārēowas āġīmelēasian þā lāre.	The teachers shall not neglect instruction.
Hiġ lǣrað manna lāra.	They teach the doctrines of men.
Ġif wē ōþre men teala lǣraþ, and hīe be ūrum lārum rihtlīce for Gode libbaþ, ðonne bringe wē Drihtne swētne stenċ on ūrum dǣdum and lārum.	If we teach others well, and by our teachings they live rightly before God, then from the Lord we bring a sweet scent onto our deeds and teachings.
Sēo ārfæste dǣd.	That goodly deed.
For þǣre dǣde.	For that deed.
Gōdum dǣdum.	By good deeds.
In his dǣdum.	In his actions.
Mid þisre dǣde.	With this deed.
Hīo spēon hine on ðā dimman dǣd.	She urged him to do that dark deed.
Opene weorþað monna dǣde.	Men's deeds shall be open.
God him ġe·unne ðæt his gōde dǣda swȳðran wearþan ðonne misdǣda.	God grant him that his good deeds be more prevailing than his misdeeds.
Menn swȳþor scamað nū for gōddǣdan þonne for misdǣdan.	Men are now ashamed more for good deeds than for misdeeds.
Sprec ofter ymb ōðres monnes weldǣda ðonne ymb ðīne āgene.	Speak more often about another man's good deeds than about thine own.

The derivational suffixes -**ung**, -**ing** and -**nes(s)** merit further illustration, since they were highly productive of abstract nouns.

From				
ācsian	'(to) ask' is derived	**ācsung**	'interrogation'
ċēapian	'(to) trade'	**ċēapung**	'trading'
costian	'(to) tempt'	**costung**	'temptation'
metgian	'(to) regulate'	**metgung**	'moderation'
ġemiltsian	'(to) pity'	**ġemiltsung**	'pity, compassion'
murcnian	'(to) complain'	**murcnung**	'complaint'
deorcian	'(to) grow dark'	**deorcnung**	'twilight'
langian	'(to) long'	**langung**	'longing'
niðerian	'(to) put bring low'	**niðerung**	'humility'
samnian	'(to) gather together'	**samnung**	'collection, assembly'
swīcian	'(to) deceive'	**swīcung**	'deceit, deception'
swīgian	'(to) be silent'	**swīgung**	'silence'
tācnian	'(to) denote'	**tācnung**	'significance'
wunian	'(to) dwell, inhabit'	**wunung**	'dwelling'
ānrǣd	'of one mind'	**ānrǣdnes**	'unanimity'
æðele	'noble'	**æðelnes**	'nobility'
blind	'blind'	**blindnes**	'blindness'
clǣne	'clean, pure'	**clǣnnes**	'purity'
ēadiġ	'wealthy; blessed'	**ēadiġnes**	'prosperity'
fæst	'secure, firm'	**fæstnes**	'security'
full	'full'	**fullnes**	'fullness'
fūl	'foul'	**fūlnes**	'foulness'
grēne	'green'	**grēnnes**	'greenness'
lufsum	'lovable'	**lufsumnes**	'pleasantness'
mildheort	'merciful'	**mildheortnes**	'mercy, mercifulness'
twirǣde	'disagreeing'	**twirǣdnes**	'disagreement'
þweorh	'crooked, perverse'	**þwēornes**	'perversity'
smēðe	'smooth'	**smēðnes**	'smoothness'
þrȳ	'three'	**ðrynes**	'trinity'
wōd	'mad'	**wōdnes**	'madness'
þicce	'thick, solid'	**þicnes**	'thickness, density'

B. Hearpe 'harp' typifies **'weak'** (or *n*-stem) **sēo-nouns**, a large class. (*OEG* 615–619 passim)

sēo	hearpe	þā	hearpan
þǣre	hearpan	þāra	hearpena
þǣre	hearpan	þǣm	hearpum
þā	hearpan	þā	hearpan

Inflection of those nouns whose stems terminate in a long vowel, as **flā** 'arrow,' are manifested only as -**n**, -**m**, -**na**: **flāna scūras** 'showers of arrows,' **þurhscoten mid ānre flān** 'shot-through with an arrow.'

Some of the common nouns of this class are **ċiriċe** 'church,' **sunne** 'sun,' **cwene** 'woman,' **eorðe** 'earth,' **heofon** 'heaven,' **heorte** 'heart,' **þrote** 'throat,' **flēoge** 'fly,' **moþþe** 'moth,' **nǣdre** 'snake.'

Sīo nǣdre ... lǣrde Ēuan on wōh. Ðā wæs Adam ... ðurh ġespan ðǣre næddran ... oferswīðed.	The serpent ... taught Eve wrongfully. Then Adam was ... overcome ... by the serpent's enticing.
Cōm of ðǣm wætre ān nǣdre,... and þā menn ealle ofslōg þe nēh ðǣm wætre cōmon.	A serpent came from the water,... and killed all the men that came near the water.
Bēo ġē swā ware suā suā nǣdran.	Be ye as watchful as serpents.
Ġē næddran and næddrena cynn.	Ye vipers and generation of vipers.
Moyses āhōf ðā næddran.... Ðā sende God fȳrene næddran.... God bebēad Moyse ðæt hē ġeworhte āne ǣrene næddran, and sette up tō tācne, and ðæt hē manode ðæt folc ðæt swā hwā swā fram ðām næddrum ābiten wǣre, besāwe up tō ðǣre ǣrenan næddran.	Moses raised up the serpent.... Then God sent fiery serpents.... God commanded Moses that he should make a brazen serpent, and set it up as an emblem, and that he should exhort the people that whoever should be bitten by the serpents should look up at the brazen serpent.
His heorte ongann wendan tō hire willan.	His heart began to turn to her will.
Heortan ġeþōhtas.	Thoughts of the heart.
Lustum heortena.	To (their) hearts' desires.
Of þǣre heortan cumaþ yfle ġeþancas.	Out of the heart proceed evil thoughts.

His mōdor ġehēold ealle þās word
  on hyre heortan.

His mother held all those words
  in her heart.

For ēower heortan heardnesse hē
  ēow wrāt þis bebod.

For the hardness of your heart he
  wrote for you this command.

Þā wæstmas þe eorþe forþbringeþ.

The fruits which the earth brings forth.

Þū eart eorþe, and þū scealt ...
  eft tō eorðan weorðan.

Thou art earth, and thou shalt ...
  become again earth.

Fēower ġesceafta [synd]: ān
  þæra is eorþe, ōþer wæter,
  þridde lyft, fēowrþe fȳr.

There are four elements: one of them
  is earth, the second water, the
  third air, the fourth fire.

Remedy for bad dreams and horrible night walkers

Ðēos wyrt þe man *betonicam* nemneð, hēo biþ cenned on mǣdum ond on
clǣnum dūnlandum, ond on ġefriþedum stōwum. Sēo dēah ġehwæþer ġe þæs
mannes sāwle ġe his līchoman. Hīo hyne scyldeþ wið unhȳrum nihtgengum ond
wið eġeslīcum ġesihðum ond swefnum. Ond sēo wyrt byþ swȳþe hāligu ond þus
þū scealt niman on augustes mōnðe būtan īserne. And þonne þū hī ġenumene
hæbbe, āhryse þā moldan of, þæt hyre nānwiht on ne clyfie, and þonne drīġ hī
on scēade swȳþe þearle ond mid wyrt-truman mid ealle ġewyrċ tō dūste. Brūc
hyre þonne, ond hyre byriġ þonne ðū beþurfe.

'This wort, which is named betony, is produced in meadows and in clean
downland (open country) and in protected places. It is good for both a man's
soul and his body. It shields him against fierce night-walkers and against terrible
visions and dreams. And that wort is extremely wholesome, and thus you must
take in the month of August, without (use of) iron. And when you have gathered
it, shake the soil from it, so that none of it clings to it, and then dry it in the
shade as thoroughly as possible, and with the roots entirely work it into dust.
Then use it, and taste of it when you have need.'

C. Other inflection patterns for **sēo**-nouns belong to (and define) statistically minor classes, most members of those classes, again, being 'everyday,' or often used, words. The classes are represented by **nosu** 'nose,' **hand** 'hand,' **mōdor** 'mother,' **dohtor** 'daughter,' **bōc** 'book,' **burg** 'fortified town.' (*OEG* 611–631 passim)

sēo	nosu	þā	nosa	sēo	hand	þā	handa
þǣre	nosa	þāra	nosa	þǣre	handa	þāra	handa
þǣre	nosa	þǣm	nosum	þǣre	handa	þǣm	handum
þā	nosu	þā	nosa	þā	hand	þā	handa

sēo	mōdor	þā	mōdra, -u	sēo	dohtor	þā	dohtor
þǣre	mōdor	þāra	mōdra	þǣre	dohtor	þāra	dohtra
þǣre	mēder	þǣm	mōdrum	þǣre	dehter	þǣm	dohtrum
þā	mōdor	þā	mōdra, -u	þā	dohtor	þā	dohtor

sēo	bōc	þā	bēċ	sēo	burg	þā	byrġ, burha
þǣre	bēċ, bōce	þāra	bōca	þǣre	byrġ, burge	þāra	burga
þǣre	bēċ, bōc	þǣm	bōcum	þǣre	byrġ, burg	þǣm	burgum
þā	bōc	þā	bēċ	þā	burg	þā	byrġ, burha

The historical-comparative classifications of these additional 'strong' declension nouns are as follows:

Bōc and **burg** are 'athematic nouns,' of which they are the most common examples; others are **hnutu** 'nut,' **lūs** 'louse,' and **mūs** 'mouse.' Like **se**-nouns **mann** and **fōt**, they have variation in root vowel resulting from operation of '*i*-umlaut.'

Mōdor and **dohtor** are 'relationship nouns,' along with **sweostor** 'sister,' the last of these not always regularly declined.

Nosu and **hand** represent '*u*-nouns,' a very small class of which **duru** 'door' is a prominent instance.

Iċ wrāt bōc.	I wrote a book.
Sēo bōc is on englisc ġewand.	The book is translated into English.
On ðǣre bēċ.	In that book.
On ðǣra cininga bōcum.	In the kings' books.

Stæfcræft is sēo cæġ þe þāra
bōca andġytt unlȳcð.

Grammar is the key that unlocks
the meaning of books.

Wē ġesetton on þissum enchiridion,
þæt ys manualis on lyden and
handbōc on englisc, maneġa þing
ymbe ġerīmcræft.

We set down in this *enchiridion*,
that is *manualis* in Latin and
handbook in English, many things
concerning arithmetic.

Ðā hālgan bēċ—saltere and
pistolbōc ... sangbōc and
handbōc.

The holy books—psalter and epistle-
book ... book of canticles and
manual.

Se cyngc hēold Apollonius hand
on handa.

The king held Apollonius hand in
hand.

Mid ðǣre ylcan hand.

With the same hand.

On ǣġðera hand.

On either hand.

Ġebindan handum and fōtum.

To bind by hands and feet.

Domicianus wearð ācweald æt his
witena handum.

Domitian was killed at the hands of
his senators.

Hēo is ealra libbendra mōdor.

She [Eve] is the mother of all living.

Se yfela willa ... is mōdor ælċes
yfeles.

The evil will ... is mother of every
evil.

[Hē] seġð his fæder and mēder.

He says to his father and mother.

[Hē] wæs Bryttisc on his mōder
healfe.

He was British on his mother's side.

Moyses cwæð, 'Wurða þīnne fæder
and þīne mōdor.'

Moses said, 'Honor thy father and
thy mother.'

His fōstormōder āne wæs him
fylġende.

His foster mother alone was
following him.

Iċ ġe·an mīnra fōstermēder ðæs
landes æt Westūne.

I give to my foster mother the land
at Weston.

For mīnes lēofan fæder sāwle and
for mīnre ealdemōdor.

For my dear father's soul and for
my grandmother's.

D. A few **sēo**-nouns are usually not inflected. **Lengu** 'length' is one, although **leng(þ)u** 'length' is inflected. **Ēa** 'water, river' is often not inflected, although such forms as **ēas** (genitive) and **ēan** (plural nominative and accusative) may occur. **Þonne þā men ... ofer þā ēa fareð, hȳ bēoð swā hrædlīce ofer þǣre ēa þæt men wēnað þæt hȳ flēogan** 'When those men ... travel across the water, they are so quickly across the water that people suppose that they fly.' **Scyld** 'crime, fault' is usually not inflected. **Ǣ** 'law' is seldom inflected: **His willa byð on Godes ǣ, ond ymb his ǣ byð smēagende dæges ond nihtes** 'His desire is in the law of God, and concerning His law he is meditating by day and by night.'

Remedy for burns

Dēos wyrt ðe man *ancusa* nemneþ byð cenned on begānum stōwum ond on smēþum, and ðās wyrte ðū scealt niman on ðām mōnþe ðe man martius hāteþ. Ðysse wyrte syndon twā cynrenu. Ān is ðe affricani *barbatam* nemnað. Ōþer ys tō lǣcedōmum swȳþe ġecoren, ond ðēos byð cenned fyrmest on ðām lande ðe man persa hāteþ. Ond hēo ys scearpan lēafon ond þurnihtum būtan stelan.

With forbærnednysse, ġenim þysse wyrte wyrt-truman ancusa on ele ġesodene ond wið wex ġemencgedne, ðām ġemete þe þū plaster oþþe clyþan wyrċ. Lege tō þām bærnytte. Wundorlīce hyt ġehǣleþ.

'This wort, which one calls *ancusa*, is produced in cultivated places and in smooth (ones), and you shall take this wort in the month which is called March. Of this wort there are two kinds. One is that which Africans call *barbatus*. The other is much favored for leechdoms, and this is produced in the land which is called Persia. And it is of sharp and thorny leaves without a stalk.

'For severe burn, take a root of this wort *ancusa* sodden (boiled/soaked) in oil and mingled with wax in the manner that you make a plaster or poultice. Lay it to the burn. It heals wonderfully.'

5.5 Þæt-nouns ('Neuter')

A. The following **'strong' nouns** have uniform inflections, except for final -*u* in plural nominative and accusative forms of words such as **hof** 'dwelling,' when a monosyllabic stem is short (see 2.6), alternating with -ø (i.e., no overt inflection), when the stem is long, in such words as **weorc** 'work, labor.' Stem variations of these 'strong' þæt-nouns are further represented by **fæt** 'vessel, vat,' **wuldor** 'glory,' **rīce** 'kingdom,' **weorod** 'troop,' **trēow** 'tree, wood,' **feoh** 'money, goods.'

þæt	weorc	þā	weorc	þæt	hof	þā	hofu
þæs	weorces	þāra	weorca	þæs	hofes	þāra	hofa
þǣm	weorce	þǣm	weorcum	þǣm	hofe	þǣm	hofum
þæt	weorc	þā	weorc	þæt	hof	þā	hofu
þæt	fæt	þā	fatu	þæt	wuldor	þā	wuldor
þæs	fætes	þāra	fata	þæs	wuldres	þāra	wuldra
þǣm	fæte	þǣm	fatum	þǣm	wuldre	þǣm	wuldrum
þæt	fæt	þā	fatu	þæt	wuldor	þā	wuldor
þæt	rīce	þā	rīcu	þæt	weorod	þā	weorod
þæs	rīces	þāra	rīca	þæs	weorodes	þāra	weoroda
þǣm	rīce	þǣm	rīcum	þǣm	weorode	þǣm	weorodum
þæt	rīce	þā	rīcu	þæt	weorod	þā	weorod
þæt	trēow	þā	trēow	þæt	feoh		
þæs	trēowes	þāra	trēowa	þæs	fēos		
þǣm	trēowe	þǣm	trēowum	þǣm	fēo		
þæt	trēow	þā	trēow	þæt	feoh		

All inflectional sets of þæt-nouns just listed illustrate 'a-stem nouns,' a collective designation of three historically different 'strong' noun classes. (*OEG* 570–584)

1. 'Pure **a**-stems,' one of these three classes, are represented by **weorc, hof, fæt, wuldor, weorod,** and **feoh.**

(a) There are no stem variations for **weorc** or **hof**; the final -*u* for plural nominative and accusative inflection of short stem **hof** is a remnant of an inflectional suffix that was lost altogether with long stem neuter nouns like **weorc** and **word.**

(b) The alternation of **fæt-** and **fat-** results from the same historical change that affected **se-**nouns such as **dæġ**.

(c) In disyllabic nouns such as **wuldor** the unstressed vowel, in the second syllable, is usually deleted when an inflectional syllable follows. **Weorod** is historically of a different pattern, but shows no stem variation in the full paradigm; on the other hand, words like **hēafod** 'head,' having a long initial syllable, delete the unstressed vowel before inflections, as **hēafdes, hēafdum,** and also plural nominative and accusative **hēafdu.**

(d) The variants in **feoh, fēos,** etc. are parallel to those of **se-**nouns **mearh** and **feorh.**

2. **Rīċe** represents 'ja-stems,' similar to **se-**nouns of the same class. Like **rīċe** are **wīte** 'punishment,' **ǣrende** 'errand.'

3. **Trēow** represents 'wa-stems,' similar to **se-**nouns of the same class.

Ealle þā word sint sōþe.	All those words are true.
Ġif þās word sind sōþ.	If these words are truth.
On frymðe wæs word and þæt word wæs mid Gode and God wæs þæt word.	In the beginning was the word and the word was with God, and the word was God.
Hē wile tō his nēhstan sprecan þā word þe hē wēnþ þæt him lēofoste sȳn tō ġehȳrenne, and þonne þenċþ hū hē hine beswīcan mæġe þurh þā swētnesse þāra worda.	He will speak those words to his neighbor that he imagines will be most pleasing to him to hear, and then (he) thinks how he can deceive him through the pleasantness of those words.
Iċ dō swā iċ ne sceolde, hwīle mid weorce, hwīle mid worde.	I do as I should not, at one time with deed, at one time with word.
Hwæðer mīn word bēo mid weorce ġefylled.	Whether my word shall be fulfilled with action (shall come to pass).
Ān weorc iċ worhte.	I have done one work.
Wæstm gōdra weorca.	The fruits of good deeds.
Ealle heora worc hiġ dōð, þæt menn hī ġesēon.	All their works they do, that men should see them.
Bēon mid bearne.	To be with child.
Þurh bearnes ġebyrd.	Through birth of a child.

Hiġ næfdon nān bearn.

Nū is þæt bearn cymen.

Þæt hīe lǣfon healdan heora
  bearnum, and heora bearna
  bearnum.

Nis ðæt nān wundor.

Ðǣr bið wundra mā ðonne hit
  æniġ mæġe āþenċan.

Wundor æfter wundre.

His wunder wǣron miclo.

Wundrum moniġo.

Wundrum lytel.

Wundrum fæġer.

Wundrum ġeġierwed.

They had no child.

Now is the child come.

What they leave to their children
  to hold, and to their children's
  children.

That is no wonder.

There are more wonders than anyone
  may think.

Wonder after wonder.

His miracles were many.

Very many.

Wondrously little.

Wondrously fair.

Wondrously arrayed.

B. Ēare 'ear' and ēage 'eye' are **'weak'** (or *n*-stem) þæt-nouns, to which class belong only these two and (with mixed declension) **wange** 'cheek.'

þæt	ēare	þā	ēaran
þæs	ēaran	þāra	ēarena
þǣm	ēaran	þǣm	ēarum
þæt	ēare	þā	ēaran

Sōþlīċe þises folces heorte is
āhyrd and hiġ hefelīċe mid
ēarum ġehȳrdon and hyra ēagan
beclȳsdon, þē-læs hiġ æfre mid
ēagum ġesēon and mid ēarum
ġehȳron and mid heortan onġyton.
... Sōþlīċe ēadiġe synt ēowre
ēagan for-þām-þe hiġ ġesēoþ
and ēowre ēaran for-þām-þe
hiġ ġehȳraþ.

Truly this people's heart is
hardened and sluggishly they
heard with ears and their eyes
they closed, lest they any time
see with (their) eyes and hear
with (their) ears and understand
with (their) heart.... Truly
your eyes are blessed because
they see and your ears because
they hear.

C. Other inflectional patterns for þæt-nouns are those of '*i*-nouns,' represented here by **spere** 'spear' and **flǣsc** 'flesh.' (*OEG* 607–610)

þæt	spere	þā	speru	þæt	flǣsc	þā	flǣsc
þæs	speres	þāra	spera	þæs	flǣsces	þāra	flǣsca
þǣm	spere	þǣm	sperum	þǣm	flǣsce	þǣm	flǣscum
þæt	spere	þā	speru	þæt	flǣsc	þā	flǣsc

Gāst næfþ flǣsc and bān.

Bān of mīnum bānum and flǣsc of
  mīnum flǣsce.

Se gāst is hræd and þæt flǣsc
  ys untrum.

Þæt þe ācenned is of flǣsce, þæt
  is flǣsc; and þæt þe of gāste is
  ācenned, þæt is gāst.

Spirit does not have flesh and bone.

Bone of my bones and flesh of
  my flesh.

The spirit is willing but the flesh
  is weak.

That which is born of flesh, that
  is flesh; and that which is born
  of spirit, that is spirit.

From Ælfric's Grammar of Latin, in a section on grammatical number

Numerus is 'ġetel': *singularis* ... '(grammatical) number'
et *pluralis* 'ānfeald oððe meniġ- ... 'singular or plural.'
feald.' Ānfeald ġetel is on . . . .
ānum, *homo* 'ān mann.' Mæniġ- . . . 'one (*or* a) man.'
feald ġetel is *homines* 'menn....' . . . . 'men.'
Witodlīċe āgene naman habbað Indeed, proper nouns have
ānfeald ġetel ond nabbað mæniġ- singular number and don't have
feald; ēac 'sunne' ond 'mōna' plural; also 'sun' and 'moon'
syndon ānfealdes ġeteles. are of singular number. There
Sindon ēac manega ōðre naman þe are also many other nouns which
æfter lēden-spræċe nabbað mæniġ- in Latin don't have plural
feald ġetel: ... *sanguis* 'blōd,' number: ... 'blood,'
... *pax* 'sibb,' *lux* 'lēoht,' ... 'peace,' 'light,'
pix 'piċ,' *fames* 'hungor,' 'pitch,' 'hunger,'
sitis 'þurst,' ... *humus* 'molde,' 'thirst,' ... 'soil,'
... *foenum* 'strēow,' *lutum* 'fenn,' ... 'straw,' 'dirt, mud,'
aeuum 'ēċnys' ... ond ælċ 'eternity,' ... and each of those
þæra þinga þe man wehð on things which one weighs on scales
wægan oððe met on fate—næfð or measures in a vessel—none of them
heora nān mæniġfeald ġetel, has plural number, although some
þēah-þe sume men be heora āgenum people by their own choice make
dōme hī āwendað mæniġfealdlīċe, them plural (-like) [forms],
þus cweþende: *frumenta* 'hwætas,' thus saying: 'wheats,'
ordea 'beras,' *fabae* 'bēana,' 'barleys,' 'beans,'
pyse 'pysan,' *uina* 'fela wīn,' 'peas,'* 'much wine,'
mella 'fela huniġ,' *et cetera.* 'much honey,' and so forth.
Sume naman syndon ēac þe nabbað There are also certain nouns that
ānfeald ġetel, ac bēoð æfre maniġ- don't have singular number, but are
fealdlīċe ġecwedene, swā swā bēoð always spoken plural, as two of
twā þæra twelf tācna: *gemini* the twelve signs are:
'ġetwisan' and *pisces* 'fixas,' and 'twins' and 'fishes,' and
manega ōðre tō ēacen þyson. many other besides these.

---

*Historically, **peas** (not **pea**) is the singular form of this noun.

Chapter 6

VERBS

6.1 Inflectional Categories of Verbs

The morphological system of Old English verbs has the pattern shown here, in the format chosen for displaying verb inflections throughout this chapter.

———	Infinitive
———	Inflected infinitive
———	Present participle
———	Passive participle
——— (þū)	Imperative singular
——— (ġē)	Imperative plural

Non-past

Person	Indicative Singular		Plural		Subjunctive Singular		Plural	
1st	(iċ)	———	(wē)	———	(iċ)	———	(wē)	———
2nd	(þū)	———	(ġē)	———	(þū)	———	(ġē)	———
3rd	(hē)	———	(hīe)	———	(hē)	———	(hīe)	———

Past

Person	Singular		Plural		Singular		Plural	
1st	(iċ)	———	(wē)	———	(iċ)	———	(wē)	———
2nd	(þū)	———	(ġē)	———	(þū)	———	(ġē)	———
3rd	(hē)	———	(hīe)	———	(hē)	———	(hīe)	———

Inflectional categories of independent verb forms in Old English include those of tense, mood, person, and number. Two tenses are distinguished, non-past and past; the three moods are indicative, subjunctive, imperative; the three persons concord with those of the personal pronouns; and number distinctions are singular and non-singular (or plural). An infinitive and two participles—a present participle and a passive participle—make up the remaining forms.

The *citation form* by convention is the infinitive—the form that serves as headword in dictionaries, glossaries, and grammars; it is given in capital letters at the top of any page displaying inflections, and the classification of the verb is also given at the top.

Not all the categories, as they intersect in verb conjugations, are represented discretely by inflectional suffixes. For example, plural forms are not distinguished for the three person categories, whether in indicative or subjunctive mood. Distinctly imperative forms are limited to second person, singular number, non-past tense. Only number and tense (but not person) distinctions occur with subjunctive forms.

Familiar verb-phrase categories of voice—active and passive—are not distinguished within Old English verb morphology. The independent verb forms are essentially 'active voice.' 'Passive voice' is a phrasal construction (as it is also in Modern English) formed by a passive participle together with an appropriately inflected form of **bēon/wesan** '(to) be' or **weorðan** '(to) become' (most frequently a past tense form); see 6.6.

Neither is the familiar category 'future' tense distinguished morphologically; regardless of contextual relations of time of action expressed in the verb, 'future' is not a formal characteristic of independent verbs. For the moment, two illustrations must suffice: **Iċ ārīse and iċ fare tō mīnum fæder and iċ secge him** ... 'I will arise and I will go to my father and I will say to him ...'; **Iċ bēo hāl** 'I shall be safe,' as contrasted with **Iċ eom** ... 'I am ....' Verb phrases formed by an infinitive together with an appropriately inflected form of **willan** '(to) desire, wish, will,' or **sculan** '(to) be obliged, shall,' are ancestral to Modern English phrases signifying future but to some extent carry the volitional or obligational meaning of these forms: **Tō dēaðe hīe þē willaþ ġelǣdan** 'They intend to lead thee to death'; **Iċ [Satan] sceal bīdan in bendum** 'I am to remain in bonds.' Non-past forms of **weorðan** '(to) become' with infinitive also signify future.

It is impractical to attempt enumeration of all formal categories *not* represented in inflections of Old English verbs—even those commonly discussed in connection with Modern English. Those of voice and future tense are especially troublesome to English speakers, though, hence their brief mention here. Likewise it is impractical to proceed from a set of conceptual categories of grammar, in the manner typified by 'Past imperfect was expressed by such-and-such,' or 'The subjunctive forms were used to express this and this and this.' (*OEG* 726–729, *OES* 600–601) Semantic categories of time and the morphological distinctions of tense simply do not square up in Old English (and they don't in Modern English, either). Meanings and forms follow different systems, and one of them cannot suitably explain the other.

On the other hand, it will be practical to illustrate the forms of principal verbs along with the principal verb classes, and also to illustrate the principal types of constructions centering on verb forms. For the first kind of illustration, verb forms will be displayed in paradigms, together with accompanying examples in sentence context; the morphology is complex in that there are many classes and subclasses of verbs, hence most space—and effort of learning—is required by the independent forms. For the second kind of illustration—a matter of syntax as well as morphology—the main classes of constructions are far fewer.

As with noun paradigms, selection of verbs for models reflects the relative frequency of occurrence of individual verb roots. The order of exposition also reflects verb frequency. The most commonly occurring verbs are morphologically anomalous—i.e., not having a set of forms consistent with those of other verbs—or they belong to small groups or subclasses of inflectionally similar verbs, just as in Modern English and the other Germanic languages: **be, do, may, can, will, see, say**, etc. According to Madden and Magoun (see 5.2), the numbers of occurrences in poetry for some of these verbs (together with derivationally related words) in the approximately 30,000 lines of verse that survive are the following: **bēon/wesan** '(to) be' occurs 4189 times, **willan** '(to) will, intend' 998, **dōn** '(to) do, make' 530, these three being anomalous; **sculan** '(to) be obligated' 794, **witan** '(to) know' 764, **cunnan** '(to) know' 539, **munnan** '(to) remember' 419, **āgan** '(to) possess' 370 are 'preterite-present' verbs, a special type to be explained later (see 6.3). **Magan** '(to) be able', occurring 1596 times, is a 'preterite-present' verb of uncertain class. **Habban** 771 '(to) have' and **secgan** '(to) say' 380 are two of a group of only four verbs called 'Weak, Class III.'

Principal parts of verbs are forms selected variously for purposes of teaching or linguistic description. Their pragmatic origin and function lie in this: that with these forms—or 'parts'—and with a knowledge of the system of which they are members, one can deduce the remaining forms of particular verbs. For further practical reasons, chiefly mnemonic ones, they are cited in the conventionalized order used in the following sections.

Concerning Verbs [Dictionary needed]

Word on englisc (þæt is, on Ælfredes cyninges ġereorde) is 'verb' on forð-
folgiende englisc (þæt is, on ūrum ġereorde), æfter Ælfriċe ðām lārēowe; ond
ælċ word hæfð tīd, þæt is 'tense,' ġemet, þæt is 'mood,' hād, þæt is 'person,'
and ġetel, þæt is 'number.' Wē wyllað nū secgan ende-byrdlīċe ond ġewīslīċe
be eallum þissum.

Twā tīda bēoð on ælcum worde ðe ful-fremed byð: andweard tīd is 'present
tense,' and forþ-ġe·witen tīd is 'past tense' (oþþe 'preterite'). Þāra worda ġe-
endunga on englisc ne ġetācniað tōwearde tīd, þæt is 'future tense,' ac swā-þēah
man mæġ secgan **iċ fare tō-meriġen** 'I go tomorrow,' **iċ ræde nū riht (oððe on
sumne tīman)** 'I will read now (or at some time).'

Ġemet, oððe þære spræċe wīse, is 'mood,' swā swā wē ær cwædon, ond
ðāra synd ðrȳ. Ġebīcniendlīċ is 'indicative,' mid þām wē ġeswuteliað hwæt
wē dōð, oððe hwæt ōðre menn dōð; iċ cweðe nū **iċ ræde** 'I read,' **hē gæþ** 'he
goeth'—þær bið mīn dæd oððe his dæd ġeswutelod. Þæt ōðer ġemet næfð nænne
naman þe ġetācnað hwæt þæt ġemet ġetācnie, ac wē magon hit ġenemnan under-
ðeodenlīċ, þæt is 'subjunctive'; hit bið ēac wiscendlīċ, oððe 'optative.' **Ġif iċ
ræde ġyrstandæġ, þonne cūðe iċ nū āġifan** 'If I had read yesterday, then I could
give back (something) now.' Þās ġemetu æt-ēowað on þām twæm tīdum ond
on þrim hādum, ac næfð unġelīċe ġe·endunga on eallum þissum. Þæt þridde
ġemet is bebēodendlīċ, þæt is 'imperative,' mid þām wē hātað ōðre menn dōn
sum þing oþþe sum ðing ðrōwian, þus: **Ræd þū,** 'Read (thou)!' **Ġehȳre ġē** 'Hear
(ye)!' Ðis ġemet næfð forð-ġe·witene tīde ond hit hæfð ðone ōðer hād ('person'),
ac næfð nā ðone forman hād ne ðone þriddan.

Þāra worda ġe·endunga æt-ēowaþ þrȳ hādas (þæt is 'persons') on ānfealdum
ġetele, ac hī synd ealle ġelīċe on mæniġfealdum ġetele. Se forma hād is, þe sprecð
be him sylfum āna, ðus: **iċ secge,** 'I say.' Se ōðer hād is, ðe se forma sprecð tō:
þū seġst 'thou sayest.' Se þridde hād is, be þām ðe se forma hād sprecð tō ðām
ōðrum hāde: **hē seġð** 'he saith'; on mæniġfealdum ġetele: **wē, ġē, hīe secgað**
'we, ye, they say.'

Ġetel ġelimpþ wordum æġðer ġe ānfeald ġe mæniġfeald; ānfeald ġetel bið
on ānum, **iċ ræde** 'I read,' and mæniġfeald tō maneġum, **wē rædað** 'we read';
ond swā forð.

Is ēac tō witenne þæt of þām worde cumað un-ġe·endelīċ word, þæt is
'infinitives,' and dæl-nimendlīċe word, þæt is 'participles.'

Contraction with negative particle

Contraction of the negative particle **ne** with certain other forms is very common. **Ne** always *immediately precedes* the form (or other sentence constituent) that it marks negation of. The form with which it contracts begins with a vowel, **w**, or **h**.

Verb forms commonly contracted with **ne** are chiefly those frequently occurring verbs that function as auxiliaries. Certain forms of **bēon/wesan** '(to) be' show this (see 6.2)—**ne wæs** contracts as **næs**, **ne wǣre** as **nǣre**, **ne is** as **nis**. Forms of **habban** '(to) have' also show this (see 6.4)—**ne hæbbe** contracts as **næbbe**, **ne hæfð** as **næfð**, etc. Another verb with contraction is **willan** '(to) will, wish' (see 6.2), so that **ne wolde** contracts as **nolde**, and so on. (Examples are also in 2.3 A illustrating /n/.)

Preterite-present verbs **witan** '(to) know' and **āgan** '(to) possess' (see 6.3) show this pattern as well: **ne wāt** contracts as **nāt**, **ne wiste** as **niste**, or **ne āh** as **nāh**, and the like.

In addition to verbs, the numeral **ān** 'one' when negated as **ne ān** contracts as **nān** 'not one, none.' Adjective **æniġ** 'any' is negated as **næniġ** 'not any.' Similarly, adverb **ǣfre** when negated as **ne ǣfre** contracts as **nǣfre** 'not ever, never.' (*OES* 1129) The pronoun **iċ** occurs with negative contraction in the response **Niċ** 'Not I.'

Two or more negated forms within a construction do not cancel each other, and in fact are quite common: **Nān wītega næfð nānne wurðscype** has negated subject **nān wītega**, negated predicate **næfð**, and negated object **nænne wurðscype**; it translates into standard Modern English as 'No prophet has...' or perhaps 'A prophet has no honor.' It translates more readily into non-standard English as 'No prophet ain't got no honor [in his own country].'

Sōðlīċe sī ēower sprǣċ, 'Hyt ys, hyt ys; hyt nys, hyt nys.' Sōðlīċe ġyf þǣr māre bið, þæt bið of yfele.	Truly, let your statement be, 'It is, it is; it isn't, it isn't.' Truly, if there be more (than these), it will be from evil.
Drihten, ġif þū wǣre hēr, nǣre mīn brōðor dēad.	Lord, if you had been here, my brother had not been dead.
Him betere wǣre ðæt hē nǣfre nǣre, ðonne hē yfele wǣre.	It were better for him that he never had been, than that he were evil.
Nafað æniġ man frēonda tō fela.	No one has too many friends.
þām bið ġeseald þe hæfð; ond þām ðe næfð, ēac þæt hē hæfð him	To that one will be given, who has; and for the one who hasn't [any-

bið ætbrōden.

Þū nāst nū þæt iċ dō, ac þū wāst syððan.	You do not know now what I do, but you will know afterwards.
Ġē ġebiddað þæt ġē nyton. Wē ġebiddaþ þæt wē witon.	You pray to that which you know not. We pray to that which we know.
Sē þe nāh [= ne āh] þā scēap, þonne hē þone wulf ġesyhþ, þonne flȳhð hē ond forlæt þā scēap.	The one who does not own the sheep, when he sees the wolf, then he flees and abandons the sheep.
Symle ġē habbað þearfan mid ēow, ac ġē nabbað mē symle.	Always you have the poor with you, but you haven't me always.
Betere wǣre þām men þæt hē nǣfre nǣre ācenned.	It were better for that man that he had never been born.
Betere him wǣre þæt se mann ācenned nǣre.	It were better for him that the man hadn't been born.
Nān witega næfð nānne wurðscype on his āgenum earde.	A prophet has not honor in his own land.
Ġif hē synful is, þæt iċ nāt. Ān þing iċ wāt: þæt iċ wæs blind and þæt iċ nū ġesēo.	If he is sinful, I know not. One thing I know: that I was blind and that now I see.
Hē cwæð ..., 'Ġē witon hwyder iċ fare ....' Thomas cwæð tō him, 'Drihten, wē nyton hwyder þū færst.'	He said ..., 'You know whither I go ....' Thomas said to him, 'Lord we don't know whither thou goest.'
Iċ cweðe nū ðæt iċ ne dearr ne iċ nelle nāne bōc æfter ðisre of Lēdene on Englisc āwendan.	I say now that I dare not and I will not any book after this (one) translate from Latin into English.

(above the table, continuing:) thing], even that which he has shall be taken away.

6.2 Anomalous Verbs

Just as Modern English and any of the other European languages, Old English had a small number of verbs whose inflectional forms did not conform to the pattern of inflections for any other verbs. Because of this there is no point in trying to list 'principal parts'; for these verbs there is no short-cut from simply listing all the forms. They are all verbs that are in constant use—the ancestral forms of **be, do, go, will**—and are among the ones learned earliest. (*OEG* 768)

Bēon/wesan '(to) be' has a number of functions. It is a copula **Ġē synd hyrdas** 'Ye are shepherds,' **Hēo wæs wudewe fēower and hundeahtatiġ ġēara** 'She was a widow eighty-four years,' **Iċ hit eom** 'It is I,' **þū hit eart** 'It is thou.' It forms phrases using the present participle **Hī ðus sprecende wæron** 'They were speaking thus,' **Hwīlum hē wæs on horse sittende, ac oftor on his fōtum gangende** 'At times he was sitting on a horse, but more often going about on his feet.' It forms phrases using the passive participle **Nū is se dæġ cumen** 'Now the day is come,' **Hyt is ġecwæden ... þæt mon sceole lufian hys nēhstan** 'It is said that one shall love his neighbor,' **Lēoð wæs āsungen** 'The song was sung (to an end).' (*OES* 651–664, 683 ff.)

Past tense forms of the verb cited as **gān** '(to) walk, go' are derived from a phonologically different verb stem from those of the present tense and infinitive, as the paradigm will show. Historically, that stem of the past tense forms has been replaced by another stem also not related to **gān**: present-day **went** derives from forms transfered from the past forms of **(to) wend**. The two phonemically unrelated stems of this verb are said to be 'in suppletion.'

The verb **dōn** '(to) do' in Old English had developed none of the auxiliary functions that it now has in Modern English: it was *not* used to carry the negative marker *He understood – He didn't understand,* or to form yes/no questions *Did he understand?* or to carry emphatic stress *He* did *understand.* (*OES* 665–669)

Willan '(to) will, etc.' had a range of meanings. Along with the preterite-present verbs (see 6.3) it also was evolving as an auxiliary, having the infinitive of another verb as its complement. It was not yet usually merely a 'future auxiliary,' although that function was developing during the period of Old English. (*OES* 1021–1023)

BĒON; WESAN '(to) be, exist, become'   Anomalous

bēon; wesan	Infinitive
	Inflected infinitive
bēonde; wesende	Present participle
	Passive participle
wes (þū)	Imperative singular
bēoþ (ġē); wesaþ (ġē)	Imperative plural

Indicative				Subjunctive		

Non-past

(iċ)	eom	(wē)	syndon,	(iċ)	sīe,	(wē)	sīen,
(þū)	eart	(ġē)	synd,	(þū)	sī,	(ġē)	sīn,
(hē)	is	(hīe)	sint	(hē)	sȳ	(hīe)	sȳn

(iċ)	bēo	(wē)	bēoþ	(iċ)	bēo	(wē)	bēon
(þū)	bist	(ġē)	bēoþ	(þū)	bēo	(ġē)	bēon
(hē)	bið	(hīe)	bēoþ	(hē)	bēo	(hīe)	bēon

Past

(iċ)	wæs	(wē)		(iċ)		(wē)	
(þū)	wære	(ġē)	wæron	(þū)	wære	(ġē)	wæren
(hē)	wæs	(hīe)		(hē)		(hīe)	

(In the plural of both indicative and subjunctive non-past, the alternate forms are no more than spelling variants.) Generally, the two non-past tense sets of forms seem to be distinguished as follows: the set **eom, eart,** ... signifies a present state of affairs without specifying its continuance, generality, or the like; the set **bēo, bist,** ... signifies future, generality (or invariability), or continuance into the future. **Ēadiġe synd ġē ðe hingriað nū, for-þām-þe ġē bēoð ġefyllede** 'Blessed are ye that hunger now, for ye shall be filled'; **Ēadiġe bēo ġē þonne ēow men hatiað** 'Blessed are ye when men hate you.' **And efne synt ȳtemeste þā ðe bēoð fyrmeste, and synt fyrmeste þā ðe bēoð ȳtemeste** 'And indeed are last those who shall be first, and are first those who shall be last'; **þū eart nū þæt iċ wæs iō, and þū byst æfter fæce þæt iċ nū eom** 'You are now what I was formerly, and you will be after a while what I now am.' (*OEG* 768, *OES* 658–664, 934–949)

Him is eall andweard, ġe ðætte ær wæs, ġe ðætte nū is, ġe ðætte æfter ūs bið.	All is present to him, that which was before, and that which now is, and that which will be after us.
Iċ bēo ġearo sōna.	I shall be ready immediately.
Iċ bēo hāl.	I shall be safe.
Sēlre bið æġhwām....	It is better for everyone....
Iċ hit eom.	It is I.
Iċ sylf hit eom.	It is I myself.
Ne mæġ iċ hēr leng wesan.	I am not able to be here longer.
Hē bið ā wesende.	He is existing forever.
Hwæt wile þis wesan?	What can this be? What is this?
Lætaþ ðis ðus wesan.	Let this be thus.
Ne bið swylċ cwēnlīċ þēaw.	Such is not a queenly custom.
Biþ storma ġehwylċ āswefed.	Every storm is (always) allayed.
Hē byð þēodum ġeseald and bið bysmrud and ġeswunġen and on-spæt.	He will be given to the people and will be mocked and scourged and spat upon.
Manega synt ġelaþode and fēawa ġecorene.	Many are called and few (are) chosen.
Þis synt wrace dagas, þæt ealle þing sȳn ġefyllede þe āwritene synt.	These are days of vengeance, that all things which are written will be fulfilled.
Nelle ġē dēman and ġē ne bēoð dēmede; nelle ġē ġenyðerian and ġē ne bēoð ġenyþerude; forġyfaþ and ēow byþ forġyfen; syllað and ēow byþ ġeseald.	Judge not and you shall not be judged; condemn not and you will not be condemned; forgive, and to you it will be forgiven; give, and it will be given to you.
Efne seofon bēoð seofon, twīa seofon bēoð fēowertȳne, þriwa seofon bēoð ān ond twentiġ, fēower siðon seofon bēoð eahta ond twentiġ, fīf siðon seofon bēoð fīf ond þrittiġ.	Just (i.e., once) seven is seven, twice seven is fourteen, thrice seven is twenty-one, four times seven is twenty-eight, five times seven is thirty-five.
Tōdæl þā nigon þurh seofon: ænne seofon bēoþ seofon; twā þær	Divide the nine by seven: one seven is seven; two are there

synt tō lāfe.

Ġedō þū tōgædere ealle þæs ġeares
dagas, þæra synt þrēo hundred
ond fīf ond syxtiġ daga....
Tōdæl þās ... þurh seofon: ...
Fīftiġ siðon seofon byð þrēo
hundred ond fīftiġ, ond ġȳt þǣr
synt fīftȳne. Tōdælað þā þurh
seofon: twia seofon bēoð
fēowertȳne; þæt ān þe þǣr ys
tō lāfe, sete on foreweardum
þām circule....

Ġif hwām ġelustfullað tō witanne
hwæt sȳ *quadrans*,... þonne
underġite hē ... þæt *quadrans*
byð se fēorða dæl þæs dæġes,
oððe ōðra þinga þe man mæġ
rihtlīċe tōdælan on fēower.

Quadrans ys fȳrðling oððe fēorðan
dæl ælċes þæra þinga þe man mæġ
tōdælan on fēower on emne.
Se fēorðan dæl byð *quadrans*
ġecīġed, bēo hit peniġ oððe
pund, swā þæt wel wāt ċeorlisc
folc. Wē magon be þām punde
rūmlicor hyt ġecȳðan. Fēower
siðon syxtī byð ān pund....
Þænne hyt ætgædere byð, twentiġ
scillingas bēoð on ānum punde,
ond twelf siðon twentiġ penega
byð ān pund.

Sum 'iċ eom' is edwistlīċ word,
and ġebyrað tō Gode synderlīċe,
for-ðan-ðe God is ǣfre un-
begunnen and un-ġe-endod.

as a remainder.

Put together all the days of the
year, of which there are three
hundred and sixty-five days....
Divide these ... by seven: Fifty
times seven is three hundred
fifty, and still there are fifteen. Divide them by seven:
twice seven is fourteen; the one
that there is as remainder, put
it at the fore of the circle
[in computation]....

If anyone desires to know what
quadrans is, ... then let him understand ... that *quadrans* is the fourth
part of the day, or other things
which one can correctly divide
in four.

Quadrans is a farthing or a fourth
part of each of those things that
one may divide in four exactly.
The fourth part is called *quadrans*,
(whether) it be a penny or a
pound, as common people well
know. We can with reference to
the pound more fully explain it.
Four times sixty is a pound....
When it is together, there are
twenty shillings in a pound, and
twelve times twenty pence is a
pound.

Sum 'I am' is a verb of being,
and it pertains to God especially,
because God is ever unbegun
and unended.

DŌN '(to) do, make, cause' Anomalous

dōn	Infinitive
(tō) dōnne	Inflected infinitive
dōnde	Present participle
(ġe)dōn	Passive participle
dō (þū)	Imperative singular
dōþ (ġē)	Imperative plural

Indicative				Subjunctive			
				Non-past			
(iċ)	**dō**	(wē)		(iċ)		(wē)	
(þū)	**dēst**	(ġē)	**dōþ**	(þū)	**dō**	(ġē)	**dōn**
(hē)	**dēþ**	(hīe)		(hē)		(hīe)	
				Past			
(iċ)	**dyde**	(wē)		(iċ)		(wē)	
(þū)	**dydest**	(ġē)	**dydon**	(þū)	**dyde**	(ġē)	**dyden**
(hē)	**dyde**	(hīe)		(hē)		(hīe)	

Iċ secge..., 'Dō þis,' and hē dēð.	I say..., 'Do this,' and he does (it).
Hwī dēst ðū wið mē swā?	Why doest thou thus toward me?
Ðæt hēo dō ðæt ðæt hēo ǣr dyde.	That she may do that which she did before.
Dōþ wel þām ðe ēow yfel dōð.	Do good to those who do you evil.
Hē dyde swā hē him bebēad.	He did as he (had) commanded him.
Hē ne cūðe hwæt þā cynn dydon.	He knew not what the people did.
Ne mōt iċ dōn þæt iċ wylle.	I cannot do what I wish.
[Þās] is rehtlīċ tō dōanne.	These (things) it is right to do.
Iċ dō þīnne ofsprincg meniġfealdne.	I will cause thine offspring to be many.
Swā ġē willaþ þæt ēow men dōn, dōþ him ġelīċe.	As you wish that men do to you, do likewise to them.

GĀN '(to) go, come, walk, move, happen'   Anomalous

gān	Infinitive
(tō) gānne	Inflected infinitive
	Present participle
(ġe)gān	Passive participle
gā (þū)	Imperative singular
gāþ (ġē)	Imperative plural

Indicative			Subjunctive		
			Non-past		
(iċ)	gā	(wē)		(iċ)		(wē)
(þū)	gǣst	(ġē) gāþ		(þū)	gā	(ġē) gān
(hē)	gǣþ	(hīe)		(hē)		(hīe)
			Past		
(iċ)	ēode	(wē)		(iċ)		(wē)
(þū)	ēodest	(ġē) ēodon		(þū)	ēode	(ġē) ēoden
(hē)	ēode	(hīe)		(hē)		(hīe)

Gǣð ā wyrd swā hīo sceal.	Fate goes ever as it must.
Ġearo tō gānne.	Ready to go.
Ēaðelīcre byð þām olfende tō gānne þurh nǣdle ēage þonne se welega on heofena rīċe gā.	It is easier for the camel to go through the eye of a needle than (that) the prosperous should go into the kingdom of heaven.
Lǣtan hī hēr beforan ūs forð gān.	Let them go forth here before us.
Hēo sōna ārās and ēode.	She straightway arose and walked.
Se mann āna gǣþ ūprihte.	Man alone walks upright.
Ġif hwā swā dyrstiġ sȳ þæt [hē] onġēan Godes lage gā....	If anyone be so presumptuous that he go against God's law....
Hē ēode þrēora sum.	He went one of three (i.e., with two others).
Hī hine ġesāwon gangende upon ðǣre sǣ.	They saw him walking upon the sea.

WILLAN '(to) will, wish, desire, be willing'   Anomalous

willan	Infinitive
	Inflected infinitive
willende	Present participle
	Passive participle
[negative only] **nyllað (ġē)**	Imperative Plural

	Indicative				Subjunctive		

Non-past

(iċ)	wil(l)e	(wē)		(iċ)		(wē)	
(þū)	wilt	(ġē)	willað	(þū)	wille	(ġē)	willen
(hē)	wil(l)e	(hīe)		(hē)		(hīe)	

Past

(iċ)	wolde	(wē)		(iċ)		(wē)	
(þū)	woldest	(ġē)	woldon	(þū)	wolde	(ġē)	wolden
(hē)	wolde	(hīe)		(hē)		(hīe)	

Þēah-hwæþere, nā swā swā iċ wylle ac swā swā þū wylt.

Nevertheless, not as I will but as thou wilt.

'Iċ wylle gān on fixað.' Þā cwǣdon hī tō him, 'And wē wyllað gān mid þē.'

'I will go fishing.' Then they said to him, 'And we wish to go with thee.'

Hwā wyle mē ... ġelǣdan?

Who will guide me forth?

Swā iċ ǣr sæġde þæt iċ dōn wolde.

As I said earlier that I would do.

Wē sceolon, wylle wē, nelle wē, ārīsan.

We must arise, whether we will it or not.

Hē cunnian wolde his Drihtnes wyllan, hū hē wolde be him.

He determined to try his Lord's will, how he willed (or intended) concerning him.

Ǣlċ mon hæfþ ðone frīodōm ðæt hē wāt hwæt hē wile, hwæt hē nele.

Each man has the freedom (of will) that he knows what he wills (and) what he doesn't will.

6.3 Preterite-Present Verbs

The small group of preterite-present verbs are best learned individually. Like anomalous verbs and Class III weak verbs, some of them occur very often, and therefore should be learned early. (*OEG* 767)

The non-past (or present tense) forms resemble the preterite (or past tense) forms of strong verb classes from which, in fact, they originated; hence the name 'preterite-present.' The past tense forms resemble those of weak verbs (see 6.4). The selection of forms for principal parts of these verbs, consequently, differs from that for either strong or weak verbs. These verbs also customarily are labeled with the strong verb class from which they originally derived (see 6.5). (The asterisk signifies that the infinitive is not recorded.)

	(Non-Past) Infinitive	Non-Past 1st Pers. Sg.	Plural	Past 1st Pers. Sg.
1	witan '(to) know'	wāt	witon	wisse, wiste
1	āgan '(to) possess'	āh	āgon	āhte
2	dugan '(to) avail'	dēag	dugon	dohte
3	unnan '(to) grant'	ann	unnon	ūðe
3	cunnan '(to) know'	cann	cunnon	cūðe
3	*durran '(to) dare'	dearr	durron	dorste
3	þurfan '(to) need'	þearf	þurfon	þorfte
4	*sculan '(to) be obligated'	sceal	sculon	scolde
4	ġe·munan '(to) remember'	ġe·man	ġe·munnon	ġe·munde
6	*mōtan '(to) be permitted'	mōt	mōton	mōste
?	magan '(to) be able'	mæġ	magon	meahte

These verbs belong together because of their morphological similarities, as explained. In their collocational characteristics, though, they are not alike. Some of them co-occur with an infinitive, resembling the so-called modal auxiliary verbs of Modern English: **Ne mihte hē þǣr nænne ġesēon þe hē ġecnāwan cūþe** 'He might not see any there whom he could recognize'; **Mōt ic þē ōhtes āhsian?** 'May I ask you something?' ... **þæt ic ne þorfte nā māre āwendan þǣre bēċ būton tō Isaac** 'that I need not translate the book except up to Isaac'; **Earm biþ sē þe sceal āna lifgan** 'Wretched is the one who must live alone.' Some of them are in fact the ancestral forms of some of the modern modal auxiliaries: **can, may, ought, must, dare** (the last of these being marginally a modal auxiliary); ***tharf** would be another if it hadn't been replaced by its semantic equivalent **need** (also a marginal member of the modern modal auxiliaries).

(The other modern modal auxiliary **will** does not descend from a preterite-present verb, however, its ancestral forms constituting one of the anomalous verbs (see 6.2).) (*OES* 990–1024; see also the detailed study by Hiroshi Ogawa, *Old English Modal Verbs: A Syntactic Study*, Anglistica vol. XXVI (1989); Jennifer Coates, *The Semantics of Modal Auxiliaries* (1983); Anthony R. Warner, *English Auxiliaries: Structure and History* (1993).)

Even so, some of the preterite-present verbs are obviously not ancestral forms of modern modal auxiliaries: **ge·munan, unnan, witan, dugan.**

Further, some of these are clearly independent verbs. This is clearest when the verb has a noun direct object, **Iċ ðā stōwe ne can** 'I do not know that place'; **Nū iċ āh mǣste þearfe** 'Now I have utmost need'; **Ðā cwæð se Hǣlend, 'Ġif þū wylt bēon fullfremed, gā and beċȳp eall þæt þū āhst and syle hyt þearfum, and þonne hæfst þū goldhord on heofone; and cum and folga me'** 'If thou wilt be complete, go and sell all that thou ownest and give it to the needy, and then hast thou treasure in heaven; and come and follow me'; **Ġif hē þæt eal ġemon** 'If he remembers that all'; **Ne þearf hē nānes þinges** 'He does not need anything'; or a noun clause may occur as direct object, **Men ne cunnon ... hwā þǣm hlǣste onfēng** 'Men know not ... who received that cargo.'

With the verb ***sculan**—as well as the weak verb **willan**—the resemblance to their Modern English descendant forms is only partial, in that the use of these with a following infinitive form did not constitute a future tense expression, even though futurity of the action expressed by the infinitive was implicit in the meaning of the phrase. This is the construction in which the phrasal future tense in English had its beginning, but it was apparently only in its very beginning in Old English. (*OES* 1021–1024)

WITAN '(to) know, be aware, "wit"'   Preterite-Present 1

witan	Infinitive
(tō) witenne	Inflected infinitive
witende	Present participle
witen	Passive participle
wite (þū)	Imperative singular
witaþ (ġē)	Imperative plural

Indicative   Subjunctive

Non-past

(iċ)	wāt	(wē)		(iċ)		(wē)	
(þū)	wāst	(ġē)	witon	(þū)	wite	(ġē)	witen
(hē)	wāt	(hīe)		(hē)		(hīe)	

Past

(iċ)	wisse, wiste	(wē)		(iċ)		(wē)	
(þū)	wistest	(ġē)	wiston	(þū)	wisse, wiste	(ġē)	wissen,
(hē)	wisse, wiste	(hīe)		(hē)		(hīe)	wisten

Ðū wāst and canst ... hū þū
lifian scealt.

You realize and know ... how you
shall live.

[Hē] manna inġehyġd wāt and can.

He knows and understands men's
intentions.

Nān þing nis behydd þæt ne sȳ
witen.

Nothing is hidden that shall not
be known.

Ðāra cynna moniġe hē wiste on
Germanie wesan.

Of those nations many he knew to
be in Germany.

Witaþ ġē ðæt hit swā nis.

Know that it is not thus.

Iċ wāt hwæt hē þenċeþ.

I know what he thinks.

Hīe wiston ġe be heora siġe, ġe ēac
be þāra hæþenra manna flēame.

They knew both about their victory
and also about the heathens' flight.

Witon wē þæt ūre Drihten mid ūs
wæs on þām scipe.

Let us know [by inference] that our
Lord was with us on the ship.

Nū wē witon þæt þū wāst ealle þing.

Now we know that you know all things.

Ēala þū mīn swuster, wistest þū þæt
iċ wāt, þās word þū ne cwede.

O thou my sister, knewest thou what I
know, these words you would not speak.

CUNNAN '(to) know; know how; be able'   Preterite-Present 3

cunnan	Infinitive
(tō) cunnene	Inflected infinitive
	Present participle
cūþ, -cunnen	Passive participle
	Imperative singular
	Imperative plural

Indicative   Subjunctive

Non-past

(iċ)	**can(n)**	(wē)		(iċ)		(wē)	
(þū)	**canst**	(ġē)	**cunnon**	(þū)	**cunne**	(ġē)	**cunnen**
(hē)	**can(n)**	(hīe)		(hē)		(hīe)	

Past

(iċ)	**cūðe**	(wē)		(iċ)		(wē)	
(þū)	**cūðest**	(ġē)	**cūðon**	(þū)	**cūðe**	(ġē)	**cūðen**
(hē)	**cūðe**	(hīe)		(hē)		(hīe)	

Iċ ēow ne con.	I know you not.
Hwanon cūðest ðū mē?	Whence did you know me?
Iċ can ēow lǣran.	I am able to teach you.
Dydon swā hīe cūðon.	They did as they could.
Ġe þā þe cunnon, ġe þā þe ne cunnon.	Both those who know and those who know not.
Hē wilnade mē tō cunenne.	He desired to know me.
Ġē ne cūðon hine. Iċ hine cann; and ġif iċ secge þæt iċ hine ne cunne, iċ bēo lēas ond ēow ġelīċ.	You have not known him. I know him; and if I should say that I know him not, I shall be false and like you.
Swīþe fēawa wǣron ... ðe hiora ðēninga cūðen understondan on Englisc.	There were very few ... who could understand their service in English.

Hē ne ðearf nā faran fram stōwe tō stōwe.

He needn't travel from place to place.

Ġē ne þurfon hēr leng wunian.

You need not remain here longer.

Iċ þē scylde, ne þearft ðū forht wesan.

I will protect you, (and for this reason) you need not be afraid.

Iċ ēow secgan mæġ, ðæt ġē ne ðyrfen leng murnan.

I am able to tell you that you haven't reason longer to care.

With these may be compared constructions with the noun **þearf**.

Nū iċ āh mæste þearfe.

Now I have greatest need.

Ðæm ðe læsan þearfe āhton.

For those who had lesser need.

Næs him æniġ þearf ðæt hē sēċan þurfe.

There wasn't any need that he be compelled to seek.

*SCULAN '(to) be obligated, shall'   Preterite-Present 4

  Present Indicative: **iċ sceal, þū scealt, hē sceal**; plural **sculon**

  Present Subjunctive: **scyle, scule**

  Preterite: **sceolde, sceoldon**

Iċ sceal ġiet sprecan.	I shall yet speak.
Hwæt sceal iċ singan?	What am I to sing?
Ġif hē āhwār byð forġyten þǣr hē bēon sceolde, þonne sceal man hine þus āmearkian ⱶ , and eft, ġif hē byð āhwār ġesett þǣr hē standan ne mæġ, þonne sceal man hine þus ġenyðerian ⱶ.	If it [H, symbol for *aspiratio*] be forgotten anywhere where it ought to be, then one should denote it thus ⱶ , and in turn if it be set anywhere where it cannot stand, then it must be suppressed thus ⱶ.
[Hē] cwæð ðæt se Hǣlend him tǣhte þone regol þæt hī sceoldon yfel mid gōde forġyldan.	He said that the Saviour taught him the rule that they should repay evil with good.
Đā andswarede se cyning ðæt hē ǣġðer ġe wolde ġe scolde ðām ġelēafan onfōn.	Then the king answered that he was both willing and bound to receive that faith.
Iċ worda ġespræc mā ðonne iċ sceolde.	I spoke more words than was fitting (*or* than I should have).
Wē dydon þæt wē dōn sceolon.	We did what we are to do.
Hē wēneþ ðæt hē sceole tō heofenum āhafen weorþan.	He imagines that he will be lifted up to heaven.
Đū eart eorþe, and þū scealt eft tō eorþan weorðan.	Thou art earth, and thou shalt turn back into earth.

MAGAN 'may, (to) avail, be able'   (Uncertain class)

magan	Infinitive
	Inflected infinitive
magende	Present participle
	Passive participle
	Imperative singular
	Imperative plural

Indicative			Subjunctive		
			Non-past		
(iċ)	mæġ	(wē)		(iċ)		(wē)
(þū)	meaht, miht	(ġē) magon		(þū)	mæġe, muge	(ġē) mæġen, mugen
(hē)	mæġ	(hīe)		(hē)		(hīe)

Past

(iċ)	meahte, mihte	(wē)		(iċ)		(wē)
(þū)	meahtest, mihtest	(ġē) mihton		(þū)	meahte, mihte	(ġē) mihten
(hē)	meahte, mihte	(hie)		(hē)		(hīe)

(Other forms: **mihton meahton, mihten meahten.**)

Ne magon hīe ond ne mōton þīnne līchoman dēaðe ġedǣlan.	They are not able and are not permitted to consign thy body to death.
Wē witon þæt wē magon ond mōton tōdæġ wel dōn; ac we nyton hwæðer wē mōton tōmorġen.	We know that we can and may (*or* that it is possible and permissible for us to) act well today, but we know not whether we may [do so] tomorrow.
Tō dēaðe hīe þē willaþ ġelǣdan, ac hī ne magon.	They intend to lead you to death, but they will not be able to.
Eaðelicor mæġ se olfend gān þurh ānre nǣdle ēage þonne se welega on Godes rīċe.	More easily may the camel go through a needle's eye than the wealthy into God's kingdom.
Magon wē nū ġehēran secgan be sumum welegum men.	Let us now hear tell concerning a certain wealthy man.

6.4 Weak Verbs

'Weak' verbs (also called 'consonantal' verbs) are characterized by past tense forms being marked by a suffix morpheme containing a dental consonant, either [d] or [t]; it follows the stem and precedes person-number inflection. There are three classes of weak verbs—Class III having only four members, at least three of them being very common in occurrence, Class II being a relatively large group with a distinctive -od- shape for the past tense morpheme, Class I being also a relatively large class, with several subclasses illustrated in the following pages. (OEG 748–766; see also Detlef Stark, *The Old English Weak Verbs, A Diachronic and Synchronic Analysis.*)

Weak verbs have three 'principal parts':

Class	Infinitive	Past 1st Sg.	Pass. Participle
III	habban '(to) have'	hæfde	hæfd
	secgan '(to) say'	sægde	sægd
	libban '(to) live'	lifde	lifd
	hycgan '(to) think'	hogde	hogod
II	lufian '(to) love'	lufode	lufod
	ācsian '(to) ask'	ācsode	ācsod
	bodian '(to) announce'	bodode	bodod
	fandian '(to) try'	fandode	fandod
	þancian '(to) thank'	þancode	þancod
	wunian '(to) dwell'	wunode	wunod
	(ġe-)miltsian '(to) pity'	ġemiltsode	ġemiltsod
I	(ġe-)hīeran '(to) hear'	ġehīerde	ġehīered
	dēman '(to) judge'	dēmde	dēmed
	herian '(to) praise'	herede	hered
	nerian '(to) save, defend'	nerede	nered
	fremman '(to) accomplish'	fremede	fremed
	fyllan '(to) fill'	fylde	fylled
	settan '(to) set'	sette	seted, set(t)
	lecgan '(to) lay'	læġde	leġd
	grētan '(to) greet, salute'	grētte	grēt(ed)

HABBAN '(to) have, possess, retain'   Weak Verb III

habban	Infinitive
(**tō**) **habbanne**	Inflected infinitive
hæbbende	Present participle
hæfd	Passive participle
hafa (**þū**)	Imperative singular
habbað (**ġē**)	Imperative plural

	Indicative				Subjunctive		
			Non-past				
(**iċ**)	**hæbbe**	(**wē**)		(**iċ**)		(**wē**)	
(**þū**)	**hæfst**	(**ġē**)	**habbað**	(**þū**)	**hæbbe**	(**ġē**)	**hæbben**
(**hē**)	**hæfð**	(**hīe**)		(**hē**)		(**hīe**)	
			Past				
(**iċ**)	**hæfde**	(**wē**)		(**iċ**)		(**wē**)	
(**þū**)	**hæfdest**	(**ġē**)	**hæfdon**	(**þū**)	**hæfde**	(**ġē**)	**hæfden**
(**hē**)	**hæfde**	(**hīe**)		(**hē**)		(**hīe**)	

Eall ... ðæt him ... wæs lēofost tō āgenne and tō hæbbenne.

All that for him it was most desirable to own and to have.

Iċ hæbbe ġeweald miċel.

I have much power.

Wē habbaþ nēd-þearfe þæt wē onġyton.

We have need to perceive.

Ðæt ċild hæfde læsse ðonne þrȳ mōnðas ðæs þriddan ġēares.

The child was not quite two years and three months old.

Æġhwilcum men biþ lēofre swā hē hæbbe holdra frēonda mā.

For each one it is the more desirable as he has more loyal friends.

Hafa þē wunden gold.

Take for thyself the twisted gold.

Wē bēoþ hæbbende ðæs ðe wē ǣr hopedon.

We shall be in possession of that which before we hoped for.

Hīe hine ofslæġenne hæfdon.

They had slain him.

Ðū hafast helle berēafod and þæs dēaþes aldor ġebundenne.

Thou hast despoiled hell and bound the prince of death.

SECGAN '(to) say, declare, recite'   Weak Verb III

secgan	Infinitive
(tō) secganne	Inflected infinitive
secgende	Present participle
sæġd	Passive participle
saga, sæġe (þū)	Imperative singular
secgaþ (ġē)	Imperative plural

	Indicative			Subjunctive		
			Non-past			
(iċ)	secge	(wē)		(iċ)		(wē)
(þū)	sæġst	(ġē)	secgaþ	(þū)	secge	(ġē) secgen
(hē)	sæġþ	(hīe)		(hē)		(hīe)
			Past			
(iċ)	sæġde	(wē)		(iċ)		(wē)
(þū)	sæġdest	(ġē)	sæġdon,	(þū)	sæġde	(ġē) sæġden
(hē)	sæġde	(hīe)	sǣdon	(hē)		(hīe)

Iċ þē secgan wille ōr and ende.

I will tell you beginning and end.

Ġif þū wille mild-heortnesse ūs dōn,
  sæġe ūs þæt hrædlīċe.

If you will show us mercy, tell us
  that quickly.

Saga mē, hwylċes cynnes ðū sī.

Tell me of what family you are.

Secgaþ mē, hwæt ġyt ġesāwon.

Tell me what you-two saw.

Ġehȳraþ hwæt hēr seġþ on þissum
  bōcum.

Hear what it says here in these
  books.

Mē lyste bet, ðæt ðū mē sǣdest
  sume hwile ymbe ðæt.

I would rather you spoke to me
  at some time about that.

'Iċ hæbbe þē tō secgenne sum ðing.'
  Þā cwæð hē, 'Lārēow, seġe þænne.'

'I have something to say to you.'
  Then he said, 'Master, speak on.'

Iċ þē hāte, þæt ðū þās ġesyhðe
  secge mannum.

I bid that thou tell this vision
  to people.

Hē for his hǣlo Drihtne þānc
  secgende wæs.

He was thanking the Lord for his
  recovery.

LUFIAN '(to) love, show love to, cherish'   Weak Verb II

lufian	Infinitive
(tō) lufienne	Inflected infinitive
lufiende	Present participle
lufod	Passive participle
lufa (þū)	Imperative singular
lufiaδ (ġē)	Imperative plural

Indicative   Subjunctive

Non-past

(iċ) **lufiġe,**	(wē)		(iċ) **lufiġe,**	(wē) **lufiġen,**
lufie			**lufie**	**lufien**
(þū) **lufast**	(ġē) **lufiaδ**		(þū)	(ġē)
(hē) **lufaδ**	(hīe)		(hē)	(hīe)

Past

(iċ) **lufode**	(wē)		(iċ)	(wē)
(þū) **lufodest**	(ġē) **lufodon**		(þū) **lufode**	(ġē) **lufoden**
(hē) **lufode**	(hīe)		(hē)	(hīe)

Ġē ġehȳrdon þæt ġecweden wæs,
  lufa þīnne nēxtan ond hata þīnne
  fēond. Sōþlīċe iċ secge ēow,
  lufiaδ ēowre fȳnd ond dōþ wel
  þām δe ēow yfel dōδ.

You have heard what has been said,
  love thy neighbor and hate thine
  enemy. Truly I say to you,
  love your enemies and do good to
  those who do you evil.

Iċ cweδe nū, *amo* 'iċ lufiġe';
  þonne cwypst þū, *quem amas*
  'hwæne lufast þū?' Iċ cweδe,
  te amo 'þē iċ lufiġe'; þonne
  befylδ mīn lufu on δē, ond þū
  miht cweδan, *amor a te* 'iċ eom
  ġelufod fram þē.'

I say now, *amo*, 'I love';
  then thou sayest, *quem amas*
  'Whom lovest thou?' I say,
  te amo 'thee I love'; then
  my love falls upon thee, and thou
  might say, *amor a te* 'I am
  loved by thee.'

Apollonius ... ongeat þæt hē ġelufod wæs fram δām mædene.

Apollonius ... perceived that he
  was loved by the maiden.

'Mōt iċ þē āhtes ācsian?'
Cwæð hē, 'Ācsa þæs þe þū
wille.'

'May I be permitted to ask you
something?' He said, 'Ask
what you will.'

Iċ ācsiġe þē hwī latast þū swā
lange.

I ask you why you delay so
long.

Heofonas bodiaþ–oððe cȳðaþ–
wuldor Godes.

The heavens declare–or make known–
the glory of God.

Ymb Bethleem bododon englas ðæt
ācenned wæs Crist on eorþan.

Near Bethlehem angels announced
that Christ was born on earth.

Wæs þæt wēa-tācen ... ġeond þā
burh bodad.

The fatal-token was proclaimed
... throughout the town.

Ne fanda þīnes Drihtnes.

Tempt not thy Lord.

Iċ wille fandiġan nū ... hwæt
þā men dōn.

I will now seek to know ... what
those men do.

Man ne sceal fandian Godes þā hwile
þe hē mæġ mid ænigum ġescēade
him sylfum ġebeorgan. Sē fandað
Godes, sē þe his āgen ġescēad
forlæt þe him God forġeaf,
and swā būtan ġescēade sēċð
Godes fultum.

One shall not seek (the help) of
God while he can protect himself
with any reasoning. He seeks
(the help) of God who relinquishes
his own understanding that God
gave him, and thus without understanding seeks God's protection.

Hē Gode þancode.

He thanked God.

Hē þæs þancode Gode.

He thanked God for it.

Đanca Gode ðīnre ġesundfulnysse.

Thank God for thy healthfulness.

Hī Gode þancodon ... þæs-þe hī
hyne ġesundne ġesēon mōston.

They thanked God ... because they
were able to see him unharmed.

Iċ wylle tō-dæġ on þīnum hūse
wunian.

I will abide today in thy house.

Iċ on wēstene wunode lange.

I remained long in a solitary place.

Medmyċel fæc nū ġȳt wuna mid ūs.

Stay with us a little while yet.

Saga mē hwær sēo rōd wuniġe.

Tell me where the Rood may be.

Hū ne ġebyrede þē ġemiltsian
þīnum efen-ðēowan swā swā iċ
þē ġemiltsode?

How does it not befit thee to show
thy fellow-servant mercy just as
I showed mercy to thee?

(ĠE-) HĪERAN   '(to) hear, obey, be subject to'   Weak Verb I

hīeran	Infinitive
(tō) hīerenne	Inflected infinitive
hīerende	Present participle
hīered	Passive participle
hīer (þū)	Imperative singular
hīeraþ (ġē)	Imperative plural

Indicative   Subjunctive
Non-past

(iċ)	hīere		(wē)		(iċ)		(wē)	
(þū)	hīerest		(ġē)	hīerað	(þū)	hīere	(ġē)	hīeren
(hē)	hīer(e)ð		(hīe)		(hē)		(hīe)	

Past

(iċ)	hīerde		(wē)		(iċ)		(wē)	
(þū)	hīerdest		(ġē)	hīerdon	(þū)	hīerde	(ġē)	hīerden
(hē)	hīerde		(hīe)		(hē)		(hīe)	

Ne hȳrde iċ ... idese lǣdan ... mæġen fæġerre.	I have not heard of ... a queen leading ... a fairer force.
Þās land hȳrað tō Swēon.	These lands belong to the Swedes.
Ne mæġ nān mon twām hlāfordum hīeran.	No man can serve two masters.
Iċ þæt ġehȳre, þæt þis is hold weorod.	I hear that this is a loyal band.
Wē þis næfre ... ġehȳrdon hæleðum cȳðan.	We never heard this declared to men.
Ġeworden iċ eom swā swā man nā ġehȳrende.	I am become as a man not hearing.
[Hē bæd] þone hālgan þæt hē his bēne ġehȳrde and him huru ġe-earnode þæt hē ġehȳran mihte.	He asked the saint that he should hear his prayer and especially obtain for him that he be able to hear.

HERIAN '(to) praise, laud'   Weak Verb I

herian	Infinitive
(tō) herienne	Inflected infinitive
heriende	Present participle
hered	Passive participle
hera (þū)	Imperative singular
heriaŏ (ġē)	Imperative plural

Indicative				Subjunctive		
			Non-past			
(iċ) **herie**	(wē)			(iċ)	(wē)	
(þū) **herest**	(ġē) **heriaŏ**			(þū) **herie**	(ġē) **herien**	
(hē) **hereþ**	(hīe)			(hē)	(hīe)	
			Past			
(iċ) **herede**	(wē)			(iċ)	(wē)	
(þū) **heredest**	(ġē) **heredon**			(þū) **herede**	(ġē) **hereden**	
(hē) **herede**	(hīe)			(hē)	(hīe)	

Hit is āwriten, 'Ne hera ŏū nænne man on his līfe.'	It is written, 'Praise no man during his life.'
Hēo Drihten herede.	She praised the Lord.
Hēo is ūs tō herianne.	She is to be praised by us.
Đū byst hered.	Thou art praised.
Dē silfne ne hera.	Praise not thyself.
Hīe heofena helm herian ne cūþon.	They knew not how to praise the heavens' protector.
Đēah hira hīeremenn hīe mid ryhte heregen for hiera āgnum ġewyrhtum.	Though their servants justly praise them before their co-workers.
Nū sculon heriġean heofonrīċes weard.	Now ought (we) praise the keeper of the kingdom of heaven.
Dæs cyninges ealdormen ... heredon hī beforan him.	The noblemen of the king [Pharaoh] ... praised her in his presence.

FREMMAN '(to) make, do, further, accomplish'   Weak Verb I

fremman	Infinitive
(tō) fremmenne	Inflected infinitive
fremende	Present participle
fremed	Passive participle
freme (þū)	Imperative singular
fremmaþ (ġē)	Imperative plural

Indicative   Subjunctive

Non-past

(iċ) fremme	(wē)		(iċ)	(wē)
(þū) frem(e)st	(ġē) fremmað		(þū) fremme	(ġē) fremmen
(hē) frem(e)ð	(hīe)		(hē)	(hīe)

Past

(iċ) fremede	(wē)		(iċ)	(wē)
(þū) fremedest	(ġē) fremedon		(þū) fremede	(ġē) fremeden
(hē) fremede	(hīe)		(hē)	(hīe)

Þæt iċ ēaðe mæġ ānra ġehwylcne fremman ond fyrþran frēonda mīnra.

That I may easily advance and further every one of my friends.

Ne fremest þū riht wīð mē.

You do not do right toward me.

Ne iċ firene fremde.

I have not commited crimes.

Ġehȳr mē ... and mē help freme.

Hear me, ... and afford me help.

... þæt iċ ... eorlscipe efnde, mǣrðo fremede.

... that I ... performed (an act of) nobility, accomplished a glorious deed.

Ǣr ġē ... fremmen ... yfel.

Before you ... commit ... evil.

Fremme sē þe wille.

Let (him) perform (it) who will.

Nīðas tō fremmanne.

To make strife.

Ne ġemune þū oft ... ealdra unrihta þe wē oft fremedon.

Remember not often ... the ancient wrongs that we often performed.

Iċ þis eal fremede for ðē.

I did this all for thee.

SETTAN '(to) set'   Weak Verb I

settan	Infinitive
(tō) settanne	Inflected infinitive
settende	Present participle
(ġe)seted, set(t)	Passive participle
sete (þū)	Imperative singular
settaþ (ġē)	Imperative plural

Indicative   Subjunctive

Non-past

(iċ)	sette	(wē)		(iċ)		(wē)	
(þū)	settst	(ġē)	settaþ	(þū)	sette	(ġē)	setten
(hē)	set(t)	(hīe)		(hē)		(hīe)	

Past

(iċ)	sette	(wē)		(iċ)		(wē)	
(þū)	settes(t)	(ġē)	setton	(þū)	sette	(ġē)	setten
(hē)	sette	(hīe)		(hē)		(hīe)	

Cum and sete þīne hand uppan hiġ, and hēo lyfað.

Come and set thy hand upon her, and she will live.

Hē hit sette on bōcum.

He set it down in books.

Þā sette hē weard, swā hit þēaw wæs, tō þām wīnġearde.

Then he set a guard, as it was the custom, to the vinyard.

Ðā beclypte hē hī and his handa ofer hī settende bletsode hī.

Then he embraced them and setting his hand on them blessed them.

Iċ sette mīn wed tō ēow and tō ēowrum ofspringe.

I establish my promise to you and to your offspring.

Iċ wylle settan mīn wed betux mē and eōw.

I will set my pledge between me and you.

Dū eart stīð man: þū nimst þæt ðū ne settest, and þū rīpst þæt ðū ne sēowe.

You are a hard man: you take up what you didn't put down, and you reap what you didn't sow.

Hit is āwriten, Ne hera ðū nænne
man on his līfe; wærlicor bið
se man ġeherod ... æfter līfe
ðonne on līfe. Hwā mæġ bēon
būton forhtunge ġeherod on ðisum
līfe, þā hwīle ðe hē besārgað his
ærran dǣda? Ac sē ðe herian
wille hāliġne mannan, heriġe hine
nā on ðisum līfe, ac æfter his
ġe·endunge þonne ne derað nān
lyffetung ðām heriġendum, ne nān
ūp-āhefednys ne costnað þone
ġeheredan. Hera ðū hine æfter
þǣre frecednysse. . . . Hera
ðone stēorman, ac nā swā ðēah
ǣrþan hē becume ġesundful tō
ðǣre hȳðe. Hera þæs heretogan
mihte, ac swā ðēah þonne hē
sīġe beġytt.

It is written, do not praise any man
during his life; more prudently
is the man praised ... after life
than in his life. Who can
without fear be praised in this
life, during the time he laments
his earlier acts? But the one
who wishes to praise a holy man,
let him not praise him in this
life, but after his ending when
no adulation can harm the one
praising, and no arrogance will
tempt the one praised. Praise
him after the danger. . . .
Praise the pilot, but not even
so before he comes sound to the
harbour. Praise the might of
the battle leader, but even so
when he has obtained victory.

Manega witegan and cyningas. . .
woldon ġehȳran þæt ġē ġehȳrað
and hiġ hit ne ġehȳrdon.

Many prophets and kings. . .
would hear that which you hear
and they heard it not.

Þā bead Iōsep his ġereuan and
cwæð, 'Fyllað heora saccas mid
hwǣte and leġe heora ælċes feoh
on his āgenne sacc.'

Then Joseph commanded his steward
and said, 'Fill their bags with
grain and put each one's money
in his own sack.'

Þonne bēoð þīne feldas fylde mid
wæstm.

Then thy fields will be filled with
fruits.

Hiġ ġegaderedon and fyldon twelf
wyliġeon fulle þǣra brytsena.

They gathered and filled twelve
baskets full of the fragments.

The following verbs are categorized as Weak, Class I, on historical principles. Within Old English they are essentially very small subclasses of verbs and
they are best learned—as they probably were learned by native speakers—as
separate, small groups. The patterns they exhibit are generally congruent with
the patterns of those with Modern English descendant forms, such as those of
seek, tell, think, buy, set. They are listed here in their three 'principal parts.'

	Infinitive	Past 1st Sg.	Pass. Participle
(1)	**tellan** '(to) tell'	**tealde**	**teald**
	sellan '(to) give; sell'	**sealde**	**seald**
	cwellan '(to) kill'	**cwealde**	**cweald**
	stellan '(to) place'	**stealde**	**steald**

Ūs sceama∂ hit nū māre tō tellanne.

It shames us now to tell more (of it).

Hiġ wæron þīne, and þū hȳ sealdest
  mē.

They were thine, and thou gavest
  them to me.

Ealle þās [rīcu] iċ sylle þē.

All these kingdoms I give to thee.

Hīe sealdon hiera suna tō gīslum.

They have given their sons as hostages.

Syllaþ þæt ġē āgon ond syllá∂
  ælmessan.

Sell what you have and give alms.

Syle eall þæt ∂ū hæfst ond syle
  eall þæt þearfum. [Latin:
  uende ... da.]

Sell all that have and give (it)
  all to the poor.

Ālȳf∂ gaful tō syllanne þām cāsere,
  hwæ∂er-þe wē ne syllá∂?

Is it permitted to give tribute
  to Caesar, or shall we not give?

Iċ sealde him þā word ∂e ∂ū
  sealdest mē.

I gave him those words that you
  gave me.

(2) **reċċan** '(to) narrate'   **reahte, rehte**   **reaht, reht**
    streċċan '(to) stretch'   **streahte, strehte**   **streaht, streht**
    tǣċan '(to) teach'   **tāhte, tǣhte**   **tāht, tǣht**
    rǣċan '(to) reach'   **rāhte, rǣhte**   **rāht, rǣht**
    sēċan '(to) seek'   **sōhte**   **sōht**
    bringan '(to) bring'   **brōhte**   **brōht**
    þenċan '(to) think'   **þōhte**   **þōht**
    þynċan '(to) seem'   **þūhte**   **þūht**
    bycgan '(to) buy'   **bohte**   **boht**
    wyrċan, '(to) make,   **worhte**   **worht**
      weorcan perform'
    lecgan '(to) lay'   **leġde**   **leġd**
    settan '(to) set'   **sette**   **sett**

Tō lang ys tō reċċenne.	It is too long to tell.
Đā reahte heora ǣġðer his spell.	Then each of them told his tale.
Wel ġestreht bed.	A well spread bed.
Đā lārēowas sceolan ... tǣċan and lǣran.	The masters ought to ... teach and instruct.
Hē wæs tǣċende dæġhwomlīċe binnan ðām temple.	He was teaching daily in the temple.
Se ōðer rǣhte forþ his hand.	The other reached out his hand.
Hwæne seċst þū?	Whom seekest thou?
Sē þe sēċð, hē hyt fint.	He who seeks will find it.
Hē āxode hine, hwæt hē sōhte.	He asked him what he sought.
[Hī] sōhton hine him tō hlāforde and tō mundboran.	They tried to get him as their lord and protector.
Secge hē hwæt iċ þenċe.	Let him say what I am thinking.
Đæt mæġ bēon, ðæt sume men þenċen, 'Hū mæġ iċ sēċan ðæt gāstlīċe lēoht?'	It may be that some think, 'How may I seek the spiritual light?'
Hīe þōhton hū hīe hine ācwellan meahton.	They thought how they might kill him.
Swā mē ðinċþ.	As it seems to me, *or* 'methinks.'

Ðūhte hēom ðæt hit mihte swā.

It seemed to them that it could
be thus.

Wirċ ðē ǣnne arc ... and ðū wirċst
wununge binnan ðām arce.

Make thee an ark ... and thou shalt
make an habitation within the ark.

Mē ġebyrað tō wyrċeanne þæs weorc
þe mē sende þā hwīle þe hit dæġ
is: niht cymþ þonne nān man
wyrċan ne mæġ.

It behooves me to work the works of
the one who sent me while it is
day: night will come when no man
can work.

Sē ðe ġelȳfð on mē, hē wyrċð þā
weorc þe iċ wyrċe.

He who believes in me will do those
works that I do.

Se cing [Herodes] cwæð þā tō ðām
mǣdene, 'Bide mē swā hwæt swā
þū wylle, and iċ þē sylle.' And hē
swōr hire: 'Sōðes iċ þē sylle
swā hwæt swā þū mē bitst....'
Hēo bæd and þus cwæð, 'Iċ wylle
þæt ðū mē hrædlīċe on ānum disce
sylle Iōhannes hēafod.' ... [Hē]
sende ǣnne cwellere and bebead
þæt man his hēafod on ānum disce
brōhte; and hē hine þā on
cwerterne behēafdode, and his
hēafod on disce brōhte and hit
sealde þām mǣdene, and þæt
mǣden hit sealde hire mēder.

The king [Herod] said to the
maiden, 'Ask of me whatever thou
will, and I will give to thee.'
And he swore to her, 'In truth
I will give thee whatever thou
askest of me.' She asked and
thus said, 'I wish that thou
quickly give me on a dish John's
head.' ... He sent an executioner
and bade that his head be brought
on a dish; and he beheaded him in
the prison, and brought his head
on a dish and gave it to the
maiden, and the maiden gave it
to her mother.

Sē ðe wille fæst hūs timbrian,
ne sceall hē hit nō settan up
on ðone hēhstan cnol,... and
eft sē ðe wille fæst hūs timbrian,
ne sette hē hit on sondbeorhas.

He who wishes to build a secure
house shall not set it on the
highest hilltop, ... and
again, he who will build a
secure house, let him not set
it on sandbanks.

Þā hē on þæt templ ēode hē ongan
drīfan of þām temple syllende
and bycgende.

When he went into the temple he
began to drive from the temple
[those] selling and buying.

6.5 Strong Verbs

'Strong' verbs (also called 'vocalic' verbs) are characterized by past and non-past forms being marked by difference in stem-vowel (and not by suffixed past tense inflection). There are seven classes of strong verbs distinguished by differences in the base form (the infinitive stem) and the ablaut series of the principal parts; in verbs, ablaut, or vowel-gradation, is essentially a systematic variation of vocalic elements in forms of the same root in relation to tense, mode, and aspect. Because past tense forms of most classes have two different stem-vowels, four 'principal parts' are conventionally cited for strong verbs. (*OEG* 730–747)

Class	Infinitive	Past 1st Sg.	Past Plural	Pass. Participle
1	stīgan '(to) ascend'	stāg, stāh	stigon	stigen
2	flēogan '(to) fly'	flēag, flēah	flugon	flogen
	būgan '(to) bend'	bēag, bēah	bugon	bogen
3	bindan '(to) bind'	band	bundon	bunden
	beorgan '(to) protect'	bearh	burgon	borgen
	sweltan '(to) die'	swealt	swulton	swolten
4	beran '(to) bear'	bær	bæron	boren
5	wrecan '(to) avenge'	wræc	wrǣcon	wrecen
6	faran '(to) proceed'	fōr	fōron	faren
7	wealdan '(to) rule'	wēold	wēoldon	wealden
	lǣtan '(to) let'	lēt	lēton	lǣten

(Ā-) STĪGAN '(to) proceed; ascend; descend' Strong Verb 1

stīgan	Infinitive
(tō) stīgenne	Inflected infinitive
stīgende	Present participle
stigen	Passive participle
stīg (þū)	Imperative singular
stīgað (ġē)	Imperative plural

Indicative			Subjunctive	
		Non-past		
(iċ) **stīge**	(wē)		(iċ)	(wē)
(þū) **stīhst**	(ġē) **stīgað**		(þū) **stīge**	(ġē) **stīgen**
(hē) **stīhþ**	(hīe)		(hē)	(hīe)
		Past		
(iċ) **stāh**	(wē)		(iċ)	(wē)
(þū) **stige**	(ġē) **stigon**		(þū) **stige**	(ġē) **stigen**
(hē) **stāh**	(hīe)		(hē)	(hīe)

Sīo sunne ofer moncyn stīhþ ā upweardes.	The sun mounts ever upward over mankind.
Ġē ġesēoð Godes englas up stīgende.	You will see the angels of God ascending.
Hē stāh up on ān trēow.	He climbed up into a tree.
Beornas on stefn stigon.	The men climbed onto the prow (of the ship).
Ne stīge hē on his hūs.	Let him not come down into his house.
Hē from helle āstāg.	He came from hell.
Ðā stīgað on helle.	Those will go down to hell.
Hē nyðer āstīhþ swā swā rēn on flȳs, and swā swā niðer āstīhþ droppetung, droppende ofer eorþan.	He shall come down as rain on a fleece, and as falling [rain] comes down, dropping over the earth.

Āstīgaþ muntas, and niðer āstīgaþ
feldas on stōwe.

The mountains ascend, and the
fields go down to their places.

Ðā steorran scīnaþ beforan ðām
mōnan, and ne scīnaþ beforan
ðǣre sunnan.

The stars shine before the moon,
and do not shine before the
sun.

Se steorra scān .iii. mōnðas.

The comet shone three months.

His ansȳn sceān swā swā sunne, and
his ġewǣda scinon on snāwes
hwītnysse.

His countenance shone as the sun,
and his garments shone with the
whiteness of snow.

On wordum and on dǣdum beorht
and scīnende.

In words and deeds bright and
shining.

'Andrēas, ārīs!' ... Andrēas þā
ārās.

'Andrew, arise!' ... Andrew then
arose.

Hē hīe āwehte and cwæð: 'Ārīsaþ!'

He awoke them and said: 'Arise!'

Se apostol cwæð tō him: 'For hwon
ārise þū swā hraðe?'

The apostle said to him: 'Why
did you arise so quickly?'

Drihten hēt ealle ārīsan þe on þām
wǣtere wǣron.

The Lord commanded all who were
in the water to arise.

Ārīsaþ þēod wið þēode.

Nation shall rise against nation.

Þā ġingran ārīsaþ wið þām yldrum.

Servants shall arise against masters.

Ydel is ēow ǣr lēohte ārīsan.

It is useless for you to arise
before light.

Ðā ārison ðā þrī weras.

Then the three men arose.

Weorod eall ārās.

The band (of men) all arose.

Sindon costinga monġe ārisene.

Many temptations are arisen.

Wrīt ðysne circul mid ðīnes cnīfes
orde on ānum stāne.

Write [or mark] this circle with
the point of your knife on a
stone.

Myċel yfel dēð sē ðe lēas wrīt
[= wrīteþ].

Great evil does he who writes
falsehood.

Hē wrāt mid his fingre on ðǣre
eorþan.

He wrote with his finger on the
earth.

Ðā wrīteras and ðā ðe hī ymbe
writon.

The writers and those they wrote
about.

FLĒOGAN '(to) fly; (to) flee'   Strong Verb 2

flēogan	Infinitive
(tō) flēogenne	Inflected infinitive
flēogende	Present participle
flogen	Passive participle
flēog (þū)	Imperative singular
flēogaþ (ġē)	Imperative plural

Indicative   Subjunctive

Non-past

(iċ)	**flēoge**	(wē)		(iċ)		(wē)	
(þū)	**flēogest**	(ġē)	**flēogaþ,**	(þū)	**flēoge**	(ġē)	**flēogen**
(hē)	**flēogeþ**	(hīe)	**flēoþ**	(hē)		(hīe)	

Past

(iċ)	**flēag, flēah**	(wē)		(iċ)		(wē)	
(þū)	**fluge**	(ġē)	**flugon**	(þū)	**fluge**	(ġē)	**flugen**
(hē)	**flēag, flēah**	(hīe)		(hē)		(hīe)	

Se fugel flēogeð.	The bird flies.
Hē flēah ofer fyðru winda.	He flew on the wings of the winds.
Iċ hæbbe swīðe swifte feðera, ðæt iċ mæġ flīogan ofer ðone hēan hrōf ðæs heofones.	I have very swift wings, that I can fly over the high roof of heaven.
Ðā englas twēġen him on twā healfa flugon.	The two angels flew on both sides of him.
Ġeseah hē ðā werian gāstas þurh ðæt fȳr flēogenne.	He saw the accursed spirits flying through the fire.
Hwā mē sealde tō flēogenne fiðeru swā culfran?	[O that] someone would give me wings like a dove to fly (away)!
[Hȳ] flēoð ... swā hrædlīċe swā is wēn þæt hȳ flēogen.	They flee ... so quickly as there is opinion that they fly [i.e., that it seems that they fly].

BŪGAN '(to) bow, bend, turn to or from, yield'   Strong Verb 2

būgan	Infinitive
(**tō**) **būgenne**	Inflected infinitive
būgende	Present participle
bogen	Passive participle
būg, būh (þū)	Imperative singular
būgaðꝺ (ġē)	Imperative plural

Indicative				Subjunctive	
		Non-past			
(iċ) **būge**	(wē)		(iċ)	(wē)	
(þū) **būgest, bȳhst**	(ġē) **būgaðꝺ**		(þū) **būge**	(ġē) **būgen**	
(hē) **būgeðꝺ**	(hīe)		(hē)	(hīe)	
		Past			
(iċ) **bēag, bēah**	(wē)		(iċ)	(wē)	
(þū) **buge**	(ġē) **bugon**		(þū) **buge**	(ġē) **bugen**	
(hē) **bēag, bēah**	(hīe)		(hē)	(hīe)	

Hī bugon ond flugon.	They yielded and fled.
Iċ sceolde ... būgan.	I must submit.
Him bēag gōd dæl þæs folces.	A good part of the people submitted to him.
Hē tō fulluhte bēah.	He submitted to baptism.
Būge iċ tō ēowerum hæðꝺenscipe.	I will turn to your heathendom.
Būh fram yfele and dō ... gōd.	Turn from evil and do ... good.
Hē forlēt woruldþing and bēah intō mynstre.	He relinquished worldly affairs and went into a monastery.
Se strēam bēah for his fōtun þæt hē mihte drȳġe ofergangan.	The stream made way for his feet so that he could cross over dry.
[Sēo ēa,] norþ būgende, ūt on ðꝺone Wendel-sǣ.	(That river,) bending northward, [proceeds] out into the Mediterranean.

It is in the root vowel of the present (or infinitive) stem that verbs represented by **flēogan** and **būgan** differ; their vowels in the rest of the ablaut series are identical. More common than **flēogan** are **bēodan** and, with consonant alternation attributable to operation of Verner's Law (see Postscript to Appendix B), **ċēosan** and **forlēosan/belēosan**.

Infinitive	Past 1st Sg.	Past Plural	Pass. Participle
bēodan '(to) command proclaim'	**bēad**	**budon**	**boden**
ċēosan '(to) choose'	**ċēas**	**curon**	**coren**
forlēosan '(to) lose'	**forlēas**	**forluron**	**forloren**

Hē bēad Iōsepe þæt hē bude his brōðrum.

He bade Joseph that he order his brothers (to do something).

Æðelstān bēot [= bēodeð] his biscopum, þæt ġē þone frið healdan.

Athelstan gives command to his bishops, that you hold the peace.

Hē him friþ bēodeð.

He announces peace to them.

Him wæs hild boden.

To them was war proclaimed.

Ċēos þē ġefēran ond feoht onġēn Amalech.

Choose out companions and fight against Amalek.

Hī ... lēofne ċēosað ofer woruldwelan.

They choose the beloved one above worldly wealth.

Drihten ðē ċist.

The Lord will choose thee.

Dæt hē ōðer līf cure.

That he should choose another life.

Ne mæġ nān man hine sylfne tō cynge ġedōn, ac þæt folc hæfð ċyre tō ċēosenne þone tō cyninge þe him sylfum līcað.

Let no man make himself king, but the people have free-choice for choosing that one as king who to themselves (it) is pleasing.

Ġif hē forlȳst ān of þām.

If he loses one of them.

Ðū nāne myrhþe ne forlure, ðā ðā ðū hīe forlure.

Thou didst lose no pleasure, when thou didst lose them.

Ðū forloren hæfst ðā woruldsælþa.

Thou hast lost worldly prosperity.

Þām ðe ær his elne forlēas.

To him who before had lost his courage.

Ne ġecure ġē mē, ac iċ ġeċēas ēow.

Ye chose not me, but I chose you.

BINDAN '(to) bind, tie, fasten'   Strong Verb 3

bindan	Infinitive
(tō) bindenne	Inflected infinitive
bindende	Present participle
bunden	Passive participle
bind (þū)	Imperative singular
bindaþ (ġē)	Imperative plural

Indicative	Subjunctive

Non-past

(iċ)	binde	(wē)		(iċ)		(wē)	
(þū)	bindest, bin(t)st	(ġē)	bindaþ	(þū)	binde	(ġē)	binden
(hē)	bindeþ, bint	(hīe)		(hē)		(hīe)	

Past

(iċ)	band	(wē)		(iċ)		(wē)	
(þū)	bunde	(ġē)	bundon	(þū)	bunde	(ġē)	bunden
(hē)	band	(hīe)		(hē)		(hīe)	

Swā hwylċe swā ġē ġebindað ofer eorþan þā bēoþ ġebundene on heofonum. And swā hwylċe swā ġē ofer eorþan unbindaþ þā bēoþ on heofonum unbundene.

Whatsoever ye shall bind on earth those shall be bound in heaven. And whatsoever ye shall loose on earth those shall be loosed in heaven.

Swā hwæt swā þū ofer eorþan ġebindst, þæt byþ on heofonum ġebunden. And swā hwæt swā þū unbindst ofer eorþan, þæt byð unbunden on heofonum.

Whatsoever thou bindest on earth, that shall be bound in heaven. And whatsoever thou unbindest on earth, that shall be unbounden in heaven.

Hē nam Simeon and band hine.

He seized Simeon and bound him.

Mid ġehāte hine sylfne bindende.

Binding himself with promises.

Hrīm hrusan bond.

Frost bound the earth.

Swelċe hwā nū delfe eorþan and
finde goldhord.... Ġif nān mon
ǣr þæt gold þǣr ne hȳdde,
þonne ne funde hē hit nō;
for-ðȳ hit næs nā wēas funden.

As if someone now should dig in the
earth and find treasure.... If no one
had earlier hidden the gold there,
then he would not have found it;
for it was not found fortuitously.

Sēo bōc on þǣre ċiriċean funden
wæs.

The book was found in the church.

Þæt hē ūs ġearwe finde.

That he may find us ready.

Ne þǣr mon his fēond findeð.

One does not find his enemy there.

For-þī ne fint ǣlċ mon þæt hē
sēċþ, for-ðȳ hē hit on riht
ne sēċþ. Ġē sēċaþ þǣr ġē
findan ne magan.

The reason each person doesn't
find what he seeks is that he
doesn't seek it aright. Ye seek
where ye are not able to find.

Ēagan mīne ġeorne sċēawedun,
hwǣr iċ trēowe funde.

Mine eyes eagerly looked for where
I should find the faithful.

Ā þū wunne æfter eorðlīcum
welum.

Ever didst thou strive for earthly
riches.

Ealle ġē þe winnaþ and ġebyrde
sindun.

All you who labor and are burdened.

Se fæder winð wið his āgenne
sunu.

The father contends against his
own son.

Hī wunnon him betwȳnan.

They contended among themselves.

Ġē wunnon onġēan Drihten.

You struggled against the Lord.

[Hagar] ongan wið Sarran winnan.

Hagar began to contend with Sarah.

Þēod winð onġēn þēode.

Nation shall strive against nation.

Hē onġēan nān ðyngc ne wan.

He did not struggle against anything.

Ēadmund cynincg ... āwearp his
wǣpna, wolde ġe-æfenlǣċan Cristes
ġebysnungum, þe forbēad Petre
mid wǣpnum tō winnenne wið þā
wælhrēowan Iūdēiscan.

King Edmund threw away his weapons,
[he] intended to emulate Christ's
example, who forbade Peter to
contend with weapons against the
bloodthirsty Jews.

Ne winne ġē onġēn þā ðe ēow
yfel dōþ.

Do not contend against those who
do you evil.

Hī wið þone here wǣron winnende.

They were fighting with the army.

BEORGAN '(to) protect, defend'   Strong Verb 3

beorgan	Infinitive
(tō) beorgenne	Inflected infinitive
beorgende	Present participle
borgen	Passive participle
beorh (þū)	Imperative singular
beorgaðˍ (ġē)	Imperative plural

Indicative			Subjunctive		
		Non-past			
(iċ) beorge	(wē)		(iċ)	(wē)	
(þū) byrhst	(ġē) beorgaðˍ		(þū) beorge	(ġē) beorgen	
(hē) byrhþ	(hīe)		(hē)	(hīe)	
		Past			
(iċ) bearh	(wē)		(iċ)	(wē)	
(þū) burge	(ġē) burgon		(þū) burge	(ġē) burgen	
(hē) bearh	(hīe)		(hē)	(hīe)	

Ġeheald mē, Drihten, and beorh mē, swā swā man byrhðˍ þām æplum on his ēagum mid his brǣwum.

Keep me, Lord, and protect me, as one protects the apples of his eyes with his eyelids.

[Hī] beorgaðˍ him bealonīþ.

They guard themselves against wickedness.

Bebeorh þē þone bealonīðˍ.

Defend thee from that wickedness.

Beorge man ġeorne þæt man þā sāwla ne forfare.

Let one diligently defend so that he not cause the soul to perish.

Āge hē þrēora nihta fierst him tō ġebeorganne.

Let him have a period of three days to save himself.

Ne mæġ nān man ōðerne wyrian and him sylfum ġebeorgan.

No man may curse another and save himself.

Hē bewand his hēafod mid ānum clāðe, and ... bearh him sylfum swīðe ġeorne.

He wrapped his head with a cloth, and ... protected himself very carefully.

Weorðan functions variously as indepedent verb, copula, and auxiliary. (*OES* 671–674)

Sceal se dæġ weorþan.	The day shall come to pass.
Hwā wæs æfre, oþþe is nū, oððe hwā wyrþ ġet æfter us?	Who ever was, or now is, or who yet will be after us?
Þæt weorþeð for þyses folces synnum, þæt ealle þās ġetimbro bēoþ tōworpene.	That happens because of the people's sins, that all these buildings shall be destroyed.
Þā hwīle þe hē þær stōd, hē wearþ færinga ġeong cniht, and sōna eft eald man.	While he stood there, he became suddenly a young boy, and immediately again an old man.
Weorðan his āgene bearn ealle stēopċild, and his wīf wyrðe wydewe.	Let his own offspring all become stepchildren, and his wife become a widow.
Ðā wearð hē druncen.	Then he became drunk.
Ðā fixas ... wurdon dēade.	The fish ... became dead.
Weorðeð tō duste.	Comes to dust.
Þū eart dust, and tō duste wyrst.	Thou art dust, and will come to be dust.
Ǣlċ þing wyrþ tō nāuhte.	Each thing comes to naught.
Nis nā gōd þæt man nime þāra bearna hlāf and hundum weorpe.	It is not good that one take children's bread and throw it to dogs.
[Hī] wurpon hine on þone bāt.	They threw him onto the boat.
Wurpaþ hit ūt on þæt wæter.	Throw it out into the water.
Hwylċ ēower sī synlēas, wurpe stān on hī.	Whichever of you is without sin, let him cast a stone at her.
Iċ ne wyrpe ūt ðone þe tō mē cymð.	I do not cast out the one who comes to me.
Hweorfað eft tō mē.	Return to me.
Hīe wǣron eft hām hweorfende.	They were returning home.
Hwider hweorfað wē?	Whither shall we turn?
Gāstas hweorfon, sōhton ... engla ēðel.	Spirits went (and) sought ... the native-land of angels.

SWELTAN '(to) die'   Strong Verb 3

sweltan	Infinitive
(tō) sweltenne	Inflected infinitive
sweltende	Present participle
swolten	Passive participle
swelt (þū)	Imperative singular
sweltaþ (ġē)	Imperative plural

<table>
<tr><td colspan="2">Indicative</td><td colspan="2">Subjunctive</td></tr>
<tr><td colspan="4" align="center">Non-past</td></tr>
<tr><td>(iċ) swelte</td><td>(wē)</td><td>(iċ)</td><td>(wē)</td></tr>
<tr><td>(þū) swyltest</td><td>(ġē) sweltaþ</td><td>(þū) swelte</td><td>(ġē) swelten</td></tr>
<tr><td>(hē) swylteþ</td><td>(hīe)</td><td>(hē)</td><td>(hīe)</td></tr>
<tr><td colspan="4" align="center">Past</td></tr>
<tr><td>(iċ) swealt</td><td>(wē)</td><td>(iċ)</td><td>(wē)</td></tr>
<tr><td>(þū) swulte</td><td>(ġē) swulton</td><td>(þū) swulte</td><td>(ġē) swulten</td></tr>
<tr><td>(hē) swealt</td><td>(hīe)</td><td>(hē)</td><td>(hīe)</td></tr>
</table>

Ne swelte iċ mid sāre.	I shall not die with sorrow.
Hē sǣde þæt hē sweltan sceolde.	He said that he would have to die.
Iċ mæġ sweltan blīðelīċe.	I am able to die joyfully.
Ealle men sweltaþ.	All men die.
Ðæt ān man swelte for folce.	That one man die for the people.
Hwī lǣddest ðū ūs þæt wē swulton on þisum wēstene?	Why leadest thou us so that we should die in this wilderness?
Hīe hungre swulton.	They died from hunger.
Þæt hē swunġen wǣre oþþæt hē swylte.	That he should be beaten until he shall die.
Oð hē fornēah hungre swealt.	Until he very nearly died from hunger.
Wē synd ġearwe tō sweltenne swyðor þonne tō forgǣgenne ūres ... drihtnes ǣ.	We are ready to die rather than to transgress our ... Lord's law.

Ðū monegum helpst.	Thou helpest many.
Hē nyle helpan ðæs folces mid-ðām-ðe hē [God] his healp.	He will not help the people when God has helped him.
Þonne þū hulpe mīn.	When thou didst help me.
Help mīn.	Help me.
God ūre helpe.	May God help us.
Ongan [hē] ... eorðan delfan.	He began ... to dig the earth.
Swelċe hwā delfe eorþan.	As if anyone should dig the earth.
Ġif se delfere ðā eorþan nō ne dulfe.	If the digger had not dug the earth.
Wæterpyttas ðe ġē ne dulfon.	Wells which ye dug not.
[Hīe] dulfon āne myċele dīċ.	They dug a great ditch.

Ġielpan '(to) boast' and ġieldan '(to) (re-)pay' have stem variation in present-tense forms, the effects of the initial palatal consonant.

Ðæt hȳ ġielpan ne þorftan.	That they needn't boast.
Ġif ðū ġilpan wille, ġilp Godes.	If thou wilt glory, glory in God.
Ġif þū þæs ġilpst, hū ne ġilpst þū heora gōdes, næs þīnes?	If you glory in that, how is it you don't glory in their good, not yours?
Nō iċ þæs ġylpe.	I boast not of that.
Hē morðres ġylpeþ.	He boasts of slaying.
Hū lange mānwyrhtan morðre ġylpað?	How long will evildoers exult in wickedness?
Hē ġealp ðæt him nōwiht wiðstandan mihte.	He boasted that nothing could withstand him.
Swīðe gulpon. Sigore gulpon. Firenum gulpon.	Boasted exceedingly. Boasted of victory. Wickedly boasted.
Hē ðē mid wīte ġieldeþ.	He will repay you with punishment.
Þis is sōðlīċe ēadiġ wer, ... [hē] nænigum yfel wið yfele ġeald.	This is truly a blessed man, ... to none [he] paid back evil for evil.
Ealle men him sceoldon gafol ġyldan.	All men must pay him tribute.
Ac hyra ār is mǣst on þām gafole þe ðā Finnas him ġyldað.	But their honor is greatest in the tribute which the Finns pay them.

BERAN '(to) bear, carry, bring forth'   Strong Verb 4

beran	Infinitive
(tō) berenne	Inflected infinitive
berende	Present participle
boren	Passive participle
ber (þū)	Imperative singular
beraþ (ġē)	Imperative plural

Indicative				Subjunctive			
			Non-past				
(iċ)	bere	(wē)		(iċ)		(wē)	
(þū)	bir(e)st	(ġē)	beraÞ	(þū)	bere	(ġē)	beren
(hē)	bir(e)Þ	(hīe)		(hē)		(hīe)	
			Past				
(iċ)	bær	(wē)		(iċ)		(wē)	
(þū)	bǣre	(ġē)	bǣron	(þū)	bǣre	(ġē)	bǣren
(hē)	bær	(hīe)		(hē)		(hīe)	

Him wæs ful boren.   To him the cup was carried.

Ġif hē tō Þǣm rīċe wæs on rihte boren.   If he to that kingdom was rightly born.

Þū eall þing birest.   Thou bearest all things.

Hē bierÞ on his heortan Þā byrÞenne Þæs bysmeres.   He bears in his heart the burden of infamy.

... þe bǣron byrþena on þises dæġes hǣtan.   ... who have born the burden in the the heat of this day.

Iċ nelle beran ēowre ġȳmelēaste.   I will not endure your negligence.

Ǣlċ gōd trēow byrþ gōde wæstmas.   Each good tree bears good fruits.

Þēos eorÞe is berende missenlīcra fugela.   This earth produces various fowl.

Fero 'iċ bere' gǣÞ Þus: *fers* 'Þū berst,' *fert* 'hē berÞ,' *ferimus* 'wē beraÞ.'   [Conjugation of] *fero* 'I carry' goes thus: 'thou bearest,' 'he beareth,' 'we bear.'

Two common Class 4 verbs have these principal parts:

Infinitive	Past 1st Sg.	Past Plural	Pass. Participle
niman '(to) take'	**nam, nōm**	**nāmon, nōmon**	**numen**
cuman '(to) come'	**c(w)ōm**	**c(w)ōmon**	**cumen**

Cum tō þām lande, þe iċ ðē
ġeswuteliġe.

Come to the land which I will point
out to you.

Þā cōmon tō him pharisei and sume
bōceras cumende fram hierusalem.

Then to him came Pharisees and
certain scribes, coming from
Jerusalem.

Oft þā forcūþestan men cumað tō
þām anwealde.

The most wicked men often come to
power.

Ġif mec hild nime.

If battle should take me.

Þā nam þæt folc miċelne andan
onġēan his lāre.

Then the people took great malice
toward his doctrine.

Graman niman. Siġe niman.
Ġelēafan niman. Suna niman.
On ġemynd niman.

To take offence. To gain victory.
To believe. To adopt a son.
To bear in remembrance.

Stelan has usual forms for its principal parts. By comparison with it,
scieran shows stem variation from diphthongization of stem-vowel by initial
palatal consonant (cf. Class 3 **ġielpan** and Class 5 **ġiefan**).

Infinitive	Past 1st Sg.	Past Plural	Pass. Participle
stelan '(to) steal'	**stæl**	**stǣlon**	**stolen**
scieran '(to) shear'	**scear**	**scēaron**	**scoren**

Ne hē his loccas mid scearum
wanode, ne his beard mid seaxe
scear.

Neither did he shorten his hair
with scissors, nor did he cut his
beard with a knife.

Ne stel þū.

Thou shalt not steal.

Þēof ne cymð būton þæt hē stele.

A thief doesn't come except to
steal.

Hēo scear hyre feax swā swā weras,
and ġeġyrede hȳ mid weres hræġle.

She cut her hair just as men, and
dressed herself with a man's garment.

Swā swā lamb þonne hit man scyrð.

As a lamb when one shears it.

Wēnst þū þæt wē þīnes hlāfordes
gold stǣlon?

Do you imagine that we stole thy
lord's gold?

WRECAN '(to) drive (out); utter; avenge' Strong Verb 5

wrecan	Infinitive
(tō) wrecenne	Inflected infinitive
wrecende	Present participle
wrecen	Passive participle
wrec (þū)	Imperative singular
wrecaþ (ġē)	Imperative plural

Indicative   Subjunctive

Non-past

(iċ)	**wrece**	(wē)		(iċ)		(wē)	
(þū)	**wric(e)st**	(ġē)	**wrecaþ**	(þū)	**wrece**	(ġē)	**wrecen**
(hē)	**wric(e)þ**	(hīe)		(hē)		(hīe)	

Past

(iċ)	**wræc**	(wē)		(iċ)		(wē)	
(þū)	**wrǣce**	(ġē)	**wrǣcon**	(þū)	**wrǣce**	(ġē)	**wrǣcen**
(hē)	**wræc**	(hīe)		(hē)		(hīe)	

Wrec mē wið mīnne wiðerwinnan.	Avenge me against mine adversary.
Ðæt wē magon wrecan Godes yrre on ðām mannum.	That we may wreak God's anger on those men.
Sēlre bið ǣġhwǣm þæt hē his frēond wrece, þonne hē fela murne.	It is better for every man that he should avenge his friend, rather than mourn much.
Ðā wræc hē his æfþancas on his fēondum.	Then he avenged his anger on hīs enemies.
Þā folc him betwēonum ful .x. winter þā ġewin wreciende wǣron.	A full ten years those people were avenging those quarrels among themselves.
[Hī] sittaþ æt symble, sōðġied wrecað.	They sit at feasting, tell true tales.
Mæġ iċ be mē sylfum sōð-ġied wrecan.	I can relate a true tale about myself.

Cweðan has alternation of its middle consonant (explained historically by operation of Verner's Law—see Postscript to Appendix B); ġiefan illustrates variation of stem vowels following an initial palatal consonant. The principal parts of these common verbs are as follows:

Infinitive	Past 1st Sg.	Past Plural	Pass. Participle
cweðan '(to) say'	cwæð	cwædon	cweden
ġiefan '(to) give'	ġeaf	ġeafon	ġiefen

Þȳ-læs ðū cweðe.	Lest thou shouldst say.
Dū cwist (= cwiþest) ðæt iċ ðē andwyrdan scyle.	Thou sayest that I must answer thee.
For þām worde þe se Wealdend cwyð.	For the word which the Lord speaks.
Hī cwædon him betwȳnan.	They spoke amongst themselves.
Ne cweþað betwux ēow.	Say not among yourselves.
Hēr Hengest and Horsa fuhton wið Wyrtgerne þām cininge on ðære stōwe ðe is cweden Ǽġeles þrep, and his brōðor Horsan man ofslōh.	Here Hengest and Horsa fought with King Vortigern in that place which is called Aylesthorpe, and his brother Horsa was slain.
Þū cwæde ðæt ðū mē woldest wel dōn.	You said that you would do well by me.
Hē wolde hyne his fæder āġyfan.	He would deliver him to his father.
Him se wer āġeaf ondsware.	To him the man returned an answer.
Syððan ġē ēowre gaful-rædenne āġifen habbað.	After ye have paid your fare.
Forġyf him.	Forgive him.
Hē forġifð hit.	He will forgive it.
Forġifaþ, ġif ġē hwæt aġēn ǣniġne habbað.	Forgive, if you have anything against any(one).
Forġyf ūs ūre gyltas swā wē forġyfað ǣlcum þāra þe wið ūs āgyltað.	Forgive us our wrongdoings as we forgive each of those who do wrong against us.
[Hē] nān ðing ne æt, ðēah-ðe ealle ōðre men ǣton....	He ate nothing, although all other men ate....

Hū lange wilt ðū, Drihten, mīn
  forġitan?

How long wilt thou, Lord, forget
  me?

Hū lange, ēalā Drihten, forġitst
  ðū mē?

How long, O Lord, forgetest thou
  me?

For-hwī forġēate ðū mīn?

Why did you forget me?

Næfre nāuht hē ne forġeat.

He has never forgotten anything.

Ne wē ne forġēaton ðē.

We did not forget thee.

Ġemunað and ne forġitað, hū swīðe
  ġē gremedon Drihten.

Remember and forget not, how much
  you vexed the Lord.

Ān ðe is forġeten.

One who is forgotten.

Maniġe licggaþ dēade, mid ealle
  forġitene.

Many lie dead, entirely forgotten.

Iċ ne sprece tō ðǣm, ac iċ sprece
  tō ðē.

I speak not to those, but I speak
  to thee.

Ne sprǣc næfre nān man swā þes
  man sprycþ.

No man ever spoke as this man
  speaks.

Þā sprǣc se ofermōda cyning.

Then spoke the arrogant king.

Nū ðū sprycst openlīċe.

Now thou speakest openly.

Hiġ spǣcon him betwȳnan.

They spoke among themselves.

Nū iċ ... begann tō sprecanne tō
  mīnum drihtne, iċ wylle sprecan
  ġit.

Now I ... have undertaken to speak
  to my lord, I will speak
  further.

Ne sint hī nō wiþ ēow tō metanne.

They are not to be compared with you.

On ðām ylcan ġemete þe ġē metaþ,
  ēow byþ ġemeten.

With that same measure that you
  mete, to you (it) shall be meted.

Thōmas ēode metende mid ānre
  mete-ġyrde þone stede.

Thomas went measuring the place
  with a measuring-rod.

Sēon '(to) see' **seah sāwon sewen** is a very common verb of this class, a
'contract verb' modified by loss of intervocalic **h** (see Appendix B).

Manega witegan and cyningas
  woldon ġesēon þæt ġē ġesēoþ,
  and hiġ hit ne ġesāwon.

Many prophets and kings wished
  to see what you see, and they
  saw it not.

FARAN '(to) go, proceed'   Strong Verb 6

faran	Infinitive
(tō) farenne	Inflected infinitive
farende	Present participle
faren	Passive participle
far (þū)	Imperative singular
faraðð (ġē)	Imperative plural

<table>
<tr><td colspan="2">Indicative</td><td colspan="2">Subjunctive</td></tr>
<tr><td colspan="4" align="center">Non-past</td></tr>
<tr><td>(iċ) fare</td><td>(wē)</td><td>(iċ)</td><td>(wē)</td></tr>
<tr><td>(þū) farest
fǣr(e)st</td><td>(ġē) faraðð</td><td>(þū) fare</td><td>(ġē) faren</td></tr>
<tr><td>(hē) fareðð,
fǣr(e)þ</td><td>(hīe)</td><td>(hē)</td><td>(hīe)</td></tr>
<tr><td colspan="4" align="center">Past</td></tr>
<tr><td>(iċ) fōr</td><td>(wē)</td><td>(iċ)</td><td>(wē)</td></tr>
<tr><td>(þū) fōre</td><td>(ġē) fōron</td><td>(þū) fōre</td><td>(ġē) fōren</td></tr>
<tr><td>(hē) fōr</td><td>(hīe)</td><td>(hē)</td><td>(hīe)</td></tr>
</table>

Iċ ārīse ond iċ fare tō mīnum fæder.	I will arise and I will go to my father.
Ēaþere ys olfende tō farenne þurh nǣdle þyrel þonne se rīca ond se welega on Godes rīċe gā.	It is easier for a camel to go through the eye of a needle than the influential and prosperous (man) go into God's kingdom.
Nū wille iċ faran.	Now I will go.
Far nū and seġe þīnum hlāforde....	Go now and say to your lord....
Swiðun hēt þæt hē fare tō Æþelwolde bisceope.	[St.] Swithin commanded that he go to Bishop Athelwold.
Þū cymst tō ðǣre stōwe ġif ðū fǣrst mid ūs nū.... Hē wearð þā swȳðe fæġen and wolde faran mid him.	You will come to that place if you go with us now.... He was then very glad and wished to go with them.

[Hīe] him þā āþas swōron ... þæt hīe hrędlīċe of his rīċe foren.

[They] then swore oaths to him ... that they quickly would go from his kingdom.

Þēodscypas winnað and sacað heom betwēonan.

Peoples will fight and contend among themselves.

Gōd sceal wið yfele, līf sceal wið dēaþe, lēoht sceal wið þȳstrum, fyrd wið fyrde, fēond wið ōðrum, lāð wið lāðe ymb land sacan.

Good shall contend with evil, life with death, light against darkness, army against army, enemy against another, foe against foe concerning the land.

Ðū mē wiðsæcst.

Thou deniest me.

Sē þe mē wiðsæcð, iċ wiþsace hine.

The one who denies me I will deny.

Sē þe mē wiðsæcð beforan mannum, sē byð wiðsacen beforan Godes englum.

He who denies me before men will be denied before the angels of God.

Ġē wiðsōcon sōðe ond rihte.

Ye denied truth and right.

Wiþsacaþ nū þām lēasum welum.

Give up now worthless riches.

Se fæder wiðsōc his bearne, and þæt bearn wiðsōc þone fæder, and æt nēxtan ǣlċ frēond wiðsōc ōðres.

The father denied his child, and the child denied the father, and finally each friend denied the other.

Standan, a very common verb in this class, has these principal parts:

Infinitive	Past 1st Sg.	Past Plural	Pass. Participle
standan '(to) stand'	**stōd**	**stōdon**	**standen**

Iċ stande beforan ðē.

I stand before thee.

Iċ niste þæt ðū stōde onġēan mē.

I didn't know that you stood [in the way] against me.

Sīo [burg] stōd bī ðǣre sǣ.

The city stood by the sea.

Nis þæt feor heonan, þæt se mere standeð.

It isn't far hence that the mere stands.

Þā þe stōdon onġēan ūs.

Those who stood against us.

Þæt wæter wæs standende and belēac þā duru þǣre ċyriċan.

The water stood [as if a wall] and closed the door of the church.

WEALDAN '(to) rule, control, have power'   Strong Verb 7

wealdan	Infinitive
(tō) wealdenne	Inflected infinitive
wealdende	Present participle
wealden	Passive participle
weald (þū)	Imperative singular
wealda𝛿 (ġē)	Imperative plural

Indicative   Subjunctive

Non-past

(iċ)	wealde	(wē)		(iċ)		(wē)	
(þū)	wealdest	(ġē)	wealdaþ	(þū)	wealde	(ġē)	wealden
(hē)	wealdeþ	(hīe)		(hē)		(hīe)	

Past

(iċ)	wēold	(wē)		(iċ)		(wē)	
(þū)	wēolde	(ġē)	wēoldon	(þū)	wēolde	(ġē)	wēolden
(hē)	wēold	(hīe)		(hē)		(hīe)	

Hī wealdaþ eorðan.

They rule the earth.

Ġif ðū hwæt on þīn druncen mis-dō, ne wīt ðū hit ðām ealoð, for-ðon ðū his wēolde ðē sylf.

If you do anything wrong in drunkenness, don't blame it on the ale, because you yourself will have caused it.

... syððan Cnut ofercōm kynn Æðelredes and Dena wēoldon dēore rīċe Engla landes.

... after Cnut overcame Æthelred's people and the Danes ruled the dear kingdom of England.

Ġelēfst ðū ðæt sēo wyrd wealde ðisse worulde?

Do you believe that fate rules this world?

His fæder ne wolde him lǣtan waldan his eorldōmes.

His father wouldn't let him rule his earldom.

Ǣlċ mon biþ wealdend ðæs ðe hē welt (= wealdeð); næfþ hē nānne anweald ðæs ðe hē ne welt.

Each man is ruler of that which he rules; he has no authority over that which he doesn't rule.

LĀTAN '(to) let, leave, permit'   Strong Verb 7

lǣtan	Infinitive
(tō) lǣtenne	Inflected infinitive
lǣtende	Present participle
lǣten	Passive participle
lǣt (þū)	Imperative singular
lǣtaþ (ġē)	Imperative plural

Indicative				Subjunctive			
				Non-past			
(iċ)	**lǣte**	(wē)		(iċ)		(wē)	
(þū)	**lǣtest**	(ġē)	**lǣtaþ**	(þū)	**lǣte**	(ġē)	**lǣten**
(hē)	**lǣteþ**	(hīe)		(hē)		(hīe)	
				Past			
(iċ)	**lēt**	(wē)		(iċ)		(wē)	
(þū)	**lēte**	(ġē)	**lēton**	(þū)	**lēte**	(ġē)	**lēten**
(hē)	**lēt**	(hīe)		(hē)		(hīe)	

Hē sceal lǣtan his unnyttan
ġeþancas of his mōde.

He must dismiss his idle thoughts
from his mind.

Ġif Drihten þē lǣteþ þone tēoþan
dǣl ānne habban.

If the Lord lets thee have the
tenth part alone.

Iċ wundriġe for-hwī God lǣte ǣniġ
yfel bēon.

I wonder why God may allow any
evil to exist.

Ðæt iċ sylf onġeat, ne lēt iċ
ðæt unwriten.

What I myself knew, I did not
leave it unwritten.

Ðæt hē his feax lēte weaxan.

That he should let his hair grow.

Ðā onlȳsde hē hine and lēt hine
fēran æfter ðām biscope.

Then he released him and allowed
him to travel after the bishop.

Hine eft ðǣm mannum hālne and
ġesundne āġeaf þǣm þe hine ǣr
dǣdne lēton.

Gave him back safe and sound
to the ones who before had left
him dead.

Because of the wide variation among the vowels in infinitive (and non-past) forms of Class 7 verbs, the past tense forms in the ablaut series are the main guides, within Old English, to their class membership. **Wealdan** and **lǣtan** represent two sub-classes distinguished by the vowel in the infinitive stem. Other subclasses are exemplified by the following verbs.

Infinitive	Past 1st Sg.	Past Plural	Pass. Participle
hātan '(to) command'	**hēt**	**hēton**	**hāten**
bēatan '(to) beat'	**bēot**	**bēoton**	**bēaten**
gangan '(to) go'	**ġēong, gēng**	**ġēongon**	**gangen**
flōwan '(to) flow'	**flēow**	**flēowon**	**flōwen**
fōn '(to) seize'	**fēng**	**fēngon**	**fangen**

Hwider wilt þū gangan? — Whither wilt thou go?

[Hīe] heonon gangaþ. — They go hence.

Hē of worulde gangende wæs. — He was going from this world.

Hē tō healle ġēong. — He went to the hall.

Gang þū hider in tō mē. — Come in hither to me.

Gangað on þās niþeran dælas þisse ċeastre. — Go into the lower parts of this city.

Iċ þē hāte ... þæt ðū þās ġesyhðe secge mannum. — I command thee ... to tell this vision to men.

Hwæt hǣtst ðū mē dōn? — What dost thou bid me do?

Wē dydon swā ðū ūs hēte. — We have done as thou didst command us.

Þā hēt hē mē on þysne sīð faran. — Then he bade me go on this journey.

Iċ hī ġelǣde of ðām earde tō gōdan lande ... þæt ðe flēowð mid meolce and mid huniġe. — I led them from that region to a good land ... which flows with milk and with honey.

Hē slōh stān and flēowon wæteru. — He struck a stone and waters flowed forth.

Þæt wæter þe of ðām stāne flēow. — The water which flowed from the stone.

Lagu flōweþ ofer foldan. — Water shall flow over the earth.

Þā ongan iċ slāpan, and slēp. — Then I began to sleep, and slept.

6.6 Passive Constructions

Ælfric explains and illustrates Latin passive verbs in this way:

Iċ cweðe nū *amo* 'ic lufiġe,' þonne
cwyþst þū *quem amas* 'hwænne
lufast þū?' Iċ cweðe *te amo*
'þē iċ lufiġe'; þonne befylð mīn
lufu on ðē, ond þū miht cweðan
amor a te 'iċ eom ġelufod fram
þē.' *Doceo te* 'iċ tǣċe þē,' ond
þū cwyþst *doceor a te* 'iċ eom
ġelǣred fram þē.'

I say now *amo* 'I love', then
sayest thou *quem amas* 'whom
lovest thou?' I say *te amo*
'thee I love'; then falleth my
love on thee, and thou mayest
say *amor a te* 'I am loved by
thee.' *Doceo te* 'I teach thee,'
and thou sayest *doceor a te* 'I
am instructed by thee.'

A. It will be clear from these examples that English passive constructions
have always had the form **bēon/wesan** + passive participle of transitive verb;
they are phrasal constructions, not inflectional ones.

Þā ðis ġefeoht ... wæs ġefohten.

When this fight ... was fought.

Wes ðū ġestrangod and ne ondrǣd
ðū ðē.

Be (thou) strengthened and fear
(thou) not.

Ūs ys ċild ācenned, and ūs ys
sunu forġifen.

To us a child is born, and to us
a son is given.

Hē bið ... bedǣled ælċes gōdes.

He will be ... deprived of each good.

Þæt þā rihtwīsan men ne bēoð
berēafode heora rihtwīsnysse
mēde.

That the righteous men shall not be
bereft of the reward of their
righteousness.

Ðā āðas and þā wedd and þā
borgas synt ealle oferhafene and
ābrocene ðe þǣr ġesealde wǣron,
and wē nytan nānum ōðrum
þingum tō ġetruwianne.

The oaths and the compacts and the
pledges are all neglected and
destroyed which were given there,
and we don't know any other
things to trust in.

Ðǣm landbūendum is beboden ðæt
ealles ðæs ðe him on heora ċēape
ġeweaxe, hiġ Gode ðone tēoðan
dǣl āġyfen.

To the farmers it is commanded
that of all that which increases
to them of their cattle, they
give the tenth part to God.

B. Passive constructions were also made with **weorðan** + passive participle of transitive verb, giving **Hēr Oswine kyning wæs ofslægen** 'Here (i.e., this year [651]) King Oswin was slain,' and **Hēr Onna cyning wearð ofslægen** 'In this year [654] King Anna was slain,' both sentences copied close together in the same manuscript.

Hē sōna wearð hāl ġeworden.	Straightway he was made whole.
... þone pytt ðe hē āworpen wearð.	... the pit that he had been thrown into.
Ġefylled wearð eall þes middanġeard monna bearnum.	All this earth was filled with the children of men.
Þā sīo stefn ġewearð ġehēred.	Then the voice was heard.
Þǣr wearð hrēam āhafen.	An outcry was there raised.
Þǣr wearð se cyng ... āflȳmed and ealle his betste men ġenumene.	There the king ... was put to flight and all his best men seized.

The examples given thus far resemble Modern English passive constructions in ways that other examples do not. **Him byð forġyfen** is closer to 'It will be forgiven him' than to 'He will be forgiven.' Or, **Him wæs þā ġe·andwyrd þus** 'To him (it) was then answered thus' beside more idiomatic 'He was then answered (thus).' Again, **Forġife ġē, and ēow bið forġifen** narrowly translated is 'Forgive (ye), and to you (it) will be forgiven,' broadly translated is 'Forgive (ye), and you will be forgiven'; the singular verb **bið** and plural **ēow**, not to mention there being no overt subject in that clause, make clear the difference between Old English and Modern English constructions of this kind. (*OES* 744–858)

C. The only remnant of an independent passive in Old English is the verb **hātte** 'is (or was) called/named' (plural **hātton**).

Saga hwæt iċ hātte.	Say what I am called. [A riddle tag]
Cwæþ þæt se hēhsta hātan sceolde Satan siððan.	Said that the highest should be called Satan afterwards.
And se munuc hātte Abbo.	And the monk was named Abbo.

When the agent of the action referred to by the verb root in a passive construction is expressed, it corresponds to the subject of a matching active construction. In Old English passive constructions a noun denoting the agent commonly is marked with a preposition preceding it—most commonly it is **fram**—although sometimes it is marked only by its oblique inflection; it is *not* in the nominative (subject) case.

Þǣr-to-ēacan wǣron swilċe wundra ġefremode þurh þone hālgan Swyðun.	Furthermore there were such miracles performed by St. Swithin.
Þurh sumne prēost hē wæs gelǣred tō Godes ġelēafan.	Through a certain priest he was persuaded to belief in God.
Þā hē þā ... tō Rome becwōm,... wæs mid dēaðe forgripen and þǣr fordferde.	When he ... had come to Rome,... he was seized with death and there departed (*or* died).
Se bysceop wæs forgripen mid wælhrēowe dēað.	The bishop was carried off by a cruel death.
Hē wearð ofslaġen fram his āgnum monnum.	He was slain by his own men.
Hē wæs ġelǣred fram ānum biscope.	He was instructed by a bishop.
Fram ðē iċ bēo ġenered.	By thee I shall be preserved.
Hēr Herebryht aldormon wæs ofslæġen from hæþnum monnum.	In this year aldorman Herebryht was slain by heathen men.
Fram þǣm þū lǣst wēnst, from þǣm þū bist beswicen.	By the one you least expect, by that one you will be deceived.
Hē onġeat þæt hē ġelufod wæs fram ðām mǣdene.	He perceived that he was loved by the maiden.
[Hī sǣdon] þæt hit drȳcræftum ġedōn wǣre.	They said that it had been done by sorcery.
Sum man wæs mid drȳcræfte bepǣht.	A certain man was deceived by magic.
Þā twelf apostolas þām ēcean Gode ġecorene wǣron.	The twelve apostles were chosen by eternal God.

From Ælfric's Grammar of Latin, on Active and Passive Verbs

Verbum is 'word.' ... *Significatio*
is 'ġetācnung'—hwæt þæt word
ġetācniġe. Ælċ ful-fremed word
[on lēden-sprǣċe] ge·endað on .o.
oððe on .or. On .o. ġe·endiað
actiua uerba (þæt synd 'dǣdlīċe
word'), þā ðe ġeswuteliað hwæt
menn dōð: *amo* 'iċ lufiġe,' ...
eall-swā *doceo* 'iċ tǣċe,' *lego*
'iċ rǣde,' *audio* 'iċ ġehȳre.' ...
Dō ǣnne .r. tō þisum wordum,
þonne bēoð hiġ *passiua* (þæt synd
'þrōwiġendlīċe')....
Þā word þe ġe·endiað on .o. ond
ne magon æfter andġite bēon
passiua, þā synd *neutra* ġehātene,
þæt is nāðres cynnes:
uiuo 'iċ libbe,' *spiro* 'iċ orðiġe,'
sto 'iċ stande,' *ambulo* 'iċ gange,'
sedeo 'iċ sitte.' Ne mæġ hēr bēon
nān *passiuum* on ðysum wordum,
for-ðan-þe heora ġetācnung ne
befylð on nānum ōðrum menn būton
on ðām þe hit cwyþ, swā þēah
sume of þysum neutrum maciað
passiuum on þām þriddan hāde,
nā tō mannum, ac tō ōðrum þingum:
aro 'iċ eriġe,' *aras* 'þū erast,'
arat 'hē erað.' Ne cweð nān
mann 'iċ eom ġe·erod,' ac on þām
þriddan hāde is ġecweden *aratur
terra* 'þæt land is ġe·erod';
bibo 'iċ drince,' *bibitur uinum*
'þæt wīn is ġedruncen';
manduco 'iċ ete,' *manducatur
panis* 'se hlāf is ġe·eten.'

Verbum is 'verb.' ... *Significatio*
is 'signification'—what the verb
may signify. Each complete verb
(in Latin) ends in *o*
or in *or*. In *o* end
actiua uerba (which are
'active verbs'), those that
show what people do: 'I love,'
... also 'I teach,'
'I read,' 'I hear.' ...
Put an *r* to these verbs,
then are they *passiua*
('passive')....
Those words that end in *o* and
may not according to sense be
passive, they are called *neutra*,
that is, of neither kind:
'I live,' 'I breathe,'
'I stand,' 'I walk,'
'I sit.' There may be here no
passive on these verbs,
because their signification
doesn't fall upon any other one
except on him who says it, even
though some of these neuters
make passive in the third person,
not for people, but for other
things: 'I plow,' 'thou plowest,'
'he ploweth.' No one says
'I am plowed,' but in the
third person is said *aratur
terra* 'the land is plowed';
'I drink,'
'the wine is drunk';
'I eat,'
'the bread is eaten.'

6.7 Imperative Constructions

Bebēodendlīċ ġemet. Þis ġemet sprecð forðwerd and næfð nānne præteritum, forþan-ðe nān man hæt dōn þæt ðe ġedōn byð; hē sprecð tō ōðrum and nā tō him sylfum, forþan-ðe ġehwā hæt ōðerne, nā hyne sylfne.	Imperative mood. This mood speaks forward and hasn't any preterite, because no one bids (someone) do what is done; he addresses another and not himself, because everyone commands another, not himself.

A. Second-person imperative constructions are the most common. Positive imperatives are illustrated first. (*OES* 883, 887–912 passim)

Iċ hæbbe þeġnas under mē, and iċ cweðe tō þissum, 'Gang!' and hē gæð; and iċ cweðe tō ōðrum, 'Cum!' and hē cymþ; tō mīnum ðēowe, 'Wyrċ þis!' and hē wyrċþ.	I have soldiers under me, and I say to this one, 'Go!' and he goes; and I say to a second, 'Come!' and he comes; to my servant, 'Do this!' and he does it.
Ġebindaþ hys handa.	Bind (ye) his hands.
Gāþ on ðā ċeastre.	Go (ye) into the city.
Biddaþ ond ēow bið ġeseald. Sēċeaþ ond ġē hit findað. Cnuciað ond ēow biþ untȳned.	Ask and to you (it) will be given. Seek and you will find it. Knock and to you (it) will be opened.
Hī cwǣdon, 'Hwār eardast ðū?' Hē cwæþ tō him, 'Cumað ond ġesēoþ.'	They said, 'Where do you dwell?' He said to them, 'Come and see.'
Ġemiltsa mē, Drihten, and ġehȳr mīn ġebed.	Pity me, Lord, and hear my prayer.
'Ārīs, nim þīn bed and gā'; ond se man nam his bed and ēode.	'Arise, take thy bed and walk'; and the man took his bed and walked.
Feoht wið þā þe wið mē feohtað.	Fight against those that fight against me.
Ġyf þū wylt bēon ful-fremed, gā and be-ċyp eall þæt þū āhst and sylle hyt þearfum, and þonne hæfst þū gold-hord on heofone; and cum and folga mē.	If thou wilt be perfect, go and sell all that thou hast and give it to the poor, and then thou shalt have treasure in heaven; and come and follow me.
Bēoð ġē under-ðēodde ēowrum worold-hlāfordum.	Be (ye) subservient to your earthly lords.

In negative second-person imperative constructions, **ne** immediately precedes the verb; **þū** or **ġē** usually occurs also, immediately following the verb. (*OES* 890–891, 913–914)

Ne sleh þū, Abraham, þīn āgen bearn.	Abraham, strike not thine own son.
Ne ondrǣd þū þē.	Fear not for thyself.
Ne ondrǣd ðū hine.	Fear him not.
Ne ondrǣde [*sic*] ġē ēow nān þing.	Fear not anything (*or* at all).
Ne ondrǣdaþ ēow.	Fear not for yourselves.
Ne bēoð ġē nū unrote, ac ġefēoþ mid mē.	Be not dejected now, but rejoice with me.
Ġif iċ ne wyrċe mīnes fæder weorc, ne ġelȳfaþ mē. Ġif iċ wyrċe mīnes fæder weorc and ġif ġē mē nellaþ ġelȳfan, ġelȳfað ðām weorcum.	If I do not work the works of my father, do not believe me. If I work my father's works, and if you will not (to) believe me, believe those works.

There are instances, chiefly in translations from Latin, in which the usual imperative inflection is replaced by -**e** with singular verbs, -**en**, -**on**, or -**an** with plural verbs.

Sunu mīn, hlyste mīnra worda.	My son, obey my words.
Ġehīere mē, Andrēas, and āræfna þās tintrego.	Hear me, Andrew, and endure these torments.
Ne wundrion ġē ðæs.	Marvel not at this.
And ġē nān ðingc ne hreppon on rēafe ne on fēo.	And touch no thing in the plunder or the goods.
Bēon ġē ġesunde.	(A salutation, literally:) Be (ye) healthy, Be (ye) sound.

B. Imperative constructions with plural first-person subject and those with either singular or plural third-person subjects are not marked by distinguishing verb inflections. First-person singular imperative constructions do not occur. (A special plural first-person imperative marked by **uton** will be illustrated separately.)

Ne ofslēa wē hine, ne wē hys blōd ne āġēoton.	Let us not slay him nor shed his blood.
Ġelȳfan wē on ūrne Drihten, and hine lufian, and his bebodu healdan.	Let us believe in our Lord, and love him, and keep his commandments.
Ne yldon wē nā from dæġe tō dæġe.	Let us not delay from day to day.
Lufian wē ūrne sceppend and hine herian.	Love we our creator and praise him.
Behealdan wē Godes Ælmihtiġes bisne.	Let us behold the example of Almighty God.
Fare wē on ġehende tūnas.	Let us go into the next towns.
Gā hē ūt.	He shall go out.
Hiġ hlyston him.	Let them hear them.
Bēon hī bēgen beworpene.	Let them both be cast down.
Sē ðe Godes ðeġn sīe, gā hider tō mē.	He who is God's servant, move hither to me.
Ġif hwā ēarran hæbbe, ġehlyste mē.	If anyone has ears, (let him) hear me.
Ne fare hē ūt.	He shall not go out.
Ne cumon ðā sacerdas nēah Drihtne, ðē-læs hī swelton.	Let not the priests come near the Lord, lest they perish.
Sē ðe hæfþ twā tunecan, sylle ðām ðe næfþ; and ðām ġelīċe dō, sē ðe mettas hæfþ.	He who has two coats, let him give to the one who hasn't (one); and let him do likewise for that one, he who has food.

Uton (**wuton**) with following infinitive constitutes a unique imperative construction, always first-person plural whether **wē** also occurs or not. **Uton** does not occur in negative constructions, except rarely in translation of Latin text. (*OES* 916–916a)

Ārīsað. Uton gān.	Arise, let us go.
Hē sǣde him: 'Cumað ond uton gān ... on wēste stōwe.'	He said to them: 'Come, let us go ... into a desert place.'
Uton tōbrecan heora bendas, and āweorpan heora ġeocu of ūs.	Let us shatter their bonds, and cast their yokes from us.
Uton nū āginnan in tō farenne tō þisses wīnġeardes weorc.	Let us now begin to fare into the work of this vineyard.
Uton sendan rāp on his swȳran and hine tēon þurh þisse ċeastre lanan, and þis uton wē dōn oþ þæt hē swelte.	Let us put a rope on his neck and draw him through the streets of this city, and let us do this until he dies.
Uton wē ðæt ġemunan.	Let us be mindful of that.
Wuton wuldrian weorada Dryhten.	Let us glorify the Lord of hosts.
Uton wē ... ġeþenċean and oncnāwan be þyses middanġeardes fruman.	Let us ... consider and understand the origin of this earth.
Uton ūrum Drihtne hȳran ġeorne and him þancas secgan ealra his ġeofena.	Let us earnestly serve our Lord and utter him thanks for all his gifts.
Uton āġifan ðǣm ēsne his wīf.	Let us restore to the man his wife.
Uton wē ārīsan and ācwellan þā apostolas.	Let us arise and kill the apostles.
Utan gangan on þissum carcerne.	Let us go into this prison.
Uton wyrċean hēr þrēo eardung-stōwa.	Let us make here three habitations.
Cumað nū ond uton niþer āstīgan ond heora ġereord þēr tōwendan.	Come now and let us go down and there confound their language.
And bringaþ ān fætt styriċ, and ofslēaþ, and uton etan and ġewistfullian.	And bring (ye) a fatted calf, and kill (it), and let us eat and feast.
Uton ġewyrċan mannan tō ūre anlīcnysse.	Let us make man in our (own) likeness.

6.8 Impersonal Constructions

A common construction incorporating certain verbs lacked a subject noun or pronoun, and the object of the verb, whether in accusative or dative case, typically preceded the verb in non-interrogative utterances. Translation into Modern English requires a subject, sometimes supplied by a word such as **it**, sometimes by transforming the object into a subject: **swā mē þincþ** 'as it seems to me,' **mē wlataþ** 'it nauseates me,' **Hyne þyrste hwȳlum and hwīlum hingrode** 'He thirsted at times and at times he hungered,' **ġif mē twēonaþ** 'if I doubt' ('if for me there is doubt'), **Hwī twȳnode þē** 'Why did it cause thee doubt?' The archaic **methinks** or better still the current colloquial ⋏ **seems to me** may stand as a near equivalent in Modern English to the Old English construction.

Constructions incorporating a form of **bēon** and an adjective are similar: **him bet wǣre** 'it would be better for him,' **þǣr þē lāþast biðʼ** 'where it will be most grievous to you.'

A complement of the verb in these constructions may be a prepositional phrase: **Ġyf mē æt enugum þingum twēonað** 'If I hesitate at anything.' A noun or pronoun complement is in genitive case, generally as a causative object: **swā ðæt him ðæs slǣpes ofþūhte** 'so that sleep was displeasing to him,' but **Hū mæġ þē nū twȳnian þæs ēċan lēohtes?** 'How are you able to doubt that eternal light?' Or a complement may be a **þæt**-clause (or, much less often, an infinitive construction): **Gode þā ofþūhte þæt hē man ġeworhte** 'It repented the Lord that he had made man' or in modern idiom, 'God regretted that he had made man.' (*OES* 1025–51; see also Michiko Ogura, *Old English 'Impersonal' Verbs and Expressions* (1986). An extensive review of recent scholarship concerning so-called impersonal constructions and verbs may be found in David Denison, *English Historical Syntax: Verbal Constructions* (1993), 61–102.)

Mē hingrode.	I hungered. (I was hungry.)
Ġif mē hingreð.	If I should hunger.
Siððan him hingrode.	Afterwards he hungered.
Hē sæġde þæt hine hingrede.	He said that he was hungry.
Þā ongan hine hingrian.	Then he began to hunger.
Cume tō mē sē ðe hine þyrste.	Let come to me the one who thirsts.
Swā hwām swā ðyrste, cume tō mē.	Whoever thirsts, let him come to me.
Ne þyrst þone.	That one shall not thirst.
'Mē hingrode ond ġē sealdon etan. Mē þyrste ond ġē mē sealdun drincan....' 'Hwænne ġesāwe wē ðē hingriendne ond wē ðē fēddon? þyrstendne ond wē ðē drinc sealdon?'	'I hungered and ye gave [something] to eat. I thirsted and ye gave me [something] to drink....' 'When did we see thee hungering and we fed thee? thirsting and we gave thee drink?'
Him twȳnode be hwām hē hit sǣde.	They were uncertain concerning whom he said it.
Hū þynċð ēow nū?	How does it seem to you now?
Ðēah monnum swā ne þinċe.	Though it may not seem so to men.
Mē ofþinċð þæt iċ hiġ worhte.	I regret that I wrought them.
Hwæt þinċð þē þæt þū sȳ?	What does it seem to you that you are?
Þā cwæð se cyncg, 'þē misþingð.'	Then said the king, 'You are mistaken.' ('You have the wrong idea.')
Þynċþ him ðæt hē næbbe ġenōg.	It seems to him that he hasn't enough.
Hine sceal on dōmes dæġ ġesceamian.	It will shame him on doomsday.
Him sceal sceamian ætforan Gode ælmihtigum.	It will cause him shame before God almighty.
Þē-lǣs ūs ġesceamiġe beforan þæs cynges dugoðe.	Lest we feel ashamed before the king's nobles.
Iċ wolde þæt þē sceamode swelċes ġedwolan.	I would that you would feel shame for such error.
Menn scamaþ for gōdan dǣdan swȳðor ðonne for misdǣdan.	People are ashamed for good deeds more than for misdeeds.
Hīe forscamiġe ðæt hīe eft swā dōn.	They are greatly ashamed that they do so again.

Ūs sceamað hit nū māre tō tellane.	It shames us now to recount it further.
Hēr is mīn se ġecorena sunu on þām mē ġelīcode.	Here is my beloved son in whom I am pleased.
Him ġelimpþ oft æfter heora willan.	Often it befalls them according to their wishes.
Hū lomp ēow on lāde, lēofa Bēowulf?	How did it come out for you on your journey, dear Beowulf?
Ġif hit ġeweorðe þæt folce mislimpe þurh here oðþon hunger.	If it should come about that it turns out bad for the people through devastation and famine.
Mīn swefen ðe mē mǣtte.	My dream that I have dreamed.
Ōðer swefen hine mǣtte.	He dreamed another dream.
Hwæt hine ġemǣtte.	What he dreamed.
Ġif [hē] secge ðæt him mǣtte swefen.	If he should say that he dreamed a dream.
Hit ġelamp þæt hine mǣtte.	It came to pass that he dreamed.
Hī hēr syngiaþ and hit him nō ne hrēowþ.	They sin here [in this world] and are not sorry for it.
Ġif ðū onġite ðæt him his synna hrēowan.	If thou perceive that his sins cause him regret.

Some of these verbs also occurred with 'personal' subjects: **Ġif iċ hyngre** 'If I hunger,' **Ēadiġe synd ġē ðe hingriað** 'Blessed are ye who hunger,' **Ġyf ġē habbað ġelēafan and ne twȳniað** 'If ye have faith and do not doubt,' **Sē ðe nā twȳnaþ on heortan his** 'He who doubts not in his heart,' etc.

Further, some verbs sometimes had **hit** as subject, apparently a late development in OE: *ningit* **hit snīwð** 'it snoweth,' *pluit* **hit rīnþ** 'it raineth,' **Hit him līcode** 'It pleased him,' **Ġif hē … cwyð, 'Hit mē ofþinċð,'** **forġyf hit him** 'If he says, "I repent it" (*or* "It causes me sorrow"), forgive him for it,' **Ne ofþingð hit ðē ġif iċ þus wer ġeċēose?** 'Doesn't it give you offence if I choose a man thus?' **Ðā ġelamp hit** 'Then it happened,' **Ġyf hyt ġelimpþ þæt hē hyt fint** (= findeð) 'If it happens that he finds it.'

PRONUNCIATION AND PHONETIC NOTATION

The phonetic symbols for vowels and consonants used in this firstbook for Old English are based on those of the International Phonetic Alphabet. This appendix brings all these symbols together and lists them with 'key word' illustrations from Modern American English whenever possible. Phonetic notation is by convention enclosed in square brackets, phonemic notation enclosed by a pair of virgules. (The symbols for all the sounds of Modern English can be found in any of the good collegiate dictionaries of English.) First, the vowels.

Phonetic Symbol	Modern English Key Word	Phonetic Notation	Old English Spelling	Editorial Symbol
i:	bee	[bi:]	i	ī
ɪ	bit	[bɪt]	i	i
ü:	(1)		y	ȳ
ü	(2)		y	y
e:	bay	[be:]	e	ē
ɛ	bet	[bɛt]	e	e
æ:	(3)		æ	ǣ
æ	bat	[bæt]	æ	æ
ɑ	bot	[bɑt]	a	a
ɔ	bought	[bɔt]	a	a
ɑ:	bah!	[bɑ:]	a	ā
ɒ	hot [British]	[hɒt]	o	o
o:	know	[no:]	o	ō
ʊ	look	[lʊk]	u	u
u:	new	[nu: nju:]	u	ū

[ə], as in **attack** [ətæk], is the neutral unstressed vowel.

(1) German **kühn, grün**.
(2) German **müssen**, French **reçu**.
(3) The [æ] sound lengthened.

Old English diphthongs are all 'falling'—that is, the onset carries the stress or syllable beat, and the following off-glide is toward a target point that is another part of the overall vocalic 'grid.' The phonetic notation represents the onset vowel and the target with two symbols; see 2.1 C. (Modern English has an entirely different set of diphthongs.)

The consonant symbols are the following.

Phonetic Symbol	Modern English Key Word	Phonetic Notation	Old English Spelling	Editorial Symbol
p	pip	[pɪp]	p	p
b	bib	[bɪb]	b	b
t	tote	[tot]	t	t
d	did	[dɪd]	d	d
k	kick	[kɪk]	c, k	c, k
g	gig	[gɪg]	g	g
m	maim	[mem]	m	m
n	noon	[nun]	n	n
ŋ	sing	[sɪŋ]	n	n
l	loll	[lɑl]	l	l
r	roar	[ror]	r	r
w	week	[wik]	p, u, uu	w
h	hit	[hɪt]	h	h
s	cease	[sis]	s	s
z	zones	[zonz]	s	s
f	fife	[faɪf]	f	f
v	valve	[vælv]	f, rarely u	f
θ	think	[θɪŋk]	þ, ð	þ, ð
ð	breathe	[brið]	þ, ð	þ, ð
x	(4)		h	h
ɣ	(5)		g	g
j	yet	[jɛt]	g	ġ
tʃ or č	chill	[čɪl]	c	ċ
dʒ or ǰ	edge	[ɛj]	cg, g	cg, ĝ
ʃ or š	shoe	[šu:]	sc	sc

(4) German **machen**, Johann Sebastian **Bach**.
(5) A voiced velar spirant. (North German **sagen**)

Appendix B

ALTERNATIONS IN FORMS AND SPELLINGS

Old English had a number of common variants in spellings and alternations of sounds within words. For someone learning the language these alternations and variants will be only troublesome and frustrating until the handful of regular underlying patterns are recognized—something on the order of the patterns that in Modern English relate **design** and **designate, tooth–teethe, denounce–denunciation, deride–derision, rite–ritual, strife–strive**, or **color–colour, center–centre**. This appendix illustrates the most common of these patterns by which, for instance, **ġeong** and **iung** 'young' or **þeġn** and **þēn** 'servant' can be recognized as the same word; or by which **fēores** and **mēares** are recognized as inflected forms of **feorh** 'life' and **mearh** 'horse'; or **scrȳdan** '(to) clothe' may be recognized as a verb incorporating the same root that occurs in **scrūd** 'clothing,' similar to the way **fēdan** '(to) feed' and **fōd** 'food' derive from a common root; or membership in Class 5 strong verbs is assigned to both **sprecan** '(to) speak' and **ġiefan** '(to) give.' Most of these variants are called **morphophonemic alternations**. The historical causes of these alternations are then assembled in chronological order at the end of this appendix.

The arrangement here is once again based on practical considerations of the initial efforts necessary to learn Old English. Less limited ways to use this kind of information have had remarkable development in the well established discipline historical phonology. Reconstructing phonological changes that preceded historical Old English is a subject in itself, one that is as interesting as it is demanding. More recent formulations purport to give an account of the 'phonological component' of the grammar of Old English conceived in the transformational-generative mode. The efforts to account in terms of a system of rules for so-called surface structure and corresponding phonetic representation constitute an enterprise separate from that of learning Old English. Be it that sufficient unto the day is the phonology thereof.

A systematic description of the historical changes that gave rise to most of these alternate forms and spellings, which aims to help students make sense of Old English phonology—and the 'professional' writings about it—is in Chapter 3, 'Evolution of Old English Phonology: The Major Early Sound Changes,' in Roger Lass, *Old English: A Historical Linguistic Companion* (1994).

Alternation of a and o

This is a spelling alternation before nasal consonant **m** or **n**.

mann	**monn**	'man'	**standan**	**stondan**	'(to) stand'
hand	**hond**	'hand'	**maniġ**	**moniġ**	'many'
bana	**bona**	'slayer'	**gangan**	**gongan**	'(to) go, walk'
land	**lond**	'land'	**and**	**ond**	'and'
fram	**from**	'from'	**gram**	**grom**	'fierce'

It also occurs in past tense singular forms of some Class 3 strong verbs.

bindan	'(to) bind'	**band**	**bond**	'(he) bound'
climban	'(to) climb'	**clamb**	**clomb**	'(I) climbed'
ġelimpan	'(to) happen'	**ġelamp**	**ġelomp**	'(it) happened'
onginnan	'(to) begin'	**ongann**	**ongonn**	'(he) began'

Alternation of a and æ

Historically, the following changes occurred in stressed syllables: **a** > **æ** unless followed by a nasal consonant (**m, n**); but also

æ > **a**, 'was retracted,' before consonantal **u** (spelled **w**),

æ > **a**, 'was restored,' in open syllable preceding a single consonant or geminate, followed by back vowel (**u, o, a**), and

æ > **a** and **a** > **æ** 'by leveling' within paradigms.

The principal change appears clearly in **a**-stem **se**-nouns and **þæt**-nouns (see 5.3 and 5.5).

se	stæf	þā	stafas	þæt	fæt	þā	fatu
ðæs	stæfes	þāra	stafa	þæs	fætes	þāra	fata
ðæm	stæfe	þæm	stafum	þæm	fæte	þæm	fatum
ðone	stæf	þā	stafas	þæt	fæt	þā	fatu

So	stæf	stafas	'staff, staves'		fæt	fatu	'vessel, vessels'
	dæġ	dagas	'day, days'		bæc	bacu	'back, backs'
	pæð	paðas	'path, paths'		bæð	baðu	'bath, baths'
	hwæl	hwalas	'whale, whales'	cf.	baðian		'(to) bathe'
but	cræft	cræftas	'craft, crafts'		baðode		'(he) bathed'

Here is an adjective declension with normal admixture of 'leveling.'

	Singular			Plural	
Masc	Fem	Neuter	Masc	Fem	Neuter
hwæt	hwatu, hwæt	hwæt	hwate	hwate	hwatu
hwates	hwætre	hwates	hwætre	hwætra	hwætra
hwatum	hwætre	hwatum	hwatum	hwatum	hwatum
hwætne	hwate	hwæt	hwate	hwate	hwæt

Like **hwæt** 'active, brave,' are **hræd** 'swift,' **sæd** 'sated,' **glæd** 'glad, courteous.'

The alternation also occurs in adjective comparison:

Uncompared **hwæt**	Comparative **hwætra**	Superlative **hwatost**
glæd	**glædra**	**gladost**

In addition, **a** > **æ** in a stressed syllable by a later phonological change of palatal mutation ('i-umlaut'). This was a part of a set of phonological changes conditioned by **ī** or **i** or **j** in the following syllable; the conditioning sound was subsequently either modified or lost.

This alternation is prominent within the **habban** '(to) have' conjugation.

	habban	'(to) have'	ic	hæbbe	'I have'
hīe	habbað	'they have'	hē	hæfð	'he hath'
	hafa	'have!'	hē	hæfde	'he had'

Strong verbs of Class 6 have alternation of **a** and **æ** in forms incorporating the non-past stem.

	faran	'(to) travel'		þū	fær(e)st	'thou goest'
hīe	farað	'they travel'		hē	fær(e)ð	'he travels'
	far	'go!'	but	ic	fare	'I (shall) go'

Like **faran** are **dragan** '(to) draw, drag' and **sacan** '(to) contend.'

Alternation of ǣ and ēa, and æ and ea

Historically, two processes of changes produced **ēa** and **ea** in the West Saxon form of Old English. In stressed syllables **ǣ > ēa** and **æ > ea** first by development of a vocalic glide, called 'breaking,' when followed by **h** or by **r** or **l** and another consonant, later by development of a vocalic glide from a preceding (syllable-initial) palatal consonant (**ċ, ġ,** or **sc**).

This alternation appears prominently in the past tense stem of strong verbs Classes 3, 4, and 5.

4	**beran**	'(to) bear'	**bær**	'(I) carried'	**bǣron**	'(we) bore'
	scieran	'(to) cut'	**scear**	'(I) sheared'	**scēaron**	'(we) cut'
5	**sprecan**	'(to) speak'	**spræc**	'(I) spoke'	**sprǣcon**	'(we) spoke'
	ġiefan	'(to) give'	**ġeaf**	'(I) gave'	**ġēafon**	'(we) gave'
3	**breġdan**	'(to) brandish'	**bræġd**	'(he) brandished'		
	weorðan	'(to) become'	**wearð**	'(it) became'		
	weorpan	'(to) throw'	**wearp**	'(he) threw'		
	ġieldan	'(to) pay'	**ġeald**	'(I) paid'		
	helpan	'(to) help'	**healp**	'(he) helped'		

With no limitation of the phonological change in word roots, there is consequently no alternation of these pairs of sounds in noun roots such as

(*scæft	>)	sceaft	'shaft'	(*scǣp	>)	scēap	'sheep'
(*ċæster	>)	ċeaster	'city'	(*ċǣce	>)	ċēace	'jaw'
(*ġæt	>)	ġeat	'gate'	(*ġǣr	>)	ġēar	'year'
(*mæht	>)	meaht	'might'	(*-x = -hs)		feax	'hair'
(*bærn	>)	bearn	'child'			fleax	'flax'
(*scætt	>)	sceatt	'treasure'			weax	'wax'

or in adjective roots such as **wearm** 'warm,' **heard** 'hard,' **eald** 'old,' or in verb forms such as **iċ sceal** 'I shall,' **þū scealt** 'thou shalt,' or **healdan** '(to) hold,' or in **ġēa** 'yea,' **eahta** 'eight,' **healf** 'half.'

Alternation of e and   eo, and e and ie

Historically, the 'breaking' that produced alternation of æ and ea and of æ and ea also produced alternation of e and eo, as in the infinitive of Class 3 strong verbs **weorðan** '(to) become' and **weorpan** '(to) cast,' beside **helpan** '(to) help.' Glide that developed in the vowel of a stressed syllable from articulation of a preceding palatal consonant **ċ, ġ,** or **sc** also produced alternation of e and ie, as in infinitives (and present tense forms) of strong verbs of Class 3 **ġieldan** '(to) pay,' beside **meltan** '(to) melt,' Class 4 **scieran** '(to) cut' beside **stelan** '(to) steal,' Class 5 **ġiefan** '(to) give' beside **tredan** '(to) step, traverse.'

Alternation of Single and Double Consonants

Historically, the principal source of alternation of single and double consonants in writing Old English was a lengthening of consonants in speech, usually called **gemination**; this was a phonological change occurring in West Germanic, well before the separate development of Old English. Every consonant except **r** which was preceded by a short vowel and followed by a consonantal **i** (often represented as **j**, a palatal consonant) was lengthened. The lengthened consonants of descendent forms in Old English were then spelled by double consonant letters. The **i** subsequently underwent further change, prior to the earliest records of Old English. (*OEG* 407–408; also 453–455)

The alternation of single and double consonants in spellings of Class I weak verbs shows up like this: **iċ fremme, wē fremað**, or **fremman fremede fremed**; see the full paradigm in 6.4. Less conspicuous is the alternation in **sellan** '(to) give' but **sealde**, or in **sċieppan** '(to) create' but **scapen.**

In adjectives of historically **ja**- or **jo**-stem classes, the alternation shows up for example as **midde, middum**, but **midre, midra** 'middle.'

At the end of a word lengthened and non-lengthened consonants (spelled double and single, respectively) did not contrast linguistically.

Alternation of ū and ȳ, and u and y

Historically, ū > ȳ and u > y in a stressed syllable by a process of palatal mutation, generally referred to as 'i-umlaut.' This was a part of a set of phonological changes conditioned by ī or i or j in the following syllable; the conditioning sound was subsequently either modified or lost.

Derivation from adjective **full** 'full' produced ***fulljan** '(to) fill,' which then evolved into **fyllan**. Both forms are related to **fyllu** 'fullness.' Or, with adverb comparison there is **tulge** 'firmly' beside **tylġ**, **tylġest** 'more, most firmly.' By word-derivation and by inflection the alternation shows up variously in this group of words:

cuman	'(to) come'	**iċ**	**cume**	'I come'
cyme	'advent, coming'	**þū**	**cymst**	'thou comest'
cuma	'comer, guest'	**hē**	**cymþ**	'he cometh.'

It also appears in declension of certain nouns: **þā cwōman wē tō sumre byriġ. Sēo burh wæs on midre þǣre ēa ... ġe·timbrod** 'Then we came to a certain fortified city. That city was build in the middle of the river.'

The alternation of ū and ȳ is conspicuous in singular-plural nominative forms of **mūs–mȳs** 'mouse–mice,' and of **lūs–lȳs** 'louse–lice.' The process of word derivation underlies ū ȳ alternations such as appear in this set of forms:

cūþ	'known'	**cȳþan**	'(to) make known'
hlūd	'loud'	**hlȳdan**	'(to) made a loud noise'
tūn	'enclosed place'	**tȳnan**	'(to) enclose, close'
scrūd	'clothing'	**scrȳdan**	'(to) clothe'
fūl	'foul'	**fȳlan**	'(to) foul, defile'
		fȳlð	'filth'
dūst	'dust'	**dȳstiġ**	'dusty'

The alternation also appears within conjugation of Class 2 strong verbs:

brūcan	'(to) use, enjoy	**þū brȳcst**	'thou usest'	**hē brȳcð**	'he useth'
lūcan	'(to) lock'	**þū lȳcst**	'thou lockest'	**hē lȳcð**	'he locketh.'

Alternation of o and e, and ō and ē

Historically, **o** > **œ** > **e** and **ō** > **œ̄** > **ē** in a stressed syllable by palatal mutation ('i-umlaut') when **ī**, **i**, or **j** occurred in the following syllable; the **ī**, **i**, or **j** subsequently was lost or in turn was changed.

There aren't many instances of alternation of these short vowels. The paradigm of **dohtor** 'daughter' has dative singular **dehter**, and **efstan** '(to) hasten' is related to **ofost** 'haste.' Normally, though, native words did not have **o** in word structures that produced the change **o** > **œ** > **e**, and there were very few loan words in Old English.

The alternation **ō** and **ē** is conspicuous in singular-plural (nominative) word-pairs **tōð–tēð** 'tooth–teeth,' **gōs–gēs** 'goose–geese,' **fōt–fēt** 'foot–feet' as well as **bōc–bēċ** 'book–books,' and **brōc–brēċ** 'covering(s) for the leg.'

Derivation underlies **ō** and **ē** alternations in such word-pairs as the following.

bōt	'compensation'	**bētan**	'(to) compensate (for)'
dōm	'judgment'	**dēman**	'(to) judge'
fōd	'food'	**fēdan**	'(to) feed'
cōl	'cool, chill'	**cēlan**	'(to) make cool'
sōfte	'softly'	**sēft**	'more softly'
sōhte	'(he) sought'	**sēċan**	'(to) seek'
sōð	'true'	**sēðan**	'(to) declare true'
wōd	'mad'	**wēdan**	'(to) be mad, rage'

Ġif iċ dēme, mīn dōm is sōð.   If I judge, my judgment is true.

Ne dēme ġe be ansyne, ac dēmað rihtne dōm.   Judge not by appearance, but judge righteous judgment.

The alternation is also conspicuous in singular present indicative forms of **dōn** '(to) do': **iċ dō**, **þū dēst**, **hē dēþ** (see 6.2).

Alternation of ā and ǣ

Historically, by an early phonological change ǣ > ā in West Saxon—ǣ 'was retracted'—when before **w** and when before a **p**, **g**, or **k** followed by a back vowel (**u**, **o**, or **a**), generally, but with a mixing of forms. From this there is the alternation in **mǣġ** 'kinsman' **magas** 'kinsmen,' and in the noun **slǣp** 'sleep' together with both Class 7 strong verb **slāpan** and Class I weak verb **slǣpan** '(to) sleep.'

In addition, ā > ǣ in a stressed syllable by palatal mutation ('i-umlaut'). Derivation underlies ā and ǣ alternations in such word-pairs as these:

hāl	'whole, sound'	**hǣlan**	'(to) heal'
		hǣlu	'health'
		hǣlþ	'health'
lār	'teaching, lore'	**lǣran**	'(to) teach'
swāt	'sweat; blood'	**swǣtan**	'(to) sweat; bleed'
brād	'broad, spacious'	**brǣdan**	'(to) broaden'
		brǣdu	'breadth'
stān	'stone'	**stǣnen**	'of stone'
ān	'one'	**ǣniġ**	'any'
sāl	'rope, cord'	**sǣlan**	'(to) fasten with cord'
hāt	'hot'	**hǣtan**	'(to) heat'
		hǣte	'heat'

Within present tense indicative conjugation of **gān** (see 6.2) are these instances of the alternation:

gān	'(to) go'	**þū gǣst**	'thou goest'
hīe gāð	'they go'	**hē gǣþ**	'he goeth'

Or within Class 7 strong verb conjugation, for example, **hātan** '(to) bid, command,' **þū hātest, hǣtst** and **hē hǣt(t), hāteþ**.

Alternation of a and e

Historically, **a** > **æ** > **e** in a stressed syllable by palatal mutation ('i-umlaut'). This alternation is conspicuous in the nominative case singular and plural forms **mann–menn** 'man–men.'

Derivation underlies the same alternation in the following word-pairs:

strang	'strong'	**strengþ(o)**	'strength'
		strengu	'strength'
wlanc	'high spirited, proud'	**wlenco, -u**	'high spirit, pride'

The same alternation occurs within these instances of adjective comparison.

lang	'long'	**lengra**	**lengest**
strang	'strong'	**strengra**	**strengest**

Alternation of e and i

This alternation is probably a product of palatal mutation **e** > **i**, but whatever the circumstance of the phonological change, **e** and **i** are commonly in alternation in present tense indicative verb conjugation. The 2nd and 3rd person singular forms regularly have **i** where **e** occurs in the other forms. For instance:

helpan	'(to) help'	**þū hilpst**	**hē hilpð**
beran	'(to) bear'	**þū birst**	**hē birð**
brecan	'(to) break'	**þū bricst**	**hē bricð**
cweðan	'(to) say'	**þū cwist**	**hē cwið**

Alternation of diphthongs īo io, īe ie, ēa ea, ēo eo, etc.

In West Saxon, **ēo** and **īo**, and **eo** and **io** 'had become equivalent in force'
as spellings 'by the time of the oldest manuscripts' (Campbell, *OEG* 296). Alternation also occurs between **īe** and both **ī** and **ȳ**, and between **ie** and both **i**
and **y**. For instance, **plīoh, pleoh** 'risk, peril'; **līoht, lēoht** 'light'; **fird, fyrd, fierd**
'army'; **ġehīran, ġehȳran, ġehīeran** '(to) hear.'

There are historical drifts and some phonological conditioning of choice
between given pairs of spellings, but there is in general a great deal of inter-
changeability. Hence the regularities of alternation that result from phonological
change do not appear as prominently or as extensively with these paradigms.
Feorr 'far' is related to **fierr** 'farther' and to **āfierran** '(to) expel, put away' (beside **āfeorran**), and present indicative inflection of **weorpan** '(to) throw, cast'
includes **þū wierpst** 'thou throwest,' **hē wierpþ** 'he throweth'; palatal mutation
io > ie is the ultimate source of this alternation. It also shows up in the singular-
plural contrasts (nominative) **fēond–fīend** 'enemy–enemies' and **frēond–frīend**
'friend–friends.' Palatal mutation is reflected in the **ēo** alternation with **īe** in
verb conjugations such as **ċēosan** '(to) choose,' **ċīest** 'he chooseth.'

More notable is the alternation **ea** and **ie**, resulting from palatal mutation
('i-umlaut'), that appears in derivationally related pairs of words such as the
following.

hleahtor	'laughter'	**hliehhan**	'(to) laugh'
eald	'old'	**ieldra**	'older'
beald	'bold'	**bieldan**	'(to) make bold'
		bieldu	'boldness'
earm	'poor, wretched'	**iermþ(o)**	'poverty'

Palatal mutation **ēa > īe** produced the alternation of these diphthongs in
a few very common words: **nēah–nīehsta** 'near–nearest,' **hēah–hīehra/hīerra**
'high–higher,' **ēaþ(e)–īeþ** 'easily–more easily.'

Alternation of -h- and -ø-

Historically, medial -h- was lost after a stressed vowel when it occurred between voiced sounds (either vowel or voiced consonant); normally there was 'compensatory lengthening' of the preceding vowel if it was short. This change occurred just before the time of the earliest records of Old English.

In nouns, a stem may have final -h but will lack medial -h- in forms with overt inflection.

feorh	'life'	beside	(*feorhes >)	fēores, etc.
mearh	'horse'		(*mearhes >)	mēares
feoh	'wealth'			fēos
eoh	'war-horse'			ēos
hōh	'heel'			hōs
scōh	'shoe'			scōs
þēoh	'thigh'			þēona

In adjectives, the same pattern is found with grammatical inflections as well as with comparative or derivational suffixes.

hēah	'high'	beside	hīerra	'higher'
			hēanis	'highness'
wōh	'twisted'		wōre, wōn	
			wōra	
			wōlíc	'wrong, perverse'
fāh	'hostile'		fā (nom. pl.),	
			fāra, etc.	

In strong verbs, syncopation of the unstressed vowel of the inflection for 2nd and 3rd person present tense indicative forms retained the -h- while in other inflectional forms this -h- was lost.

sēon	'(to) see'	þū sīehst	'thou seest'	hē sīehþ	'he seeth'
flēon	'(to) flee'	þū flīehst		hē flīehþ	
fōn	'(to) seize'	þū fēhst		hē fēhþ	
slēan	'(to) strike'	þū sliehst		hē sliehþ	

Alternation of V́ġ- and V-

Historically, in late West Saxon the spirant/glide ġ was lost between a stressed vowel and **d** or **n** or **þ**; usually there was 'compensatory lengthening' of the preceding vowel if it was short (that is, the consonant was vocalized). Thus the same word may appear in texts—or in the same text—spelled alternately.

reġn	**rēn**	'rain'	**þeġn**	**þēn**	'servant'
wæġn	**wǣn**	'wagon, wain'	**þeġnung**	**þēnung**	'service'
mæġden	**mǣden**	'maiden'	**þeġnian**	**þēnian**	'(to) serve'
sæġde	**sǣde**	'(he) said'	**friġnan**	**frīnan**	'(to) ask'
bræġd	**brǣd**	'(he) brandished'	**fræġn**	**frǣn**	'(I) inquired'
riġnan	**rīnan**	'(to) rain'	**liġ(e)ð**	**līð**	'(he) lieth'
iġl	**īl**	'hedgehog'			

Alternation of ġ and i

This is a spelling alternation for the consonant (not for a vowel).

iū	**ġiō, ġeō**	'of old'	**herian**	**herġan**	'(to) praise'
iung	**ġiong, ġeong**	'young'	**nerian**	**nerġan**	'(to) save'
iā	**ġēa**	'yea, yes'	**neri(ġ)end**	**nerġend**	'savior'
iūl	**ġēol**	'yule'	**werian**	**werġan**	'(to) defend'
iuc	**ġeoc**	'yoke'	**weri(ġ)end**	**werġend**	'protector'

Chronology of Principal Phonological Changes Affecting Old English

The history of the continuous and differential changes in the phonological systems of Indo-European languages has been reconstructed in detail, as a way of accounting for the systematic correspondences among the various language groups and among the individual languages within them. The patch of that history having direct usefulness to the learning of Old English concerns first some changes within West Germanic that eventuated in the phonology of Old English (as well as that of Old Saxon, Old High German, and others), and then some changes within Prehistoric Old English. The main changes whose effects are evident in the alternations described in this Appendix are listed here in chronological order: because knowledge of them depends on historical reconstruction rather than on contemporary documentation, the chronology can only be relative.

West Germanic Gemination

Within a word-stem, any consonant except **r** was lengthened when it was preceded by a short vowel and followed by **-j-**. Because length of a consonant was signified in writing by doubling the letter representing the consonant, the term 'gemination' has come to be used to label this change. (Some long consonants in Old English have other historical sources.)

Fronting of a to æ and Fronting of ā to ǣ

Within a word-stem **a** was changed to **æ** in a closed syllable (see 2.6), when followed by **h**, or in an open syllable followed by a single consonant and a front vowel. See 'Alternation of **a** and **æ**.' Similarly, **ā** was changed to **ǣ** except when followed by **w**, **p**, **g**, or **k** followed in turn by a back vowel. See 'Alternation of **ā** and **ǣ**.'

Shortening of Final Long Consonants

Length of a consonant became non-distinctive in the final position in a word: **mann** or **man** 'man,' **bedd** or **bed** 'bed,' **feorr** or **feor** 'far.'

Palatalization of West Germanic ʒ, k and their Geminates

At the beginning of a word-stem, one of these consonants was fronted in its articulation when followed by a front vowel or diphthong. This is the source of /ċ/ and the origin of many of the stems beginning with /ġ/ (**ċinn**, **ċeaster**, or **ġeard**, **ġēar**).

'Breaking' of Front Vowels æ, e, ǣ, i

Within a word-stem a simple front vowel developed into a diphthong by accretion of a vocalic glide when followed by **h** or by **r** or **l** and another consonant. See 'Alternation of ǣ and ēa, and æ and ea,' and 'Alternation of ē and ēo....'

'Diphthongization' of e, æ, ǣ by Initial Palatal Consonant

Within a word-stem, certain front vowels developed into diphthongs by accretion of a vocalic glide when preceded by a palatal consonant, **ċ** or **ġ**, or by the cluster **sc.** See 'Alternation of ǣ and ēa, æ and ea ' and 'Alternation of ... e and ie.'

Palatal Mutation ('i-umlaut')

The thoroughgoing set of changes described among the alternations of forms and attributed to palatal mutation perhaps can be summarized best in diagrammatic representation.

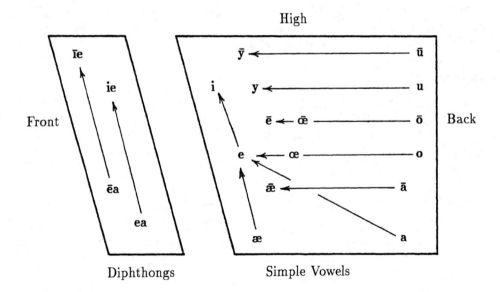

This is a considerable simplification of the general shifting of vowel qualities in word-stems when the succeeding syllable contained a palatal vowel ī or i or the palatal consonant represented as **j** (or as **i**); the mutation of the diphthongs, in particular, occurred only in West Saxon, and they in turn merged with simple vowels in many instances.

Syncopation of Vowels

Unstressed vowels—chiefly **e**, **i**, and **o**—were cut short enough ultimately to be eliminated in certain word patterns. The most important of these is in the unstressed syllables of verb inflections, so that **dēmest** > **dēmst**, **dēmeþ** > **dēmþ**, and the like. When the vowel of the inflectional syllable was **i**, it caused palatal mutation; but when it was lost between stem and inflectional consonants (or changed to **e** and then was lost), only the effect of its earlier presence remains in the alternation of stem vowels in such verb sets as **cuman cymst cymþ** or in **helpan hilpst hilpþ**. These are typically two-syllable words.

Typical of syncopation in three-syllable words is the loss of the vowel in the second of two syllables of a stem, falling as it does between the stressed stem vowel and the vowel of the grammatical inflection. This is the source of the morphophonemic variation in the stem of such words as **engel**, inflected as **engles**, etc., or **hālig** inflected as **hālgum**, etc.

Loss of Intervocalic h

This was a very late change in the prehistory of Old English word-stems, in which an **h** occurring between voiced sounds—either vowel or consonant—was lost. When the preceding stressed vowel was short, it usually became lengthened with the loss of the **h** consonant. See 'Alternation of -h- and -ø-.'

Because syncope occurred earlier than this change, the **h** that was lost in such forms as infinitive **seohan** > **sēon** '(to) see' remains in inflected forms as **siehst siehþ**.

Simplification of ie and īe to i and ī

This occurred within the historical period of Old English.

Merging of ȳ and ī and of y and i

With loss of phonemic distinction between /ȳ/ and /ī/ and between /y/ and /i/ the letters **y** and **i** used to represent these phonemes became interchangeable.

Loss of Postvocalic ġ

In a word-stem, $\dot{g}$ was lost between a stressed vowel and **d**, **n**, or **þ**. See 'Alternation of **V́ġ** and **V**.'

The consonant was also lost progressively in final position in a word, including the end of an unstressed syllable, most notably in the suffix **iġ** > **ī**.

POSTSCRIPT

'Grimm's Law' is the familiar label for a systematic shift among certain consonants that occurred in the Germanic branch of the Indo-European languages; it is so named because it is associated with a pioneering philologist Jakob Wilhelm Grimm. The more formal name is 'The First Germanic Consonant Shift.' The shift occurring in the Germanic branch alone makes its effects a distinguishing feature of the Germanic languages.

Grimm's Law formulates a simple and fundamental set of correspondences between phonemic structure of cognate words in Germanic languages in contrast to other Indo-European languages, **p** → **f**, for example, represented in Latin *piscus* beside Old English *fisc*, Latin *nepos*, Old English *nefa*; or **k** → **h**, or Latin *canem* beside Old English *hund* (Modern English *hound*). A lengthy summary can be readily found in Joseph Wright and Elizabeth Mary Wright, *Old English Grammar*, 3rd ed. (Oxford 1925), sections 229–237. It is represented in simplified diagrammatic form on p. 12.

'Verner's Law', named for Karl Verner, is the familiar name of another regular pattern of consonant alternation caused by historical change, in this instance conditioned by the placement of principal accent within words in early Germanic. The effects of this change on the structure Old English are noticeable in a several words—see, for example, p. 179 **ċēosan** and **forlēosan**, or p. 183 infinitive **weorðan** but past plural **wurdon**, or p. 189, **cweðan**. Briefly, this law accounts for apparent exceptions to the operation of Grimm's Law, by which (voiced) **f**, **d**, **g**, **r** occur where **f**, **þ**, **h**, **s** would otherwise be expected. A summary can be readily found in Joseph Wright and Elizabeth Mary Wright, *Old English Grammar*, sections 238–39.

NUMBER, GENDER, CASE

In Old English, nouns and pronouns are said to be 'inflected for number, gender, and case.' Adjectives are inflected for the same three grammatical categories, and according to two separate systems. The other principal constituents of noun-phrase constructions are said to be inflected for the same categories as well (they are called variously articles, demonstratives, designators, determiners, and the like). And so are first and second person possessive pronouns. Such formulations of the inflectional variations of nouns, pronouns, adjectives, and the rest have the value of any long-polished epitome. They also have the liabilities of in-group formulations, not to mention those of analytical obsolescence.

This appendix sets out some plain points about the morphological categories of number, gender, and case in the inflectional system for constituents of noun-phrase constructions, and explains grammatical government with each of them. The exposition of these categories is offered first in ordinary (lineal) verbal presentation, and then in the form of diagrammatic (two-dimensional) representation.

In conventional terms for describing this language, a noun-phrase (NP) part of any sentence (S) will be typically the subject of the sentence, a complement of a verb, or the complement of a preposition.

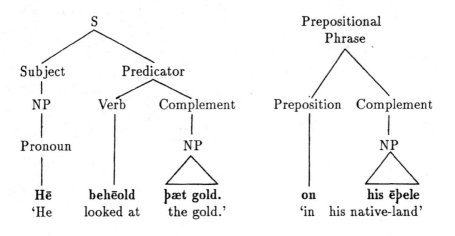

A noun-phrase typically has as its head a pronoun or a noun. If it is a noun, the NP may be expanded to include a designator, adjectives (and their modifiers), other NPs (as modifiers), possessive pronouns, or relative clauses— or any combinations of them.

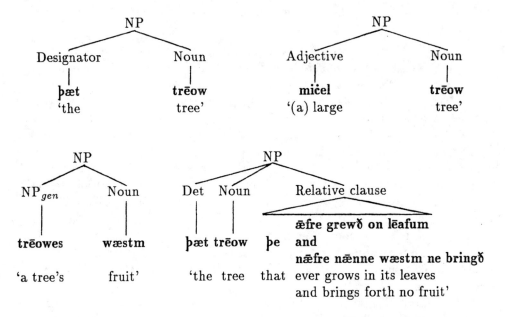

1. **Number** is one of the categories in the morphology of NP constituents. For nouns and much of the time for personal pronouns, number is not determined by syntax. Rather, selection of singular or plural (which is obligatory) is made on the basis of reference to something outside the grammar of the sentence. Or to put it the other way about, number selection of the grammatical inflection signifies a referential feature: the noun refers to one thing, or to more than one.

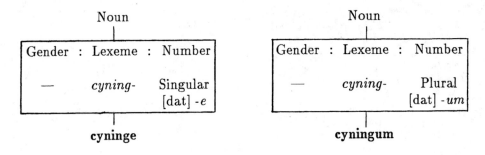

(The boxing and the colons signify that the constituents are all parts of a single word, and that all are present in every occurrence of a word that is the part of speech named above the box.)

When the number has been selected, of course, it may govern other elements of the sentence. The number of a noun selects the number of any designators and adjectives that are immediate co-constituents with it in a NP: **þes mōnað** 'this month,' **þās twelf mōnðas** 'these twelve months.' A pronoun or pronominal referring to a noun is also governed for number by the number of the noun (its 'antecedent').

Another obvious case is that of a noun that heads a Subject NP: its number governs the number category of the verb in the Predicator, as in singular **iċ wæs** plural **wē wǣron** 'I was,' 'we were'; singular **se cyning fōr of Rome** 'the king traveled from Rome,' plural **twēġen cyningas fōron of Rome** 'two kings traveled from Rome.' The horizontal arrow signifies the number of the Subject NP governing the number of the verb in the Predicator.

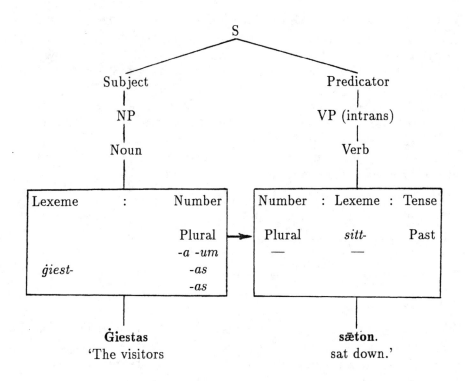

Also, any qualifier—'modifier'—that precedes a noun is governed for grammatical number by the number of the noun. (For Quantifiers see 3.B, below.)

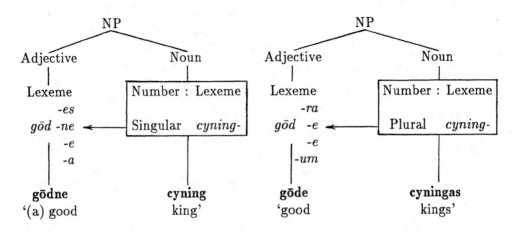

2. **Gender** is another category in the morphology of NP constituents. For Other (3rd person) pronouns, it is referential in respect to sex: a pronoun referring to a male person is one that is marked as masculine gender, one for a female person is marked as feminine gender, etc. Speaker and Addressee forms are not marked morphologically for gender. (See 3.1).

For nouns, gender is not selected, and it has no sexual reference. Rather, it is an inherent feature of any noun: **stān** 'stone,' **dæġ** 'day' are *masculine*; **lufu** 'love,' **niht** 'night' are *feminine*; **trēow** 'tree,' **wīf** 'woman,' **ċild** 'child' are *neuter*. As with number, gender will be represented with horizontal bracketing. (Number is omitted in the diagrams, to simplify them.)

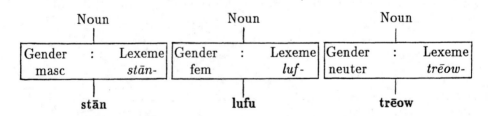

The pragmatic sense of the gender terms is defined entirely by the co-occurrence patterns in the syntax. For pronominals, designators, and adjectives, the gender is selected automatically—is 'governed'—by the gender of the noun which the form is directly linked to. (See 5.2.)

(A set of inflectional suffixes does not define the gender of a noun. The plural set -**as**, -**a**, -**um**, -**as**, for example, does not make a noun 'masculine,' although it may be a useful reminder of the gender of the noun. It partially defines a sub-type of masculine nouns (see 5.3, for instance).)

For pronominals, designators, and adjectives, on the other hand, grammatical selection of the gender class is a matter of grammatical concord solely (not one of (sex-)reference).

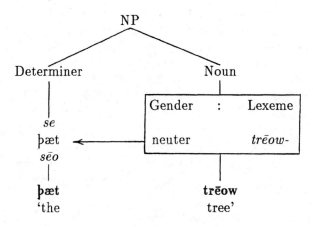

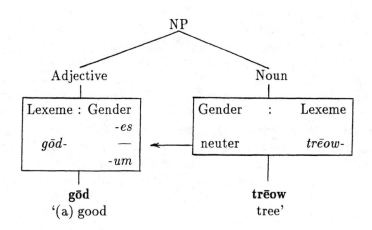

3. Case is the third category in the morphology of NP constituents, with a far more elaborate system of grammatical government than the systems for number and gender.

The terminology for the case categories almost universally is taken over from Latin grammar—nominative, genitive, dative, accusative cases chiefly, with instrumental and vocative often used as well. The scheme is useful, because the inflectional cases of Old English are generally limited in number to four (or rarely, to five). The terminology has such a long, extensive, and interlingual application as to be unexceptionable.

Misunderstanding often results, though, from asking 'What is nominative?' 'What is accusative?' and so on, in expectation of a simple statement of what the case *is* or what it *does*. Notional definitions, such as these two from Ælfric's Grammar, are of little help: **Nominatiuus is nemniġendlīċ: mid þām casu wē nemnað ealle þing, swilċe þū cweðe hic homo equitat 'þes mann rīt'** 'Nominative [in Latin] is "naming-like": with that case we name all things, as when you say "this man rides."' **Accusatiuus is wrēġendlīċ: mid þām casu bið ġeswutelod hū menn sprecað be ælcum þinge. Hunc hominem acuse 'Ðysne mann iċ wrēġe'** 'Accusative is "accusing": with that case is shown how people speak concerning each thing. "This man I accuse."'

Attempts to state what a case means, or what 'idea(s)' may be expressed by it, have always been partial and misleading; at best they take the form of listings—possessive, subjective, objective, partitive genitive, then genitive of measure, genitive of composition, genitive of material, and so on. But to say, for instance, that accusative case is used for the direct object of a verb is true enough, as **Ðysne man iċ wrēġe** has just illustrated; or **Hīe ġeflīemdon þone here** 'They put to flight that army.' Yet other verbs have single complements with genitive case inflection: **Hē āxode hine and fandode hys** 'He asked him and tested him'; **Fandiaþ þises goldes and ðissera ġymstāna** 'Test this gold and these gemstones'; **Hwæs anbīdie iċ, būtan þīn, Drihten?** 'Whom do I wait for but thee, Lord?' Objects of verbals have inflection in the same case that is called for by the lexical valence of the corresponding finite verb forms: **Hī āxodon hwæðer ālȳfð ænegum men his wīf forlætan, his þus fandiġende** 'They asked whether it was permitted for any man to put away his wife, thus testing him.' And other verbs have single objects with dative case inflection: **Hē folgude ānum burh-sittendan men** 'He followed [attached himself to] a citizen (of that land).' Some of these seem very like direct objects. In addition, accusative case inflection occurs regularly with objects of certain prepositions (see Section C) and with the subject of an infinitive: **Ðā ġeseah hēo licgan ðone hring on ðām weġe** 'Then she saw the ring lying on the path.'

A model emulating standard transformational grammar may also lead to confusion if it is based on Modern English. If it has this form—

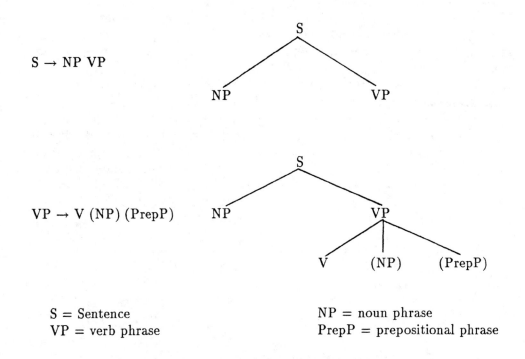

S → NP VP

VP → V (NP) (PrepP)

S = Sentence   NP = noun phrase
VP = verb phrase   PrepP = prepositional phrase

—then it will not begin to be useful until further rules specify all the ways any NP on the right (a complement of the verb) is distinguished from the NP on left (the subject) by the grammatical case of the pronoun or the noun (with its modifiers) that actualizes it. For learning Old English—and understanding its structure—probably the best approach is through syntax and lexicon together. (The historical developments that help in understanding this state of affairs are illustrated in 'The syntax of OE cases in historical perspective,' pp. 228–40, in Roger Lass, ed., *Old English: A historical linguistic comparison* (1994).)

Case is 'governed.' That is to say, grammatical case inflection is determined by relation of a case-inflected form to some other constituent of a sentence. For nouns and pronouns, the primary relation may be that of (a) complement of a finite verb, or (b) complement of a preposition. Or it may be (c) that of a noun or pronoun dependent on another noun, or (d) a noun dependent on a quantifier. Or it may be (e) the relation of a noun to a predicate adjective. Each of these types of case government will be described next.

A. A sentence in Old English regularly contains a 'finite' verb form, which is to say, a verb form inflected for tense, for mood, and for person and number. (This leaves aside response-sentences such as Ġēa, Nese, Niċ, Ðæs cāseres.) Most other elements may or may not occur in a sentence. Some are 'adjuncts,' which are optional in the syntax no matter how important they may be to the shading, the precision, or the tone of the utterance. The others are 'complements' of the verb form chosen, entailed by it.

To represent this aspect of the syntax of Old English, the diagrams that follow have as their centers the finite verb. The core verb—the lexeme for it, actually—is printed in large type. Above it is a heavy horizontal line linking all the elements of syntactic structure connected directly to the central ('finite') verb form. Above this line are the obligatory categories of inflectional variation of the verb: tense, mood, and person and number. Below it, together with the verb, are the verb's complements. For example:

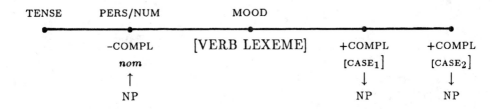

Nearly every verb occurs with -COMPL (the 'subject'). If the -COMPL is a noun or pronoun it is regularly nominative case. In any event, it also determines the person and number inflection of the finite verb (shown by an up-arrow).

There may be other complements of the verb in the more usual sense, typically 'objects' of transitive verbs, or 'complements' of copula verbs, as they are usually called. The verb lexeme determines which of these complements will occur in association with it. They are distinguished then as +COMPL. The verb also determines the case inflection if the +COMPL is headed by a pronoun or noun or adjective (shown by a down-arrow). A +COMPL may be in any of the four cases. The case transmitted by a verb to a +COMPL is fixed in the lexeme itself. That is why terms such as 'direct object' and 'indirect object' (among others) are not appropriate to describing morphosyntactic aspects of OE sentences. And that is why it is necessary for the diagrams regularly to include the case specification of any +COMPL with each verb lexeme.

The illustrations of case government in this section will be limited to simple declarative sentences.

The unmarked form of a noun or name is selected for nouns and names 'used in direct address'; these stand outside the syntactic structure of any predicating sentence. On the model of Latin grammar, they are said to be in vocative case. **Lēofe dohtor** 'Dear daughter,' **Menn þā lēofestan** 'Most beloved men.'

With 'intransitive' verbs (those without +COMPL), only the case of the subject (the -COMPL) is determined by the finite verb. It is nominative case: **Bēowulf maþelode** 'Beowulf spoke-formally'; **Se Hǣlend wēpte** 'The Savior wept.'

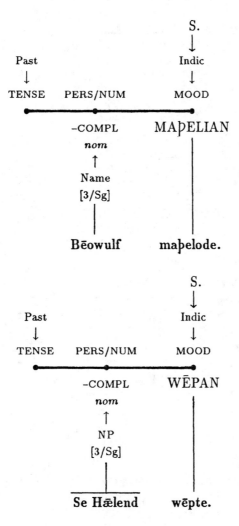

'Copula' (or 'linking') verbs select nominative case for both -COMPL and +COMPL: **Ić hit eom** 'It is I'; **Hē wearð fǣringa iung man** 'He suddenly turned into a young man.'

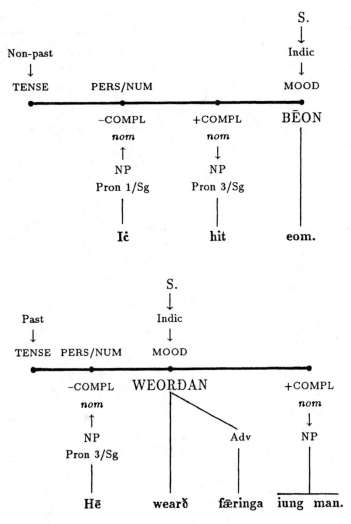

If the verb is 'transitive,' the case of the inflection for any +COMPL will be other than nominative. It may be accusative, as in **Ić hine cann** 'I know him'; **Hī lēofne ćēoseð ofer worldwelan** 'They choose the beloved (one) over worldly wealth'; **Ālȳs ūs of yfele** 'Deliver us from evil.' (*HSEL* 418 ff.)

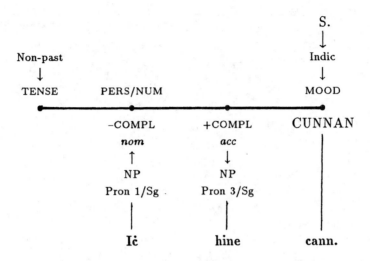

Or it may be dative, as in **Hē þancode Gode** 'He thanked God.'

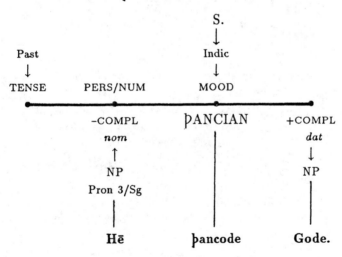

Verbs governing dative case complements gather into several sense-groups: serving or obeying (**folgian, hīeran, þēowian**), liking or disliking (**līcian, lāðian**); saying, confessing, cursing, etc. (**andswarian, ċīdan, bebēodan**); injuring or protecting (**derian, beorgan**); pleasing or its opposite (**līðian**), believing or trusting or their opposite (**trēowian, swīcan**), approaching (**nēalǣċan**), touching (**hrīnan**), and others. (*HSEL* 316–369)

Or it may be genitive, as in **Iċ ġe·feah þæs weorces** 'I rejoice-in that work.'
Fandiað ðises goldes 'Test this gold,' **Helpe mīn** 'Help me,' **God ūre helpe** '(May)
God help us'; or two of the Ten Commandments, **Ne ġewilna ðū ōðres mannes
wīfes** 'Desire (thou) not another man's wife,' **Ne ġewilna ðū ōðres mannes æhta**
'Desire (thou) not another man's goods.'

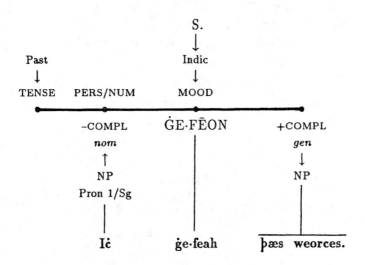

Many of the verbs governing genitive case complements share semantic features
of desiring, hoping, needing (**wilnian, ġiernan, hopian, behofian**); enjoying or
rejoicing or their opposite (**fæġnian, ġielpan, sargian, sceamian**); using (**brūcan**);
granting (**unnan**); acquiring or losing (**earnian, losian**); helping (**helpan**); testing
(**fandian, cunnian**), and others. (*HSEL* 378–91)

Genitive case complement of both verb **wilnian** and predicate adjective
ġeornful (derived from **ġiernan**), employed for rhetorical parallelism, still is
preserved in an early Middle English copy of an Ælfredian text: **ælċ þāra þe
hys wilnað and þe his ġeornful by[þ]** 'each of those who desire it and who is
yearnful [i.e., desirous] of it.'

If the verb is 'ditransitive,' the case inflections of the two +COMPL constituents are nearly always different from each other. (*HSEL* 676–698, *OES* 1092) For example, Accusative + Dative **Hē sealde his sweord þām cyninge** 'He gave his sword to the king'; Dative + Genitive **Hē þāra ġifena Gode þancode** 'He thanked God for the gifts' (the root **þanc–** governs case similarly when it occurs in a noun derivative: **Iċ ðæs þoncunge dō grēca heriġe** 'For that I do (i.e., give) thanks to the Greek army'); Accusative + Genitive **Hē hīe bereafade heora wǣpna** 'He deprived them of their weapons.'

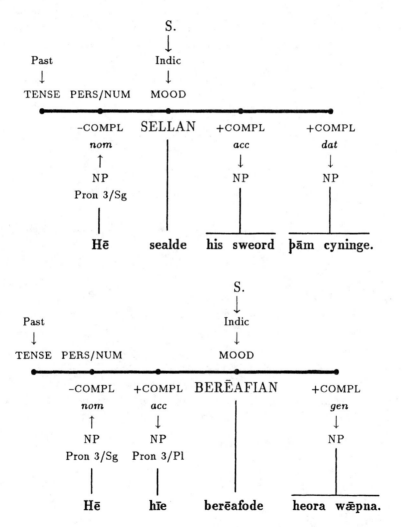

'Impersonal' verbs are an anomaly from the point of view of most verb-centered patterns: **Mē hingrode** 'I hungered.'

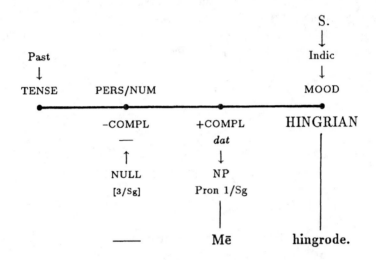

B.   Government of case by preposition is a structurally simple matter, because prepositions are single lexical items and any preposition governs directly the head of its complement: **[Hē] sette his hand ofer þāra wera ēagan** 'He set his hand on (the) eyes of the/those men'— **ofer** governing the case of **ēagan** but not the case of **þāra wera** (which is governed as shown in Section C, next).

Case governance with prepositions did not follow a one-for-one scheme over the historical span and geographical spread of Old English. Ælfric, for example, in reworking texts of his homilies after they had begun to circulate, changed case forms from dative to accusative frequently with **þurh** and several times with **ofer**. What follows therefore is a simple listing of the main prepositions and their characteristic case governance. (Tom Lundskaer-Nielson, *Prepositions in Old and Middle English* (1993), especially Chapter 2, is helpful on this.)

æfter 'after, along, according to'; with dative, usually.

ǣr 'before [time]'; with dative.

æt 'at, by, on, upon'; with dative, and accusative.

andlang 'along,' with genitive.

be/bī 'by, along,' with dative, and instrumental.

beġondan 'beyond'; with dative.

beheonan 'on this side of,' behindan 'behind,' beneoþan 'beneath,' be·ūtan 'outside'; all with dative.

betwēoh betwēonum betwēonan 'between, among'; with dative and accusative.

būtan 'without, except'; with dative, and accusative.

for, fore 'for'; with dative, and accusative.

fram 'from, by'; with dative, and instrumental.

ġeond 'through'; with accusative, and dative.

in 'in'; with dative, and accusative.

mid 'with'; with dative, and instrumental.

of 'from, away from, out of'; with dative.

ofer 'over, across, beyond, opposed to'; with accusative.

on 'on, in, among, (on)to'; with accusative, and dative/instrumental.

onġēan ongeġn ongēn 'opposite, against'; with dative, and accusative.

tō 'to, into, at, by'; with dative, usually.

tōweard, tō .. weard 'toward(s)'; with dative.

þurh 'through, during'; with accusative, usually.

under 'under'; with dative, and accusative.

wiþ 'towards, against'; with genitive, and accusative, and dative.

ymb 'about, around (a place), after (time)'; with accusative and dative.

Many of these prepositions have Modern English cognates with the same functions: fram dēaðe tō līfe 'from death to life,' þurh ðā duru 'through the door,' on ðone seofoðan dæġ 'on the seventh day.' But some have been replaced by other forms: Hīe ymb ðā gatu feohtende wǣron 'They were fighting around the gate'; Ealle þās þing [hē] sprǣc mid biġ-spellum ... and nān þing ne sprǣc būtan biġ-spellum 'All these things he spoke with parables, and no thing did he speak without parables.' Some have remained in the language but have changed meaning: ġif iċ ... him gulde yfel wið yfle 'if I ... should repay him evil for evil.' Of has split into two forms, Modern English of and off. And so on.

C. Another kind of government by syntactic structure alone is that of a nominal occurring within a noun phrase (NP), when it is an immediate dependent (rather than the head) of that NP. It is functionally adjectival, and in every instance it is marked by genitive inflection: **mīn fæder** 'my father,' **Bēowulfes sīþ** 'Beowulf's venture,' **ðæs cyninges þegnas** 'thanes of the king.'

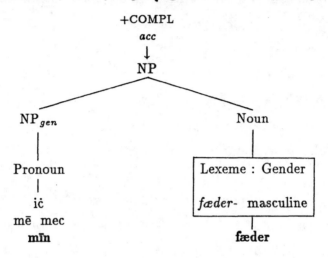

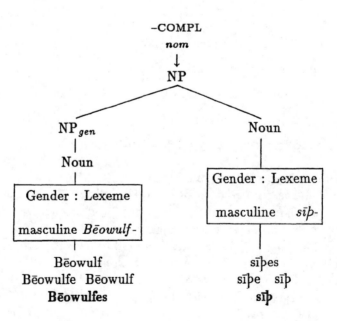

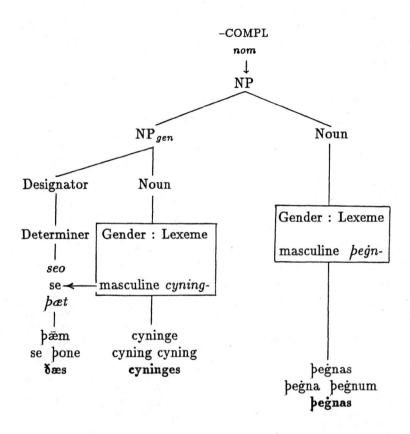

The same principle of government holds, of course, when there has been deletion of the head noun to eliminate unneeded repetition. **Hwæs sunu ys hē? ... Dauides.** 'Whose son is he? ... David's.'

Þā brōhton hī him [þone peniġ].
 Þā sǣde hē him, 'Hwæs is þēos anlīcnys and þis ġewrit?'
 Hī cwǣdon, 'Ðæs cāseres.'
 Ðā cwæð se hǣlend tō him,
 'Āġyfað þām cāsere þā þing þe þæs cāseres synd, and Gode þā ðe Godes synd.'

Then they brought him the penny.
 Then he said to them, 'Whose is this image and this inscription?'
 They said, 'Caeser's.' Then said the Saviour to them,
 'Give to Caeser those things which are Caeser's, and to God those which are God's.'

In the same way, any constituent modifier has the same genitive inflection as does that of the genitive noun which heads its immediate phrase: þæs
ælmihtigan godes sunu '(the) son of the-almighty-God'; ælċes libbendes mannes
mæġen ... is īdelnes 'the virtue of every living person is vanity.'

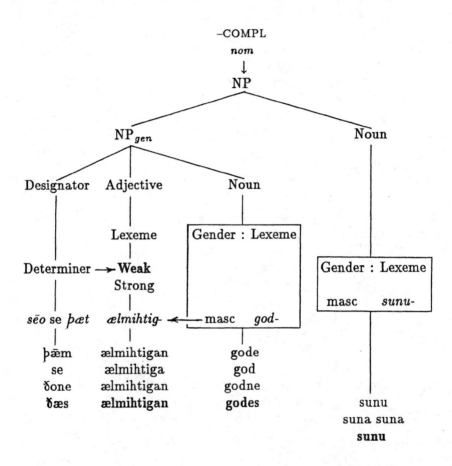

When a determiner occurs with the noun that heads a dominant NP, a dependent NP follows the head of that NP (rather than preceding it): **ġe·earnode him þā ġife Hālġes Gāstes** '(he) earned the gift of the holy spirit'; **þæt ġē cunnon ðā ġerȳnu godes rīċes** 'that ye may know the secrets of the kingdom of God'; **Se heofonlīca mete hæfde þā ġetācnunge ūres Hælendes Cristes, þe cōm of heofonum tō ūs** 'The heavenly food [manna] has the signification [i.e., symbolic meaning] of our Saviour Christ, who came from heaven to us.'

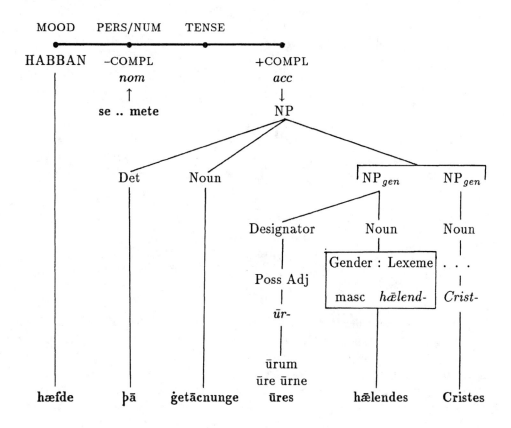

This pattern holds as well when the dominant NP has its head noun modified by a fraction adjective: **Se healfa dæl þæra prēosta** 'the half part [i.e., half] of the priests.'

However, a differing case inflection for a form preceding the noun in the
dependent NP marks it as not belonging to that dependent NP construction:
in **Ān sunu, mǣre meotudes bearn** 'One son, illustrious child of the Creator,'
the constituent structure is **mǣre ... bearn**, and not **mǣre meotudes**.

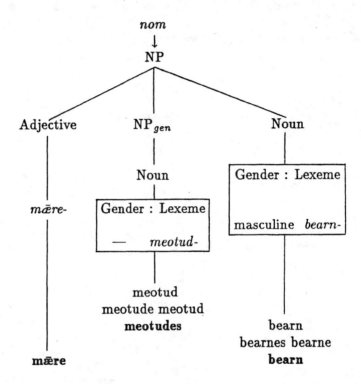

Not only is any nominal marked by genitive case inflection when it is a
dependent (rather than head) in a noun phrase, but any nominal dominated
in turn by such a dependent NP is also marked by its own (separate) genitive
inflection, as illustrated by one of the genitive forms being singular, the other
plural, in **Ēow is ġeseald tō witanne heofona rīċes ġerȳnu** 'To you is given to
know the secrets of the kingdom of the heavens,' and in **Đā slōh hyra ān þāra
sacerda ealdres þēow** 'Then one of them struck (the) servant of (the) chief of the
priests.' In Modern English the layering of the structure is similar, but reversed
in sequence and converted to phrasal (not inflectional) marking. (With both
dependent NPs in singular form, the pattern is the same: **on Godes mæġnes
swȳþran healfe** 'on the right side of the power of God.') Periphrastic genitive
(constructed with *of*) evolved only later in the history of English.

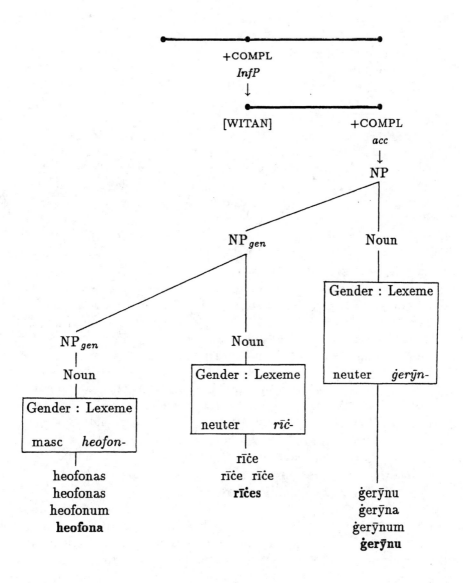

D. Another system of case governance involves quantifiers. Old English had a system of quantification within NP structure that has both syntactic and morphological features. It is embedded only in part in number inflection (singular, non-singular). Some of it is carried in sets of quantifying lexemes such as numerals: **fiftiġ scyllinga** 'fifty shillings,' **syxtiġ furlanga** 'sixty furlongs,' **þrēo and twentiġ stafa** 'twenty-three letters,' **þūsend wintra** 'a thousand years,' **ān hund daga and fiftiġ daga** 'one hundred fifty days,' **ān ðæra twelfa Drihtnes þeġena** 'one of the twelve servants of the Lord,' or in the fraction-words **healf** 'half,' **twæde** 'two-thirds, two of three parts.' It may be carried in collectives of number or enumeratives, such as **fela daga** 'many days,' **fēawa daga** 'a few days,' **hyra ælċ** 'each of them,' **ēower ælċ** 'each of you,' **hiera ān** 'one of them,' **ælċ þāra þinga** 'each of those things,' **ōþer twēġa** 'either of two (things).' (*OES* 1296–1299, 1332) Or in terms of degree or size **miċel** 'much,' **lȳtel** 'little.' Other aspects of quantification have expression in words for unit of measure—all nouns—of which there are many: **pund** 'pound,' **mancus** 'mancus, one-eighth of a pound,' **hȳpe** 'heap, large quantity,' and the like.

Yet another aspect is the distinction between quantity that is counted with numerals and quantity that is not. Any noun will name something conceived of as countable—**ċild** – **ċildru** 'child, children,' **hwæl** – **hwalas** 'whale, whales,' **fōt** – **fēt** 'foot, feet'—or as representing something conceived of as quantity that can be increased or diminished by measure other than number—**slæp** 'sleep,' **meolc** 'milk,' **ofermōd** 'pride,' **ġestrēon** 'property, treasure,' **seolfer** 'silver,' **gold** 'gold.' These types of nouns are commonly referred to as 'count nouns' and 'non-count nouns,' respectively. Any noun will carry one of these features, somewhat in the way it carries a feature of grammatical gender. The determination is made not by whether the speaker has counted what the noun refers to, but by whether quantity of what the noun names ordinarily is measured by counting.

The counting system begins from *one*. That is, any quantity greater than one, whether **siex** 'six,' **hundtwelftiġ** 'one hundred twenty,' **þridda healf** 'two and one-half,' **fela** 'many,' **fēawa** 'few,' requires the noun representing the things to be countable to have plural inflection. There is no counting 'backwards' from one in the numeral lexicon. *One* can be divided into parts, though, as with **healf, twæde, þridda dæl** 'half, two-thirds, one-third (a third part).'

The relations among these elements within NP-structure are interactive. First determination seems to be whether the thing being quantified is countable or not. If it is not, as for **gold**, the quantifier selected will be one that represents quantity that is measured in non-numerical terms: **pund** 'pound,' **mancus** 'mancus,' **hȳpe** 'heap,' **miċelnesse** 'abundance, quantity,' and the like: **ān pund goldes** 'one pound of gold,' **fela goldes** 'much gold.' If it is countable, as **pund** or **mancus**, **lēap** 'basket, leap,' or **dæġ** 'day,' **ċild** 'child,' etc., its quantifier will be a numerative lexical form, from the cardinal numerals (**fēower**, **tīen**, etc.), or of another type illustrated above. In any case, it is the NP of 'thing measured' that determines the type of quantifier immediately co-occurring with it in the NP. On the other hand the NP of 'thing measured' is dominated by the NP containing a quantifier, and is marked regularly by genitive-case inflection. For example, **fēower daga** 'four days' has this structure:

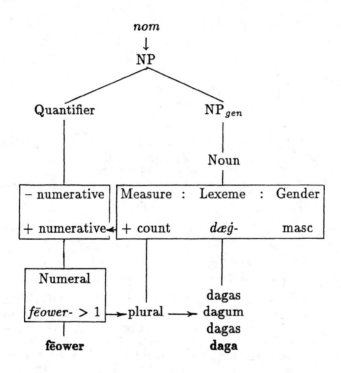

A bit more complex is the structure of **hundtwelftiġ punda goldes** 'one hundred twenty pounds of gold.' In this the NP of 'thing measured' is expressed by a 'non-count noun' *gold-*, and is quantified by a non-numerative noun *pund-*; but **pund** is at the same time a 'count noun,' so that it is quantified in turn by a numerative form **hundtwelftiġ**. Each of the nouns quantified is marked by genitive-case inflection, its number determined by its being 'count' or 'non-count,' and if 'count' whether its quantifier is greater than *one* or not. It is only the initial quantifier, then, that has its case marked by the governance of an element of the sentence lying outside the overall NP structure.

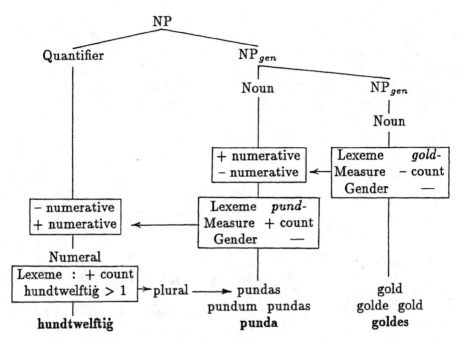

Both the quantifier and the noun of 'thing measured' may have dependent forms, as **for þǣre miċelnisse þæs goldes** 'because of the quantity of gold'; **and nam him þā gōd dǣl goldes and ġeband hit innen āne clāþe** 'and took for himself then a good share of gold and tied it in a cloth.' A quantitative form such as **hȳpe** 'heap, large quantity' is ambivalent for number, as the complement NPs show in **him tō brōhton goldes ... and ... ġymma unġerīme hȳpan** 'and (they) brought him an immeasurable quantity of gold and jewels.'

    E. Certain adjectives occurring as complements of **bēon** also govern their complements by marking them with genitive inflection: **hī bēoð grǣdiġ goldes** 'they are greedy for gold,' **ġeorn wīsdōmes** 'desirous of wisdom,' **orwēna līfes** 'despairing of life,' **wordes cræftiġ** 'crafty/skilful in words.' As the translations show, this pattern has been replaced in Modern English by phrasal constructions requiring a preposition. Typical adjectives in this construction are these (*OES* 197–210, 219):

ġesund	ormōd	orwēna	ēste	spēdiġ	earm	þearfa
cēne	brād	ġemyndiġ	ġeorn	dēop	cræftiġ	andbīdiġend.

Dative case complements of some other adjectives occurring as complements of **bēon** were also common in Old English: **þæt wæs monegum cūþ** 'that was known to many'; **bĭð him ēac uncūð hwæ̆ðer ...** 'it is also unknown to him whether ...'; **hit is swīþe uncūþ ūs eallum, hwænne ...** 'it is entirely unknown to us, when ...'; **hīe sint wilcuman Deniga lēodum** 'they are welcome to the people of the Danes'; **Sē wæs him dȳre** 'He was dear to them.' As the translations illustrate, this construction, too, has been superseded in Modern English by a pattern requiring a preposition to mark the complement; and while a complement in Modern English—whether for pronoun or noun—normally follows the adjective, the position was variable in Old English. (*OES* 192–219, *HSEL* 333–347)

Hē wæs lēof Gode.

He was dear to God.

Hē wæs eallum his ġefērum lēof.

He was dear to all his companions.

Gode is swīðe lēof ðæt ġē earmum monnum syllon.

It is very acceptable to God that you give to poor people.

Lēofre mē ys ðæt iċ hiġ sylle ðē ðonne ōðrum men.

It is more acceptable to me (or I would rather) that I give her to thee than to another man.

Ūs biþ ðonne lēofre ðonne eal eorþan wela ġif hē ūs miltsian wile.

It shall then be more desirable to us than (*or* we shall prefer it over) all the earth's wealth, if he will show mercy to us.

Sē wæs lāð Gode.
Ġif him is lāð tō dōnne þis.

He was loathsome to God.
If it is grievous to him to do this.

Him wæs lāð tō āmyrrene his āgenne folgað.

It was displeasing to him (*or* he was loath) to injure his own followers.

Þā ðe him ... lāðost wæron.

Those who were most hateful to him.

Hē wolde on eallum ðingum him ġehȳrsum bēon.

He wished to be obedient to him in all things.

Hē nāt hwæt him tōweard biþ.

He doesn't know what is in store for him.

And uton ġeþenċan, þæt ūs ys uncūð sēo tīd and sēo dæġ, þe wē sceolon þās lǣnan woruld forlǣtan.

And let us consider that to us is unknown the time and the day that we shall relinquish this transitory world.

Ðæt bið ēac swīðe hefiġ broc ðǣm lārēowe
ðæt hē scyle, on ġemǣnre lāre,
ðǣr ðǣr hē eall folc ætsomne lǣrð,
ðā lāre findan ðe hī ealle behofiġen;
forðǣm hira wanan bīoð swīðe unġelīċe.

Part Two

READINGS

HOW THE TEXTS HAVE BEEN PREPARED

Each text has been copy-edited differently in order to illustrate some significant aspects of the ways Old English texts may appear in print, and to match them to some differing pedagogical uses.

The first two, Ælfric's Sermon on the Nativity of Christ, and his homily on St. Edmund, are printed with punctuation resembling that of the manuscript sources. Although this punctuation does not provide the help with sentence structure that a beginner in Old English would find in modern punctuation for the text, the help is nonetheless available in the fully punctuated translation which runs parallel, virtually line by line: it can be transfered as needed, in the process of construing the Old English. Lineation of the Nativity Sermon is determined solely by the width of the text space and the size of the type, while for the homily on St. Edmund the lineation is that of the strings of words as they have been cast into rhythmic units by Ælfric. Both of these texts are based on *Ælfric's Lives of Saints, ... edited from Manuscript Julius E. vii in the Cottonian Collection ...,* ed. Walter W. Skeat, EETS 76, 82. A critical edition of the St. Edmund homily, with glossary, is provided by G. I. Needham, ed., *Lives of Three English Saints* (London 1966); a discussion of the editorial options—and rationales—for Ælfric's distinctive prose may be found in Paul Szarmach, 'Ælfric's Rhythmical Prose and the Computer Age,' in *New Approaches to Editing Old English Verse*, ed. S. L. Keefer and K. O'Brien O'Keefe, 95–108 (Cambridge, 1998). A very good website, which includes manuscript facsimile of the St. Edmund text, is **http://www.wmich.edu/medieval/rawl/edmund/index.html.**

For approximately the first half of The Legend of St. Andrew the translation is placed below the text, so that text (with translation) can be printed with the same line-division and page-division as that of the manuscript source on which this text is based. One can place the text beside the facsimile edition (cited in the headnote) to understand how a modern printed text compares to the original Old English text. The latter half merely presents the text spread to fill the size of the printed page. And because this text is highly repetitive in formulaic phrases, the latter half has been left untranslated. Punctuation throughout is modern. (The source for this text, like that for the remaining texts, is given in the headnote.)

Ælfric's homily on the creed is printed with punctuation resembling the manuscript source, and is given without translation: use of a dictionary will be the only help for reading this one.

The Harrowing of Hell has modern lineation and punctuation. Because of the extensive repetition of formulas and phrases, it is also given without translation. Paragraphing is used to signal only the onset and the end of the sweeping, seamless narrative of the harrowing.

Blickling Homily X, on the then soon-expected end of the world, is edited with punctuation, paragraphing, section numbers, and intervening blank lines that are altogether modern: they are modern conventions of textual presentation that record the editor's sense of the rhetorical structure of the homily and some of its elocutionary potentials. This homily is so highly charged for oral style (which is not to claim refinement for it) that it is left without translation in the hope that a reader's translating it will be no more than a step towards appreciating the text as it was composed in Old English—in keeping with the goal of this entire first-book of Old English.

A few of the printed characters vary from those in the grammar section. 'Insular g' (ᵹ ᵹ) is used regularly instead of **G g**. In the last prose text, Anglo-Saxon wynn (Ƿ ƿ) is not replaced by **W w**. In that same text the common abbreviation symbol þ (for þæt) is retained.

DECEMBER 25. THE NATIVITY OF OUR LORD JESUS CHRIST

Most beloved men, we told you sometime before how our Saviour Christ on this day was born in true human nature of the holy Virgin Mary. We now desire, nevertheless, for the honor of this day, to stir up your minds by spiritual teaching for your happiness, through (the grace of) God. There were certain heretics deceived by the devil, so that they said that Christ, God's Son, was not eternally dwelling with the Holy Father, but there was a certain (period of) time before He was born. But the holy Gospel has very often surpassed the understanding of such heretics. The Jews asked Christ who He was. He then answered them thus: *Ego sum principium qui et loquor vobis* 'I who speak to you am the beginning.'* Now you have heard how the Saviour spoke concerning Himself, that he is the Originator and Beginning of all things, (together) with His Heavenly Father and with the Holy Ghost. The Father is the Beginning, and the Son is the Beginning, and the Holy Ghost is the Beginning; yet they are not three Beginnings, but they are all three one Beginning, and one Almighty God, ever unbegun and unended. But that man is mad who wishes to have anything before a beginning; because, the Holy Trinity is the Beginning and the one Creator of all creatures, and no thing (ever) was or (now) is existing that the One Worker did not create. If any heretic or frenzied person should wish to inquire further and go beyond the beginning—with foolish presumption—he is like that man who raises up a high ladder, and climbs by the ladder's steps until he comes to the end; and desires to climb then yet higher: climbs then without the steps until without a (standing) place, he falls with a much worse fall as he further climbed.

There are three things on the earth: one is transitory, which has both beginning and end; such are beasts, and all soulless things which began when God created them, and afterward come to an end and turn to nothing. The second thing is eternal, so that it has beginning and hasn't an end; such are angels and souls of men, which began when God created them but they never end. The third thing is eternal, so that it has neither beginning nor end; such is the One

---

*John VIII.25. Ðā cwǣdon hī tō him, 'Hwæt eart þū?' Se Hǣlend cwǣð tō him, 'Ic eom fruma þe tō ēow sprece.'

UIII KALENDAS IANUARII . NATIVITAS DOMINI
NOSTRI IESU CHRISTI*

Men ðā lēofestan hwīlon ǣr wē sǣdon ēow hū ūre hǣlend crist
on þisum dæʒe on sōðre menniscnysse ācenned wæs of þǣm hālʒan
mǣdene marian · Nū wylle wē swā-þēah for ðyses dæʒes mǣrðe
ēower mōd mid þǣre ʒāstlican lāre onbryrdan ēow tō blisse þurh
5 ʒod · Sume ʒedwol-menn wǣron þuruh dēoful beswicene swā þæt
hī cwǣdon þæt crist ʒodes sunu nǣre [= ne wǣre] ǣfre mid þām
hālʒan fæder wuniende · ac wǣre sum tima · ǣr-þan-þe hē ācenned
wǣre · ac þæt hāliʒe ʒodspell hæfð ofer-swīðod swylċera ʒedwolena
andʒit for-oft · Þā iūdēiscan āxodon crist hwæt hē wǣre · Ðā and-
10 wyrde hē him þus · Ego sum principium · qui et loquor uobis ·
Iċ eom anʒinn · þe ēow tō sprece · Nū ʒē habbað ʒehēred hū se
hǣlend be him sylfum sprǣc · þæt hē is ordfruma · and anʒin ealra
þinʒa · mid his heofonlīcan fæder · and mid þām hālʒan ʒāste · Se
fæder is anʒin · and se sunu is anʒin · and se hālʒa ʒāst is anʒin ·
15 ac hī ne synd nā þrēo anʒinnu · ac hī ealle þrȳ syndon ān anʒin ·
and ān ælmihtiʒ ʒod ǣfre unbeʒunnen · and unʒe·endod · ac se man
wēt þe wyle habban ǣniʒ þinʒ ǣr anʒinne · for-þan-ðe sēo hāliʒe
þrynnes · is anʒinn · and ān scyppend ealra ʒesceafta and nān þinʒ
næs ne nys wuniende þe se ān wyrhta ne ʒescēope; Ʒif hwylċ ʒedwola ·
20 oððe āwoffod man · wyle furðor smēaʒan and þæt anʒinn ofer-stīʒan ·
mid dysilīċere dyrstiʒnesse · þonne bið hē þām men ʒelīċ þe ārǣrþ
sume hēaʒe hlǣddre · and stīhð be þǣre hlǣddre stapum · oð-þæt hē
tō ðǣm ende becume · and wylle þonne ʒit stīʒan ufor · āstīhð þonne
būton stapum · oð-þæt hē stedelēas fylþ mid mycclum wyrsan fylle swā
25 hē furðor stāh · Ðrēo þinʒ synd on middan-earde · ān is hwīlwendlīc ·
þe hæfð ǣʒðer ʒe ord-fruman ʒe ende · þæt synd nȳtenu · and
ealle sāwul-lēase þinʒ þe on-ʒunnon þā þā hī ʒod ʒescēop · and eft
ʒe·endiað and tō nāhte ʒewurðaþ · Ōðer þinʒ is ēċe · swā þæt hit
hæfð ord-fruman · and næfð nǣnne ende · þæt synd enʒlas and manna
30 sāula · þe onʒunnon ðā þā hī ʒod ʒescēop · ac hī ne ʒe·endiað nǣfre ·
Ðridde þinʒ is ēċe · swā þæt hit næfð nāðor ne ord-fruman ne ende ·

---

*Several spellings in this text have been normalized without notice.

Almighty God in Trinity, and in Unity, continuing ever inscrutable and
unspeakable. The Father is the Beginning, of none other; and the Son
is the Beginning, eternally begotten of the Father; and the Holy Ghost
is the Beginning, eternally of the Father and of the Son, not begotten,
but proceeding; because the Son is the Father's Wisdom, of Him, and
with Him; and the Holy Ghost is the Will of them both and the Love, of
Them both, and with Them both. In this one God we must believe, and
honor Him with (our) works, because all the holy books, both in the Old
Law and in the New, truly speak concerning the Holy Trinity and the
True Unity.

   This One Creator knows all things, and sees both that which has
been, and that which now is, and that which is to come; He no thing
forgets, nor may anything escape Him. He does not fear anything, because He has none more powerful (than Himself), nor even any equal to
Him. Ever He is giving, and He nevertheless does not diminish any
part of Himself, neither is anything needful to Him. Always He is
Almighty God, because He forever wills good and never evil, but He
hates the evil-doers and the unrighteous. The creatures whom this one
Creator created are manifold, and of various form, and move diversely.
Some are invisible spirits, without body, as are the angels in Heaven.
Some creep on the earth, with the whole body, as worms do. Some go
on two feet, some on four feet; some fly with wings, some swim in the
waters, and yet they all are bowed down earthward, and thither [do
they] desire, either because it pleases them or because they needs
must; but man alone goes upright, which signifies that his thoughts
should be more upward than downward, lest the mind be lower than
the body; and that he ought to seek after the eternal life for which he
was created, rather than after earthly things, even as his stature
shows him.

   All these creatures have a beginning, and some also an end, as
we before said. But the true Creator has no beginning, because He
is Himself the beginning, neither created nor made. He made all
things, and continues always and forever [lit., ever, in eternity]:
nothing could make Him, because nothing was before Him; and if He
had been made, then had He never been Almighty God. Again, if any
witless man think that God made Himself, then we ask (him) how He
could have made Himself if He had not existed before? He was ever
unmade, and ever continues unending. We may wonder at Him, but we

þæt is se āna ælmihtiᵹa ᵹod on þrynesse · and on ānnysse · æfre
wuniende un-āsmēaᵹendlīċ · and un-āsecᵹendlīċ · Se fæder is anᵹin ·
of nānum ōðrum · and se sunu is anᵹin · æfre of þām fæder ācenned ·
35 and se hālᵹa ᵹāst is anᵹin · æfre of þām fæder · and of þām sunu ·
nā ācenned ac forð-steppende for-ðan-þe se sunu is þæs fæder wīsdōm ·
of him · and mid him · and se hālᵹa ᵹāst is heora beᵹra wylle · and
lufu · of him bām · and mid him bām · On ðisne ǽnne ᵹod wē
sceolon ᵹelēafan · and hine mid weorcum wurðian · for-þan-þe ealle
40 þā hālᵹan bēċ æᵹðer ᵹe on þære ealdan ·ǽ· ᵹe on þære nīwan sōðlīċe
sprecað be þære hālᵹan ðrynysse · and sōðre ānnysse · Þes ān scyppend wāt ealle þinᵹ · and ᵹesīhð ᵹe þæt ᵹedōn is · ᵹe þæt þe nū is ·
ᵹe þæt ðe tō-weard is · ne hē nān þinᵹ ne for-ᵹīt · ne him nān þinᵹ
æt-flēon ne mæᵹ · Ne on-dret hē him nānes þinᵹes · for-ðan-þe hē
45 næfð nænne riċċran · ne furðon nānne him ᵹelīċne · Symble hē bið
ᵹyfende · and hē ne wanað swā-þēah nān þinᵹ his · ne him nānes
þinᵹes nis nēod-þearf · Symble hē bið ælmihtiᵹ ᵹod · for-ðan-ðe hē
symble wyle ᵹōd · and næfre nān yfel · ac hē hatað þā yfel-
wyrċendan · and þā unriht-wīsan · Ðā ᵹesceafta þe þes ān scyppend
50 ᵹescēop syndon mæniᵹ-fealde · and mislīċes hīwes · and unᵹelīċe
farað · Sume sindon un-ᵹesewenlīċe ᵹāstas · būtan līċhoman swā swā
synd enᵹlas on heofonum · Sume syndon crēopende on eorðan · mid
eallum līċhoman · swā swā wurmas dōð · Sume ᵹāð on twām
fōtum · sume on fēower fōtum · Sume flēoð mid fyðerum · sume on
55 flōdum swimmað · and hī ealle swā-þēah ālotene bēoð tō þære
eorðan weard · and þider wilniað · oððe þæs-þe him lyst · oððe þæs-
þe hī beþurfon · ac se man āna ᵹæð ūprihte · þæt ᵹetācnað · þæt hē
sceall mā þenċan ūpp · þonne nyðer · þe-læs-þe þæt mōd sȳ neoðer ·
þonne se līċhoma and hē sceal smēaᵹan embe þæt ēċe līf · þe hē tō
60 ᵹesceapen wæs · swīðor þonne embe þā eorðlīcan þinᵹ · swā swā his
wæstm him ᵹebīcnað · Ealle þās ᵹesceafta habbað anᵹinn · and sume
ēac ende swā swā wē ær cwædon · ac se sōða scyppend næfð nān
anᵹin · for-ðan-þe hē is him sylf anᵹin · nā ᵹesceapen · ne ᵹeworht ·
Sē ᵹeworhte ealle þinᵹ · and wunað ·ā· on ēċnysse · Hine ne mihte
65 nān þinᵹ ᵹewyrċean · for-ðon-þe nān þinᵹ næs ær hē · and ᵹif hē
ᵹeworht wære ne wurde hē næfre ælmihtiᵹ ᵹod · Eft ᵹif hwylċ ᵹewyt-
lēas man · wēnð þæt hē hine sylfne ᵹeworhte · þonne āxie wē hū hē
mihte hine sylfne ᵹewyrċean ᵹif hē ær næs · Hē wæs æfre un-ᵹeworht ·
and æfre wunað un-ᵹe·endod · His wē maᵹon wundrian · and wē ne

may not, and must not, inquire further concerning this, if we would
not destroy ourselves. The sun which lights up the whole earth is
God's creature, and we can understand that its light is from itself,
(and) not it from the light; and the heat proceeds alike from the sun
and from its light. In such manner the Son of Almighty God is
eternally begotten of the Father, true light and true wisdom; and the
Holy Ghost is eternally of them both, not begotten, but proceeding;
and the Son alone took human nature, and on this day was born as
man, to the end that He might bring us to His kingdom. There is to any
man living in this mortal life nothing so needful as that he should know
the Almighty God by faith, and afterwards [know] his own soul.

　　We have often spoken to you of your faith concerning the Holy
Trinity. Now will we tell you something about your own souls, briefly
if we can. All the orthodox fathers who wrote God's teaching spoke
undoubtingly and agreed unanimously that God creates each man's soul,
and the soul is not of God's own nature. If it were taken from God's
nature, certainly it could not sin.

　　It is natural to man that he should love that which is good; who
is good but God only, who is supreme goodness, without whom no man
can have anything (that is) good? This goodness, from which comes to
us every good thing, we must continually love; but the love of this
goodness cannot exist except in the soul, and only that soul is nobly-
born that loves that from whom it came, who created it such that it
might have God's image and likeness in its understanding, and should
be worthy of this (thing), (namely,) that God should dwell in it.
Philosophers say that the soul's nature is threefold: the first part
in her is capable of desire, the second (capable) of anger, the third
(capable) of reason. Two of these parts beasts and cattle have (in
common) with us—that is, desire and anger; man only has reason and
speech and intelligence. Desire is given to man to desire that which
profits him, both in things needful and for everlasting salvation; then
if the desire be perverted, it begets Gluttony, and Lechery, and
Avarice. Anger is given to the soul to the end that it may be angry
against vice, and be subject to no sins,
for Christ said, 'Whosoever commits sins is the servant
of sins.' If anger be turned to evil, then from it come
Wrath and Sloth. Reason is given to the soul to direct
and govern its own life and all its deeds; from reason, if it be

70 maʒon · ne ne mōtan · nā furðor embe þis smēaʒan · ʒif wē nellað
   ūs sylfe for-pǣran · Sēo sunne þe on-līht ealne mid-eard is ʒodes
   ʒesceaft · and wē maʒon understandan þæt hyre lēoht is of hyre · nā
   hēo of þām lēohte · and sēo hǣtu ʒǣð of þǣre sunnan · and of hire
   lēohte ʒelīce · Swā ēac þæs ælmihtiʒan ʒodes sunu is ǣfre of þǣm
75 fæder ācenned · sōð lēoht · and sōð wīsdōm · and se hālʒa ʒāst is
   ǣfre of him bām · nā ācenned · ac forð-steppende · and se sunu āna ·
   underfēnʒ mennisc-nysse and on þisum dæʒe wearð tō menn ʒeboren ·
   tō-þī-þæt hē wolde ūs tō his rīce ʒefeccan · Nis nānum menn on ðisum
   dēadlīcan līfe libbendum nānes þinʒes · swā myċel nēod · swā him biþ
80 þæt hē cunne þone ælmihtiʒan ʒod mid ʒelēafan · and siþþan his
   āʒene sāwle : Wē habbað ēow oft ʒesǣd ēowerne ʒelēafan be þǣre
   hālʒan ðrynysse · Nū wylle wē ēow sum þinʒ be ēowre sāwle secʒan ·
   sceortlīce ʒif wē maʒon · Ealle þā ʒelēaffullan fæderas þe ʒodes lāre
   āwriton · sǣdon untwȳlīce · and ʒeþwǣr-lēhton on þām ānum · þæt
85 ʒod ʒescypð ælces mannes sāwle · and sēo sāwl nis nā of ʒodes
   āʒenum ʒecynde · Ʒif hēo wǣre of ʒodes ʒecynde ʒenumen ·
   witodlīce ne mihte hēo sinʒian · Þām men is ʒecyndelīc þæt hē
   lufiʒe þæt þæt ʒōd is · Hwæt is ʒōd būtan ʒode ānum sē þe is
   hēalīc ʒōdnisse · būtan þām ne mæʒ nān man nān þinʒ ʒōdes habban ·
90 Ðās ʒōdnysse wē sceolan simble lufian þe ūs ælċ ʒōd of-cymþ · ac
   þissere ʒōdnysse lufu ne mæʒ bēon būtan on þǣre sāwle · and sēo
   ān sāwul is æðel-boren þe ðone lufað þe hēo fram cōm · þe hī
   þyllīce ʒescēop þæt hēo on hire andʒyte habban mihte ʒodes anlīcnesse and ʒelīcnesse · and þæs wyrðe wǣre · þæt hyre ʒod on-
95 wunode · Ūp-wytan secʒað · þæt þǣre sāwle ʒecynd is ðrȳ-feald ·
   Ān dæl is on hire ʒewylniʒend-līc · ōðer yrsiʒend-līc · þrydde ʒe-
   scēadwīs-līc · Twēʒen þissera dǣla habbað dēor and nȳtenu mid ūs ·
   þæt is ʒewylnunʒe and yrre · Se man āna hæfð ʒescēad · and rǣd ·
   and andʒit · Ʒewylnunʒ is þām menn for-ʒifen tō ʒewilnienne þā
100 ðinʒ þe him fremiað tō nit-wyrðum þinʒum and tō þǣre ēcan hǣle ·
   Þonne ʒif sēo ʒewylnunʒ mis-went · þonne ācenð hē[o] ʒyfernesse ·
   and forlyʒr and ʒītsunʒe · Yrre is ðǣre sāwle for-ʒifen · tō-ðȳ-þæt
   hēo yrsīʒe onʒēan leahtres · and ne bēo nā synnum under-þēodd ·
   for-þan-ðe crist cwæð · ælċ þāra þe synna wyrċð · is þǣre synna
105 ðēow · Ʒif þæt yrre bið on yfel āwend · þonne cymð of þām un-
   rōtnisse · and ælmylnysse · Ʒescēad is ðǣre sāwle for-ʒifen tō
   ʒewyssienne and tō stȳrenne hire āʒen līf · and ealle hire dǣda ·

perverted, proceed Pride and Vainboasting. Reason, not the soul, waxes in children; and the soul increases in virtues, yet is it no larger than it was at the beginning, but becomes better, though it receives no bodily greatness.

The soul has (as we said before) in its nature a likeness to the Holy Trinity, in that it has memory and understanding and will. It is one soul, and one life, and one substance, which has in itself these things; and these three things are not three lives, but one, not three substances, but one. The soul, or the life, or the substance are considered by themselves (separately); and the memory, or the understanding, or the will, are considered relatively to certain things, and these three have unity amongst themselves. I understand that which I will to understand and remember, and I will that which I understand and remember. Wherever memory is, there is understanding and will.

Let us now consider the wonderful swiftness of the soul: it has so great swiftness that at the same time, if it so will, it contemplates heaven and flies over the sea, traverses lands and cities, and in thought disposes all these things in its vision; and as soon as it hears the name of the city that it knew before, so soon can it in thought create that city, whatsoever it be. So also, as to every other thing that it before knew or knew not, it can create them in the mind whenever it hears them spoken of. And so active is the soul, that even in sleep it does not rest; but when it thinks of the city of Rome it cannot at the same time think of Jerusalem, or when it is thinking about one thing it cannot at the same time think of another, but is busied with that one thing until that thought (shall) depart and another come.

Truly, God Almighty knows all things at the same time, and has all things in His presence, and they are ever in His sight, and never unknown to Him; and this is that which is said, that 'God is, everywhere, all things'; because all things that ever were, or now are, or those that are to come, they are all present to God's sight, not once but always. The soul truly is the life of the body, and the life of the soul is God.

If the soul leave the body, then the body dies, and if God leave the soul because of very-grievous sins, then it dies in its better part, so that it is lost to eternal life; but nevertheless it never comes to an end in (its) eternal punishment. This death betides it [the soul] if

Of þām ᵹescēade ᵹif hit miswent · cymð mōdiᵹnysse and ȳdel ᵹylp ·
ᵹescēad wexð on ċildrum nā sēo sāwul · and sēo sāwul þīhþ on mæᵹ-
110 enum · and ne bið nā-māre þonne hēo æt fruman wæs ac bið betere
ne hēo ne underfēhð līċhomlīċe myċelnysse · Sēo sāwul hæfð swā
swā wē ǣr cwǣdon on hire ᵹecynde · þǣre hālᵹan þrynysse anlīċnysse ·
on-þan-þe hēo hæfð ᵹemynd · and andᵹit · and wyllan · Ān sāwul
is · and ān līf · and ān edwist · þe þās ðrēo þinᵹ hæfð on hire · and
115 þās ðrēo þinᵹ nā synd nā ðrēo līf ac ān · ne þrēo edwiste ac ān ·
Sēo sāwul · oððe þæt līf · oððe sēo edwist · synd ᵹecwedene tō
hyra sylfra · and þæt ᵹemynd · oððe þæt andᵹit · oððe sēo wylla ·
bēoð ᵹecwedene tō sumum þinᵹa · ed-lesendlīċe · and þās ðrēo þinᵹ
habbað ānnysse him betwȳnan · Iċ underᵹyte · þæt iċ wylle under-
120 ᵹytan and ᵹemunan · and iċ wylle þæt iċ underᵹyte and ᵹemune ·
þǣr þǣr þæt ᵹemynd bið · þǣr bið þæt andᵹyt and se wylla · Uton
nū behealdan þā wundorlīcan swyftnysse þǣre sāwle · hēo hæfð swā
myċele swyftnysse þæt hēo on ānre tīde ᵹif hēo swā wyle · be-
scēawað heofonan and ofer sǣ flȳhð · land · and burᵹa ᵹeond-fǣrð ·
125 and ealle þās þinᵹ mid ᵹeþōhte on hire sihðe ᵹeset · and swā
hraðe swā hēo ᵹehȳrð þǣre burᵹe naman · þe hēo ǣr cūðe · swā
hraðe hēo mæᵹ þā burh on hire ᵹeþōhte ᵹescyppan hwylċ hēo bið ·
Eal swā be ᵹehwylcum ōðrum þinᵹum þe hēo ǣr cūðe · oððe ne
cūðe · hēo mæᵹ on hire mōde ᵹescyppan · þonne hēo ᵹehȳrð be
130 þām sprecan · And swā styriᵹende is sēo sāwul · þæt hēo furðon
on slǣpe ne ᵹestylþ · ac ðonne hē[o] smēað be rōme byriᵹ ne mæᵹ
hēo þā hwīle smēaᵹan be hierusalem · oððe þonne hēo smēað be
ānum þinᵹ · ne mæᵹ hēo þā hwȳle be ōðrum þinᵹe smēaᵹan ·
ac biþ ᵹebysᵹod mid þām ānum ðinᵹe oð-þæt þæt ᵹeþōht ᵹe-wȳte ·
135 and ōðer cume · Witodlīċe ᵹod ælmihtiᵹ wāt ealle þinᵹ tōᵹædere ·
and ealle þinᵹ hæfð on his andwerdnysse · and hī ǣfre bēoþ
on his ᵹesihþe · and nǣfre him uncūþe · and þis is þæt ᵹecweden
is þæt ᵹod is ǣᵹhwǣr eall · for-ðan-ðe ealle þinᵹ þe ǣfre wǣron
oððe nū synd · oþþe ðā þe tō-wearde synd · ealle hī synd on ᵹodes
140 ᵹesihðe · an-wearde · nā ǣne · ac ǣfre · Sēo sāwul sōðlīċe is
þæs līċhoman līf · and þǣre sāwle līf is ᵹod · Ᵹif sēo sāwul for-lǣt
þone līċhoman þonne swelt [se] līċhoma · and ᵹif ᵹod for-
lǣt þā sāwle for or-mǣttum synnum · þonne swelt hēo on þām sēlran
dǣle swā þæt hēo bið for-loren þām ēċan līfe · and swā-þēah nǣfre
145 ne ᵹe·endað on þām ēcum wȳtum · Þes dēað hire ᵹelimpð · ᵹif

it allow desire and anger to rule in it, rather than reason, which
should always direct it to good deeds. Through that [faculty of] reason
alone we are better than the irrational beasts.

With two dignities Almighty God adorned man's soul, that is (to
say), with immortality and happiness: but it lost happiness when it
sinned; and (yet) immortality it cannot lose, because it shall never
end. The beauty of the soul is to have power so that it may turn aside
from evil; and it will be deformed through vices if it be subject unto
them.

The soul's powers are these four foremost and best ones.
Prudentia, that is, prudence, by which it must understand its Creator
and love Him, and discern good from evil. The second virtue is
Justitia, that is, righteousness [Justice], by which it must worship
God and live uprightly. The third virtue is *Temperantia*, that is,
moderation [Temperance], with which the soul must measure all things,
that it be neither excessive nor too slight, because it is written,
Omnia nimia nocent: 'All excesses [lit., things overdone] are
hurtful.' With certainty, moderation is the mother of all virtues.
The fourth virtue is *Fortitudo*, that is, strength or constancy, by
which the soul should, with steadfast mind, endure hardship for God's
love, and never yield to the Devil to its own destruction. These four
virtues have one crown, that is, the true love of God and Man, because
the soul is blessed that loves the Creator who created it and its
fellow-pilgrims, and [desires] to do good to them as it best may.

The soul is a rational spirit, ever quick [i.e., living], and is
capable of following either a good desire or an evil (one) according to
its own choice. The benevolent Creator lets it have the rule over its
own choice; then became it corrupt by its own free-will, through the
Devil's teaching. It shall again be delivered through the favor of
God, if it obey God. It is invisible and incorporeal, without weight
and without color, enveloped with the body, and dwelling in all the
limbs. It cannot by its own power depart out of the body, nor return
again except He who made it and sent it into the body should so will.

It is called by various names in books, according to its services
of deed. Its name is *Anima*, that is, soul, and the name befits its
life; and *Spiritus*, (that is,) spirit, which appertains to its
contemplation. It is *Sensus*, that is, perception or sensation, when
it perceives. It is *Animus*, that is, intellect, when it knows. It is

hēo lǣt rīxian on hire þā ȝewilnunȝe and þæt yrre · swīðor þonne
þæt ȝescēad þe hī ȝewȳsiȝan sceall tō wel-dǣdum ·ā· Ðuruh þæt
ȝescēad āna wē synd sēlran þonne þā un-ȝesceadwȳsan nȳtenu ·
Mid twām wurðscipum ȝeȝlænȝde se ælmihtiȝa scyppend þæs
150 mannes sāwle · þæt is mid ēċċnysse · and ēadiȝnysse · Ac hēo forlēas þā ēadiȝnysse þā ða hē[o] āȝylte · and hēo ne mihte þā ēċnysse
for-lēosan for-ðan-þe hēo ne ȝe·endað nǣfre · Ðǣre sāwle wlyte
is · þæt hēo hæbbe mihte · swā þæt hēo leahtres for-būȝe · and
hēo bið atolīċ þurh leahtras ȝif [hēo] him under-līð · Ðǣre sāwle
155 mihta syndon þās fēower fyrmestan · and sēlestan · prudentia ·
þæt is snoternysse · þurh þā hēo sceal hyre scippend understandan ·
and hine lufian · and tō-scēadan ȝōd from yfele · Ōðer mæȝen
is · Iustitia · þæt is rihtwīsnys · þurh þā hēo sceal ȝod wurðiȝan ·
and rihtlīċe libban · Ðæt ðrydde mæȝen is · temperantia · þæt is
160 ȝemeteȝunȝ · mid þǣre sceall sēo sāwul ealle þinȝ ȝemeteȝian · þæt
hit tō swīþe ne sȳ · ne tō hwonlīċe · for-ðan-þe hit is āwryten ·
Omnia nimia nocent · þæt is ealle ofer-dōne þinȝ deriað · Witodlīċe
ȝemeteȝunȝ is eallra mæȝenra mōdor · Ðæt fēorðe mæȝen is ·
Fortitudo · þæt is strenȝð · oððe ān-rædnyss · þurh þā sceal sēo
165 sāwul for-beran earfoðnysse mid ān-rædum mōde · for ȝodes lufan ·
and nǣfre þām dēofle ne ābūȝan tō for-wyrde · Ðās fēower mæȝenu
habbað ǣnne kynehelm · þæt is sēo sōðe lufu · ȝodes · and manna ·
for-ðan-þe sēo sāwul is ȝesǣliȝ · ðe þone scyppend lufað þe hī
ȝescēop · and hire ȝefēran · and him fremian [wile] swā hēo fyrmest
170 mæȝe · Sēo sāwul is ȝescēadwīs ȝāst · ǣfre cucu and mæȝ under-
fōn ȝe ȝōdne wyllan · and yfelne · æfter āȝenum ċyre · Se wēl-
willende scyppend lǣt hī habban āȝenes ċyres ȝeweald · þā wearð
hēo be āȝenum wyllan ȝewemmed þurh þæs dēofles lāre · Hēo
wearð eft ālȳsed þuruh ȝodes ȝife · ȝif hēo ȝode ȝehȳrsumað ·
175 Hēo is un-ȝesewenlīċ · and un-līċhomlīċ · būtan hefe and būtan
blēo · mid þām līċhaman befanȝen · and on eallum limum wuniȝende ·
Ne hēo ne mæȝ be hyre āȝenre mihte of þām līċhoman ȝewȳtan · ne
eft onȝēan ċyrran · būtan se wylle þe hī ȝeworhte · and on þone
līċhaman āsende · Hēo is on bōcum maneȝum naman ȝecȳȝed · be
180 hyre weorces þēnunȝum · Hyre nama is anima þæt is sāwul and [sē]
nama ȝelympð tō hire līfe · And spiritus ȝāst · belimpð tō hire ymb-
wlātunȝe · Hēo is sensus · þæt is andȝit · oððe fēlnyss · þonne hēo
ȝefret · Hēo is animus · þæt is mōd · þonne hēo wāt · Hēo is mens ·

Mens, that is, mind, when it understands. It is *Memoria*, that is, memory, when it remembers. It is *Ratio*, that is, reason, when it reasons. It is *Voluntas*, that is, will, when it wills anything; nevertheless all these names are one soul. Every soul is a spirit, but nevertheless every spirit is not a soul. The Apostle Paul distinguished between these names of spirit and mind, thus saying: *Psallam spiritu, psallam et mente.* That is, in English, 'I will sing with the spirit, and I will sing with the mind.' He sings with the spirit who utters the words with his mouth and understands not the signification of their meaning; and he sings with the mind who understands the signification of their meaning. The soul is the mistress of the body, and governs the five senses of the body, as from a royal throne. These senses are thus named: *Visus*, that is, sight; *Auditus*, hearing; *Gustus*, taste, with the mouth; *Odoratus*, smelling, with the nose; *Tactus*, touching, or feeling, with all the limbs but most usually with the hands. The soul directs these five senses according to its will, and it behoves it that, as a mistress, it should carefully consider (in advance) what it commands each limb to do, or what it permits to each limb as regards its natural desire, that nothing unseemly should befall in any limb's service.

Like as God Almighty excels all creatures, so excels the soul all created bodies by the dignity of its nature, and no bodily creature may be compared with it. We said before that it [the soul] was without color, because it is incorporeal. A body has color, and the soul will be adorned (according) as it has merited on earth: concerning this Christ spoke in His Gospel, *Tunc justi fulgebunt sicut sol in regno patris eorum.* That is, in English, 'Then shall the righteous shine as the sun in their Father's kingdom.' Verily, the wicked shall be like their own evil deeds.

It is not our breath [*spiritus*] or our soul that we blow out and draw in, but air, in which all bodily things live, except fishes alone that live in the waters. Often the soul is so busy about one thing or one thought, that it heeds not who may be near at hand, though it may be looking (at him); and though it hear a voice, it understands it not; though any touch it, it feels it not. Sometimes it sorrows for its body's pains, sometimes it rejoices in good fortune; sometimes it thinks of things that it knew before; sometimes it desires to know those things that it knew not before. Some things it wills, some things

þæt is mōd þonne hēo understent · Hēo is memoria · þæt is ʒemynd
185 þonne hēo ʒemanð · Hēo is ratio · þæt is ʒescēad · þonne hēo
tō-scæt · Hēo is uoluntas · þæt is wylla · þonne hēo hwæt wyle ·
Ac swā-þēah ealle þās naman syndon sāwul · ælċ sāwul is ʒāst ·
ac swā-þēah nis nā ælċ ʒāst sāwul · Se apostol paulus tōtwæmde
þæs ʒāstes naman · and þæs mōdes þus cweðende · Psallam spiritu
190 psallam et mente · Þæt is on enʒlisc · Iċ sinʒe mid ʒāste · and
iċ sinʒe mid mōde [·] Sē sinʒð mid ʒāste · sē ðe clypað þā
word mid mūðe · and ne understænt þæs andʒites ʒetācnunʒe ·
and sē sinʒð mid mōde sē ðe þæs andʒites ʒetācnunʒe understænt · Sēo sāwul is þæs līchoman hlæfdiʒe · and hēo ʒewissað
195 þā fīf andʒitu þæs līchaman · swā swā of cyne-setle · Þā andʒitu sint ʒehātene þus · Uisus · þæt is ʒesihð · auditus · hlyst ·
Ʒustus · swæc on þām mūðe · Odoratus · stenċ · on þæra nosa ·
tactus · hrepunʒ · oððe ʒrāpunʒ · on eallum limum · ac þēah ʒe-
wunelicost on þām handum · Ðās fīf andʒitu ʒewisseð sēo sāwul
200 to hire wyllan · and hyre ʒedafnað þæt hēo swā swā hlæfdiʒe · ʒeornlīce fore-scēawiʒe hwæt hēo ʒehwylcum lime bebēode tō dōnne ·
oððe hwæt hēo ʒehwylcum lime ʒeþafiʒe on ʒewylnunʒe his ʒecyndes ·
þæt þær nān þinʒ unþæslīce ne ʒelympe on nānes limes þēnunʒe · Swā
swā ʒod ælmihtiʒ ofer-stīhð ealle ʒesceafta · swā ofer-stīhð sēo
205 sāwul ealle līchamlīce ʒesceafta mid wurðfulnysse hyre ʒecyndes ·
and nān līchamlīċ ʒesceaft ne mæʒ bēon hyre wið-meten · Wē cwædon
ær þæt hēo wære būtan blēo · for-þan-ðe hēo nis nā līchamlīċ · On
līchaman bið blēoh · and sēo sāwul bið swā ʒewliteʒod · swā hēo on
worulde ʒe·earnode · Be þām cwæþ crist on his ʒodspelle · Tunc
210 iusti fulgebunt sicut sol in regno patris eorum · Þæt ys
on enʒlisc · þonne scīnað þā riht-wīsan swā swā sunne on heora
fæder rīce · Witodlīce þā ār-lēasan bēoð heora yfelum weorcum
ʒelīce · Nis sēo orþunʒ þe wē ūt blāwaþ · and in ātēoð oþþe ūre
sāwul ac is sēo lyft þe ealle līchamlīce þinʒ on lybbað · būtan
215 fixum ānum þe on flōdum lybbað · Oft bið sēo sāwul on ānum þinʒe ·
oððe on ānum ʒeþōhte · swā bysiʒ þæt hēo ne ʒȳmð hwā hyre ʒehende
bið · þēah-ðe hēo on-lōcie · ne þēah hēo sume stemne ʒehȳre ·
hēo hit ne understent · ne þēah hī hwā hreppe hēo hit ne ʒefret ·
Hwīlon hēo besārʒað hyre līchoman sārnissa · hwīlon hēo ʒladað on
220 ʒōdum ʒelimpum · hwīlon hēo þencð þā ðinʒ þe hēo ær cūðe · hwīlon
hēo wyle wytan þā ðinʒ þe hēo ær ne cūðe · Sume þinʒ hēo wyle ·

it wills not; and every form of corporeal things it can shape within
itself, and so shaped retain them in its mind.

The soul's beauty is that it may love wisdom; not that earthly
wisdom of which it is thus written, *Sapientia hujus mundi stultitia est
apud deum*: 'The wisdom of this world is foolishness before God.' But
this wisdom it should learn—that it love God and ever honor Him in all
its works, and learn those things which please God, and forsake those
things which are displeasing to Him. This wisdom is written of in Holy
Scripture, and it is said of it, *Omnis sapientia a Domino Deo est*:
'Every wisdom is of God.' Wherefore every man is happy and blessed
who is wise toward God, and if he order his deeds by the aid of wisdom.
Concerning this spoke blessed Job, 'Man's wisdom is righteousness, and
his true knowledge is to depart from evil.'

Certainly, that is true wisdom, that one desire the true life in
which he may live for ever with God in glory, if he merit it in this
world. To that may the dear Lord Christ bring us, he who is the true
Wisdom, and the Life of souls, he who with his Eternal Father and
with the Holy Ghost lives for ever and ever. Amen.

sume ðinȝ hēo nele · and ealle līċhamlicra þinȝa hīw hēo mæȝ on
hyre sylfre ȝehīwian · and swā ȝehīwode on hyre mōde ȝehealdan ·
Dǣre sāwle wlyte is þæt hēo wīsdōm lufie · nā ðone eorðlican wīsdōm
225 be þām þe þus āwriten is · Sapientia huius mundi · stultitia est
apud deum · Þysses middan-eardes wȳsdōm · is stuntnis æt-foran
ȝode · Ac þone wīsdōm hēo sceal leornian · þæt hēo lufie ȝod ·
and hine ǣfre wurðiȝe on eallum hyre weorcum · and þā þinȝ leorniȝe
þe ȝode līciað · and þā þinȝ forlǣte þe him lāðe syndon · Þes
230 wīsdōm is āwryten on hālȝum bōcum · and be ðām is þus ȝecweden ·
Omnis sapientia a domino deo est · Ǣlċ wīsdōm is of ȝode · Is nū
for-ðȳ ǣlċ man ēadiȝ and ȝesǣliȝ · sē ðe for ȝode wīs bið ·
and ȝif [hē] his weorc mid wīsdōme ȝefadað · Be þǣm cwæð se ēadiȝa
iōb · Þæs mannes wīsdōm is ārfæstnys · and sōð in-ȝehyd · þæt
235 [hē] yfel for-būȝe · Witodlīċe þæt is sōþ wȳsdōm · þæt man ȝewylniȝe
þæt sōðe līf on þām þe hē ǣfre lybban mæȝ mid ȝode on wuldre ȝif hē
hit on þyssere worulde ȝe·earnað · Tō þām ūs ȝelǣde se lēofa drihten
crist · sē ðe is sōð wȳsdōm and sāwla līf · sē ðe mid his ēċan fæder ·
and mid þām hālȝan ȝāste · ā on ēċnysse leofað · Amen ·

Nov. 20. PASSION OF ST. EDMUND, KING AND MARTYR

A certain very learned monk came from the south, over the sea, from Saint Benedict's Stow, in King Æthelred's day, to Archbishop Dunstan, three years before he died; and that monk was called Abbo. Then they were in conversation until Dunstan told (him) about Saint Edmund, just as Edmund's sword-bearer told it to King Athelstan when Dunstan was a young man, and the sword-bearer a very old man. Then the monk set down all this account in a book, and afterwards when the book had come to us within a few years, we turned it into English just as it stands hereafter. That monk Abbo then within two years went home to his minster, and was straightway appointed abbot in that same minster.

Edmund the blessed, king of the East Angles,
was wise and honourable, and ever glorified
by his excellent conduct Almighty God.
He was humble and devout, and continued so steadfast
5   that he would not yield to shameful sins,
nor in any direction did he bend aside his practices,
but was always mindful of the true doctrine
'[If] thou art made a chief-man, exalt not thyself,
but be amongst men as one of them.'
10   He was bountiful to the poor and to widows just as a father,
and with benevolence guided his people
ever to righteousness, and controlled the violent,
and lived happily in the true faith.
Then at last it came about that the Danish people
15   came with a fleet, harrying and slaying
widely throughout the land, as their custom is.
In that fleet were their foremost chief-men,
Hingwar and Hubba, brought together by the devil,
and they landed in Northumbria with their ships,
20   and wasted the land and slew the people.
Then Hingwar turned eastward with his ships,
and Hubba remained behind in Northumbria,
having won the victory by means of cruelty.

XII. KAL. DECEMBRES. PASSIO SANCTI EADMVNDI REGIS ET MARTYRIS

Sum swȳðe ʒelǣred munuc cōm sūþan ofer sǣ fram sancte benedictes stōwe
on æþelredes cynincʒes dæʒe tō dūnstāne ærċe-bisceope þrim ʒēarum ǣr hē
forð-fērde · and se munuc hātte abbo · Þā wurdon hī æt sprǣċe oþ-þæt dūnstān
rehte be sancte ēadmunde · swā swā ēadmundes swurd-bora hit rehte æþelstāne
cynincʒe þā þā dūnstān iunʒ man wæs · and se swurd-bora wæs for-ealdod
man · Þā ʒesette se munuc ealle þā ʒereccednysse on ānre bēċ · and eft ðā þā
sēo bōc cōm tō ūs binnan fēawum ʒēarum þā āwende wē hit on enʒlisc · swā
swā hit hēr-æfter stent · Se munuc þā abbo binnan twām ʒēarum · ʒewende
hām tō his mynstre and wearð sōna tō abbode ʒeset on þām ylcan mynstre ·

Ēadmund se ēadiʒa   ēast-enʒla cynincʒ
wæs snotor and wurðful · and wurðode symble
mid æþelum þēawum   þone ælmihtiʒan ʒod ·
Hē wæs ēad-mōd · and ʒeþunʒen · and swā ān-rǣde þurh-wunode
5 þæt hē nolde ābūʒan   tō bysmorfullum leahtrum ·
ne on nāþre healfe   hē ne āhylde his þēawas ·
ac wæs symble ʒemyndiʒ   þǣre sōþan lāre ·
[ʒif] þū eart tō hēafod-men ʒeset · ne āhefe þū ðē ·
ac bēo betwux mannum   swā swā ān man of him ·
10 Hē wæs ċystiʒ wǣdlum   and wydewum swā swā fæder ·
and mid wel-willendnysse   ʒewissode his folc
symle tō riht-wīsnysse · and þām rēþum stȳrde ·
and ʒesǣliʒlīce leofode   on sōþan ʒelēafan ·
Hit ʒelamp ðā æt nēxtan   þæt þā deniscan lēode
15 fērdon mid scip-here   herʒiende and slēande
wīde ʒeond land   swā swā heora ʒewuna is ·
On þām flotan wǣron   þā fyrmestan hēafod-men
hinʒuar and hubba · ʒe-ānlǣhte þurh dēofol ·
and hī on norð-hymbra-lande   ʒelendon mid æscum ·
20 and āwēston þæt land · and þā lēoda of-slōʒon ·
Þā ʒewende hinʒuar   ēast mid his scipum ·
and hubba belāf   on norð-hymbra-lande ·
ʒewunnenum siʒe · mid wæl-hrēownysse ·

Hingwar then came rowing to East Anglia
25 in the year that Alfred the atheling was one and twenty years old,
he who afterward became the renowned king of the West-Saxons.
And the aforesaid Hingwar suddenly, like a wolf,
stalked over the land and slew the people,
men and women, and witless [i. e., innocent] children,
30 and shamefully tormented the innocent Christians.
He sent then immediately to the king
an arrogant message, that he must bow down
to do him homage, if he recked of his life.
The messenger came then to King Edmund,
35 and speedily announced to him Hingwar's message.
'Hingwar our king, brave and victorious
by sea and by land, hath rule over many peoples,
and has landed here suddenly (even) now with an army,
that he may take up his winter-quarters here with his forces.
40 Now he commandeth thee to divide thy secret treasures
and thine ancestors' wealth quickly with him,
and thou be his under-king, if thou desire to live,
because thou hast not the power that thou mayst withstand him.'
So, Edmund then called a bishop
45 who was handiest to him, and consulted with him
how he should answer the savage Hingwar.
Then the bishop feared for this sudden misfortune,
and for the king's life, and said that it seemed best to him
that he should submit to that which Hingwar bade him.
50 Then the king was silent and looked on the ground,
and said to him at last even like a king,
'Behold, thou bishop, the poor people of this land
are brought to shame, and it were now dearer to me
that I should fall in fight against him who would possess
55 my people's inheritance.' And the bishop said,
'Alas, thou beloved king, thy people lie slain,
and thou hast not the forces that thou canst fight,
and these seamen will come and will bind thee alive,
unless thou save thy life by means of flight,
60 or thou protect thyself thus, that thou submit to him.'
Then said Edmund the king, full brave as he was;

Hinȝuar þā becōm   tō ēast-enȝlum rōwende ·
25 on þām ȝēare þe ælfred æðelincȝ · ān and twentiȝ ȝēare wæs ·
se̅ þe west-sexena cynincȝ   siþþan wearð mǣre ·
And se fore-sǣda hinȝuar   fǣrlīċe swā swā wulf
on lande bestalcode · and þā lēode slōh
weras and wīf · and þā unȝewittiȝan ċild ·
30 and tō bysmore tūcode   þā bilewitan cristenan ·
He̅ sende ðā sōna   syððan tō þām cyninȝe
bēotlīċ ǣrende · þæt hē ābūȝan sceolde
tō his man-rǣdene   ȝif hē rōhte his fēores ·
Se ǣrend-raca cōm þā   tō ēadmunde cynincȝe
35 and hinȝuares ǣrende   him ardlīċe ābēad ·
Hinȝuar ūre cyninȝ   cēne and siȝe-fǣst ·
on sǣ and on lande · hæfð fela [þ]ēoda ȝewyld ·
and cōm nū mid fyrde   fǣrlīċe hēr tō lande
þæt hē hēr winter-setl   mid his werode hæbbe ·
40 Nū hēt hē þē dǣlan   þīne dīȝelan ȝold-hordas ·
and þīnra yldrena ȝestrēon   ardlīċe wið hine ·
and þū bēo his under-kyninȝ · ȝif ðū cucu bēon wylt ·
for-ðan-þe ðū næfst þā mihte   þæt þū maȝe him wið-standan ·
Hwæt þā ēadmund   clypode ǣnne bisceop ·
45 þe him þā ȝehendost wæs   and wið hine smēade
hū hē þām rēþan hinȝuare   andwyrdan sceolde ·
Þā forhtode se bisceop   for þām fǣrlican ȝelimpe ·
and for þæs cynincȝes līfe · and cwæþ þæt him rǣd þuhte
þæt hē tō þām ȝebūȝe   þe him bēad hinȝuar ·
50 Þā suwode se cynincȝ   and beseah tō þǣre eorþan ·
and cwæð þā æt nēxtan   cynelīċe him tō ·
Ēalā þū bisceop   tō bysmore synd ȝetāwode
þās earman land-lēoda · and mē nū lēofre wǣre
þæt iċ on feohte fēolle · wið þām þe mīn folc mōste
55 heora eardes brūcan · and se bisceop cwæð ·
Ēalā þū lēofa cyninȝ   þīn folc līð of-slaȝen ·
and þū næfst þone fultum   þæt þū feohtan mæȝe ·
and þās flot-men cumað · and þē cucenne ȝebindað
būtan þū mid flēame   þīnum fēore ȝebeorȝe ·
60 oððe þū þē swā ȝebeorȝe   þæt þū būȝe tō him ·
Þā cwæþ ēadmund cyninȝ   swā swā hē ful cēne wæs ·

'This I desire and wish in my mind,
that I should not be left (behind) after my dear thanes,
who in their beds, with their bairns and their wives,
65   have by these seamen been suddenly slain.
It was never customary in me that I take flight,
but I would rather die, if I must,
for my own land; and almighty God knoweth
that I will never turn aside from His worship,
70   nor from His true love, whether I die or live.'
After these words he turned to the messenger
which Hingwar had sent to him, and said to him unafraid:
'Truly thou wouldest be worthy of death now,
but I will not defile my clean hands
75   with thy foul blood, because I follow Christ,
who hath so given example to us, and I will joyfully
be slain by you, if God hath so ordained.
Go now very quickly, and say to thy cruel lord,
Edmund will never bow in life to Hingwar,
80   to the heathen leader, unless he will first bow,
in this land, to Jesus Christ with faith.'
Then went the messenger quickly away,
and met on the way the bloodthirsty Hingwar
with all his army hurrying to Edmund,
85   and told that wicked one how he was answered.
Hingwar then arrogantly commanded his ship-forces
that they should all of them take the king alone,
who had despised his command, and instantly bind him.
So then King Edmund, when Hingwar came,
90   stood within his hall mindful of the Saviour,
and threw away his weapons: he intended to imitate
Christ's example, who forbade Peter
to fight with weapons against the bloodthirsty Jews.
So those wicked men then bound Edmund,
95   and shamefully insulted him, and beat him with clubs.
And afterward they led the faithful king
to an earth-fast tree, and tied him thereto
with hard bonds, and again scourged him
a long while with whips, and ever he called,

þæs iċ ȝewilniȝe   and ȝewisce mid mōde ·
þæt iċ āna ne belīfe   æfter mīnum lēofum þeȝnum
þe on heora bedde wurdon   mid bearnum · and wīfum ·
65 færlīċe of-slæȝene   fram þysum flot-mannum ·
Næs mē næfre ȝewunelīċ   þæt iċ worhte flēames ·
ac iċ wolde swīðor   sweltan ȝif iċ þorfte
for mīnum āȝenum earde · and se ælmihtiȝa ȝod wāt
þæt iċ nelle ābūȝan   fram his biȝ-ȝenȝum æfre ·
70 ne fram his sōþan lufe · swelte iċ · lybbe iċ ·
Æfter þysum wordum   hē ȝewende tō þām ærend-racan
þe hinȝuar him tō sende · and sæde him unforht ·
Witodlīċe þū wære   wyrðe sleȝes nū ·
ac iċ nelle āfȳlan   on þīnum fūlum blōde
75 mīne clænan handa · for-ðan-þe iċ criste folȝie
þe ūs swā ȝebysnode · and iċ blīðelīċe wille bēon
of-slaȝen þurh ēow · ȝif hit swā ȝod fore-sċeawað ·
Far nū swīþe hraðe · and seȝe þīnum rēþan hlāforde ·
ne ābīhð næfre ēadmund   hinȝware on līfe
80 hæþenum here-toȝan · būton hē tō hælende criste
ærest mid ȝelēafan   on þysum lande ȝebūȝe ·
þā ȝewende se ærend-raca   ardlīċe aweȝ ·
and ȝemētte be wæȝe   þone wæl-hrēowan hinȝwar
mid eallre his fyrde   fūse tō ēadmunde ·
85 and sæde þām ārlēasan   hū him ȝe·andwyrd wæs ·
Hinȝwar þā bebēad   mid bylde þām scip-here
þæt hī þæs cynincȝes ānes   ealle cēpan sceoldon ·
þe his hæse forseah · and hine sōna bindan ·
Hwæt þā ēadmund cynincȝ   mid-þām-þe hinȝwar cōm ·
90 stōd innan his healle   þæs hælendes ȝemyndiȝ ·
and āwearp his wæpna   wolde ȝe·æfen-læċan
cristes ȝebysnunȝum · þe forbēad petre
mid wæpnum tō winnenne   wið þā wæl-hrēowan iūdēiscan ·
Hwæt þā ārlēasan þā   ēadmund ȝebundon
95 and ȝebysmrodon huxlīċe · and bēoton mid sāȝlum ·
and swā syððan læddon   þone ȝelēaf-fullan cyninȝ
tō ānum eorð-fæstum trēowe · and tīȝdon hine þær-tō ·
mid heardum bendum · and hine eft swuncȝon ·
lanȝlīċe mid swipum · and hē symble clypode

100   between the blows, with true faith,
        on Jesus Christ; and then the heathen
        on account of his faith were madly angry,
        because he called upon Christ to help him.
        They shot at him with javelins as if for their amusement,
105   until he was all beset with their shots,
        as with a porcupine's bristles, even as Sebastian was.
        When Hingwar, the wicked seaman,
        saw that the noble king would not deny Christ,
        but with steadfast faith ever called upon Him,
110   then he commanded (men) to behead him, and the heathen did so.
        While he was yet calling upon Christ,
        the heathen drew away the saint, for slaying,
        and with one blow struck off his head;
        and his soul departed joyful to Christ.
115   There was a certain man at hand, kept by God
        hidden from the heathen, who heard all this,
        and told it afterward just as we tell it here.
        So then the seamen went again to ship,
        and hid the head of the holy Edmund
120   in the thick brambles, that it might not be buried.
        Then after a space, after they were gone away,
        came the country-folk, who were still left there,
        to where their lord's body lay without the head,
        and were exceedingly sore at heart because of his murder,
125   and chiefly because they had not the head with the body.
        Then said the witness who previously beheld it
        that the seamen had taken the head with them,
        and it seemed to him, even as it was quite true,
        that they had hidden the head in the wood somewhere about.
130   Then they all went together at last in the wood,
        seeking everywhere among the brush and brambles
        if anywhere they might find the head.
        Was also a great wonder, that a singular wolf was sent,
        by God's direction, for guarding the head
135   against the other animals by day and night.
        They went then seeking and continually calling out,
        as it is the wont of those who go often through woods,

100 betwux þām swinᵹlum   mid sōðan ᵹelēafan
   tō hǣlende criste · and þā hǣþenan þā
   for his ᵹelēafan wurdon   wōdlīċe yrre
   for-þan-þe hē clypode   crist him tō fultume ·
   Hī scuton þā mid ᵹafelucum   swilċe him tō ᵹamenes tō ·
105 oð þæt hē eall wæs besæt   mid heora scotunᵹum
   swilċe iᵹles byrsta · swā swā sebastiānus wæs ·
   Þā ᵹeseah hinᵹwar   se ārlēase flot-man ·
   þæt se æþela cyninᵹ   nolde criste wið-sacan ·
   ac mid ānrǣdum ᵹelēafan   hine ǣfre clypode ·
110 hēt hine þā behēafdian   and þā hǣðenan swā dydon ·
   Betwux-þām-þe hē clypode   tō criste þā-ᵹit
   þā tuᵹon þā hǣþenan   þone hālᵹan tō slǣᵹe ·
   and mid ānum swencᵹe   slōᵹon him of þæt hēafod ·
   and his sāwl sīþode   ᵹesǣliᵹ tō criste ·
115 Þǣr wæs sum man ᵹehende   ᵹehealden þurh ᵹod ·
   behȳd þām hǣþenum · þe þis ᵹehȳrde eall ·
   and hit eft sǣde   swā swā wē hit secᵹað hēr ·
   Hwæt ðā se flot-here   fērde eft tō scipe ·
   and behȳddon þæt hēafod   þæs hālᵹan ēadmundes ·
120 on þām þiccum brēmelum   þæt hit bebyrᵹed ne wurde ·
   Þā æfter fyrste   syððan hī āfarene wǣron
   cōm þæt land-folc tō   þe þǣr tō lāfe wæs þā ·
   þǣr heora hlāfordes līċ   læᵹ būtan hēafde ·
   and wurdon swīðe sāriᵹe   for his sleᵹe on mōde ·
125 and hūru þæt hī næfdon   þæt hēafod tō þām bodiᵹe ·
   Þā sǣde se scēawere   þe hit ǣr ᵹeseah
   þæt þā flot-men hæfdon   þæt hēafod mid him ·
   and wæs him ᵹeðuht   swā swā hit wæs ful sōð
   þæt hī behȳddon þæt hēafod   on þām holte forhweᵹa ·
130 Hī ēodon þā . . . ealle   endemes tō þām wuda ·
   sēċende ᵹehwǣr   ᵹeond þȳfelas and brēmelas
   ᵹif hī ā-hwǣr mihton   ᵹemēton [sic] þæt hēafod ·
   Wæs ēac miċel wundor   þæt ān wulf wearð āsend
   þurh ᵹodes wissunᵹe   tō beweriᵹenne þæt hēafod
135 wið þā ōþre dēor · ofer dæᵹ · and niht ·
   Hī ēodon þā sēċende · and symle clypiᵹende ·
   swā swā hit ᵹewunelīċ is   þām ðe on wuda ᵹāð oft ·

'Where art thou now, comrade?' And the head answered them,
'Here, here, here.' And so it called out repeatedly,

140   answering them all, as oft as any of them called,
until they all came to it by means of those cries.
At that time the gray wolf lay (there), who guarded the head,
and with his two feet had embraced the head,
greedy and hungry, and on account of God durst not

145   taste the head, but kept it against (other) animals.
Then they were astonished at the wolf's guardianship,
and carried the holy head home with them,
thanking the Almighty for all His wonders;
but the wolf followed forth with the head

150   until they came to the town, as if he were tame,
and turned back then towards the wood.
Then the country-people afterward laid the head
by the holy body, and buried him
as best they might in such haste,

155   and soon built a church over him.
Then again, after a space, after many years,
when the harrying had ceased and peace was given back
to the oppressed people, then they came together,
and built this church worthily to the saint,

160   because frequently miracles were done at his burial-place,
at the bede-house where he was buried.
They desired then to carry the holy body
with popular honour, and to lay (it) within the church.
Then was a great wonder, that it was just as whole

165   as if he were alive, with clean body,
and his neck was healed which before was cut through,
and there was as it were a silken thread about his neck red,
as evidence for men how he was slain.
And in the same way the wounds, which the bloodthirsty heathen

170   had made in his body by their repeated shots,
were healed by the heavenly God;
and so he lieth uncorrupt until this present day,
awaiting resurrection and the eternal glory.
His body which lieth undecayed maketh known to us

175   that he lived without fornication here in this world,

Hwǣr eart þū nū ʒefēra? and him andwyrde þæt hēafod ·
Hēr · hēr · hēr · and swā ʒelōme clypode

140 andswariʒende him eallum · swā oft swā heora ǣniʒ clypode ·
op-þæt hī ealle becōmen þurh ðā clypunʒa him tō ·
Þā lǣʒ se ʒrǣʒa wulf þe bewiste þæt hēafod ·
and mid his twām fōtum hæfde þæt hēafod beclypped ·
ʒrǣdiʒ · and hunʒriʒ · and for ʒode ne dorste

145 þæs hēafdes ābyrian · [ac] hēold hit wið dēor ·
Þā wurdon hī ofwundrode þæs wulfes hyrd-rǣdenne ·
and þæt hāliʒe hēafod hām fēredon mid him ·
þanciʒende þām ælmihtiʒan ealra his wundra ·
ac se wulf folʒode forð mid þām hēafde ·

150 op-þæt hī tō tūne cōmon · swylċe hē tam wǣre ·
and ʒewende eft siþþan tō wuda onʒēan ·
Þā land-lēoda þā siþþan lēdon þæt hēafod
tō þām hālʒan bodiʒe · and bebyriʒdon hine
swā swā hī sēlost mihton on swylċere hrǣdinʒe

155 and ċyrċan ārǣrdan sōna him on-uppon ·
Eft þā on fyrste æfter fela ʒēarum ·
þā sēo herʒunʒ ʒeswāc and sibb wearð forʒifen
þām ʒeswenċtan folce · þā fēnʒon hī tōʒædere
and worhton āne ċyrċan wurðlīċe þām hālʒan ·

160 for-þan-ðe ʒelōme wundra wurdon æt his byrʒene
æt þām ʒebæd-hūse þǣr hē bebyrʒed wæs ·
Hī woldon þā ferian mid folclicum wurðmynte
þone hālʒan līċhaman · and læcʒan innan þǣre ċyrċan ·
Þā wæs miċel wundor þæt hē wæs eall-swā ʒehāl

165 swylċe hē cucu wǣre mid clǣnum līċhaman ·
and his swura wæs ʒehālod þe ǣr wæs forslaʒen ·
and wæs swylċe ān seolcen þrǣd embe his swuran rǣd
mannum tō sweotelunʒe hū hē ofslaʒen wæs ·
Ēac swilċe þā wunda þe þā wæl-hrēowan hǣþenan

170 mid ʒelōmum scotunʒum on his līċe macodon ·
wǣron ʒehǣlede þurh þone heofonlican ʒod ·
and hē līþ swā ansund oþ þisne and-werdan dæʒ ·
andbīdiʒende ǣristes · and þæs ēċan wuldres ·
His līċhama ūs cȳð þe līð unformolsnod

175 þæt hē būtan forliʒre hēr on worulde leofode ·

and by pure life passed to Christ.

   A certain widow called Oswyn dwelt
near the saint's burial-place in prayers
and fastings for many years after.

180 She would every year cut the hair of the saint,
and cut his nails soberly and lovingly,
and keep them in a shrine as relics on the altar.
Then the people of the land faithfully venerated the saint;
and Bishop Theodred exceedingly [enriched the church]

185 with gifts in gold and silver, in the saint's honour.

   Then on a certain occasion came some un-blessed thieves,
eight in one night, to the venerable saint,
planned to steal the treasures which people had brought thither,
and tried by crafty ways how they might get in.

190 One struck at the hasp violently with a hammer;
one of them filed about it with a file;,
one dug under the door with a spade;
one of them by a ladder wished to unlock the window:
but they toiled in vain, and fared miserably,

195 such that the holy man wondrously bound them,
each as he stood, toiling with his implement,
so that none of them could do that evil deed,
nor stir thence; but they stood just so until morning.
Men then wondered about it, to see how the criminals hung there,

200 one on a ladder, one bent down to his digging,
and each was fast bound in his own work.
Then they were all brought to the bishop,
and he commanded them all hang them on a high gallows;
but he was not mindful how the merciful God

205 spake through His prophet these words which here stand;
Eos qui ducuntur ad mortem eruere ne cesses:
'Those who are led to death deliver thou alway.'
And also the holy canons forbid clerics,
both bishops and priests, to be concerned about thieves,

210 because it becometh not them that are chosen
to serve God, that they should consent
to any man's death, if they be the Lord's servants.
Afterwards when Theodred had afterwards searched his books,

and mid clǣnum līfe   tō criste sīþode ·
Sum wudewe wunode ōswyn ȝehāten
æt þæs hālȝan byrȝene on ȝebedum
and fæstenum maneȝa ȝēar syððan ·
180 sēo wolde efsian ǣlċe ȝēare þone sanct ·
and his næȝlas ċeorfan sȳferlīċe · mid lufe ·
and on scrȳne healdan   tō hāliȝ-dōme on wēofode ·
þā wurðode þæt land-folc   mid ȝelēafan þone sanct ·
and þēodrēd bisceop   þearle mid ȝifum
185 on ȝolde and on seolfre · þām sancte tō wurðmynte ·
þā cōmon on sumne sǣl   unȝesǣliȝe þēofas
eahta on ānra nihte   tō þām ārwurðan hālȝan
woldon stelan þā māðmas   þe men þyder brōhton ·
and cunnedon mid cræfte   hū hī in cumon [*sic*] mihton ·
190 Sum slōh mid slecȝe   swīðe þā hæpsan ·
sum heora mid fēolan   fēolode abūtan ·
sum ēac under-dealf   þā duru mid spade ·
sum heora mid hlǣddre   wolde unlūcan þæt æȝðyrl ·
Ac hī swuncon on īdel · and earmlīċe fērdon ·
195 swā þæt se hālȝa wer   hī wundorlīċe ȝeband ·
ǣlcne swā hē stōd   strūtiȝende mid tōle ·
þæt heora nā ne mihte   þæt morð ȝefremman ·
ne hī þanon āstyrian · ac stōdon swā oð merȝen ·
Men þā þæs wundrodon   hū þā wearȝas hanȝodon ·
200 sum on hlǣddre · sum lēat tō ȝedelfe ·
and ǣlċ on his weorce   wæs fæste ȝebunden ·
Hī wurdon þā ȝebrōhte   tō þām bisceope ealle ·
and hē hēt hī hōn   on hēaȝum ȝealȝum ealle ·
Ac hē næs nā ȝemyndiȝ   hū se mild-heorta ȝod
205 clypode þurh his wīteȝan   þās word þe hēr standað ·
Eos qui ducuntur ad mortem eruere ne cesses ·
þā þe man lǣt tō dēaðe   ālȳs hī ūt symble ·
and ēac þā hālȝan canōnes   ȝehādodum forbēodað
ȝe bisceopum ȝe prēostum · tō bēonne embe þēofas ·
210 for-þan-þe hit ne ȝebyraþ   þām þe bēoð ȝecorene
ȝode tō þeȝniȝenne   þæt hī ȝeþwǣr-lǣċan sceolon ·
on ǣniȝes mannes dēaðe · ȝif hī bēoð drihtnes þēnas ·
Eft þā ðeodrēd bisceop   scēawode his bēċ syððan

(he) rued with lamentation that he had awarded such a cruel doom
215 to these unhappy thieves, and ever deplored it
to his life's end; and earnestly prayed the people
that they fast with him fully three days,
praying the Almighty that He would have mercy upon him.
In that land was a certain man called Leofstan,
220 rich in worldly things, and ignorant towards God;
this man rode with great insolence to the saint's shrine,
and very arrogantly commanded (them) to show him
the holy saint, whether he were sound [i. e., incorrupt];
but as soon as he saw the saint's body,
225 then he straightway raved and roared horribly,
and miserably ended by an evil death.
This is like that which the orthodox pope
Gregory said in his writing
concerning the holy Lawrence who lieth in the city of Rome,
230 that men were always wishing to see how he lay,
both good and evil, but God checked them,
so that there died in the looking all at once
seven men together; then the others desisted
from looking at the martyr with human error.
235 We have heard of many wonders in the popular talk
about the holy Edmund which we will not here
set down in writing; but every one knoweth them.
In this saint is manifest and in others like him,
that Almighty God can raise man
240 again in the day of judgment, incorruptible from the earth,
He who preserveth Edmund whole in his body
until the great day, though he was made of earth.
Worthy is the place for the sake of the venerable saint
that men should venerate it, and will provide it
245 with God's pure servants, to Christ's service,
because the saint is greater than men may imagine.
The English nation is not deprived of the Lord's saints,
since in English land lie such saints
as this holy king is, and the blessed Cuthbert,
250 and Saint Athelthryth [Audrey] in Ely, and also her sister,
incorrupt in body, for the confirmation of the faith.

behrēowsode mid ʒeōmerunʒe · þæt hē swā rēðne dōm sette
215 þām unʒesæliʒum þēofum · and hit besārʒode æfre
oð his līfes ende · and þā lēode bæd ʒeorne ·
þæt hī him mid fæstan fullīce þrȳ daʒas ·
biddende þone ælmihtiʒan · þæt hē him ārian scolde ·
On þām lande wæs sum man · lēofstān ʒehāten ·
220 rīce for worulde · and unwittiʒ for ʒode ·
sē rād tō þām hālʒan mid riccetere swīðe ·
and hēt him æt-ēowian orhlīce swīðe ·
þone hālʒan sanct hwæþer hē ʒesund wære ·
ac swā hraðe swā hē ʒeseah þæs sanctes līchaman ·
225 þā āwēdde hē sōna · and wæl-hrēowlīce ʒrymetede ·
and earmlīce ʒe·endode yfelum dēaðe ·
Þis is ðām ʒelīc þe se ʒelēaffulla pāpa
ʒreʒōrius sæde on his ʒesetnysse
be ðām hālʒan laurentię ðe lið on rōme-byriʒ ·
230 þæt menn woldon scēawian symle hū hē lāʒe ·
ʒe ʒōde ʒe yfele · ac ʒod hī ʒestilde ·
swā þæt þær swulton on þære scēawunʒe āne
seofon menn ætʒædere · þā ʒeswicon þā ōþre
tō scēawiʒenne þone martyr mid menniscum ʒedwylde ·
235 Fela wundra wē ʒehȳrdon on folclicre sprǣce ·
be þām hālʒan ēadmunde þe wē hēr nellaþ
on ʒewrite settan · ac hī wāt ʒehwā ·
On þyssum hālʒan is swutel · and on swilcum ōþrum ·
þæt ʒod ælmihtiʒ mæʒ þone man ārǣran
240 eft on dōmes dæʒ andsundne of eorþan
sē þe hylt ēadmunde hālne his līchaman ·
oð þone micclan dæʒ þēah-ðe hē of moldan cōme ·
Wyrðe is sēo stōw for þām wurðfullan hālʒan
þæt hī man wurþiʒe and wel ʒeloʒiʒe
245 mid clǣnum ʒodes þēowum · tō cristes þēow-dōme ·
for-þan-þe se hālʒa is mærra þonne men maʒon āsmēaʒan ·
Nis anʒel-cynn bedæled drihtnes hālʒena ·
þonne on enʒla-landa licʒaþ swilce hālʒan
swylce þæs hālʒa cyninʒ is and cūþberht se ēadiʒa ·
250 and sancte æþeldryð on ēliʒ · and ēac hire swustor
ansunde on līchaman ʒelēafan tō trymminʒe ·

There are also many other saints among the English,
who work many miracles, as it is widely known,
in praise to the Almighty in whom they believed.

255 Christ showeth to men, through His illustrious saints,
that He is Almighty God who causeth such wonders,
although the miserable Jews altogether denied Him,
because they are accursed, as they desired for themselves.
There are no wonders wrought at their sepulchres,

260 because they believe not in the living Christ;
but Christ signifieth to men where the true faith is,
when He worketh such miracles by His saints
widely throughout the earth; wherefore to Him be Glory
ever with His Heavenly Father, and with the Holy Ghost,
        for ever and ever. Amen.

Synd ēac fela ōðre   on anȝel-cynne hālȝan
þe fela wundra wyrċað · swā swā hit wīde is cūð
þām ælmihtiȝan tō lofe · þe hī on ȝelȳfdon ·
255 Crist ȝeswutelaþ mannum   þurh his mæran hālȝan
þæt hē is ælmihtiȝ ȝod   þe macað swilċe wundra
þēah-þe þā earman iūdēi   hine eallunȝe wið-sōcen ·
for-þan-þe hī synd āwyrȝede   swā swā hī wiscton him sylfum ·
Ne bēoð nāne wundra   ȝeworhte æt heora byrȝenum ·
260 for-ðan-þe hī ne ȝelȳfað   on þone lifiȝendan crist ·
ac crist ȝeswutelað mannum   hwǣr se sōða ȝelēafa is ·
þonne hē swylċe wundra   wyrèð þurh his hālȝan
wīde ȝeond þās eorðan · Þæs him sȳ wuldor
ā mid his heofonlican fæder · and þām hālȝan ȝāste
(ā būton ende) · Amen ·

THE LEGEND OF ST. ANDREW

[The text here is based on *The Blickling Homilies*, edited by Richard Morris for the Early English Text Society, and on a subsequent collation. The manuscript now called The Blickling Homilies, since 1938 in The John H. Scheide Library, Princeton, is incomplete; Morris's text supplied the missing parts from Cambridge MS. CCC 198, the other manuscript containing this legend in Old English. A complete facsimile edition of The Blickling Homilies is edited by Rudolph Willard as the tenth volume of *Early English Manuscripts in Facsimile*.]

Hēr seʒð þæt æfter-þām-þe Drihten Hǣlend Crist tō heofonum
āstāh, þæt þā apostoli [= apostolas] wǣron æt-somne; and hīe
sendon hlot him betwēonum, hwider hyra ʒehwylċ faran scolde
tō lǣranne. Seʒþ þæt se ēadiʒa Matheus ʒehlēat tō
5 Marmadonia þǣre ċeastre; seʒð þonne þæt þā men þe on þǣre
ċeastre wǣron, þæt hī hlāf ne ǣton, ne wǣter ne druncon, ac
ǣton manna līċhaman, and heora blōd druncon. And ǣʒhwylċ
man þe on þǣre ċeastre cōm ælþēodisc, seʒð þæt hīe hine sōna
ʒenāmon and his ēaʒan ūt-āstunʒun, and hīe him sealdon āttor
10 drincan þæt mid myclan lyb-cræfte wæs ʒeblanden; and mid-þȳ-
þe hīe þone drenċ druncon, hraþe heora heorta wæs tō-lēsed
[= tō-līesed] and heora mōd onwended. Se ēadiʒa Matheus þā
in-ēode on þā ċeastre, and hraðe hīe hine ʒenāmon and his
ēaʒan ūt-āstunʒon; and hīe him sealdon āttor drinccan, and hine

Here it says that after the Lord Saviour Christ ascended to heaven, that the apostles were together, and they cast lots among them whither each of them should go to teach. It says that the blessed Matthew drew by lot [was allotted to] the city of Marmadonia. It says moreover that the men who were in that city, that they did not eat bread, nor drink water, but ate the bodies of men and drank their blood. And whatever person came to that city a foreigner, it says that they straightway seized him and pierced out his eyes; and they gave him poison to drink that was blended with great magic: and when they had drunk the drink, immediately their heart was dissolved and their mind changed. The blessed Matthew then entered into that city, and straightway they seized him and pierced out his eyes; and they gave him poison to drink, and

[The text on pp. 285-92 here matches that of The Blickling Homilies page for
page and line for line.]

    sendon on carcern[e], and hīe hine hēton þæt āttor   [*fol. 136r*
    etan; and hē hit etan nolde. Forðon-þe his heorte
    næs tōlȳsedu, ne his mōd næs onwended; ah hē   [= tō-līesed
    wæs simle hine tō Drihtne ȝebiddende mid myc-
5   lum wōpe, and cwæð tō him: 'Mīn Drihten Hǣlend Crist,
    forðon wē ealle forlēton ūre cnēorisne and wǣ-   [= cnēoresse
    ron þē fylȝende, and þū eart ūre ealra fultum,   [= folȝiende
    ðā þe on þē ȝelȳfað: beheald nū and ȝeseoh hū þās   [= ȝelīefað
    men þīnum ðēowe dōþ; and iċ þē bidde, Dryhten,
10 þæt þū mē forȝife mīnra ēaȝena lēoht, þæt iċ ȝe-
    sēo þā [ðe] mē onȝinnað dōn on þisse ċeastre
    ðā werrestan tintreȝa; and ne forlǣt mē, mīn   [= wierrestan
    Drihten Hǣlende Crist, ne þū mē ne syle on þone
    biterestan dēað.' And mid-þȳ-þe hē þis ȝebed, se
15 ēadiȝa Matheus, ȝecweden hæfde, myċel lēoht
    and frea-beorht onlȳhte þæt carcern, and Drihtnes [= onlīehte
    stefn wæs ȝeworden tō him on þǣm lēohte
    cweþende, 'Matheus, mīn se lēofa, beheald on
    mē.' Se ēadiȝa Matheus þā lōciende ȝeseah
20 Drihten Crist; and eft Drihten wæs cweþende:
    'Matheus, wes þū ȝestranȝod and ne ondrǣd þū þē,

sent him to prison and commanded him to eat the poison; but he would not eat it. For this
reason his heart was not dissolved nor was his mind changed. But he was continually praying
to the Lord with great weeping, and said to Him: 'My Lord Saviour Christ, forasmuch as
we all forsook our kin and followed thee, and thou art the support of us all who believe on
thee: behold now and see how these men act towards thy servant; and I pray thee, Lord, that
thou give back the light of mine eyes, so that I may see those who will (try to) do to me in
this city the worst of torments; and forsake me not, my Lord Saviour Christ, and deliver me
not to that bitterest death.' And when he, the blessed Matthew, had uttered this prayer, a
great and very bright light lighted the prison, and the Lord's voice was manifest to him in
that light saying, 'Matthew, my beloved, look on me.' The blessed Matthew then looking saw
the Lord Christ; and again the Lord was speaking: 'Matthew, be thou strengthened and fear
thou not,

forþon ne forlǣte iċ þē ǣfre; ah iċ þē ġefrēol-   *[fol. 136v*
siġe of ealre frēcennesse and ealle þīne brōþor,
and ealle þā þe on mē ġelȳfað eallum tīdum on
ēċnesse. Ac onbīd hēr seofon and twēntiġ nihta;
5   ǣfter-þon iċ sende tō þē Andreas þīnne brōþor,
þæt hē þē ūt-ālǣdeþ of þyssum carcerne, and ealle þā
ðe mid þē syndon.' And mid-þȳ-þe þis ġecweden wæs,
Drihten him eft tō cwæð, 'Sib sȳ mid þē, Matheus.'
Hē þā þurhwuniġende mid ġebedum wæs Driht-
10   nes lof sinġende on þǣm carcerne. And þā unrih-
tan men in-ēodan on þæt carcern, þæt hīe þā men ūt
lǣdan woldon and him tō mete dōn. Se ēadiġa
Matheus þā betȳnde his ēaġan, þ[ȳ]-lǣs þā cwelle-
ras ġesāwon þæt his ēaġan ġe·openode wǣron.
15   And hīe cwǣdon him betwēonum, 'Þrȳ daġas
nū tō lāfe syndon, þæt wē hine willað ācwellan
and ūs tō mete ġedōn.' Se ēadiġa Matheus þā
ġefylde .xx. daġa. Þā Drihten Hǣlend Crist
cwæð tō ðǣm hālġan Andrea his apostole,
20   mid-þȳ-þe hē wæs in Achaia þǣm lande and þǣr
lǣrde his discipuli; hē cwæð: 'Ʒanʒ on Merme-

for I will never forsake thee; but I will deliver thee from all danger, and all thy brothers, and all those who believe on me in all times forever. But abide here twenty-seven days; after that I will send to thee Andrew thy brother so that he will lead thee from this prison, and all those who are with thee.' And when this was said, the Lord again addressed him: 'Peace be with thee, Matthew.' He then dwelt continually in prayer singing praise of the Lord in that prison. And the wicked men came into the prison, (for the reason) that they intended to lead the men out and prepare them as food. The blessed Matthew then shut his eyes lest the murderers saw that his eyes had been opened; and they said among themselves, 'Three days now remain (until the time) that we will kill him and make food for us.' The blessed Matthew had then fulfilled twenty days. Then the Lord Saviour Christ said to the holy Andrew his apostle, when he was in the land of Achaia and taught there his disciples: 'Go in to the city of

donia ċeastre and ālæde þonon Matheum   [*fol. 137r*
þīnne brōþor of þæm carcerne, forþon-
þe nū ᵹīt þrȳ daᵹas tō lāfe syndon, þæt hīe
hine willa𝛿 ācwellan and him tō mete dōn.' Se hālᵹa

5 Andreas him andswarede and hē cwæ𝛿: 'Mīn Drihten
Hǣlende Crist, hū mæᵹ iċ hit on þrim daᵹum ᵹe-
faran? Ac mā wēn is þæt þū onsende þīnne enᵹel,
sē hit mæᵹ hrædlīcor ġefēran; for𝛿on, mīn Drihten, þū wāst þæt iċ eom flǣsclīc man and iċ hit ne mæᵹ

10 hrædlīce þider ᵹefēran, for𝛿on-þe, mīn Drihten,
se sīþfæt is þyder tō lanᵹ, and þone weᵹ iċ ne con.'
Drihten Crist him tō cwæ𝛿: 'Andreas, ᵹehȳre mē,
for𝛿on-þe iċ þē ᵹeworhte, and iċ þīnne sīþfæt ᵹesta-
𝛿elode and ᵹetrymede. Ᵹanᵹ nū tō 𝛿æs sǣs waro𝛿e

15 mid þīnum discipulum; and þū þǣr ᵹemētst scip
on þǣm waro𝛿e; and āstīᵹ on þæt mid þīnum discipulum.' And mid-þȳ-þe hē þis cwæ𝛿, Drihten Hǣlend
𝛿ā-ᵹīt wæs sprecende and cwæ𝛿, 'Sib mid þē and mid
eallum þīnum discipulum'; and hē āstāᵹ on heofe-

20 nas. *Tunc Sanctus Andreas surens mane abiit*
ad mare cum discipulis suis, et uidit nauiculam

Marmadonia and bring thence Matthew thy brother from the prison; for three days yet remain (until the time) that they will kill him and eat him. Saint Andrew answered him, and he said: 'My Lord Saviour Christ, how am I able to accomplish it (the journey) in three days? There is greater expectation that [i.e., more probably] thou shouldst send thine angel, who can travel more quickly; for, my Lord, thou knowest that I am a man of flesh, and I am not able to travel thither (very) quickly, for, my Lord, the voyage thither is too long and I do not know the way.' The Lord Christ said to him: 'Andrew, attend to me, for I wrought thee, and I fixed and appointed thy journey. Go now to the shore of the sea with thy disciples; and there thou wilt encounter a ship at the shore; climb aboard that (ship) with thy disciples.' And when he had said this the Lord Saviour was speaking further and said, 'Peace [be] with thee and with all thy disciples'; and he ascended into heaven....

in litore, et intra naue sedentes tres uiros.   [*fol. 137v*

Se hālʒa Andreas þā ārās on morʒen and hē ēode
tō þǣre sǣ mid his discipulum; and hē ʒeseah
scip on þǣm warþe and þrȳ weras on þǣm sit-
5 tende; and hē wæs ʒefēonde myclum ʒefēan, and him
tō cwæþ: 'Brōþor, hwyder wille [ʒē] fēran mid þys
medmyclum scipe?' Drihten Hǣlende Crist
wæs on þǣm scipe swā se stēorrēþra, and his twēʒen enʒlas mid him; þā wǣron ʒehwyrfde on
10 manna onsȳne. Drihten Crist him þā tō
cwæð: 'On Mermedonia ċeastre.' Se hālʒa
Andreas him andswerede and cwæð: 'Brōðor, onfōh ūs
mid ēow on þæt scip and ʒelǣdaþ ūs on þā ċeastre.'
Drihten him tō cwæð: 'Ealle men flēoþ of þǣre
15 ċeastre; tō-hwām wille ʒē þyder faran?' Se hālʒa
Andreas him andswerede, hē cwæþ: 'Medmyċel ǣrende wē þyder habbað, and ūs is þearf þæt wē
hit þēh ʒefyllon.' Drihten Hǣlende Crist him   [= þēah
tō cwæð: 'Āstīʒað on þis scip tō ūs and syllaþ ūs
20 ēowerne fersceat.' Se hālʒa Andreas him   [= færsceat
andswerede: 'Ʒehȳraþ ʒebrōþor, ne habbað

... Then Saint Andrew arose in the morning, and he went to the sea with his disciples; and
he saw a ship at the shore and three men sitting in it; and he rejoiced with great joy, and
said to them: 'Brothers, whither do ye intend to go with this small [moderate-sized] ship?'
The Lord Saviour Christ was in the ship as the steersman, and his two angels with him; they
were changed into human appearance [form]. The Lord Christ said to him: 'To the city of
Marmadonia.' The holy Andrew answered him and said: 'Brother, take us with you into the
ship and bring us to that city.' The Lord said to him: 'All men flee from that city; for what
reason do ye wish to go thither?' The holy Andrew answered him [and] he said: 'We have a
modest mission thither, and it is necessary for us that we fulfill it even so.' The Lord Saviour
Christ said to him: 'Climb onto the ship to us, and give us your passage-money.' The holy
Andrew answered him: 'Hear (me), brothers, we do not have

wē fersceat; ah wē syndon discipuli Drih[t]nes [*fol. 138r*]
Hǣlendes Cristes þa hē ᵹeċeas; and þis bebod
hē us sealde, and hē cwæð, "Þonne ᵹē faran
ᵹodspel tō lǣrenne, þonne næbbe ᵹē mid ēow
5 hlāf, ne feoh, ne twȳ-feald hræᵹl." Ᵹif þū þonne
wille mildheortnesse ūs dōn, sæᵹe ūs þæt hrædliċe. Ᵹif þū þonne nelle, ᵹecȳþe ūs swā-þēah
þone weᵹ.' Drihten him tō cwæð: 'Ᵹif þis ᵹebod ēow
wǣre ᵹeseald fram ēowrum Drihtne, āstīᵹað
10 hider mid ᵹefēan on mīn scip.' Se hālᵹa Andreas þā āstāᵹ on þæt scip mid his discipulum, and hē ᵹesæt be þǣm stēorrēþran þæs scipes, þæt wæs Drihten
Hǣlend Crist. Drihten Hǣlend Crist him tō cwæð:
'Iċ ᵹesēo þæt þās brōþor synd ᵹeswenċede of ðisse
15 sǣwe hrēonesse; āxa hīe hweþer hīe woldon tō
eorþan āstīᵹan and þīn þǣr onbīdan, oþþæt þū ᵹe-
fylle þīne þeᵹnunᵹe tō þǣre þe þū sended eart,
and ðū þonne eft h[w]yrfest tō him.' Se hālᵹa Andreas him tō cwæð: 'Mīn bearn, willaþ ᵹē āstīᵹan
20 on eorðan and mīn þǣr onbīdan?' His discipuli him
andswaredon and cwǣdon: 'Ᵹif wē ᵹewītaþ fram þē,

passage-money; but we are disciples of the Lord Saviour Christ whom he chose; and he gave us this commandment, and he said: "When ye go to teach the gospel, have with you then neither bread, nor money, nor twofold raiment." If then thou wilt do us a kindness, tell us that quickly. If thou wilt not, yet make known to us the way.' The Lord said to him: 'If this commandment was given to you by your lord, come up hither joyfully onto my ship.' The holy Andrew came up then onto the ship with his disciples, and he sat by the steersman of the ship, who was the Lord Saviour Christ. The Lord Saviour Christ said to him: 'I see that these brothers are afflicted by the roughness of the sea; ask them whether they wish to get back to land and await thee there, until thou fulfil thy service [business] to which thou art sent, and shalt then return to them.' Saint Andrew said to them: 'My children, do ye wish to get back to land and there await me?' His disciples answered him and said: 'If we depart from thee,

þonne bēo wē fremde from eallum þǣm ʒōdum   [*fol. 138v*
þe þū ūs ʒeʒearwodest; ac wē bēoþ mid þē swā
hwyder swā þū færest.' Drihten Hǣlend him tō
cwæþ...: 'Ʒif þū sȳ sōþlīċe his discipul sē is cwe-
5 den Crist, sprec tō þīnum discipulum be þǣm mæʒe-
num þe þīn lārēow dyde, þætte sȳ ʒeblissad heora
heorte, and hīe sȳn oferʒytende þisse sǣwe eʒe.'   [oferʒieten
Se hālʒa Andreas þā cwæð tō his discipulum: 'Sumre
tīde mid-þȳ-þe wē wǣron mid ūrum Drihtne, wē ā-
10 stiʒon mid him on scip, and hē ætēowde ūs swā hē slǣpende wǣre, tō costianne; and dyde swīþe hrēonesse
ðǣre sǣwe; fram þǣm winde wæs ʒeworden swā þæt
þā sylfan ȳþa wǣron āhafene ofer þæt scip. Wē ūs þā
swīþe ondrēdon and ceʒdon tō him Drihtne Hǣlendum [= cīeʒdon
15 Criste. And hē þā ārās and bebēad þǣm winde þæt hē ʒestilde;
ðā wæs ʒeworden myċel smyltnes on þǣre sǣ. And hī hine
ondrēdon, ealle þā þe his weorc ʒesāwon. Nū þonne,
mīn bearn, ne ondrǣdaþ ʒē ēow, forþon-þe ūre Ʒod
ūs ne forlǣteþ.' Ond þus cweþende se hālʒa An-
20 dreas āsette his hēafod ofer ānne his discipula
and hē onslēp. Drihten Hǣlende Crist þā wiste for-

then we will be estranged from all the good things that thou hast prepared for us; but we will
be with thee wheresoever thou goest.' The Lord Saviour said to him...: 'If thou be truly his
disciple—the one who is called Christ—speak to thy disciples concerning the miracles which
thy teacher did, so that their hearts shall be gladdened and they may be disregarding of the
terror of the sea.' The holy Andrew then said to his disciples: 'On a certain occasion when
we were with our Lord, we went with him aboard a ship, and he appeared to us as he were
sleeping, for testing (us); and (he) caused a great roughness of the sea: from the wind it came
about that the very waves were raised over the ship. We were then greatly afraid and called
to him, the Lord Saviour Christ. And then he arose and commanded the wind that it be
stilled; then there was a great calm on the sea. And they feared him, all those who saw his
work. Now therefore, my children, fear ye not, for our God will not forsake us.' And saying
thus the holy Andrew laid his head upon one of his disciples, and he slept. The Lord Saviour
Christ then knew

ðon-þe se hālʒa Andreas þā slēp; hē cwæþ tō his [*fol. 139r*
enʒlum: 'Ʒenimaþ Andreas and his discipuli and āset-
tað hīe beforan Mermedonia ċeastre, and mid-þȳ-
ðe ʒē hīe þǣr āsetton, hweorfað eft tō mē.' Þā enʒlas
5 þā dydon swā him beboden wæs; and hē āstāʒ on heofenas.
Ðā se morʒen ʒeworden wæs beforan Mermedonia
ċeastre; and his discipulos ðǣr slǣpende wǣron mid
him, and hē hie āwehte and cwæð: 'Ārīsað ʒē, mīne bearn,
and onʒytað Ʒodes mildheortnesse, sēo is nū mid ūs
10 ʒeworden. Witon wē þæt ūre Drihten mid ūs wæs on þǣm
scipe, and wē hine ne onʒēaton; hē hine ʒe-ēaðmēdde
swā stēorrēðra, and hē hine ætēowde swā swā man ūs
tō costianne.' Se hālʒa Andreas þā locode on
heofenas and hē cwæð: 'Mīn Drihten Hǣlend Crist, iċ wāt
15 þæt þū ne eart feor fram þīnum þēowum; and iċ þē behēold
on þǣm scipe, and iċ wæs tō ðē sprecende sw[ā] tō men.
Nū þonne, Drihten, iċ þē bidde þæt þū mē þē ætēowe
on þisse stōwe.' Þā ðis ʒecweden wæs, Drihten him ætēowde,
his onsȳne on fæʒeres ċildes hēowe,
20 and him tō cwæð: 'Andreas, ʒefeoh [? ʒeseoh] mid þīnum discipulum.'
Se hālʒa Andreas þā hine ʒebæd and cwæð: 'Forʒif mē,

by that that the holy Andrew slept then; he said to his angels: 'Take Andrew and his disciples
and set them before the city of Marmadonia, and when ye have placed them there, return
to me.' The angels did then as to them was commanded; and he ascended to heaven. Then
morning came before the city of Marmadonia; and his [Andrew's] disciples were sleeping there
with him, and he awoke them and said: 'Arise, my children, and perceive the mercy of God
which is now come to pass with us. We know that our Lord was with us on the ship, and we
did not recognize him; he humbled himself (to be) as the steersman, and he showed himself to
us as a man, to test us.' Saint Andrew then looked to heaven and he said: 'My Lord Saviour
Christ, I know that thou art not far from thy servants; and I beheld thee in the ship and spoke
to thee as to a man. Now therefore, Lord, I pray thee that thou appear to me in this place.'
When this was said, the Lord appeared to him, his face in the appearance of a fair child, and
said to him: 'Andrew, rejoice [? look on (me)], with thy disciples.' The holy Andrew then
prayed him and said, 'Forgive me,

Drihten, þæt iċ tō ðē sprecende wæs swā tō men; wēn is   *[fol. 139v*
þæt iċ ġefyrenode forðon-þe iċ þē [ne] onġēat.' Drihten
him þā tō cwæð: 'Andreas, ne ġefyrenodest þū nān
wuht; ah forðon ðū cwæde þæt þū hit ne mihte on
5 ðrim daʒum hider ġefaran, forþon iċ þē swā ætēowde: forþon iċ eom mihtiʒ mid worde swā eal tō
dōnne, and ānra ġehwylcum tō ætēowenne swā hwæt
swā mē līcað. Nū þonne ārīs and ʒanʒ on ðā ċeastre
tō Matheum þīnum brēþer, and ālæde þonne hine
10 of ðære ċeastre and ealle þā ðe mid him syndon. Eno iċ þē [= heonu
ġecȳþe, Andreas, forþon-þe maneʒa tintreʒa hīe þē
on brinʒað, and þīnne līċhoman ġeond þisse ċeastre
lanan hīe tōstenċeað, swā þætte þīn blōd flēwþ ofer
eorðan swā swā wæter. Tō dēaðe hīe þē willaþ ġe-
15 lædan, ac hī ne maʒon; ac maneʒa earfoðnessa
hīe þē maʒon on ġebrinʒan. Ah þonne hweþre
āræfne þū þā ealle, Andreas, and ne dō þū æfter
heora unġelēaffulnesse. [Ġemune ġē hū maneʒa earfoðnesse]
                fram Iudeum iċ wæs
ðrōwiende; hīe mē swunʒon, and hī me spætlædon on mīnne
20 ondwleotan. Ah eal iċ hit āræfnede þæt iċ   [= andwlitan
ēow ætēowe hwylcum ġemete ġē sceolan āræfnan.

Lord, that I spoke to thee as to a man; I expect that I sinned, because I knew thee not.' The
Lord said then to him: 'Andrew, thou didst not sin at all; but because thou saidst that thou
couldst not travel hither in three days, for that reason I appeared to thee thus: for I am mighty
in word to do all things and to appear to everyone as it pleaseth me. Now therefore arise and
go into the city to Matthew thy brother, and lead him out of the city and all those who are
with him. Behold, I make known to thee, Andrew, that they shall bring many torments upon
thee, and thy body they shall scatter through the streets of the city, so that thy blood shall
flow upon the earth like water. They will lead thee forth to death, but they shall not be able
[to kill thee]. But many afflictions they may bring upon thee. But do thou nonetheless endure
all [these things], Andrew, and do not thou according to their unbelief. Remember how many
afflictions I suffered of the Jews; they scourged me, and they spat upon my countenance. But
I endured it all that I might show you in what measure ye will have to suffer.

ᵹehīere mē, Andreas, and āræfna þās tintreᵹo, forþon maniᵹe synt on þisse
ċeastre þā sculon ᵹelēofan on mīnne naman.' Mid-þī hē þis cwæð, Drihten
Hǣlend Crist, hē āstāh on heofenas. Se hāliᵹa Andreas þā in-ēode on þā ċeastre
mid his discipulum, and nǣniᵹ man hine ne mihte ᵹesēon. Mid-þī-þe hīe cōmon
tō þæs carcernes duru, hīe þǣr ᵹemētton seofon hyrdas standan. Se hāliᵹa
Andreas þā ᵹebæd on his heortan, and rāðe hīo wǣron dēade. Se hālᵹa Andreas
þā ēode tō þæs carcernes duru, and hē worhte Cristes rōdetācen, and raþe þā
dura wǣron ontȳnede, and hē in-ēode on þæt carcern mid his discipulum, hē
ᵹeseah þone ēadiᵹan Matheus ǣnne sittan sinᵹende. Se ēadiᵹa Matheus þā and
se hāliᵹa Andreas, hīe wǣron cyssende him betwēonum. Se hāliᵹa Andreas him
tō cwæð: 'Hwæt is þæt, brōþor? Hū eart þū hēr ᵹemēt? Nū þrȳ daᵹas tō lāfe
syndon þæt hīe þē willaþ ācwellan, and him [i. e., þē] tō mete ᵹedōn.' Se hāliᵹa
Matheus him andswarode, and hē cwæð: 'Brōþor Andreas, ac ne ᵹehȳrdest þū
Drihten cweþende, "Forþon-þe iċ ēow sende swā swā scēap on middum wulfum?"
Þanon wæs ᵹeworden, mid-þȳ-þe hīe mē sendon on þis carcern, iċ bæd ūrne
Drihten þæt hē hine ætēowde; and hraþe hē mē hine ætēowde, and hē mē tō
cwæð: "Onbīd hēr .xxvii. daᵹa, and æfter-þon iċ sende tō þē Andreas þīnne
brōþor, and hē þē ūt-ālæt of þissum carcerne and ealle þā [þe] mid þē syndon."
Swā mē Drihten tō cwæþ, iċ ᵹesīe [= ᵹesēo]. Brōðor, hwæt sculon wē nū dōn?'
Se hāliᵹa Andreas þā and se hāliᵹa Matheus ᵹebǣdon to Drihtne, and æfter þon
ᵹebede se hāliᵹa Andreas sette his hand ofer þāra wera ēaᵹan þe þǣr on lande
wǣron, and ᵹesihþe hīe onfēnᵹon. And eft hē sette his hand ofer hiora heortan,
and heora andᵹeat him eft tō-hwirfde. Se hāliᵹa Andreas him tō cwæð: 'ᵹanᵹað
on þās niþeran dǣlas þisse ċeastre, and ᵹē þǣr ᵹemētað myċel fictrēow: sittað
under him and etað of his wæstmum oð þæt iċ ēow tō cyme.' Hī cwǣdon tō
þām hālᵹan Andreas: 'Cum nū mid ūs, forþon-þe þū eart ūre wealdend, þȳ-lēas
wēn is þæt hī ūs eft ᵹenimon and on þā wyrstan tintreᵹu hīe ūs on ᵹebrinᵹan.'
Se hāliᵹa Andreas him tō cwæð: 'Farað þider, forþon-þe ēow nǣniᵹ wiht ne
derað ne ne swenċeþ.' And hraðe hīe þā ealle fērdon swā him se hālᵹa Andreas
bebēad. And þǣr wǣron on þǣm carcerne twā hund and eahta and fēowertiᵹ
wera, and niᵹon and fēowertiᵹ wīfa, ðā se hāliᵹa Andreas þanon onsende. And
þone ēadiᵹan Matheum hē ᵹedyde ᵹanᵹan tō þām ēast-dǣle mid his discipulum.
And ... [hīe] āsetton on þā dūne þǣr se ēadiᵹa Petrus se apostol wæs. And hē
þǣr wunode mid him. Se hāliᵹa Andreas þā ūt-ēode of þǣm carcerne, and hē
onᵹan ᵹanᵹan ūt þurh midde þā ċeastre, and hē cōm tō sumre stōwe, and hē
þǣr ᵹeseah swēr standan, and ofer þone swēr ǣrne onlīcnesse. And hē ᵹesæt
be þǣm swēre anbīdende hwæt him ᵹelimpan scolde. Ðā unrihte men þā ēodon
þæt hīe þā men ūt-ᵹelǣddon and hīe tō mete ᵹedōn. And hīe ᵹemētton þæs
carcernes duru opene, and þā seofon hyrdas dēade licᵹan. Mid-þȳ-þe hīe þæt

ʒesāwon, hīe eft hwirfdon tō hiora ealdormannum, and hīe cwǣdon: 'Þīn carcern
open wē ʒemētton, and inʒanʒende nǣniʒe wē þǣr ʒemētton.' Mid-þī-þe hīe
ʒehȳrdon, þāra sacerda ealdormen,... hīe cwǣdon him betwēonan, 'Hwæt wile
þis wesan? Wēn is þæt hwilċ wundor in-ēode on þæt carcern and þā hyrdas
ācwǣlde, and somnunʒa [alȳsde þā] þe þǣr betȳnede wǣron.' Æfter þiossum
him ætēowde dēofol on cnihtes onlīcnysse, and him tō cwæð: 'Ʒehȳrað mē, and
sēċað hēr sumne ælþēodiʒne man þæs nama is Andreas, and ācwellað hine. Hē
þæt is sē þā ʒebundenan of þissum carcerne ūt-ālǣdde, and hē is nū on þisse
ċeastre. Ʒē hine nū witon; efstað, mīne bearn, and ācwellað hine.' Se hāliʒa
Andreas þā cwæð tō þām dēofle: 'Ana [= heonu], þū heardeste strǣl tō æʒ-
hwilċre unriht[n]esse, þū þe simle fihtest wið manna cyn. Mīn Drihten Hǣlend
Crist þē ʒehnǣde in helle.' Þæt dēofol þā hē þis ʒehȳrde, hē him tō cwæð,
'Þīne stefne iċ ʒehīere, ac iċ ne wāt hwǣr þū eart.' Se hāliʒa Andreas him tō
cwæð, 'Forþon-þe þū eart blind þū ne ʒesihst ǣniʒne of Ʒodes þām hālʒum.'
Þæt dēofol þā cwæð tō þām folce: 'Behealdað ēow and ʒesēoð hine, forþon-
þe hē þæt is sē þe wið mē sprǣc.' Ðā burhlēode þā urnon, and hī betȳndon
þǣre ċeastre ʒatu, and hīe sōhton þæne [= þone] hālʒan Andreas þæt hīe hine
ʒenāmon. Drihten Hǣlend hine þā ætēowde þām hāliʒan Andrea, and him
tō cwæð: 'Andreas, ārīs and ʒecȳð him þæt hīe onʒieton mīn mæʒen on þē
wesan.' Se hāliʒa Andreas þā ārās on þæs folces ʒesihþe, and hē cwæð, 'Iċ eom
sē Andreas þe ʒē sēċaþ.' Þæt folc þā arn, and hīe hine ʒenāmon and cwǣdon,
'Forþon þū ūs þus dydest, wē hit þē forʒyldað.' And hīe þōhton hū hīe hine
ācwellan meahton. Þā wæs se dēofol in-ʒanʒende [hiora ānne], and cwæð tō þām
folce: 'Ʒif ēow swā līciʒe, uton sendan rāp on his swȳran, and hine tēon þurh
þisse ċeastre lanan, and þis uton wē dōn oþþæt hē swelte. And mid-þī-þe hē
dēad sīe, uton wē dǣlan his līċhaman ūrum burhlēodum.' And þā eall þæt folc
þæt ʒehīerde, hit him līcode, and hraðe hīe sendon rāp on his swēoran, and hīe
hine tuʒon ʒeond þǣre ċeastre lanan. Mid-þī-þe se ēadiʒa Andreas wæs toʒen,
his līċhama wæs ʒemenʒed mid þǣre eorðan, swā þæt blōd flēow ofer eorðan
swā wæter. Ðā ǣfen ʒeworden wæs, hī hine sendon on þæt carcern, and hīe
ʒebundon his handa behindan, and hīe hine forlēton; and eall his līċhama [wæs]
ʒelȳsed. Swilċe ōþre dæʒe þæt ilce hīe dydon. Se hāliʒa Andreas þā wēop, and
hē cwæð: 'Mīn Drihten Hǣlend Crist, cum and ʒeseoh þæt hīe mē dōð þīnum
þēowe; and eall iċ hit ārǣfnie for þīnum ʒebode þe þū mē sealdest, and þū
cwǣde, "Ne dō [ðū] æfter hiora unʒelēafulnesse." Beheald, Drihten, and ʒeseoh
hū hīe mē dōð.' Mid-þī hē þus cwæð, þæt dēofol cwæð tō þām folce, 'Swinʒað
hine on his mūð, þæt hē þus ne sprece.' Ðā ʒeworden wæs þæt hīe hine eft
betȳndon on þām carcerne. Ðæt dēofol þā ʒenam mid him ōþre seofon dēoflo,
þā þe [se] hāliʒa Andreas þanon āflīemde, and in-ʒanʒende on þæt carcern

hīe ʒestōdon on ʒesihþe þæs ēadiʒan Andreas,... hine bismriende mid myclere bismre, and hīe cwædon: 'Hwæt is þæt þū hēr ʒemētest? Hwilċ ʒefrēolseð þē nū of ūrum ʒewealde? Hwǣr is þīn ʒilp and þīn hiht?' Þæt dēofol þā cwæð tō þām ōðrum dēoflum, 'Mīne bearn, ācwellað hine, forþon hē ūs ʒescende and ūre weorc.' Þā dēofla þā blǣston hīe ofer þone hālʒan Andreas, and hīe ʒesāwon Cristes rōdetācen on his onsīene; hī ne dorston hine ʒenēalǣċan, ac hraðe hīe on weʒ fluʒon. Þæt dēofol him tō cwæð: 'Mīne bearn, for-hwon ne ācwealdon ʒē hine?' Hīe him andswarodon and hīe cwædon: 'Wē ne mihton, forþon-þe Cristes rōdetācn on his onsīene wē ʒesawon, and wē ūs ondrēdon. Wē witon forþon-þe, ǣr hē on þæs earfoðnesse cōm, hē ūre wæs wealdend. Ʒif þū mæʒe, ācwel hine. Wē þē on þissum ne hērsumiað, þȳ-lǣs wēn sīe þæt hine Ʒod ʒefrēolsiʒe and ūs sende on wyrsan tintrego.' Se hāliʒa Andreas him tō cwæð: 'Þēah-þe ʒē mē ācwellen, ne dō iċ ēowerne willan, ac iċ dō willan mīnes Drihtnes Hǣlendes Cristes.' And þus hīe ʒehērdon and on weʒ fluʒon. On merʒen þā ʒeworden wæs, eft hīe tuʒon þone hālʒan Andreas, and hē cīʒde mid mycle wōpe tō Drihtne, and cwæð: 'Mīn Drihten Hǣlend Crist, mē ʒenihtsumiað þās tintrega, forþon iċ eom ʒetēorod. Mīn Drihten Hǣlend Crist, āne tīd on rōde þū þrōwodest and þū cwæde, "Fæder, for-hwon forlēte þū mē?" Nū .iii. daʒas syndon syððan iċ wæs ʒetoʒen þurh þisse ċeastre lanum. Þū wāst, Drihten, þā menniscan tȳddernysse: hāt onfōn mīnne ʒāst. Hwǣr syndon þīne word, Drihten, on þām þū ūs ʒestranʒodest, and þū cwæde, "Ʒif ʒē mē ʒehȳrað and ʒē mē bēoð fylʒende, ne ān loc of ēowrum hēafde forwyrð?" Beheald, Drihten, and ʒeseoh... [hū mīn] līċhama and loccas mīnes hēafdes mid þisse eorðan synd ʒemenʒde. Āne, .iii. daʒas syndon syððan iċ wæs ʒetoʒen tō þǣm wyrstan tintreʒum, and þū mē ne ætēowdest. Mīn Drihten Hǣlend Crist, ʒestranʒa mīne heortan.' Ðus ʒebiddende, þǣm hælʒan Andrea Drihtenes stefn wæs ʒeworden on Ebreisc cweþende, 'Mīn Andreas, heofon and eorðe mæʒ ʒewītan; mīn word nǣfre ne ʒewītaþ. Beheald æfter þē and ʒeseoh þīnne līċhaman and loccas þīnes hēafdes, hwæt hīe syndon ʒewordene.' Se hāliʒa Andreas þā lōciende, hē ʒeseah ʒeblōwen trēow wæstm-berende; and hē cwæð: 'Nū iċ wāt, Drihten, forþon þæt þū ne forlēte mē.' On ǣfenne þā ʒeworden, hīe hine betȳndon on þām carcerne, and hīo cwǣdon him betwȳnum, 'Forþon-þe þisse nihte hē swelt.' Him ætēowde Drihten Hǣlend Crist on þǣm carcerne, and hē āþenede his hand and ʒenām, and hē cwæð: 'Andreas, ārīs.' Mid-þī-þe hē þæt ʒehȳrde, hraþe hē þā ārās ʒesund, and hē hine ʒebæd and hē cwæð: 'Þancas iċ þē dō, mīn Drihten Hǣlend Crist.' Se hāliʒa Andreas þā lōciende, hē ʒeseah on middum þǣm carcerne swēr standan, and ofer þone swēr stǣnenne anlīcnesse. And hē āþenede his handa and hiere tō cwæð: 'Ondrǣd þē Drihten and his rōdetācn, beforan þǣm forhtiʒað heofon and eorþe. Nū þonne, anlīcnes, dō þæt iċ bidde

on naman mīnes Drihtnes Hǣlendes Cristes: sænd myċel wæter þurh þīnne
mūþ, swā þæt sīen ᵹewemmede ealle þā on þisse ċeastre syndon.' Mid-þī hē
þus cwæð, se ēadiᵹa Andreas, hraþe sīo [stænene] onlīcnes sendde myċel wæter
þurh hiora mūþ swā sealt, and hit æt manna līċhaman, and hit ācwealde heora
bearn and hyra nȳtenu. And hīe ealle woldon flēon of þǣre ċeastre. Se hāliᵹa
Andreas þā cwæð: 'Mīn Drihten Hǣlend Crist, ne forlǣt mē, ac send mē þīnne
enᵹel of heofonum on fȳrenum wolcne, þæt þā embᵹanᵹe ealle þās ċeastre þæt
ne maᵹen ᵹenēosian for þǣm fȳre.' And þus cweþende, fȳren wolc[en] āstāh
of heofonum and hit ymbsealde ealle þā ċeastre. Mid-þȳ þæt onᵹeat se ēadiᵹa
Andreas, hē blētsode Drihten. Þæt wæter wēox oþ mannes swūran, and swiþe
hit æt hyra līċhaman. And hīe ealle cīᵹdon and cwǣdon, 'Wā ūs, forþon-þe
þās ealle ūp cōman for þissum ælþēodiᵹum þe wē on þissum carcerne betȳned
hæbbað. Hwæt bēo wē dōnde?' Sume hīe cwǣdon: 'Ᵹif ēow swā ... þuhte,
utan ᵹanᵹan on þissum carcerne and hine ūt forlǣtan, þȳ-lǣs wēn sīe þæt wē
yfele forweorþon; and uton wē ealle cīᵹean and cweþan, forþon-þe wē ᵹelēofað
on Drihten þyses ælþēodiᵹan mannes; þonne āfyrseþ hē þās earfoðnesse fram
ūs.' Mid-þī se ēadiᵹa Andreas onᵹeat þæt hīe tō Drihtene wǣron ᵹehwerfede,
hē cwæð tō þǣre stǣnenan anlīcnesse, 'Āra nū þurh mæᵹen ūres Drihtenes, and
mā wæter of þīnum mūþe þū ne send.' And þā ᵹecweden, þæt wæter oflan, and
mā of heora mūþe hit ne ēode. Se hāliᵹa Andreas þā ūt-ēode of þām carcerne,
and þæt selfe wæter þeᵹnunᵹe ᵹearwode beforan his fōtum. And þā þǣr tō lāfe
wǣron, hīe cōmon tō þæs carcernes duru, and hīe cwǣdon, 'Ᵹemiltsa ūs, Ᵹod,
and ne dō ūs swā swā wē dydon on þisne ælþēodiᵹan.' Se hāliᵹa Andreas þā
ᵹebæd on þæs folces ᵹesihþe, and sēo eorþe hīe ontȳde and hīo forswealh þæt
wæter mid þām mannum. Þā weras þā þæt ᵹesāwon, hīe him swiþe ondrǣdon,
and hīe cwǣdon: 'Wā ūs, forþon-þe þes dēað fram Ᵹode is, and Hē ūs wile
ācwellan for þissum earfoðnessum þe wē þissum mannan dydon. Sōðlīċe fram
Ᵹode hē is send, and hē is Ᵹodes þēowa.' Se hǣlᵹa Andreas him tō cwæð:
'Mīne bearn, ne ondrǣdaþ ᵹē ēow forþon-þe þās þe on þis wætere syndon, eft
h[ī]e libbað. Ac þis is forþon þus ᵹeworden þæt ᵹē ᵹelēofon on mīnum Drihtne
Hǣlendum Criste.' Se hāliᵹa Andreas þā ᵹebæd tō Drihtne and cwæð: 'Mīn
Drihten Hǣlend Crist, send þīnne þone Hālᵹan Ᵹāst, þæt āweċċe ealle þā þe
on þisse wætere syndon, þæt hīe ᵹelīefen on þīnne naman.' Drihten þā hēt
ealle ārīsan þe on þām wætere wǣron. And æfter þissum se hāliᵹa Andreas hēt
ċyriċan ᵹetimbrian on þǣre stōwe þǣr se swēr stōd. And hē him sealde bebodu
Drihtnes Hǣlendes Cristes, 'And lufiað hine forþon myċel is his mæᵹen.' And
ǣnne of heora aldormannum tō bisceope hē him sette. And hē hī ᵹefullode
and cwæð: 'Nū þonne iċ eom ᵹearo þæt iċ ᵹanᵹe tō mīnum discipulum.' Hīe
ealle hine bǣdon and hīe cwǣdon: 'Medmyċel fæc nū ᵹȳt wuna mid ūs, þæt

þū ūs ʒedēfran ʒedō, forþon-þe wē nīwe syndon tō þissum ʒelēafan ʒedōn.' Se
hālʒa Andreas hīe þā nolde ʒehīeran, ac hē hīe ʒrētte and hīe swā forlēt. Him
fylʒede myċel maniʒo þæs folces wēpende and hrȳmende. And þā āscān lēoht
ofer hieora hēafod. Mid-þī se hālʒa Andreas þanon wæs farende, him ætīwde
Drihten Hǣlend Crist on þām weʒe on ansīne fæʒeres ċildes, and him tō cwæð:
'Andreas, for-hwan ʒæst þū swā būton wæstme þīnes ʒewinnes, and þū forlēte
þā þe þē bǣdon, and þū nǣre miltsiend ofer heora ċild þā þe wǣron fyliende and
wēpende? Þāra ċirm and wōp tō mē āstāh on heofonas. Nū þonne hwyrf eft on
þā ċeastre and bēo þǣr seofon daʒas, oþþæt þū ʒestranʒie heora mōd on mīnne
ʒelēafan. Ʒanʒ þonne tō þǣre ċeastre mid þīnum discipulum, and [þā þe] on
mīnne ʒelēafan ʒelēofan.' Mid-þī hē þis cwæð, Drihten Hǣlend Crist, hē āstāh
on heofonas. Se ēadiʒa Andreas þā wæs eft hwyrfende on Marmadonia ċeastre,
and hē cwæð: 'Iċ þē blētsiʒe, mīn Drihten Hǣlend Crist, þū þe ʒehwyrfest
ealla sāula, forþon þū mē ne forlēte ūt-ʒanʒan mid mīnre hāt-heortan of þisse
ċeastre.' Hīo wǣron ʒefēonde mid myċle ʒefēan, and hē þǣr wunode mid him
seofon daʒas, lǣrende and stranʒende hira heortan on ʒelēafan ūres Drihtnes
Hǣlendes Cristes. Mid-þī-þe þā wǣron ʒefyllede seofon daʒas swā swā him
Drihten bebēad, hē fērde of [Mar]madonia ċeastre efstende tō his discipulum.
And eall þæt folc hine lǣdde mid ʒefēan, and hīe cwǣdon: 'Ān is Drihten Ʒod,
sē is Hǣlend Crist, and se Hālʒa Ʒāst, þām is wuldor and ʒeweald on þǣre
Hālʒan Þrȳnysse þurh ealra worulda woruld sōðlīċe ā būtan ende.'

FERIA IIIIa DE FIDE CATHOLICA

[The text here is transcribed from the facsimile of this homily, item XX, folios 96v–103, in *Ælfric's First Series of Catholic Homilies* (British Museum Royal 7 c. xii), ed. Norman Eliason and Peter Clemoes, Early English Manuscripts in Facsimile, Vol. XIII (1966). The punctuation markings, as noted, resemble those in the manuscript (even if the question mark is shaped quite differently); not imitated here, though, is the spacing of letter-strings in the manuscript, which is an additional method of representing togetherness of word sequences or separation between them. This homily, and the others which it belongs with, are edited by Benjamin Thorpe, *The Homilies of the Anglo-Saxon Church, The First Part, Containing the Sermones Catholici, or Homilies of Ælfric* (1843–6).]

Ælċ cristen man sceal æfter rihte cunnan æჳþer ჳe his paternoster ჳe his crēdan; Mid þām paternostre hē sceal hine ჳebiddan · mid þām crēdan hē sceal his ჳelēafan ჳetrymman; wē habbað ჳesæd ymbe þæt paternoster nū wē wyllað secჳan ēow þone ჳelēafan þe on þām crēdan stent · swā swā se wīsa auჳustinus be þære hālჳan þrynnysse trahtnode; Ān scyppend is ealra þinჳa ჳesewenlīcra and unჳesewenlīcra · and wē sceolon on hine ჳelӯfan · for-þān-ðe hē is sōð ჳod · and ān ælmihtiჳ · sē þe næfre ne onჳan ne anჳin næfde ac hē sylf is anჳinn · and hē eallum ჳesceaftum anჳinn and ordfruman forჳeaf þæt hī bēon mihton and þæt hī hæfdon āჳen ჳecynd swā swā hit ðære ჳodcundlīcan fadunჳe ჳelīcode; Enჳlas hē worhte · þā sind ჳāstas · and nabbað nænne līċhaman; Men hē ჳescōp mid ჳāste and mid līċhaman; Nӯtenu · and dēor⁓ fixas · and fuჳelas⁓ hē ჳescēop on flæsce būton sāwle; Mannum hē sealde ūprihtne ჳanჳ⁓ þā nӯtenu hē lēt ჳān alotene; Mannum hē forჳeaf hlāf tō biჳleofan · and þām nӯtenum ჳærs; Nū māჳe ჳē brōðru understandan ჳif ჳē willað þæt twā þinჳ sindon ān is scyppend ōðer is ჳesceaft; Hē is scyppend sē ðe ჳescēop · and ჳeworhte ealle ðinჳ of nāhte; ðæt is ჳesceaft þæt se sōþa scyppend ჳescēop · þæt sind ærest · heofenas and enჳlas · þe on heofenum wuniað · and syððan þēos eorðe mid eallum ðām ðe hire on eardiað · and sæ mid eallum þām ðe hire on swymmað · nū ealle ðās þinჳ sind mid ānum naman ჳenemnode ჳesceaft; Hī næron æfre wuniende ac ჳod hī ჳescēop; Đā ჳesceafta sind fela ān is se scyppend þe hī ealle ჳescēop · se āna is ælmihtiჳ ჳod; hē wæs æfre · and æfre hē bið þurhwuniende on him sylfum and þurh hine sylfne; Ġif hē onჳunne and anჳin hæfde būton twӯn ne mihte hē bēon ælmihtiჳ ჳod; Sōðlīċe þæt ჳesceaft þe onჳan and ჳesceapen is næfð nāne ჳodcundnysse · for-þī ælċ edwist þætte ჳod nis · þæt is ჳesceaft; And þæt ðe

ᵹesceaft nis · þæt is ᵹod; Sē ᵹod wunað on þrynnysse untōdǣledlīċ · and on
ānnysse ānre ᵹodcundnysse; Sōðlīċe ōðer is se fæder · ōþer is se sunu ōðer is sē
hālᵹa ᵹāst ac þeah-hwǣþere þæra ðreora is ān ᵹodcundnyss and ᵹelīċ wuldor ·
and efeneċe mæᵹenþrymnyss; Ælmihtiᵹ ᵹod is se fæder · ælmihtiᵹ ᵹod is se
sunu ælmihtiᵹ ᵹod is se hālᵹa ᵹāst; Ac þeah-hwǣþere ne sind þrȳ ælmihtiᵹe
ᵹodas · ac ān ælmihtiᵹ ᵹod; þrȳ hī sind on hādum and on naman and ān on
ᵹodcundnysse; þreo for-ðī-þe se fæder bið æfre fæder · and se sunu bið æfre
sunu · and se hālᵹa ᵹāst bið æfre hāliᵹ ᵹāst · and heora nān ne āwent næfre
of þān þe hē is; Nū habbað ᵹē ᵹehȳred þā hālᵹan þrynnysse · ᵹē sceolon eac
ᵹehȳran þā sōðan ānnysse; Sōðlīċe sē fæder and se sunu · and se hālᵹa ᵹāst
habbað āne ᵹodcundnysse · and ān ᵹecynd · and ān weorc; Ne worhte se fæder
nān þinᵹ ne ne wyrċð būton þām suna · oððe būton þām hālᵹan ᵹāste; Ne heora
nān ne wyrċð nān þinᵹ būton ōþrum ac him eallum is ān weorc · and ān ræd ·
and ān willa; Æfre wæs se fæder and æfre wæs se sunu · and æfre wæs se hālᵹa
ᵹāst ān ælmihtiᵹ ᵹod; Sē is fæder sē þe nis nāðer ne ᵹeboren ne ᵹesceapen
fram nānum ōþrum · sē is fæder ᵹehāten for-þān-ðe hē hæfð sunu · þone ðe hē
of him sylfum ᵹestrȳnde būton ælċere mēder; Se fæder is ᵹod of nānum ᵹode ·
se sunu is ᵹod of þām fæder ᵹode; Se hālᵹa ᵹāst is ᵹod forðstæppende of þām
fæder · and of þām suna; þās word sind sceortlīċe ᵹesæde · and ēow is neod
þæt wē hī swutelīcor ēow onwreon; hwæt is se fæder? ælmihtiᵹ scyppend꞉ nā
ᵹeworht ne ācenned · ac hē sylf ᵹestrynde bearn him sylfum efeneċe; Hwæt is
se sunu? hē is þæs fæder wīsdōm · and his word and his miht · þurh ðone sē
fæder ᵹesceōp ealle þinᵹ · and ᵹefadode; Nis se sunu nā ᵹeworht ne ᵹesceapen
ac hē is ācenned; Ācenned hē is and þeah-hwǣðere hē is efeneald · and efeneċe
his fæder; Nis nā swā on his ācennednysse swā swā bið on ūre ācennednysse;
ðonne se man sunu ᵹestrȳnþ and his ċild ācenned bið · þonne bið se fæder māre ·
and se sunu læsse; hwī swā? for-þī꞉ þonne se sunu wyxð þonne ealdað se fæder;
Ne fintst þū nā ᵹelīċe on mannum · fæder and sunu; Ac iċ ðē sylle bysne hū ðū
ᵹodes ācennednysse þȳ bet understandan miht; fȳr ācenð of him beorhtnysse ·
and seo beorhtnys is efeneald þām fȳre; Nis nā þ fȳr of þære beorhtnysse · ac
seo beorhtnys is of þām fȳre; ðæt fȳre ācenð þā beorhtnysse · ac hit ne bið
næfre būton þære beohtnysse; Nū þū ᵹehȳrst þæt seo beorhtnys is eallswā eald
swā ðæt fȳr þe hēo of cymð꞉ ᵹeþāfa nū for-þī þæt ᵹod mihte ᵹestrȳnan eallswā
eald bearn and eallswā ēċe swā hē sylf is; Sē ðe mæᵹ understandan þæt ūre
hælend crist is on þære ᵹodcundnysse eallswā eald swā his fæder · hē þancie
þæs ᵹode · and blissiᵹe; Sē þe understandan ne mæᵹ · hē hit sceal ᵹelȳfan · þæt
hē hit understandan mæᵹe꞉ for-þan þæs wīteᵹan word ne mæᵹ bēon ā·ȳdlod þe
ðus cwæð; Būton ᵹē hit ᵹelȳfon ne maᵹe ᵹē hit understandan; Nū hæbbe ᵹē
ᵹehȳred þæt se sunu is of þām fæder būton ælcum anᵹinne · for-þan-ðe hē is

þæs fæder wīsdōm · and hē wæs æfre mid þām fæder and æfre bið; Uton nū
ʒehȳran be þām hālʒan ʒāste · hwæt hē sȳ; hē is se willa · and sēo sōðe lufu
þæs fæder and þæs suna · þurh ðone sind ealle þinʒ ʒelīffæste · and ʒehealdene·
bē ðām is þus ʒecweden; Godes ʒāst ʒefylð ealne ymbhwyrft middaneardes ·
and hē hylt ealle ðinʒ · and hē hæfð inʒehyd ælċes ʒereordes; Nis hē ʒeworht
ne ʒesceapen ne ācenned · ac hē is forðstæppende · þæt is ofʒanʒende · of þām
fæder · and of þām suna þām hē is ʒelīċ · and efenēċe; Nis se hālʒa ʒāst nā
sunu · for-þān-ðe he nis nā ācenned · ac hē ʒæð of þām fæder · and of þām suna
ʒelīċe · for-þān-ðe hē is heora beʒra willa · and lufu; .Crist cwæð þus be him
on his ʒōdspelle; se frōforʒāst þe iċ ēow āsendan wille · ʒāst þære sōðfæstnysse
þe of mīnum fæder ʒæð hē cȳð ʒecȳðnysse be mē þæt is · hē is mīn ʒewīta þæt
iċ eom ʒodes sunu; and ēac se rihta ʒeleafa ūs tæċð þæt wē sceolon ʒelȳfan on
þone hālʒan ʒāst · hē is se līffæstenda ʒod sē ʒæð of þām fæder and of þām
suna; hū ʒæð hē of him? se sunu is þæs fæder wīsdōm æfre of þām fæder ·
and se hālʒa ʒāst is heora beʒra willa · æfre of him bām; Is for-ðī þonne ān
fæder sē þe æfre is fæder · and ān sunu sē þe æfre bið sunu · and ān hāliʒ ʒāst ·
sē þe æfre is hāliʒ ʒāst; Æfre wæs se fæder būton anʒinne · and æfre wæs se
sunu mid þām fæder for-þān-ðe hē is ðæs fæder wīsdōm; æfre wæs se hālʒa
ʒāst sē þe is heora beʒra willa and lufu; Nis sē fæder of nānum ōþrum · ac
hē wæs æfre; Se sunu is ācenned of þām fæder ac hē wæs æfre on ðæs fæder
bōsme · for-þān-ðe hē is his wīsdōm and hē is of þām fæder eall ðæt hē is; Æfre
wæs se hālʒa ʒāst for-þān-þe hē is swā wē ær cwædon willa and sōð lufu þæs
fæder and þæs suna; Sōðlīċe willa and lufu ʒetācniað ān þinʒ; þæt ðæt þū
wilt þæt þū lufast · and þæt ðū nelt þæt ðū ne lufast; [Sēo sunne ðe ofer ūs
scīnð is līċhamlīċ ʒesceaft · and hæfð swā-ðeah ðrēo āʒennyssa on hire; Ān
is sēo līċhamlīċe edwist · þæt is ðære sunnan trendel; Oðer is se lēoma oððe
beorhtnys · æfre of ðære sunnan sēo ðe onlīht ealne middanʒeard; þridde is sēo
hætu · þe mid þām lēoman becymð tō ūs; Sē lēoma is æfre of ðære sunnan · and
æfre mid hire; And ðæs ælmihtiʒan ʒodes sunu is æfre of ðām fæder ācenned ·
and æfre mid him wuniʒende; Bē ðām cwæð sē apostol · þæt hē wære his fæder
wuldres beorhtnys; ðære sunnan hætu ʒæð of hire · and of hire lēoman · and
se hālʒa ʒāst ʒæð æfre of ðām fæder · and of þām suna ʒelīċe; Bē ðām is þus
āwriten; Nis nān þe hine behȳdan mæʒe · fram his hætan; Fæder and sunu and
haliʒ ʒāst · ne maʒon bēon tōʒædere ʒenamode · ac hī ne bēoð swā-ðeah nāhwār
tōtwæmede;] Nis sē ælmihtiʒa ʒod nā þrȳfeald · ac is þrynnys; God is se fæder ·
and se sunu is ʒod · and se hālʒa ʒāst is ʒod; Nā þrȳ ʒodas· ac hī ealle ðrȳ
ān ælmihtī ʒod; se fæder is ēac wīsdōm of nānum ōþrum wīsdōme· Se sunu is
wīsdōm of þām wīsan fæder· se hālʒa ʒāst is wīsdōm · ac þeah-hwæðere hī sind
ealle ætʒædere ān wīsdōm; Eft se fæder is sōð lufu · and se sunu is sōð lufu ·

and se hālʒa ʒāst is sōð lufu · and hī ealle ætʒædere ān ʒod and ān sōð lufu;
Ēac swilċe is se fæder ʒāst and hāliʒ and se sunu is ʒāst and hāliʒ untwȳlīċe
þeah-hwæþere se hālʒa ʒāst is synderlīċe ʒehāten hāliʒ ʒāst · ðæt þæt hī ealle
ðrȳ synd ʒemænelīċe; Swā miċel ʒelīcnys is on þyssere hālʒan þrynnysse þæt
se fæder nis nā māre þonne se sunu on þǣre ʒodcundnysse · ne se sunu nis māre
þonne se hālʒa ʒāst · ne nān heora ān nis nā læsse · þonne eall sēo þrynnyss;
Swā hwǣr swā heora ān bið þǣr hī bēoð ealle ðrȳ æfre ān ʒod untōdǣledlīċ; Nis
heora nān māre þonne ōðrum ne nān læssa ðonne ōðer · ne nān beforan ōþrum ·
ne nān bæftan [= be·æftan] ōðrum · for-ðān swā hwæt swā læsse bið þonne
ʒod · þæt ne bið nā ʒod; þæt ðæt lator bið þæt hæfð anʒinn ac ʒod næfð nān
anʒin; Nis nā se fæder āna ðrynnys · oððe se sunu þrynnyss · oþðe se hālʒa
ʒāst þrynnyss · ac þās þrȳ hādas sindon ān ʒod on ānre ʒodcundnysse · þonne
þū ʒehȳrst nemnan þone fæder · þonne understenst þū ðæt hē hæfð sunu; Eft
ðonne ðū cwyst sunu · þū wāst būton twȳn þæt hē hæfð fæder; Eft wē ʒelȳfað
þæt se hālʒa ʒāst is ǣʒðer ʒe þæs fæder ʒe þæs suna ʒāst; Ne bepæċe nān
man hine sylfne swā ðæt hē secʒe oððe ʒelȳfe þæt þrȳ ʒodas sindon · oððe æniʒ
hād on þǣre hālʒan ðrynnysse sȳ unmihtiʒra þonne ōðer · ælċ ðæra þrēora is
ʒod þēah-hwæðere hī ealle ān ʒod for-þān-ðe hī ealle habbað ān ʒecynd and
āne ʒodcundnysse · and āne edwiste · and ān ʒeþeaht · and ān weorc and āne
mæʒenþrynnysse · and ʒelīċ wuldor · and efenēċe rīċe; Is hwæþere se sunu āna
ʒeflǣschamod and ʒeboren tō men of þām hālʒan mædene marian; Ne wearð
se fæder mid menniscnysse befanʒen ac hwæðere hē asende his sunu tō ūre
ālȳsednysse and him æfre mid wæs ǣʒðer ʒe on līfe ʒe on þrōwunʒe · and on
his ǣriste · and on his ūpstīʒe; Eac eal ʒodes ʒelaðunʒ andet on þām rihtum
ʒeleāfan þæt crist is ācenned of þām clǣnan mædene marian · and of þām
hālʒan ʒāste; Nis se hālʒa ʒāst þēah-hwæðere cristes fæder · ne nān cristen
man þæt nǣfre ne sceal ʒelȳfan; Ac sē hālʒa ʒāst is willa ðæs fæder · and
þæs suna for-þī þonne swīðe rihtlīċe is āwriten on ūrum ʒeleafan þæt cristes
menniscnys wearð ʒefremmed þurh þone hālʒan willan; Beheald þās sunnan
mid ʒlēawnysse · on þǣre is swā wē ǣr cwǣdon hætu and beorhtnyss · ac sēo
hætu drīʒð · and sēo beo[r]htnys onlīht; Ōðer þinʒ dēð sēo hætu and ōþer sēo
beorhtnys · and þēah-ðe hī ne maʒon bēon tōtwǣmede belimpð hwæðere þēah
sēo hæþunʒ tō þǣre hǣtan · and sēo onlīhtinʒ belimpð tō þǣre beorhtnysse;
Swā ēac crist āna underfenʒ þā menniscnysse and nā se fæder ne se hālʒa ʒāst ·
þēah-hwæðere hī wǣron æfre mid him on eallum his weorcum · and on ealre his
fare; Wē sprecað ymbe ʒod · dēadlīċe bē undēadlīcum tȳddre bē ælmihtiʒum ·
earminʒas bē mildheortum · ac hwā mæʒ wurðfullīċe sprecan bē þām ðe is
unāsecʒendlīċ; hē is būton ʒemete · for-þī-ðe hē is ǣʒhwǣr; Hē is būton ʒetele
for-þān-ðe hē is æfre; hē is būton hefe for-þān-ðe hē hylt ealle ʒesceafta būton

ʒeswinċe; and hē hī ealle ʒelōʒode on þām ðrim ðinʒum · þæt is on ʒemete
and on ʒetele · and on hefe; Ac wite ʒē þæt nān man ne mæʒ fullīċe ymbe ʒod
sprecan · þonne wē furþon ðā ʒesceafta þe hē ʒescēop ne maʒon āsmēaʒan ·
ne āreccan; hwā mæʒ mid wordum þære heofenan freatewunʒe āsecʒan? oððe
hwā ðære eorðan wæstmbærnysse? oððe hwā hereð ʒenihtsumlīċe eallra tīda
ymhwyrft? oððe hwā ealle ōðre þinʒ? þonne wē furðon þā līchamlīcan þinʒ ·
þe wē on lōciað ne maʒon fullīce befoon [sic] mid ūre ʒesihðe? Efne þū ʒesihst
þone mannan beforan ðē · ac on þære tīde þe ðū his neb ʒesihst þū ne ʒesihst nā
his hricʒ · eallswā ʒif þū sumne clāð sċēawast · ne miht þū hine ealne tōʒædere
ʒesēon · ac wēntst ābūton þæt ðū ealne hine ʒesēo; Hwilċ wundor is ʒif sē
ælmihtiʒa ʒod is · unāsecʒendlīċ · and unbefanʒennlīċ: sē þe æʒhwær is eall ·
and nāhwār tōdæled; Nū smēað sum undēop-ðancol man hū ʒod maʒe bēon
æʒhwær ætʒædere · and nāhwār tōdæled; Beheald þās sunnan hū hēaʒe hēo
āstīhð · and hū hēo āsent hire lēoman ʒeond ealne middaneard · and hū hēo
onlīht ealle ðās eorþan þe mancyn on-eardað; Swā hraðe swā hēo upāsprinʒð on
ærne meriʒen · hēo sċīnð on hierusalem and on romebyriʒ and on ðisum earde:
and on eallum eardum ætʒædere · and hwæþere hēo is ʒesceaft · and bē ʒodes
dihte ʒæð; Hwæt wēnst þū · hū miccle swīðor is ʒodes andwerdnys · and his
miht · and his nēosunʒ æʒhwær · him ne wiðstent nān þinʒ nāðor ne stænen
weal ne breden wāh swā swā hī wiðstandað þære sunnan; him nis nān ðinʒ
diʒele ne uncūð; ðū sċēawast þæs mannes neb · and ʒod sċēawað his heortan;
Godes ʒāst āfandað ealra manna heortan · and þā ðe on hine ʒelȳfað · and hine
lufiað þā hē clænsað · and ʒeʒladað mid his nēosunʒe · and þæra unʒelēaffulra
manna heortan hē forbīhð · and āscunað; wite ēac ʒehwā þæt ælċ man hæfð
þrēo þinʒ on him sylfum untōdæledlīċe and tōʒædere wyrċende · swā swā ʒod
cwæð þā þā hē ærest man ʒescōp; Hē cwæð uton ʒewyrċan mannan tō ūre
anlīcnysse · and hē worhte þā adam tō his anlīcnysse; On hwilcum dæle hæfð
se man ʒodes anlīcnysse · on him? on þære sāwle nā on þām līċhaman; þæs
mannes sāwul hæfð on hire ʒecynde þære hālʒan þrynnysse anlīcnysse · for-
þan-ðe hēo hæfð on hire ðrēo ðinʒ · þæt is ʒemynd · and andʒit · and willa;
þurh ðām ʒemynde · se man ʒeþenċð þā ðinʒ ðe hē ʒehȳrde · oððe ʒeseah ·
oððe ʒeleornode; þurh ðæt andʒit hē understent ealle þā ðinʒ þe hē ʒehȳrð
oððe ʒesīhð; Of þām willan cumað ʒeþōhtas · and word and weorc · æʒðer
ʒe yfele · ʒe ʒōde; Ān sāwul is · and ān līf and ān edwist sēo þe hæfð þās
þrēo þinʒ on hire tōʒædere wyrċende untōdæledlīċe for-þī þær ðæt ʒemynd bið
þær bið þæt andʒit and se willa · and æfre hī bēoð tōʒædere; ðēah-hwæðere
nis nān þæra þrēora sēo sāwul ac sēo sāwul þurh ðæt ʒemynd ʒemanð · þurh
þæt andʒit hēo understent · þurh ðone willan hēo wile swā hwæt swā hire līcað
and hēo is hwæþere ān sāwul and ān līf; Nū hæfð hēo for-ðī ʒodes anlīcnysse

on hire · for-þān-ðe hēo hæfð þrēo þinʒ on hire untōdæledlīċe wyrċende; Is
hwæþere sē man ān man · and nā þrynnys; God soðlīċe · fæder · and sunu and
hāliʒ ʒāst þurhwunað on þrynnysse · hāda: and on ānnysse ānre ʒodcundnysse;
Nis nā se man on þrynnysse wuniende swā swā ʒod ac hē hæfð hwæþere ʒodes
anlīcnysse on his sāwle þurh ðā ðrēo þinʒ þe wē ær cwædon; Arrius hātte ān
ʒedwolman sē flāt wið ānum biscope þe wæs ʒenemned alexander wīs · and
riht-ʒelȳfed; ðā cwæð se ʒedwolman þæt crist ʒodes sunu ne mihte nā bēon
his fæder ʒelīċ · ne swā mihtiʒ swā hē and cwæð ðæt se fæder wære ær se
sunu and nam bysne bē mannum hū ælċ sunu bið ʒynʒra þonne se fæder on
þysum līfe; ðā cwæð se hālʒa biscop alexander him tōʒeanes; God wæs æfre
and æfre wæs his wīsdōm of him ācenned · and se wīsdōm is his sunu · eallswā
mihtiʒ swā se fæder; þā beʒeat se ʒedwola þæs caseres fultum tō his ʒedwylde
and cwæð ʒemōt onʒean þone biscop · and wolde ʒebīʒan eall þæt folc tō his
ʒedwyldum; þā wacode se biscop āne niht on ʒodes ċyrċan and clypode tō his
drihtne · and þus cwæð; Dū ælmihtiʒa ʒod dēm rihtne dōm betwux mē and
arrium; Hī cōmon þā ðæs on meriʒen tō þām ʒemōte; þā cwæð se ʒedwola tō
his ʒefērum þæt hē wolde ʒān ymbe his nēode forð; þā ðā hē tō ʒanʒe cōm ·
and hē ʒesæt · þā ʒewand him ūt eall his innewearde æt his settle · and hē sæt
þær dēad; ðā ʒeswutelode ʒod · þæt hē wæs swā ʒe·æmtoʒod on his innoðe
swā swā he wæs ær on his ʒeleafan; Hē wolde dōn crist læssan þonne hē is ·
and his ʒodcundnysse wurðmynt wanian · þā wearð him swā bysmorlīċ dēað
ʒeseald swā swā hē wel wyrðe wæs; Ōðer ʒedwolman wæs sē hātte sabellius ·
hē cwæð þæt se fæder wære · þā ðā hē wolde fæder and eft ðā ðā hē wolde hē
wære sunu · and eft ðā ðā hē wolde wære hāliʒ ʒāst · and wære for-ðī ān ʒod;
ðā forwearð ēac þes ʒedwola mid his ʒedwylde; Nū eft þæt iudeisce folc þe crist
ofslōʒon swā swā hē sylf wolde · and ʒeþafode: secʒað ðæt hī wyllað ʒelȳfan
on þone fæder and nā on þone sunu þe heora maʒas ofslōʒon; Heora ʒelēafa
is nāht · and hī for-þī losiað; for ūre ālysednysse crist ʒeþafode þæt hī hine
ofslōʒon; Hit ne mihte eall mancyn ʒedōn ʒif hē sylf nolde; Ac sē hālʒa fæder
ʒescēop and ʒeworhte mancyn þurh his sunu · and hē wolde eft þurh ðone ylcan
ūs ālȳsan fram helle-wīte · þā ðā wē forwyrhte wæron; Būton ælċere þrōwunʒe
hē mihte ūs habban ac him þūhte þæt unrihtlīċ; Ac se dēofol forwyrhte hine
sylfne þā ðā hē tihte þæt iudēisce folc tō þæs hælendes sleʒe and wē wurdon
ālȳsede þurh his unscyldiʒum dēaðe fram þām ēċan dēaðe; Wē habbað þone
ʒelēafan þe crist sylf tæhte his apostolum · and hī eallum mancynne: and þone
ʒelēafan ʒod hæfð mid maneʒum wundrum ʒetrymmed and ʒefæstnod; Ærest
crist þurh hine sylfne dumbe and dēafe · healte and blinde · wōde and hrēofliʒe
ʒehælde · and þā dēadan tō līfe ārærde · and syððan þurh his apostolas and ōþre
hāliʒe men ðās ylcan wundra ʒeworhte · nū ēac on ūrum tīman ʒehwær þær ðær

hāliʒe men hī restað · æt heora dēadum bānum ʒod wyrcð fela wundra tō-ðī-ðæt
hē wile folces ʒelēafan mid þām wundrum ʒetrymman;　Ne wyrcð ʒod nā þas
wundra æt nānes iudēisces mannes byrʒene ne æt nānes ōðres ʒedwolan · ac æt
riht-ʒelȳfedra manna byrʒenum þā ðe ʒelȳfdon on þǣre hālʒan þrynnysse · and
on sōþre ānnysse ānre ʒodcundnysse; wite ʒehwā eac þæt nān man ne mōt bēon
tuā ʒefullod · ac ʒif se man æfter his fulluhte āslīde wē ʒelȳfað þæt hē maʒe
bēon ʒehealden ʒif hē his synna mid wōpe behrēowsað · and bē lārēowa tǣcunʒe
hī ʒebet;　Wē sceolon ʒelȳfan þæt ælċes mannes sāwul bið þurh ʒod ʒesceapen
ac hwæðere hēo ne bið nā of ʒodes āʒenum ʒecynde;　Dæs mannes līċhaman
antimber bið of þām fæder and of þǣre mēder꞉ ac ʒod ʒescȳpð þone līċhaman
of þām antimbre and āsent on þām līċhaman sawle;　Ne bið sēo sāwul nāhwǣr
wuniende ǣror ac ʒod hī ʒescȳpð þǣrrihte · and beset on þām līċhaman and lǣt
hī habban āʒenne cyre swā hēo synʒie swā hēo synna forbuʒe;　ðēah-hwæðere
hēo behōfað æfre ʒodes fultumes · þæt hēo maʒe synna forbūʒan · and eft tō
hyre scyppende ʒecuman þurh ʒōdum ʒe·earnunʒum · for-þān-ðe nān man ne
dēð būton ʒode nān þinʒ tō ʒōde;　Ēac wē sceolon ʒelȳfan þæt ælċ līċhama þe
sāwle underfēnʒ sceal ārīsan on dōmes dæʒe mid þām ylcan līċhaman þe hē nū
hæfð · and sceal onfōn edlēan ealra his dæda · þonne habbað þā ʒōdan ēċe līf
mid ʒode and hē sylð þā mēde ælcum bē his ʒe·earnunʒum;　ðā synfullan bēoð
on hellewīte · ā · þrōwiʒende and heora wīte bið ēac ʒemeteʒod ælcum bē his
ʒe·earnunʒum;　Uton for-þī ʒe·earnian þæt ēċe līf mid ʒode þurh ðisne ʒelēafan
and þurh ʒōdum ʒe·earnunʒum · sē ðe þurhwunað on þrynnysse · ān ælmihtiʒ
ʒod · ā · on ēċnysse · AMEN;

THE HARROWING OF HELL

[From The Gospel of Nicodemus, Camb. Univ. Lib. MS. Ii.2, 11, ff. 173v–93, printed by W. H. Hulme, *PMLA*, New Series VI (1898), pp. 457–541. Another manuscript of this gospel, in BL. Cotton Vitellius A. 15, survives incomplete. In the Cambridge manuscript this apocryphal gospel follows texts of the four canonical gospels. The narration of the harrowing of hell makes up about three-eighths of the whole Gospel of Nichodemus.]

. . . And hlystað mē nū ðā: Ealle wē cūðon þone ēadegan Symeon, and þone mǣran mæsseprēost þe ðone Hǣlend ǣrost on hys earmum intō þām temple bær, and ealle wē wyton þæt hē twēȝen sunu hæfde, þā wǣron hātene se ōðer Carinus, and se ōðer Leuticus. . . . Heom cōm þā stefen of heofenum and wæs þus cweðende: 'Wrȳtað and ȝeswuteliað hyt.' Hiȝ þā swā dydon. Karinus and Leuticus þus hyt āwryton and þus cwǣdon.

Efne þā wē wǣron myd eallum ūrum fæderum on þǣre hellican dēopnysse, þǣr becōm sēo beorhtnys on þǣre þēostra dymnysse, þæt wē ealle eondlȳhte [= ȝeondlīehte] and ȝeblyssiȝende wǣron. Þǣr wæs fǣrinȝa ȝeworden on ansȳne swylče þǣr ȝylden sunna onǣled wǣre, and ofer ūs ealle eondlȳhte, and Satanas þā and eall þæt rēðe werod wǣron āfyrhte, and þus cwǣdon: 'Hwæt ys þys lēoht þæt hēr ofer ūs swā fǣrlīče scȳneð?' Þā wæs sōna eall þæt mennisce cynn ȝeblyssiȝende, ūre fæder Adam myd eallum hēah-fæderum and myd eallum wȳteȝum for þǣre myclan beorhtnysse, and hiȝ þus cwǣdon: 'Þys lēoht ys ealdor þæs ēčan lēohtes, eall swā ūs Dryhten behēt, þæt hē ūs þæt ēce lēoht onsendan wolde.' Þā clypode Ysaias se wȳteȝa and cwǣð: 'Þys ys þæt fæderlīce lēoht and hyt ys ȝodes sunu, eall swā ič forsǣde þā ič on eorðan wæs, þā ič cwæð and forewīteȝode þæt ðæt land Zabulon and þæt land Neptalim wyð þā ēa Iordanen, and þæt folc þæt on þām þȳstrum sæt sceoldon mǣre lēoht ȝesēon; and þā ðe on dymmum rȳče wunedon, ič wīteȝode þæt hiȝ lēoht sceoldon onfōn: and nū hyt ys tōcumen, and ūs onlȳht þā ðe ȝefyrn on dēaðes dymnysse sǣton. Ac uton ealle ȝeblyssian þæs lēohtes.' Se wȳteȝa þā Symeon, heom eallum ȝeblyssiȝendum, heom tō cwæð: 'Wuldriað þone Dryhten Cryst ȝodes sunu, þone þe ič bær on mȳnum earmum in-tō þām temple; and ič þā ðus cwæð, "Þū eart lēoht and frōfer eallum þēodum, and þū eart wuldor and wurðmynt eallum Ysrahela folce."' Symeone þā ðus ȝesprecenum, eall þæt werod þǣra hālȝena þā wearð swȳðe ȝeblyssiȝende. And æfter þām þǣr cōm swylče þunres sleȝe, and ealle þā hālȝan onȝēan clypodon and cwǣdon, 'Hwæt eart þū?' Sēo stefen heom

andswarode and cwæð: 'Ić eom Iohannes þæs hēhstan wīteᵹa, and ić eom cumen
tō-foran hym, þæt ić his weᵹas ᵹeᵹearwian sceal, and ᵹe·īċan þā hǣle hys folces.'
Adam þā wæs þys ᵹehȳrende and tō his suna cweðende, sē wæs ᵹenemned Seth;
hē cwæð: 'Ᵹereċe þȳnum bearnum and þysum hēah-fæderum ealle þā ðinᵹ þe ðū
fram Mychaele þām hēah-enᵹle ᵹehȳrdest, þā ðā ić þē āsende tō neorxna-wanᵹes
ᵹeate, þæt ðū sceoldest Dryhten byddan þæt hē myd þē his enᵹel āsende, þæt hē
þē ðone ele syllan sceolde of þām trēowe þǣre myldheortnysse, þæt ðū myhtest
mȳnne lȳċhaman myd ᵹesmyrian, þā ðā ić myd eallum untrum wæs.' Seth,
Adames sunu, wæs þā tō-ᵹenēalǣċende þām hālᵹum hēah-fæderum and þām
wȳteᵹum, and wæs cweðende: 'Efne þā ić wæs Dryhten byddende æt neorxna-
wanᵹes ᵹeate, þā ætȳwde mē Michael se hēah-enᵹel and mē tō cwæð: "Ić eom
āsend fram Dryhtne tō ðē, and ić eom ᵹesett ofer ealle mennisce līċhaman. Nū
secᵹe ić þē, Seth: ne þearft þū swincan byddende ne þȳne tēaras āᵹēotende, þæt
ðū þurfe biddan þone ele of þām trēowe þǣre myldheortnysse, þæt ðū Adam
þȳnne fæder myd smyrian mōte for his līċhaman sāre; for-þām-ðe ᵹȳt ne syndon
ᵹefyllede þā fīf þūsend wyntra and þā fīf hund wyntra þe sceolon bēon āᵹāne ǣr
hē ᵹehǣled wurðe; ac þonne cymð se myldheortesta Cryst Ᵹodes sunu and ᵹelǣt
þȳnne fæder Adam on neorxna-wanᵹ tō þām trēowe þǣre myldheortnysse."' Þā
ðys wǣron eall ᵹehȳrende—ealle þā hēah-fæderas and þā wȳteᵹan, and ealle þā
hālᵹan þe þǣr on þām cwicsusle wǣron—hiᵹ wǣron swȳðe ᵹeblyssiᵹende and
Ᵹod wuldriᵹende. Hyt wæs swȳðe anᵹrislić þā ðā Satanas þǣre helle ealdor and
þæs dēaðes heretoᵹa cwæð tō þǣre helle: 'Ᵹeᵹearwa þē sylfe þæt ðū mæᵹe Cryst
onfōn, sē hyne sylfne ᵹewuldrod hæfð, and ys Ᵹodes sunu and ēac man, and ēac
se dēað ys hyne ondrǣdende; and mȳn sāwl ys swā unrōt þæt mē þynċð þæt
ić ālybban ne mæᵹ: for-þiᵹ hē ys myċel wyðerwynna and yfel-wyrċende onᵹean
mē and ēac onᵹean þē. And fæla þe ić hæfde tō mē ᵹewyld and tō ātoᵹen,
blynde and healte, ᵹebȳᵹede and hrēoflan—ealle hē fram þē ātȳhð.' Sēo hell þā
swīðe ᵹrymme and swȳðe eᵹeslīċe andswarode . . . Satanase þām ealdan dēofle
and cwæð: 'Hwæt ys sē þe ys swā stranᵹ and swā myhtiᵹ, ᵹif hē man ys, þæt hē
ne siᵹ þone dēað ondrǣdende þe wyt ᵹefyrn beclȳsed hæfdon? For-þām ealle þā
ðe on eorðan anweald hæfdon, þū hiᵹ myd þȳnre myhte tō mē ᵹetuᵹe and ić hiᵹ
fæste ᵹehēold. And ᵹif þū swā myhtiᵹ eart swā þū ǣr wǣre, hwæt ys se man
and se hǣlend, þe ne siᵹ þone dēað and þȳne myhte ondrǣdende? Ac tō sōðan
ić wāt, ᵹif hē on mennyscnysse swā myhtiᵹ ys þæt hē nāðer ne unc ne ðone dēað
ne ondrǣt, þæt ić wāt, þæt swā myhtiᵹ hē ys on ᵹodcundnysse, þæt hym ne
mæᵹ nā þynᵹ wyðstandan. And ić wāt ᵹif se dēað hyne ondrǣt, þonne ᵹefōhð
hē þē, and þē byð æfre wā tō ēċere worulde.' Satanas þā, þæs cwycsusles ealdor,
þǣre helle andswarode and þus cwæð: 'Hwæt twȳnað þē, oððe hwæt ondrǣtst
þū ðē þone Hǣlend tō onfōnne, mȳnne wyðerwynnan and ēac þȳnne? For-þon

iċ hys costnode, and iċ ġedyde hym þæt eal þæt Iudeisce folc þæt hiġ wæron onġēan hyne myd yrre and myd andan āwehte. And iċ ġedyde þæt hē wæs myd spere ġesticod. And iċ ġedyde þæt hym man drincan menġde myd ġeallan and myd eċede. And iċ ġedyde þæt man hym trēowene rōde ġeġearwode and hyne þǣr on āhēnġ, and hyne myd næġlum ġefæstnode. And nū æt nēxtan iċ wylle hys dēað tō ðē ġelǣdan, and hē sceal bēon underþēod æġðer ġe mē ġe þē.' Sēo hell þā swȳðe anġrysenlīċe þus cwæð: 'Wyte þæt ðū swa dō þæt hē ðā dēadan fram mē ne ātēo, for-þām-þe hēr fæla syndon ġeornfulle fram mē, þæt hiġ on mē wunian noldon. Ac iċ wāt þæt hiġ fram mē ne ġewȳtað þurh heora āġene myhte, būton hiġ se ælmyhtyġa Ġod fram mē ātēo, sē ðe Lazarum of mē ġenam, þone þe iċ hēold dēadne fēower nyht fæste ġebunden, and iċ hyne eft cwycne āġeaf þurh hys bebodu.' Þā andswarode Satanas and cwæð: 'Sē ylca hyt ys, sē ðe Lazarum of unc bām ġenam.' Sēo hell hym þā ðus tō cwæð. 'Ēalā, iċ hālsiġe þē þurh þȳne mæġenu and ēac þurh mȳne, þæt ðū nǣfre ne ġeþāfiġe þæt hē in on mē cume; for-þām þā iċ ġehȳrde þæt word hys bebodes, iċ wæs myd myclum eġe āfyriht and ealle mȳne ārlēasan þēnas wǣron samod myd mē ġedrehte and ġedrēfede, swā þæt wē ne myhton Lazarum ġehealdan. Ac hē wæs hyne āsceacende eal swā earn þonne hē myd hrǣdum flyhte wyle forð āflēon; and hē swā wæs fram ūs rǣsende, and sēo eorðe þe Lazarus dēadan līċhaman hēold, hēo hyne cwycne āġeaf. And þæt iċ nū wāt, þæt se man þe eall þæt ġedyde, þæt hē ys on Ġode stranġ and myhtiġ, and ġif þū hyne tō mē lǣdest, ealle þā ðe hēr syndon on þysum wælhrēowan cwearterne beclȳsede, and on þysum bendum myd synnum ġewryðene, ealle hē myd hys ġodcundnysse fram mē ātȳhð and tō lȳfe ġelǣt.' Ac amanġ-þām-þe hiġ þus sprǣcon, þǣr wæs stefen and ġāstlīċ hrēam swā hlūd swā þunres sleġe, and wæs þus cweðende: '*Tollite portas, principes, uestras, et eleuamini porte eternales et introibit rex ġlorie.*' Þæt byð on enġlisc, 'Ġē ealdras, tō-nymað þā ġatu, and ūp āhebbað þā ēcan ġatu, þæt mæġe in-ġān se cynġ þæs ēcan wuldres.' Ac þā sēo hell þæt ġehȳrde, þā cwæð hēo tō þām ealdre Satane: 'Ġewȳt raðe fram mē, and far ūt of mȳnre onwununġe. And ġif þū swā myhtiġ eart swā þū ǣr ymbe sprǣce, þonne wyn þū nū onġēan þone wuldres cyninġ; and ġewurðe þē and hym.' And sēo hell þā Satan of hys setlum ūt ādrāf, and cwæð tō þām ārlēasum þēnum: 'Belūcað þā wælhrēowan and þā ǣrenan ġatu, and tō-foran onscēotað þā ȳsenan scyttelsas, and heom stranġlīċe wiðstandað, and þā hæftinġa ġehealdað, þæt wē ne bēon ġehæfte.' Þā þæt ġehȳrde sēo mæniġeo þǣra hālġena þe ðǣr ynne wǣron, hiġ clypedon ealle ānre stefne and cwǣdon tō þǣre helle: 'Ġe-opena þȳne ġatu, þæt mæġe in-ġān se cyninġ þæs ēcan wuldres.' Þā cwæð Dauid þā-ġȳt: 'Ne forewīteġode iċ ēow þā ðā iċ on eorðan lyfiġende wæs, "Andettað Dryhtne hys myldheortnysse, for-þām-ðe hē hys wundra wyle manna bearnum ġecȳðan, and

þā ǣrenan ᵹatu and þā ȳsenan scyttelas tōbrecan; and hē wyle ᵹenyman hiᵹ
of þām weᵹe heora onrihtwȳsnysse."' Æfter þām þā cwæð se wȳteᵹa Īsaias tō
eallum þām hālᵹum þe ðǣr wǣron: 'And ne foresǣde iċ ēow, þā ðā iċ on eorðan
lyfiᵹende wæs, þæt dēade men ārȳsan sceoldon, and mæniᵹe byrᵹena ᵹe·openod
weorðan; and þā sceoldon ᵹeblyssian þe on eorðan wǣron: for-þām-ðe hym fram
Dryhtne hǣl sceolde cuman.' Þā ealle þā hālᵹan þys wǣron ᵹehȳrende fram þām
wīteᵹan Īsaiam, hiᵹ wǣron cweðende tō þǣre helle: 'Ᵹe·opena þȳne ᵹatu. Nū
þū scealt bēon untrum and unmyhtiᵹ, and myd-eallum oferswȳþed.' Heom þā
ðus ᵹesprecenum, þǣr wæs ᵹeworden sēo myċele stefen swylċe þunres sleᵹe and
þus cwæð: 'Ᵹē ealdras, tō-nimað ēowre ᵹatu and ūp-āhebbað þā ēċan ᵹatu, þæt
mæᵹe in-ᵹān se cyninᵹ þæs ēċan wuldres.' Ac sēo hell þā þæt ᵹehȳrde þæt
hyt wæs tuwa swā ᵹeclipod, þā clypode hēo onᵹēan and þus cwæð: 'Hwæt ys
se cyninᵹ þe siᵹ wuldres cyninᵹ?' Dauid hyre andswarode þā and cwæð: 'Þās
word iċ oncnāwe, and ēac iċ þās word ᵹeᵹyddode þā ðā iċ on eorðan wæs;' and
iċ hyt ᵹecwæð: þæt se sylfa Drihten wolde of heofenum on eorðan besēon, and
þǣr ᵹehȳran þā ᵹeōmrunᵹe his ᵹebundenra þēowa. Ac nū þū fūluste and þū
fūl stincendiste hell, ᵹe·opena þȳne ᵹatu, þæt mæᵹe in-ᵹān þæs ēċan wuldres
cyninᵹ.' Dauide þā þus ᵹesprecenum, þǣr tō becōm se wuldorfulla cyninᵹ on
mannes ᵹelȳcnysse—þæt wæs ūre heofenlīca Dryhten—and þār þā ēċan þȳstro
ealle ᵹeondlȳhte. And þār þā synbendas hē ealle tō-brǣc, and hē ūre ealdfæderas
ealle ᵹenēosode, þǣr þǣr hiᵹ on þām þȳstrum ǣr lanᵹe wuniᵹende wǣron. Ac
sēo hell and se dēað and heora ārlēasan þēnunᵹa, þā ðā hiᵹ þæt ᵹesāwon and
ᵹehȳrdon, wǣron āforhtode myd heora wælhrēowum þēnum, for-þām-ðe hiᵹ
on heora āᵹenum rīċe swā myċele beorhtnysse þæs lēohtes ᵹesāwon; and hiᵹ
fǣrinᵹa Cryst ᵹesāwon on þām setle syttan þe hē him sylfum ᵹe·āhnod hæfde.
And hiᵹ wǣron clypiᵹende and þus cweðende: 'Wē syndon fram þē oferswȳðde.
Ac wē ācsiað þē, hwæt eart þū, þū ðe būtan ǣlcon ᵹeflyte and būtan ǣlċere
ᵹewemminᵹe myd þȳnum mæᵹenþrymme hæfst ūre myhte ᵹenyðerod. Oððe
hwæt eart þū swā myċel and ēac swā lȳtel and swā nyðerlīċ, and eft ūp swā
hēah, and swā wunderlīċ on ānes mannes hȳwe ūs tō oferdrȳfenne? Hwæt: Ne
eart þū sē ðe lāᵹe dēad on byrᵹene, and eart lyfiᵹende hyder tō ūs cumen? And
on þȳnum dēaðe ealle eorðan ᵹesceafta and ealle tunᵹla syndon āstyrode. And
þū eart freoh ᵹeworden betwȳnan eallum ōðrum dēadum, and ealle ūre ēoredu
þū hæfst swīðe ᵹedrēfed. And hwæt eart þū þe hæfst þæt lēoht hyder eond-[=
ᵹeond-] send, and myd þȳnre ᵹodcundan myhte and beorhtnysse hæfst āblend
þā synfullan þȳstro? And ᵹelȳċe ealle þās ēoredu þyssa dēofla syndon swȳðe
āfyrhte.' And hiᵹ wǣron þā ealle þā dēoflu clypiᵹende ānre stefne: 'Hwanon
eart þū, lā, Hǣlend, swā stranᵹ man and swā beorht on mæᵹenþrymne būtan
ǣlcon womme, and swā clǣne fram ǣlcon leahtre? Eall eorðan myddan-eard

ūs wæs symble underþēod oð nū. And eornostlīċe wē āhsiað þē, hwæt eart þū,
þū ðe swā unforht ūs tō eart cumen? And þār-tō-ēacan ūs wylt fram āteon
ealle þā ðe wē ġefyrn on bendum hēoldon? Hwæðer hyt wēn siġ þæt ðū siġ se
ylca Hǣlend þe Satan ūre ealdor ymbe spæc and sǣde þæt ðurh þȳnne dēað hē
wolde ġeweald habban ealles myddan-eardes?' Ac se wuldorfǣsta cyninġ and
ūre heofenlīca hlāford þā nolde þǣra dēofla ġemaðeles [nā] māre habban, ac
hē þone dēoflīcan dēað feor nyðer ātrǣd; and hē Satan ġeġrāp and hyne fæste
ġeband; and hyne þǣre helle sealde on anġeweald. Ac hēo hyne þā underfēnġ
eall swā hyre fram ūre heofenlīcan hlāforde ġehāten wæs. Þā cwæð sēo hell tō
Satane: 'Lā, ðū ealdor ealre forspyllednysse; and lā, ðū *ordfruma* ealra yfela;
and lā, ðū fæder ealra flȳmena; and lā, ðū þe ealdor wǣre ealles dēaðes; and lā,
ordfruma ealre mōdiġnysse: for-hwiġ ġedyrstlǣhtest þū þē þæt ðū þæt ġeþanc
on þæt Iudeisce folc āsendest þæt hiġ þysne Hǣlend āhēnġon? And þū hym
nænne ġylt on ne oncnēowe. And þū nū þurh þæt trȳw [= trēow] and þurh
þā rōde hæfst ealle þȳne blysse forspylled. And þurh-þæt-þe ðū þysne wuldres
cyninġ āhēnġe, þū dydest wyðer-werdlīċe onġēan þē and ēac onġēan mē. And
oncnāw nū hū fæla ēċe tyntreġa and þā unġe-endodan sūslo þū byst þrōwiġende
on mȳnre ēċan ġehealtsumnysse.' Ac þā ðā se wuldres cyninġ þæt ġehȳrde,
hū sēo hell wyð þone rēðan Satan spræc, hē cwæð tō þǣre helle: 'Bēo Satan
on þȳnum anwealde, and ġyt būtū on ēċum forwyrde, and þæt bēo æfre tō
ēċere worulde on þǣre stōwe þe ġē Adam and þǣra wīteġena bearn ǣr lanġe
on ġehēoldon.' And se wuldorfulla Dryhten þā his swȳðran hand āðenede and
cwæð: 'Ealle ġē mȳne hālġan, ġē þe mȳne ġelȳcnysse habbað, cumað tō mē; and
ġē þe þurh þæs trēowes blēda ġenyðerude wǣron, ġē sēoð nū þæt ġē sceolon
þurh þæt trēow mȳnre rōde, þe iċ on āhanġen wæs, ofer-swȳðan þone dēað
and ēac þone dēofol.' Hyt wæs þā swȳðe raðe þæt ealle þā hālġan wǣron
ġenēalēċende tō þæs Hǣlendes handa. And se Hǣlend þā Adam be þǣre riht
hand ġenam, and hym tō cwæð: 'Syb siġ myd þē, Adam, and myd eallum
þȳnum bearnum.' Adam wæs þā nyðer āfeallende and þæs Hǣlendes cnēow
cyssende, and myd tēarġēotendre hālsunġe and myd myċelre stefne þus cwæð:
'Iċ heriġe þē, heofena hlāford, þæt ðū mē of þysse cwycsūsle onfōn woldest.'
And se Hǣlend þā his hand āðenede and rōdetācen ofer Adam ġe-worhte, and
ofer ealle his hālġan. And hē Adam be þǣre swȳðran handa fram helle ġetēh,
and ealle þā hālġan heom æfter-fyliġdon. Ac se hālġa Dauid þā ðus clypode
myd stranġlīcre stefne and cwæð: 'Sinġað Dryhtne nȳwne lofsanġ, for-þām-ðe
Dryhten hæfð wundra eallum þēodum ġeswutelod, and hē hæfð hys hǣle cūðe
ġedōn tō-foran ealre þēode ġesyhðe, and his ryhtwȳsnysse onwriġen.' Ealle þā
hālġan hym þā andswaredon and cwǣdon: 'Þæs siġ Dryhtne mǣrð and eallum
hys hālġum wuldor. Amen. ALLELUIA.' Se hālġa Dryhten wæs þā Adames

hand healdende, and hiʒ Michaele þām hēahenʒle syllende, and hym sylf wæs
on heofenas farende. Ealle þā hālʒan wæron þā Mychaele þām hēah-enʒle æfter-
fyliʒende, and hē hiʒ ealle in-ʒelædde on neorxena-wanʒ myd wuldorfulre blysse.
Ac þā hiʒ in-weard fōron, þā ʒemȳtton [= ʒemētton] hiʒ twēʒen ealde weras.
And ealle þā hālʒan hiʒ sōna ācsedon and heom þus tō cwædon: 'Hwæt syndon
ʒē þe on helle myd ūs næron, and ʒē nū ʒȳt dēade næron, and ēower lȳċhaman
swā-þēah on neorxna-wanʒe tōʒædere syndon?' Se ōðer hym þā andswarode
and cwæð: 'Iċ eom Enoch, and iċ þurh Dryhtnes word wæs hyder ālædd. And
þys ys Helias Thesbyten þe myd mē ys. Sē wæs on fȳrenum cræte hyder ʒeferod.
And wyt ʒȳt dēaðes ne onbyriʒdon. Ac wyt sceolon myd ʒodcundum tācnum
and myd forebēacnum Antecrystes ʒe·anbȳdian and onʒēan hyne wynnan. And
wyt sceolon on Hierusalem fram hym bēon ofslaʒene, and hē ēac fram ūs. Ac
wyt sceolon bynnan fēorðan healfes dæʒes fæce bēon eft ʒe·edcwycode, and
þurh ʒenypu ūp onhāfene.' Ac onmanʒ-þām-ðe Enoch and Elias þus spræcon,
heom þær tō becōm sum wer þe wæs earmlīces hȳwes, and wæs berende ānre
rōdetācen on uppan his exlum. Ac þā hālʒan hyne þā sōna ʒesāwon and hym
tō cwædon: 'Hwæt eart þū þe ðȳn ansȳn ys swylċe ānes sceaðan; and hwæt
ys þæt tācen þe ðū on uppan þīnum exlum byrst?' Hē hym andswarode and
cwæð: 'Sōð ʒē secʒað þæt iċ sceaða wæs, and ealle yfelu on eorðan wyrċende.
Ac þā Iudeas mē wyð þone Hælend āhēnʒon, and iċ þā ʒeseah ealle þā ðinʒ
þe be þām Hælende on þære rōde ʒedōne wæron; and iċ þā sōna ʒelȳfde þæt
he wæs ealra ʒesceafta scyppend, and se ælmyhtiʒa cyninʒ, and iċ hyne ʒeorne
bæd, and þus cwæð: "Ēalā, Dryhten, ʒemun þū mȳn þonne þū on þȳn rȳċe
cymest." And hē wæs mȳne bēne sōna onfōnde, and hē mē tō cwæð: "Tō sōðan
iċ þē secʒe: tō-dæʒ þū byst myd mē on neorxna-wanʒe." And hē mē þysse
rōde-tācen sealde and cwæð, "ʒā on neorxna-wanʒ myd þysum tācne. And ʒif
se enʒel þe ys hyrde tō neorxna-wanʒes ʒeate ðē in-ʒanʒes forwyrne, ætȳw hym
þysse rōdetācen and seʒe tō hym þæt se Hælenda Cryst, ʒodes sunu, þe nū wæs
anhanʒen, þē þyder āsende. And iċ þā ðām enʒle þe ðær hyrde wæs eall hym
swā āsæde, and hē mē sōna in-ʒelædde on þā swȳðran healfe neorxna-wanʒes
ʒeates; and hē mē ʒe·anbȳdian hēt, and mē tō cwæð: "ʒe·anbȳda hēr oð-þæt
in-ʒā eall mennisc cynn þe se fæder Adam myd eallum his bearnum and myd
eallum hālʒum þe myd hym wæron on þære helle."' Ac ðā ealle hēah-fæderas
and þā wȳteʒan þā hiʒ ʒehȳrdon ealle þæs sceaðan word, þā cwædon hiʒ ealle
ānre stefne: 'Siʒ ʒebletsod se ælmyhtiʒa Drihten, and se ēca Fæder, sē ðe swylċe
forʒifenysse þīnum synnum sealde, and myd swylċere ʒife þē tō neorxna-wanʒe
ʒelædde.' Hē andswarode and cwæð, 'Amen.'

Ðis syndon þā ʒodcundan and þā hālʒan ʒerynu þe ðā twēʒen wȳteʒan
Carinus and Leuticus tō sōðon ʒesāwon and ʒehȳrdon, eall swā iċ ær hēr beforan

sǣde, þæt hiʒ on þysne dæʒ myd þām Hǣlende of dēaðe āryson, eall swā hiʒ se
Hǣlend of dēaðe āwehte. And þā hiʒ eall þys ʒewryten and ʒefylled hæfdon, hiʒ
ūp āryson and þā cartan þe hiʒ ʒewryten hæfdon þām ealdrum āʒēafon; Carinus
his cartan āʒeaf Annan, and Caiphan, and Ʒamaliele, and ʒelīċe Leuticus his
cartan āʒeaf Nychodeme, and Iosepe, and heom þus tō cwǣdon: 'Sybb siʒ myd
ēow eallum fram þām sylfan Dryhtne Hǣlendum Cryste, and fram ūre ealra
Hǣlende.' And Carinus and Leuticus wǣron þā fǣrinʒa swā fæʒeres hȳwes swā
sēo sunne þonne hē beorhtost scȳneð; and on þǣre beorhtnysse hyʒ of þām folce
ʒewyton, swā þæt þæs folces nāwyht nyston hwǣder hiʒ fōron. Ac þā ealdras
þā and þā mæsseprēostas þā ʒewrytu rǣddon þe Carinus and Leuticus ʒewryten
hæfdon, þā wæs æʒðer ʒelīċe ʒewryten, þæt nāðer næs ne lǣsse ne māre þonne
ōðer be ānum stafe—ne furðon, be ānum prican. . . .

[The remaining text relates how Joseph and Nicodemus told Pilate about
Karinus and Leuticus, and Pilate sent a letter to Claudius reporting the events
concerning the crucifixion and resurrection.]

BLICKLING HOMILY X

Men ðā lēofestan, hꝓæt! Nū ānra manna ȝehpilcne iċ mynȝie and lǣre, ȝe peras ȝe pīf, ȝe ȝeonȝe ȝe ealde, ȝe snottre ȝe unpīse, ȝe þā peleȝan ȝe þā þearfan, þ ānra ȝehpylċ hine sylfne scēapiȝe and onȝyte; and spā hꝓæt spā hē on mycclum ȝyltum oþþe on medmycclum ȝefremede, þ hē þonne hrædlīċe ȝecyrre tō þām sēlran and tō þon sōþan lǣċedōme. Þonne maȝon pē ūs ȝod ælmihtiȝne mildne habban, forþon-þe Drihten pile þ ealle men sȳn hāle and ȝesunde, and tō þon sōþan andȝite ȝecyrran.

Spā Dāuid cꝓæþ, þā ēaðmōdan heortan, and þā forhtȝendan, and þā bifiȝendan, and þā cꝓaciȝendan, and þā ondrǣdendan heora Scyppend: ne forhoȝaþ þā næfre ȝod ne ne forsyhþ, ah heora bēna hē ȝehȳreð, þonne hīe tō him cleopiað and him āre biddað.

.i.

Maȝon pē þonne nū ȝesēon and oncnāpan and spīþe ȝearelīċe onȝeotan þ þisses middanȝeardes ende spīþe nēah is, and maniȝe frēcnessa ætēopde, and manna pōhdǣda and pōnessa spīþe ȝemoniȝfealdode. And pē fram dæȝe tō ōþrum ȝe·āxiað unȝecyndelico pītu and unȝecyn[d]elīċe dēaþas ȝeond þēodland tō mannum cumene. And pē oft onȝytaþ þ ārīseþ þēod piþ þēode and unȝelimplico ȝefeoht on pōlīcum dǣdum. And pē ȝehȳraþ oft secȝȝan ȝelōme porldrīcra manna dēaþ þe heora līf mannum lēof pǣre, and þūhte fæȝer and plitiȝ heora līf and pynsumlīċ. Spā pē ēac ȝe·āxiað mislīċe ādla on maneȝum stōpum middanȝeardes and hunȝras pexende. And maniȝ yfel pē ȝe·āxiaþ hēr on life ȝelōmlīcian and pæstmian, and næniȝ ȝōd āpuniȝende, and ealle porldlicu þinȝ spīþe synlicu. And cōlaþ tō spīþe sēo lufu þe pē tō ūrum Hælende habban sceoldan, and þā ȝōdan peorc pē ānforlætaþ þe pē for ūre sāule hæle beȝān sceoldan.

Þās tācno þyslico syndon þe iċ nū hꝓīle biȝ sæȝde be þisse porlde earfoþnessum and fræcnessum. Spā Crist sylfa his ȝeonȝrum sæȝde: þ þās þinȝ ealle ȝepeorþan sceoldan ǣr þisse porlde ende.

Uton pē nū efstan ealle mæȝene ȝōdra peorca and ȝeornfulle bēon ȝodes miltsa, nū pē onȝeotan maȝon þ þis nēalǣċþ porlde forpyrde. Forþon iċ mynȝiȝe and maniȝe manna ȝehpylcne þ hē his āȝene dǣda ȝeorne smēage, þ hē hēr on porlde for ȝode rihtlīċe lifȝe and on ȝesyhþe þæs hēhstan Cyninȝes.

Sȳn pē rūmmōde þearfendum mannum, and earmum ælmesȝeorne; spā ūs ȝod sylfa bebēad þ pē sōþe sibbe hēoldan and ȝeþþærnesse ūs betpēonon habban. And þā men þe bearn habban, lǣran hīe þām rihtne þēodscipe and him tǣċean līfes peӡ and rihtne ӡanӡ tō heofonum; and ӡif hīe on ǣniӡum dǣle pōlīċe libban heora līf, sӯn hīe þonne sōna from heora pōnessum onpende, and fram heora unrihtum onċyrron, þ pē þurh þ ealle Ӡode līcian. Spā hit eallum ӡelēaffullum folcum beboden standeþ. Nǣs nā þām ānum þe Ӡode sylfum underþēodde syndon mid myclum hādum—biscopas and cyninӡas and mæsseprēostas and hēahdīaconas—ac ēac sōþlīċe hit is beboden subdīaconum and munecum, and is eallum mannum nēdþearf and nytlīċ: þ hīe heora fulpiht [and] hādas pel ӡehealdan.

Ne bēo nǣniӡ man hēr on porldrīċe on his ӡeþōhte tō mōdiӡ, ne on his līċhoman tō stranӡ, ne nīþa tō ӡeorn, ne bealpes tō beald, ne breӡda tō full; ne inpit tō lēof, ne prōhtas tō pebӡenne, ne searo tō rēniӡenne.

Ne þearf þæs nān man pēnan þ his līċhama mōte oþþe mæӡe þā syn-byrþenna on eorþscrafe ӡebētan; ah hē þǣr on moldan ӡemolsnaþ and þǣr pyrde bīdeþ, hponne se ælmihtiӡa Ӡod pille þisse porlde ende ӡepyriċean. And þonne hē his byrnspeord ӡetȳhþ and þās porld ealle þurhslyhþ and þā līċhoman þurhscēoteð and þysne middanӡeard tōclēofeð and þā dēadan ūp āstandaþ: biþ þonne se flǣschoma āscȳred spā ӡlæs; ne mæӡ ðæs unrihtes bēon āpiht bedīӡled. Forðon pē habbaþ nēdþearfe þ pē tō lanӡe ne fylӡeon inpitpeorcum; ac pē sce-olan ūs ӡe·earnian þā siblecan pǣra Ӡodes and manna and þone rihtan ӡelēafan fæste staðelian on ūrum heortum, þ hē ðǣr punian mæӡe and mōte, and þǣr ӡrōpan and blōpan. And pē sceolan andettan þā sōþan ӡelēaffulnesse on ūrne Drihten Hǣlende Crist and on his ðone ā[n]cendan Suna and on ðone Hālӡan Ӡāst, sē is efnēċe Fæder and Sunu. And pē sceolan ӡehyhtan on Ӡodes þā ӡehālӡodan ċyriċean and on ðā rihtӡelēfedan. And pē sceolan ӡelȳfan synna forlǣtnessa and līċhoman ǣristes on domes dæӡ. And pē sceolan ӡelēfan on þ ēċe līf and on þ heofonlīċe rīċe þ is ӡehāten eallum þe nū syndan on ӡōdes pyrhtan. Þis is se rihta ӡelēafa þe æӡhpylcum men ӡebyreð þ hē pel ӡehealde and ӡelǣste, forðon-þe nān pyrhta ne mæӡ ӡōd peorc pyrċean for Ӡode būton lufon and ӡelēafan. And ūs is myċel nēdþearf þ pē ūs sylfe ӡeðenċean and ӡemu-nan, and þonne ӡeornost þonne pē ӡehȳron Ӡodes bēċ ūs beforan reċċean and rǣdan and ӡodspell secӡӡean and his puldorþrymmas mannum cȳþan.

.ii.

Uton pē þonne ӡeorne teolian þ pē æfter-þon ðē beteran sӯn and þē sēlran for ðǣre lāre ðe pē oft ӡehȳrdon.

Ēalā men ðā lēofostan, hpæt: pē sceolan ӡeðenċean þ pē ne lufian tō spȳþe þ þæt pē forlǣton sceolan, ne þæt hūru ne forlǣtan tō spīþe þ pē ēċelīċe habban sceolan.

ʒeseō þē nū forʒeorne þ nǣniʒ man on porlde tō-ðæs myċelne pelan nafað,
ne tō-ðon mōdelico ʒestrēon hēr on porlde, þ sē on medmycclum fyrste tō ende
ne cume and þ eall forlǣteð þ him ǣr hēr on porlde pynsumlīċ pæs and lēofest
tō āʒenne and tō hæbbene. And se man nǣfre tō-ðon lēof ne bið his nēhmāʒum
and his porldfrēondum, ne heora nān hine tō-þæs spīþe ne lufað, þ hē sōna
syþþan ne sȳ onscunʒend, seoþþan se līċhoma and se ʒāst ʒedǣlde bēoþ, and
þinċð his nēapist lāþlico and unfæʒer.

Nis þ nān pundor. Hpæt biþ hit, lā, elles būton flǣsc, seoððan se ēċea dǣl
of biþ, þ is sēo sāpl? Hpæt biþ, lā, elles sēo lāf būton pyrma mete?

Hpǣr bēoþ þonne his pelan and his pista? Hpǣr bēoð þonne his plencea
and his anmēdlan? Hpǣr bēoþ þonne his īdlan ʒescyrplan? Hpǣr bēoþ ðonne
þā ʒlenʒeas and þā mycclan ʒeʒyrelan þe hē þone līċhoman ǣr mid frætpode?
Hpǣr cumaþ þonne his pillan and his fyrenlustas ðe hē hēr on porlde be·ēode?
Hpæt, hē þonne sceal mid his sāule ānre ʒode ælmihtiʒum riht āʒyldan ealles
þæs þe hē hēr on porlde tō pommum ʒefremede.

Maʒon pē nū ʒehēran secʒʒean be [sumum peleʒum men] and porldrīcum.
Āhte hē on þysse porlde myċelne pelan and spīðe mōdelico ʒestrēon and maniʒ-
fealde, and on pynsumnesse lifde. Þā ʒelamp him þ his līf pearð ʒe·endod
and fǣrlīċ ende on becōm þisses lǣnan līfæs. Þā pæs his nēhmāʒa sum and
his porldfrēonda þ hine spȳþor lufode þonne ǣniʒ ōþer man. Hē þā for þǣre
lanʒunʒa and for þǣre ʒeōmrunʒa þæs ōþres dēaþes lenʒ on þām lande ʒepunian
ne mihte. Ac hē unrōtmōd of his cȳþþe ʒepāt and of his earde, and on þǣm
lande feala pintra punode, and him nǣfre sēo lanʒunʒ ne ʒetēorode, ac hine
spīþe ʒehyrde and þrēade. Þā onʒan hine eft lanʒian on his cȳþþe, forþon þ
hē polde ʒesēon eft and sceapian þā byrʒenne, hpylċ sē þǣre þe hē oft ǣr mid
plite and mid pæstmum fæʒerne mid [mannum] ʒeseah. Him þā tō cleopodan
þæs dēadan bān and þus cpǣdon: 'For-hpon cōme þū hider ūs tō sceapiʒenne?
Nū þū miht hēr ʒesēon moldan dǣl and pyrmes lāfe, þǣr þū ǣr ʒesāpe ʒodpeb
mid ʒolde ʒefāʒod. Sċēapa þǣr nū dūst and drȳʒe bān, þǣr þǣr þū ǣr ʒesāpe
æfter flǣsclicre ʒecynde fæʒre leomu on tō sēonne. Ēalā þū frēond and mīn
mǣʒ, ʒemyne þis and onʒyt þē sylfne, þ þū eart nū þ iċ pæs iō, and þū byst
æfter fæce þ iċ nū eom. Ʒemyne þis and oncnāp þ mīne pelan þe iċ iō hæfde
syndon ealle ʒepitene and ʒedrorene, and mīne herepīċ syndon ʒebrosnode and
ʒemolsnode. Ac onpend þē tō þē sylfum and þīne heortan tō rǣde ʒeċyr, and
ʒe·earna þ þīne bēna sȳn ʒode ælmihtiʒum andfenʒe.'

Hē þā spā ʒeōmor and spā ʒnornʒende ʒepāt from þǣre dūstsċēapunʒa,
and hine þā onpende from ealre þisse porlde beʒanʒum. And hē onʒan ʒodes
lof leornian and þ lǣran and þ ʒāstlīċe mæʒen lufian, and þurh þ ʒe·earnode
him þā ʒife hāliʒes ʒāstes, and ēac þæs ōþres sāule of pītum ʒenerede and of

tintreȝum ālēsde.

Maȝon pē þonne, men þā lēofestan, ūs þis tō ȝemyndum habban and þās bysene on ūrum heortum staþelian, þ pē ne sceolan lufian porlde ȝlenȝas tō spīþe, ne þysne middanȝeard, forþon-þe þēos porld is forpordenlīċ and ȝedrorenlīċ and ȝebrosnodlīċ and feallendlīċ, and þēos porld is eal ȝepiten.

.iii.

Uton pē þonne ȝeornlīċe ȝeþenċean and oncnāpan be þyses middanȝeardes fru-man. Þā hē ærest ȝesceapen pæs, þā pæs hē ealre fæȝernesse full and hē pæs blōpende on him sylfum on spȳþe maniȝfealdre pynsumnesse. And on þā tīd pæs mannum lēof ofor eorþan, and hālpende and hēal smyltnes pæs ofor eorþan, and sibba ȝenihtsumnes and tūddres æþelnes. And þes middanȝeard pæs on þā tīd tō-þon fæȝer and tō-þon pynsumlīċ þ hē tēah men tō him, þurh his plite and þurh his fæȝernesse and pynsumnesse, fram þon ælmihteȝan Ȝode. And þā hē þus fæȝer pæs and þus pynsum, þā pisnode hē on Cristes hāliȝra heortum.

. . . . and is nū on ūrum heortum blōpende, spā hit ȝedafen is. Nū is æȝhponon hrēam and pōp. Nū is hēaf æȝhponon and sibbe tōlēsnes. Nū is æȝhponon yfel and sleȝe. And æȝhponon þes middanȝeard flȳhþ from ūs mid myċelre biternesse, and pē him flēondum fylȝeaþ and hine feallendne lufiaþ. Hpæt: pē on þām ȝecnāpan maȝon þ þēos porld is scyndende and heononpeard.

Uton pē þonne þæs ȝeþenċean, þā hpīle þe pē maȝon and mōton, þ pē ūs ȝeorne tō Ȝode þȳdon.

Uton ūrum Drihtne hȳran ȝeorne and him þancas secȝȝan ealra his ȝeofena and ealra his miltsa and ealra his ēaðmōdnessa and fremsumnessa þe hē piþ ūs æfre ȝecȳþde. Þæm heofonlīcan Cininȝe [sȳ lof, sē] þe leofað and rīxað on porlda porld aa būton ende on ēċnesse. Amen.

HOW THE TEXTS HAVE BEEN PREPARED

The texts have been copy-edited in a generally uniform style. The verse texts are printed with the conventions of a separate line for each metrical 'line,' and the established line numbering has been supplied as well. Division of morphic elements is at word boundaries only. Vowel length is marked, but the spellings **c** and **g** are not marked for their different phonetic values except in the glosses. Modern punctuation is provided, as is also customary (with exception of 'The Wanderer').

Instead of a running translation (as with most of the prose readings), the accompanying linguistic information is reduced to a running gloss. The lemmata are in the conventional forms used in glossaries and dictionaries, that is, verbs cited by infinitive, nouns by nominative singular, adjectives by nominative singular (masculine). When the morphemic structure is not simple the structure is signaled by hyphen between root forms, or by the raised point separating the **ge-** prefix from the stem. Parts of speech and major class of verbs and nouns are identified after each lemma with these symbols:

1, 2, 3, 4, 5, 6, 7	strong verb class
W1, W2, W3	weak verb class
pret pres	preterite-present verb
impers	impersonal verb
m, f, n	gender class of nouns
m/n etc.	either gender
aj	adjective
av	adverb
num	numeral
prep	preposition
interj	interjection
conj	conjunction
comp aj	comparative adjective
ppl aj	participial adjective

A few further notes are included for syntactical features, such as

w dat   (verb or preposition) with dative complement
w gen   (verb or preposition) with genitive complement
mpl   masculine plural

So, for example, **brūcan** 2 (w gen) signifies a strong verb, class 2, with complement having genitive case form.

The method of glossing for semantic features should be carefully noted. The glosses are *not* snippets of translation that have been set alongside the text—the kind of glossing provided by editors and glossators who present a text as a dark saying needing precisely the illumination which only they can provide. Rather, the norm is to offer two Modern English words selected to identify the semantic range of the Old English stem. Occasionally, any given pair of glosses will not be adequate to indicate the area of meaning for every occurrence of a single word, hence in one text **tēona** is glossed in one place as 'iniquity, shame' and in another as 'hurt, trouble.' Sometimes one of these words—sometimes either one—will fit into an accurate and smooth translation; but sometimes neither one may be a suitable direct substitute in a modern English rendering. And sometimes the Old English word—or phrase—is idiomatic or context-specific; in these instances the gloss is given in inverted commas: **ġe·fēran** 'accomplish' is the meaning in a specific context, or **hran-rād** whale's riding place, 'sea' offers a literal gloss (for a kenning) followed by a simple idiomatic gloss, or **þurh ealra worulda world** 'for ever,' for Old English text that is a calque on a Latin formula. An asterisk (*) in the glossing indicates a word found in that text only. In short, the scheme of glossing of the verse texts is another part of the plan for this firstbook of Old English—to help a student learn to read Old English texts in Old English. This scheme also entails omitting glosses altogether for the most commonly occurring words.

Two texts are given without glosses of any kind.

blētsian W2 bless; consecrate. blīðe aj joyful, pleasant.
innera aj'l n inner, interior. þæne = þone. nama m name.
bealde av boldly, freely.
ofer-ġitol aj forgetful, oblivious.

mān-dǣd f evil deed, sin. miltsian W2 have pity on, show mercy.
ādl f disease, sickness. ġe·hǣlan W1 heal; save. ā-lȳsan W1 let loose;
    redeem. for-wyrd f destruction, ruin.
fyllan W1 fulfill; satisfy. willa m will, desire. fæġere av gently, fairly.
ġe·siġe-fæstan W1 make triumphant. sōð aj true. milts f kindness, mercy.
mild-heorte aj kind-hearted, merciful. ġe·trymman W1 encourage; set in
    order. ed-neowe aj renewed. earn m eagle. ġe·līċe aj alike, similar.
ġeoguð f youth. glēaw aj wise, sagacious.
milde aj mild, gentle. miht/meaht f might, ability. strang aj strong,
    mighty. dōm m judgment, ruling. dēope av deeply, earnestly.
treaflīċe av grievously, painfully. tēona m hurt, trouble. þolian W2 suffer,
    undergo. weġ m way.
Moyse Moses. mǣre aj illustrious, famous. tīd f time, season, while.
wer m man; person.
ġe·þyldiġ aj patient, quiet.

cȳðan W1 make known, show forth.
yrre n anger, wrath.
āwa av always, for ever. belgan 3 become angry, avenge oneself.
ġe·wyrht n work, desert. wealdend m ruler, sovereign.

EXCERPTS FROM THE PARIS PSALTER

[The Paris Psalter (Paris, Bibliothèque Nationale, MS Fonds Latin 8824) contains the psalms in both Latin and Old English, the English translations for the first fifty in prose, those for the other two fifties in verse. Three of them, numbered 102, 120, and 129 are given here, with the verse divisions of the manuscript represented by the hanging indentations. The numbers of these psalms in the English Authorized bible are respectively 103, 121, 130.]

Psalm 102

Blētsa, mīne sāwle, blīðe drihten,
  and eall mīn inneran his þæne ēcean naman.
Blētsiʒe, mīne sāwle, bealde dryhten,
  ne wylt þū oferʒeottul æfre weorðan
  ealra ʒōda, þe hē þē ær dyde.
Hē þīnum māndædum miltsade eallum
  and þīne ādle ealle ʒehælde.
He ālȳsde þīn līf lēof of forwyrde,
  fylde þīnne willan fæʒere mid ʒōde.
Hē þē ʒesiʒefæste sōðre miltse
  and ðē mildheorte mōde ʒetrymede;
  eart þū edneowe earne ʒelīcast
  on ʒeoʒoðe nū ʒlēawe ʒeworden.
Hafast þū milde mōde, mihta stranʒe,
  drihten, dōmas eallum þe dēope hēr
  and full treaflīce tēonan þolian.
Hē his weʒas dyde wīse and cūðe
  Moyse þām mæran on mæniʒe tīd,
  swylce his willan ēac werum Israhela.
Mildheort þū eart and mihtiʒ, mōde ʒeþyldiʒ,
  ēce drihten, swā þū ā wære;
  is þīn milde mōd mannum cȳðed.
Nelle þū oð ende yrre habban,
  ne on ēcnesse ðē āwa belʒan.
Nā þū be ʒewyrhtum, wealdend, ūrum

womm m/n stain, disgrace. **wyrht** f doing, work.

un-riht n wrong, wickedness, evil. **ġieldan** 3 render, requite.

hēah-weorc n lofty work.

mild-heortness f mercy, loving kindness.

lustum 'gladly, joyfully.' **lufedan** = **lufodon.**

folde f earth; ground. **fæðm** m embrace, expanse. **be-windan** 3
    surround, enwrap. **ēast-rodor** m eastern part of heaven.

tēona m (cf sixth verse) iniquity, shame.

ā-fyrran W1 remove, expel. **simble** av ever, always.

þenċan W1 think of; remember; wish. **bearn** n child, son, offspring.

milde aj merciful, gentle.

līðe aj gentle, mild, kind.

þearf f need, want.

ġe·munan pret pres remember, be mindful. **molde** f dust, soil.

māwan 7 mow. **hīeġ** n hay, cut grass.

blostma m blossom, flower.

lǣne aj lent, transitory.

of-ġiefan 5 give up, leave. **gærs-bedd** n grass-bed, 'grave.'

wunian W2 dwell, exist, remain. **wīde-ferð** av 'always,' 'eternally.'

stōw f site, position, place.

þurh .. woruld 'forever.'

ġe·dēfe aj befitting; gentle; good. **on-drǣdan** W1 dread, be afraid.

sōð-fæstness f truthfulness; fidelity.

be-bod n command, order.

ġe·mynd fn remembrance; thought.

wīs-fæst aj wise; learned. **wynnum** 'joyfully.' **æfnan** W1 carry out;
    fulfill.

hēah-setl n exalted seat, throne. **hrōr** aj strong. **timbrian** W2 build,
    erect. **eorð-rīċe** n earthly kingdom.

blētsian, bealde cf opening two verses. **frēa** m lord, king.

mǣre aj great; sublime.

hyġe m thought; intention.

þrēat m host, troop, throng.

wommum wyrhtum   woldest ūs dōn,
ne æfter ūrum unryhte   āhwǣr ʒyldan.
Forðon þū æfter hēahweorce   heofenes þīnes
  mildheortnysse,   mihtiʒ drihten,
  lustum cȳðdest,   þām þe lufedan þē.
Swā þās foldan   fæðme bewindeð
  þes ēastrodor   and æfter west,
  hē betwēonan þām   tēonan and unriht
  ūs fram āfyrde   æʒ[h]wǣr symble.
Swā fæder ðenceð   fæʒere his bearnum
  milde weorðan,   swā ūs mihtiʒ ʒod,
  þām þe hine lufiað,   līðe weorðeð,
  forðan hē ealle can   ūre þearfe.
Ʒemune, mihtiʒ ʒod,   þæt wē synt moldan and dust;
  bēoð mannes daʒas   māwenum heʒe
  æʒhwǣr anlīce,   eorðan blostman,
  swā his līfdaʒas   lǣne syndan.
Þonne hē ʒāst ofʒifeð,   syþþan hine ʒærsbedd sceal
  wunian wīdefyrh,   ne him man syððan wāt
  āhwǣr elles   æniʒe stōwe.
Þīn mildheortnes,   mihtiʒ drihten,
  þurh ealra worulda woruld   wīslīc standeð,
  dēorust and ʒedēfust   ofer ealle þā þe .. ondrǣdað him.
Swā his sōðfæstnyss   swylce standeð
  ofer þāra bearna bearn   þe his bebodu healdað,
  and þæs ʒemynde   mycle habbað,
  þæt hēo his wīsfæst word   wynnum efnan.
On heofenhāme   hāliʒ drihten
  his hēahsetl   hrōr timbrade,
  þanon hē eorðrīcum   eallum wealdeð.
Ealle his enʒlas   ēcne drihten
  blētsian bealde,   heora blīðne frēan,
  mæʒyn and mihta,   þā his mǣre word
  habbað and healdað   and hyʒe fremmað.
Blētsian drihten   eal his bearna mæʒen
  and his ðeʒna ðrēat,   þe þæt þence nū,
  þæt hī his willan   wyrcean ʒeorne.

ġe·weorc n work; deed; action.
stede m place, site, station.
eġsa m awe, fear.

hebban 6 lift up, raise; exalt. **hēah** aj high. **beorg** m mountain, hill.
fultum m help; protection. **fǽle** aj trusty; good. **þearf** f need; want.

wyrċan W1 make; perform; prepare. **hrūse** f earth; soil.
fēond m adversary, enemy. **ġe·weald** n power; control; possession.

hygd fn mind, thought.
swefan 5 sleep, slumber.

mund-bora m protector, guardian. **mihtiġ** aj mighty; able.
swīðre hand right hand.
sōl n sun. **bærnan** W1 (cause to) burn.

yfel aj evil.

ūtgang m going out, departure. **ingang** m going in, entrance.

āwā tō worulde 'for ever,' 'evermore.'

Eall his āȝen ȝeweorc ēcne drihten
  on his āȝenum stede ēac blētsiȝe,
  þǣr him his eȝsa, anweald, standeð;
  blētsiȝe mīn sāwl blīðe drihten.

Psalm 120

Hōf ic mīne ēaȝan tō þām hēan beorȝe,
  þǣr ic fultum fand fǣlne æt þearfe.
Is mīn fultum ēac fæȝer æt drihtne,
  sē ðe heofon worhte, hrūsan swylce.
Ne sylle hē þīnne fōt on fēondes ȝeweald,
  ne hycȝe tō slǣpe sē ðe healdeð þē.
Efne sē on hyȝde hūru ne slǣpeð
  ne swefeð swȳðe, sē þe sceal healdan nū
  Israela folc ūtan wið fēondum.
Ȝehealde þē hāliȝ drihten,
  and þīn mundbora mihti[ȝ] weorðe
  ofer þā swīðran hand symble æt þearfe.
Ne þē sunne on dæȝe sōl ne ȝebærne
  ne þē mōna on niht mīn ne ȝeweorðe,
  ac þē ȝehealde hāliȝ drihten
  wyð yfela ȝehwām æȝhwǣr ȝeorne
  and ðīne sāwle swylce ȝe[he]alde.
Ūtȝanȝ þīnne and inȝanȝ ēce drihten,
  sāwla sōðcynincȝ, symble ȝehealde
  of þisson forð āwā tō worulde.

grund m ground; abyss; depths. **ġeōmor** aj troubled, sad. **clipian** W2
  speak; cry out.
ġe·bed n prayer, supplication. **bēn** f prayer, request.
hīeran W1 listen to.

esne m servant; slave; retainer.
unriht n wrong; sin, iniquity.

ġe·æfnan W1 endure, sustain.
mild-heort-ness f mercy, kindness.
ǣ f law, covenant.
ēaðe av easily, lightly. **ā-ræfnian** W1 carry out; endure; ponder.

ġe·trēowan W1 hope; trust in; be faithful to.

mǣre aj splendid; famous; excellent. **morgen-tīd** f (time of) morning.
ǣfen n/m evening, eventide.

ā-līesan W1 redeem, let loose, absolve. **lustum** 'willingly.'
hyht m/f hope, trust; joy.

Psalm 129

Ic of ʒrundum tō þē ʒeōmur cleopode;
  drihten, drihten, dō þū nū ðā,
  þæt þū mīnes ʒebedes bēne ʒehȳre.
Wesan þīne ēaran ēac ʒehȳrende
  and beheldende mid hiʒe swylce
  on eall ʒebedd esnes þīnes.
Ʒif þū ūre unriht wilt eall behealdan,
  drihten, drihten, hwā ʒedēð æfre
  þæt hē þæt ʒeefne eall mid rihte?
Ys sēo mildheortnes mid þē, mihta wealdend,
  and ic for ðīnre ǣ, ēce drihten,
  þās oþer eall ēaðe ārǣfniʒe.
Hwæt, þæt sāwl mīn symble ārǣfnede,
  þæt ic on þīnum wordum mē wel ʒetrēowde;
  forðon mīn sāwl on þē symble ʒetrēoweð.
Fram þǣre mǣran merʒentīde
  oðþæt ǣfen cume ylda bearnum,
  Israhelas on drihten ā ʒetrēowen.
Forðon is mildheortnesse miht on drihtne
  and hē ālȳseð lustum ealle,
  þā ðe hiht on hine habbað fæste.
Hē Israhelas ealle ālȳseð
  of unrihte æʒhwǣ[r] symble.

eorl m nobleman, (noble) warrior. **dryhten** m lord, prince.

beorn m man, warrior. **bēag-ġifa** m giver of rings.

æþeling m member of royal family; prince. **ealdor-lang*** aj eternal. **tīr** m
glory. **ġe·slēan** 6 obtain by fighting. **sæcce** f strife, contest. **ecg** f edge.

bord-weall m wall of shields. **clēofan** 2 cleave, split.

hēawan 7 hew. **heaþo-lind*** f shield. **hamor** m hammer. **lāf** f remnant, thing
left. **eafora** m offspring, child. **ġe·æþele*** aj natural, suitable.

cnēo-mǣġ m kinsman; ancestry. **camp** m battle, warfare.

lāþ aj hostile, hated (one). **ġe·hwā** each. **ealgian** W2 defend, protect.

hord n/m treasure. **hām** m home. **hettend** m enemy. **cringan** 3 die, fall (in
battle). **Scottas** mpl Scots. **lēode** mpl people, men. **scip-flota*** m sailor.

fǣġe aj doomed (to death). **feallan** 7 fall. **feld** m field. **dunnian** W2 become
dark. **secg** m man, warrior. **swāt** n (m?) 'blood.' **sunne** f sun.

morgen-tīd f morning. **mǣre** aj famous, glorious. **tungol** m/n heavenly
body. **glīdan** 1 glide. **grund** plain, land. **candel** f candle. **beorht** aj bright.

ēċe aj eternal. **æþele** aj noble, glorious. **ġe-sceaft** f/n created thing.

sīgan 2 sink, set (of the sun). **setl** n setting place. **licgan** 5 lie. **secg** cf 13.

gār m spear. **ā-ġīetan** W1 destroy, waste. **guma** m man.

scield m shield. **scēotan** 2 shoot, pierce. **Scyttisc** aj Scottish.

wēriġ aj weary, exhausted. **wīg** n war. **sæd** aj sated. **West-seaxe** mpl West
Saxons. **and-lang** aj entire (period of time). **ēored-ċyst** f troop, company.

on lāst leġdon 'pursued.' **lāþ** aj hostile. **þēod** f people, nation. **hēawan** cf 6.

here-flīema* m 'fugitive soldier.' **hindan** av from behind. **þearle** av sorely.

'THE BATTLE OF BRUNANBURH'

[The text of *The Battle of Brunanburh* is incorporated in the Anglo-Saxon Chronicles as the entry for the year 937. Of the four extant versions of this poem, the 'Parker Chronicle' copy is the oldest (now Corpus Christi College, Cambridge, MS 173, folios 26r–27r). All four copies are believed to be independently derived from one original text providing a second continuation of the Chronicle. The text here is based on Alistair Campbell's critical text, in *The Battle of Brunanburh* (London 1938). It is not normalized, however, and a number of forms, especially inflections, differ from those that may be expected on the basis of paradigms that are based on Early West Saxon: preterite plural -*on* is often replaced by -*an*, dative plural -*um* replaced by -*an*, and so on.]

Hēr Æþelstān cyninჳ,   eorla dryhten,
beorna bēahჳifa,   and his brōþor ēac,
Ēadmund æþelinჳ,   ealdorlanჳne tīr
ჳeslōჳon æt sæcce   sweorda ecჳum
5 ymbe Brūnanburh.   Bordweal clufan,
hēowan heaþolinde   hamora lāfan
afaran Ēadweardes,   swā him ჳeæþele wæs
from cnēomæჳum,   þæt hī æt campe oft
wiþ lāþra ჳehwæne   land ealჳodon,
10 hord and hāmas.   Hettend crunჳun,
Sceotta lēoda   and scipflotan
fæჳe fēolan.   Feld dunnade
secჳa swāte,   siðþan sunne ūp
on morჳentīd,   mære tunჳol,
15 ჳlād ofer ჳrundas,   ჳodes condel beorht,
ēces Drihtnes,   oð sīo æþele ჳesceaft
sāh tō setle.   Þær læჳ secჳ mæniჳ
ჳārum āჳēted,   ჳuma norþerna
ofer scild scoten,   swilce Scittisc ēac,
20 wēriჳ, wīჳes sæd.   Wesseaxe forð
ondlonჳne dæჳ   ēorodcistum
on lāst leჳdun   lāþum þēodum,
hēowan hereflēman   hindan þearle

mēċe m sword. **mylen-scearp*** aj sharp. **Myrċe** mpl Mercians. **wiernan** W1
refuse. **hand-plega** m fighting. **hæleð** m man, hero.

ēar-ġe·bland n commotion of the sea.

lid n ship. **bōsm** m bosom. **ġe-sēċan** W1 seek, visit, invade.

fǣġe cf 12. **ġe·feoht** n battle, action of fighting. **fīf** num five. **licgan** 5 lie.

camp-stede m battlefield. **ġeong** aj young.

ā-swebban W1 put to sleep, kill. **seofon** num seven.

un-rīm n countless number. **here** m army, predatory troop.

flota m sailor. **ġe·flīeman** W1 put to flight.

brego m prince, chief. **nīed** f force, necessity. **ġe·bǣdan** W1 compel, impel.

lid cf 27. **stefn** m prow. **werod** n troop, band, throng. **crūdan** 2
crowd, press. **cnear*** m? ship. **flot** n? water. **ġe·wītan** 1 go, depart.

fealo aj fallow, yellowish. **flōd** m/n water, sea. **feorh** n life. **ġe·nerian** W1
save. **frōd** aj old, wise. **flēam** m flight, fleeing.

cȳþþ f native land, (place of) fellow countrymen.

hār aj gray, hoary. **hilde-rinc** m warrior. **hrēman** W1 exult.

mæcg m man. **ġe·māna** m fellowship, meeting. **mǣġ** m kinsman. **sceard** aj
deprived. **be-flellan** W1 deprive (cf **be-feallan**). **folc-stede** m 'battlefield.'

be-slēan 6 strike, deprive by violence. **sæcc** cf 4. **for-lǣtan** 7 leave.

wæl-stōw f slaughter-place, battlefield. **wund** f wound. **for-grindan** 3
destroy. **ġeong** cf 29. **gūþ** f war. **ġielpan** 3 boast, exult.

beorn m man, warror. **blanden-feax** aj having hair mixed (with gray).

bill-ġe·slieht* n sword-clash, battle. **inwidda** m evil or deceitful one.

here-lāf f remnant of an army, 'booty.' **hliehhan** 6 laugh, rejoice.

beadu-weorc n warlike deed, fighting.

camp-stede cf 29. **cumbol-ġe·hnāst*** n clash of banners, battle.

gār-mitting* f meeting of spears. battle. **guma** cf 18. **ġe·mōt** n meeting,
wǣpen-ġe·wrixl n conflict. **wæl-feld*** m 'battlefield' (dat sg).

eafora cf 7. **plegian** W2 'play,' be active, busy oneself.

ġe·wītan cf 35 (pret pl). **næġled-cnearr*** m nailed ship.

drēoriġ aj sad, mournful. **daroð** m spear. **lāf** f remnant, survivors.

Dinges-mere*? **Dyflen** Dublin. **sēċan** W1 seek, visit.

Īras mpl Irish. **ǣwisc-mōd** aj feeling of shame or dishonor.

ġe·brōþor m (collective pl) brothers. **æt-samne** av together.

æþeling cf 3. **cȳþþ** cf 38. **sēċan** cf 55.

wīġ cf. 20. **hrēmiġ** aj exultant, boastful.

lǣtan 7 let. **hrǣw** n/m corpse. **bryttian** W2 enjoy; divide. **salowiġ-
pād** aj dark-coated. **sweart** aj black. **hræfn** m raven. **hyrned-nebba** m

mēcum mylenscearpan. Myrce ne wyrndon
25 heardes hondpleʒan hæleþa nānum
þǣra þe mid Anlāfe ofer ēarʒebland
on lides bōsme land ʒesōhtun
fǣʒe tō ʒefeohte. Fīfe lǣʒun
on þām campstede cyninʒas ʒiunʒe
30 sweordum āswefede, swilce seofene ēac
eorlas Anlāfes, unrīm heriʒes,
flotena and Sceotta. Þǣr ʒeflēmed wearð
Norðmanna breʒu, nēde ʒebēded
tō lides stefne lītle weorode;
35 crēad cnear on flot, cyninʒ ūt ʒewāt
on fealene flōd, feorh ʒenerede.
Swilce þǣr ēac se frōda mid flēame cōm
on his cȳþþe norð, Costontīnus,
hār hilderinʒ; hrēman ne þorfte
40 mecʒa ʒemānan: hē wæs his mǣga sceard,
frēonda befylled on folcstede,
beslaʒen æt sæcce, and his sunu forlēt
on wælstōwe wundun forʒrunden,
ʒiunʒne æt ʒūðe. Ʒelpan ne þorfte
45 beorn blandenfeax bilʒeslehtes,
eald inwidda, nē Anlāf þȳ mā;
mid heora herelāfum hlehhan ne þorftun
þæt hī beaduweorca beteran wurdun
on campstede cumbolʒehnāstes,
50 ʒārmittinʒe, ʒumena ʒemōtes,
wǣpenʒewrixles, þæs hī on wælfelda
wiþ Ēadweardes afaran pleʒodan.
Ʒewitan him þā Norþmen næʒledcnearrum,
drēorig daraða lāf, on Dinʒesmere,
55 ofer dēop wæter Difelin sēcan,
eft Īra land, ǣwiscmōde.
Swilce þā ʒebrōþer bēʒen ætsamne,
cyninʒ and æþelinʒ, cyþþe sōhton,
Wesseaxena land, wīʒes hrēmʒe.
60 Lētan him behindan hrǣ bryttian
saluwiʒpādan, þone sweartan hræfn,

horny-beaked (one). **haso-pāda*** m dun-coated (one). **earn** m eagle.

æftan av from behind. **æs** n food, carrion. **brūcan** 2 (w gen) enjoy.

grǣdiġ aj greedy. **gūþ-hafoc*** m bird of war. **grǣġ** aj gray. **dēor** n animal.

weald m wood, forest. **wæl** n number of dead; slaughter.

eġ-land n island.

folc n people. **ġe·fiellan** W1 fell, slay.

bōc f book.

ūþ-wita m learned man. **ēastan** av from the east.

be-cuman 4 come, arrive.

brād aj broad. **brim** n sea. **Bryten** f Britain. **sēċan** cf 55, 58.

wlanc aj proud, bold. **wīġ-smið** m war-maker, warrior. **Wealh** m Welshman.

eorl cf 1, 31, **ār-hwæt*** aj abounding in glory. **eard** m country. **be-ġietan** 5 obtain, conquer.

hyrnednebban,   and þane hasupādan,
earn æftan hwīt,   æses brūcan—
ʒrædiʒne ʒūðhafoc—   and þæt ʒræʒe dēor,
65 wulf on wealde.   Ne wearð wæl māre
on þis ēiʒlande   æfre ʒīeta
folces ʒefylled   beforan þissum
sweordes ecʒum,   þæs þe ūs secʒað bēc,
ealde ūðwitan,   siþþan ēastan hider
70 Enʒle and Seaxe   ūp becōman,
ofer brād brimu   Brytene sōhtan,
wlance wīʒsmiþas,   Wēalas ofercōman,
eorlas ārhwate,   eard beʒēatan.

ǣdre av at once. **āġef andsware** 'answered.'
dēop aj deep. **ġe·lād** n course, way. (**dēop ġe·lād** 'the deep sea').
fōr f journey. **feor(r)** aj distant, remote. **weġ** m road, way.
hrædliċe av quickly, promptly. **scyppend** m maker, creator.
wealdend ruler, the Lord. **be-cweðan** 5 declare, command.
ēað comp av more easily. **ġe·fēran** W1 'accomplish.'
cunnan pret pres know. **holm** m sea, ocean. **be-gang** m circuit, expanse.
sǣ-strēam m ocean, current. **swān-rād** f swan's riding-place, i.e., sea.
waroð-faruð* m/n eddying surf. **ġe·winn** n strife. **wæter-brōga** m
  terrible water. **wīd-land** n broad earth. **wine** m 'lord, ruler.'
eorl m nobleman, champion. **el-þēodiġ** of another people, foreign.
hæleð m hero, warrior. **ġe-hygd** n thought. **here-strǣt** f 'highway.'

ġe·wītan 1 go, depart. **ūhte** f dawn, early morning. **ǣr-dæġ** m daybreak.
sand-hlið* n sand-hill. **sǣ** m/f ocean, sea. **faroð** m/n current, surf.
þrīst(e) aj bold, earnest. **ġe·þanc** m/n thought. **gangan** 7 go, walk.

EXCERPTS FROM *ANDREAS*

[*Andreas* is the title supplied by editors for the verse text in the Vercelli Book (Vercelli, Biblioteca Capitolare MS CXVII) which narrates the legend of St. Andrew. It has been edited fully, with introduction, commentary, and glossary, by Kenneth R. Brooks in *Andreas and The Fates of the Apostles* (Oxford, 1961). Relations of the verse narrative to prose versions (Latin as well as English) are examined by Milton Henry Riemer in *The Old English Andreas: A Study of the Poet's Response to his Source* (Ph.D. dissertation, The University of Texas, 1965). The excerpts given here parallel the prose text in The Blickling Homilies (see the Prose Readings) as follows: *Andreas* lines 189–201 corresponds to Blickling folio 137r, 5–11, and *Andreas* lines 235–369 corresponds to Blickling folio 137v, 2 to folio 138r, 13. As will be obvious, the verse text embellishes the prose narrative with both phrasal variation and expanded dialog.]

[II]

. . . . . .

Ǣdre him Andrēas aʒef andsware:

190 'Hū mæʒ ic, dryhten mīn,   ofer dēop ʒelād
fōre ʒefremman   on feorne weʒ
swā hrædlīce,   heofona scyppend,
wuldres waldend,   swā ðū worde becwist?
Ðæt mæʒ enʒel þīn   ēað ʒefēran,
195 [hāliʒ] of heofenum: con him holma beʒanʒ,
sealte sǣstrēamas   ond swanrāde,
waroðfaruða ʒewinn   ond wæterbrōʒan,
weʒas ofer wīdland.   Ne synt mē winas cūðe,
eorlas elþēodiʒe,   ne þǣr æniʒes wāt
200 hæleða ʒehyʒdo,   ne mē herestrǣta
ofer cald wæter   cūðe sindon.'

. . . .

[III]

. . . . . .

235 Ʒewāt him þā on uhtan   mid ǣrdæʒe
ofer sandleoðu   tō sǣs faruðe,
þrīste on ʒeþance,   ond his þeʒnas mid,

grēot n gravel; seashore. **gār-secg** m sea, ocean. **hlynnan** W1 resound.

bēatan 7 beat. **brim-strēam** m ocean-current. **hyht** m joy, comfort.

waroð m shore. **wīd-fæðme** aj wide-bosomed, capacious. **mōdiġ** aj brave.

ġe·mētan W1 find, encounter. **morgen-torht*** aj radiant-in-the-morning.

bēacen n sign. **beorht** aj radiant. **brim** n sea. **snēowan** 2 move, hasten.

heolstor m hiding-place, darkness. **heofon-candel** f lamp of the sky.

blāc aj shining, radiant. **lago-flōd** m ocean. **lid-weard*** m boat-guard,
    i.e., seafarer. **þrymliċ** aj glorious. **ġe·mētan** W1 meet, find.

mōdiġlīċ aj valiant. **mere-bāt*** sea-boat, ship.

sīð-from aj ready to go, eager.

dugoð f (experienced) warriors. **wealdend** m leader, ruler, lord.

ēċe aj eternal, everlasting.

ġe·scirpla m garment. **scip-ferend*** m sailor, voyager.

eorl m nobleman. **on-līċ** aj (w dat) like (to). **ēa-līðend** m seafarer.

fæðm m expanse, embrace. **feorne weġ** cf. 191.

cēol m ship. **lācan** 7 go, travel.

ġe·grētan W1 salute, hail. **grēot** cf 238.

fūs aj eager to go. **faroð** m/n 'sea.' **fæġ(e)n** aj glad, joyful.

reordian W2 speak. **līðan** 1 go, journey.

mā-cræftiġ aj of superior skill. **mere-þissa** m sea-burster, i.e., ship.

āne 'solitary.' **æġ-flota*** m sea-floater, ship. **ēagor-strēam** m ocean
    current, sea. **ȳð** f wave, billow. **ġe·wealc** n rolling, tossing.

bīdan 1 (w gen) await.

meðel-hēġende aj 'endowed with speech.'

waroð cf 240. **wið þingian** W2 speak with, address.

mæġð f nation, people. **feorran** av from afar.

fēran W1 go, journey. **flōd** m ocean, sea. **beran** 4 bear, carry. **hran-rād** f
    whale's riding place, 'sea.' **hēah-stefn** aj with high prow. **naca** m ship.

snel-liċ aj swift. **sǣ-mearh** m sea-horse, 'ship.' **sund** n water, ocean.

lēode m/f people, nation. **ġe·sēċan** W1 come to.

wær n sea. **be-wrecan** 5 drive away. **for-drīfan** 1 impel.

ēað-mōd aj humble, meek. **on-cweðan** 5 answer, reply.

biddan 5 ask, request. **þēah** conj although. **bēag** mpl treasure, money.

sinc-weorðung f costly gift. **syllan** W1 give, render.

ġe·bringan W1 convey, escort. **brant** aj high (-prowed). **cēol** cf 253, 256.

hēa = **hēah**. **horn-scip*** n beaked ship. **hwæl** m whale. **ēðel** native land.

mæġð cf 264. **meorð** f reward.

ʒanʒan on ʒrēote. Ʒārsecʒ hlynede,
bēoton brimstrēamas. Se beorn wæs on hyhte,
240 syðþan hē on waruðe wīdfæðme scip
mōdiʒ ʒemētte. Þā cōm morʒentorht
bēacna beorhtost ofer breomo snēowan,
hāliʒ of heolstre, heofoncandel blāc,
ofer laʒoflōdas. Hē ðær lidweardas,
245 þrymlīce þrȳ þeʒnas [ʒemētte],
mōdiʒlīce menn, on merebāte
sittan sīðfrome, swylce hīe ofer sǣ cōmon:
þæt wæs drihten sylf, duʒeða wealdend,
ēce ælmihtiʒ, mid his enʒlum twām.
250 Wǣron hīe on ʒescirplan scipferendum
eorlas onlīce, ēalīðendum,
þonne hīe on flōdes fæðm ofer feorne weʒ
on cald wæter cēolum lācað.
Hīe ðā ʒeʒrette, sē ðe on ʒrēote stōd,
255 fūs on faroðe, *f*æʒn reordade:
'Hwanon cōmon ʒē cēolum līðan,
mācræftiʒe menn, on mereþissan,
āne æʒflotan? Hwanon ēaʒorstrēam
ofer ȳða ʒewealc ēowic brōhte?'
260 Him ðā ondswarode ælmihti ʒod,
swā þæt ne wiste, sē ðe þæs wordes bād,
hwæt se manna wæs meðelhēʒendra,
þe hē þǣr on waroðe wið þinʒode:
'Wē of Marmedonia mæʒðe syndon
265 feorran ʒefērede. Ūs mid flōde bær
on hranrāde hēahstefn naca,
snellīc sǣmearh s*u*nde bewunden,
oðþæt wē þiss[a] lēoda land ʒesōhton,
wǣre bewrecene swā ūs wind fordrāf.'
270 Him þā Andrēas ēaðmōd oncwæð:
'Wolde ic þē biddan, þēh ic þē bēaʒa lȳt,
sincweorðunʒa, syllan meahte,
þæt ðū ūs ʒebrōhte brante cēole,
hēa hornscipe, ofer hwæles ēðel
275 on þǣre mæʒðe. Bið ðē meorð wið Ʒod,

lād f way, journey. **līðe** aj kind, gracious.

eft av afterwards, in return. **helm** m protector, 'ruler.'

ȳð-lid n wave-traveller, ship. **scyppend** cf 192.

ġe·wunian W2 remain, dwell. **wīd-fērend** aj pl travellers from afar.

el-þēodiġ aj of another people. **eard** m dwelling. **brūcan** 2 (w gen) enjoy.

ċeaster f stronghold, city. **cwealm** m death. **þrōwian** W2 undergo, suffer.

feorran cf 265. **feorh ġe·lǣdan** 'venture.'

wilnian W2 implore ('to go'). **mere** m sea, water.

fǣġð(e) f state of enmity, hostility. **feorh** n life. **spildan** W1 destroy.

ā-ġifan 5 give.

lust m desire. **hwettan** W1 urge. **lēod-mearc** f territory.

hyht m hope, expectation. **mǣre** aj famous, renowned.

þēoden m king, lord. **lēof** aj dear, beloved.

mere-faroð m ocean current. **milts** f favor, kindness. **ġe·cȳðan** W1 reveal.

þēoden cf 288.

neriġend m Saviour. **fīras** mpl men. **naca** cf 266. **stefn** prow.

ēst-liċe av willingly.

ferian W1 bear, convey. **frēo-liċe** av gladly.

efne av just, even. **lust** cf 286. **mynnan** W1 urge.

ġe·sēċan W1 reach, attain to.

gaful-rǣden f agreed tribute, 'fare.'

sceatt m coin; pl money. **ġe·scrīfan** W1 appoint. **scip-weard*** m 'crew.'

ār m attendant. **ȳð-bord** n wave-plank, i.e., ship. **unnan** pret pres decide.

ofost-līċe av with haste, speedily.

wine-þearfende aj friendless. **mǣlan** W1 speak.

fǣted ptc aj plated (with gold). **feoh-ġe-strēon** n rich treasure.

wela m prosperity. **wist** f food. **wīra ġe·spann** ornament of 'fine metalwork.'

locenra bēaga of interlocked rings. **lust ā-hwettan** W1 excite, arouse.

willa m wish, desire. **be-cweðan** cf 193.

beorn m man, hero. **brego** m prince, lord. **bolca** m gangway.

waroða ġe·weorp 'sandhills.' **wið þingian** cf 263.

hū . . þæs (ðæt) 'how did you come to.' **wine** m friend.

sǣ-beorg m cliff by the sea. **woldes = woldest.** **mere-strēam** m ocean
    current. **ġe·met** n 'expanse.' **māðm** m treasure. **be-dǣlan** W1 deprive.

clif n cliff (pl). **nēosan** W1 (w gen) seek, go to.

frōfor f help, consolation. **faroð-strǣt** f way over the sea, voyage.

hlāf m bread. **wist** cf 302. **hluttor** aj clear, pure.

drync m drink. **duguð** f 'benefit.' **drohtað** m condition, lot.

þæt ðū ūs on lāde līðe weorðe.'
Eft him ondswarode æðelinȝa helm
of ȳðlide, enȝla scippend:
'Ne maȝon þǣr ȝewunian wīdfērende,
280 ne þǣr elþēodiȝe eardes brūcað,
ah in þǣre ceastre cwealm þrōwiað,
þā ðe feorran þyder feorh ȝelǣdaþ,
ond þū wilnast nū ofer wīdne mere
þæt ðū on þā fæȝðe þīne fēore spilde?'
285 Him þā Andrēas āȝef ondsware:
'Ūsic lust hweteð on þā lēodmearce,
mycel mōdes hiht, tō þǣre mǣran byriȝ,
þēoden lēofesta, ȝif ðū ūs þīne wilt
on merefaroðe miltse ȝecȳðan.'
290 Him ondswarode enȝla þēoden,
nereȝend fīra, of nacan stefne:
'Wē ðē ēstlīce mid ūs willað
feriȝan frēolīce ofer fisces bæð
efne tō þām lande þǣr þē lust myneð
295 tō ȝesēcanne, syððan ȝē ēowre
ȝafulrǣdenne āȝifen habbað,
sceattas ȝescrifene, swā ēow scipweardas,
āras ofer ȳðbord, unnan willað.'
Him þā ofstlīce Andrēas wið,
300 wineþearfende, wordum mǣlde:
'Nǣbbe ic fǣted ȝold ne feohȝestrēon,
welan ne wiste, ne wīra ȝespann,
landes ne locenra bēaȝa, þæt ic þē mæȝe lust āhwettan,
willan in worulde, swā ðū worde becwist.'
305 Him þā beorna breoȝo, þǣr hē on bolcan sæt,
ofer waroða ȝeweorp wið þinȝode:
'Hū ȝewearð þē þæs, wine lēofesta,
ðæt ðū sǣbeorȝas sēcan woldes,
merestrēama ȝemet, māðmum bedǣle*d*,
310 ofer cald cleofu cēoles nēosan?
Nafast þē tō frōfre on faroðstrǣte
hlāfes wiste ne hlutterne
drync tō duȝoðe: is se drohtað stranȝ

lago-lād f water-way, voyage. **cunnian** W2 try, venture upon.

wīs aj wise, prudent. **ġe·wit** n mind, reason. **on-lūcan** 2 open, disclose.
ġe·dafnian W2 befit, suit. **ġifan** 5 give, grant.
wela, wist cf 302. **woruld-spēd** f worldly prosperity.
ofer-hygd f arrogance, pride.
sār-cwide m bitter retort, reproach.
ēaδ-mēdum av humbly. **ellor-fūs** aj ready to depart.
on-cnāwan 7 'address.' **cūδ-līċe** av openly, frankly. **be-bēodan** 2 command.
þrym-fæst aj powerful, glorious.
ġe·ċēosan 2 choose. **cempa** m warrior, champion.
wealdend m ruler. **wyrhta** m maker. **wuldor-þrym** m glorious majesty.
ēċe aj eternal, everlasting. **ġe·sceaft** thing created, creature.
be-fōn 7 encompass, envelop.
miht f might, strength.
sigor m (divine) power.
fēran W1 go, proceed. **hātan** 7 command.
ginn aj spacious, wide. **grund** m ground, earth. **strēonan** W1 win over, gain.
faran 6 go. **scēat** m corner, region.
emne = efne. **be-būgan** 2 surround, encompass.
stede-wang m 'plain.' **strǣt** f street, road. **ġe·licgan** 5 be situated.
bodian W2 'preach.' **æfter** 'through.' **burg** f city. **ġe·lēafa** m belief, faith.
folde f earth. **fæδm** cf 252. **freoδo** f peace, protection.
þurfan pret pres need (pres pl). **fōr** f journey. **frætwa** f 'money.' **lǣdan**
    W1 'bring.' **gōd** n good (-ness), benefit. **āgen** aj own.
dōm m 'choice, wish.' **ēst** f 'liberal supply.' **ā-hwettan** W1 'provide.'
sīδ m journey, expedition.
ġe·hȳran W1 find out, understand. **hyge-þancol** aj prudent, wise.
cunnan pret pres know. **duguδ** f 'benefit.'

þrym m glory, majesty. **ā-hebban** 6 exalt, raise up.

ġe·healdan 7 keep, observe. **bēodan** 2 command.
ġe·fēa m joy, happiness. **ferian** W1 convey, carry.
brim-strēam m ocean current. **bēna** m petitioner, one who asks a favor.
stīgan 1 ascend; embark. **collen-fer(h)δ** aj bold-hearted.
ellen-rōf aj famed for courage, valiant.
mere-faroδ cf 289. **ġe·blissian** W2 comfort, gladden.

þām þe laʒolāde lanʒe cunnaþ.'
315 Đā him Andrēas ðurh ondsware,
wīs on ʒewitte, wordhord onlēac:
'Ne ʒedafenað þē, nū þē dryhten ʒēaf
welan ond wiste ond woruldspēde,
ðæt ðū ondsware mid oferhyʒdum,
320 sēce sārcwide. Sēlre bið æʒhwām
þæt hē ēaðmēdum ellorfūsne
oncnāwe cūðlīce, swā þæt Crist bebēad,
þēoden þrymfæst. Wē [h]is þeʒnas synd
ʒecoren tō cempum. Hē is cyninʒ on riht,
325 wealdend ond wyrhta wuldorþrymmes,
ān ēce ʒod eallra ʒesceafta,
swā hē ealle befēhð ānes cræfte,
hefon ond eorðan, hālʒum mihtum,
siʒora sēlost. Hē ðæt sylfa cwæð,
330 fæder folca ʒehwæs, ond ūs fēran hēt
ʒeond ʒinne ʒrund ʒāsta strēonan:
"Farað nū ʒeond ealle eorðan scēatas
emne swā wīde swā wæter bebūʒeð,
oððe stedewanʒas strǣte ʒelicʒaþ.
335 Bodiað æfter burʒum beorhtne ʒelēafan
ofer foldan fæðm. Ic ēow freoðo healde.
Ne ðurfan ʒē on þā fōre frætwe lǣdan,
ʒold ne seolfor. Ic ēow ʒōda ʒehwæs
on ēowerne āʒenne dōm ēst āhwette."
340 Nū ðū seolfa miht sīð ūserne
ʒehȳran hyʒeþancol. Ic sceal hraðe cunnan
hwæt ðū ūs tō duʒuðum ʒedōn wille.'
Him þā ondswarode ēce dryhten:
'ʒif ʒē syndon þeʒnas þæs þe þrym āhōf
345 ofer middanʒeard, swā ʒē mē secʒaþ,
ond ʒē ʒehēoldon þæt ēow se hālʒa bēad,
þonne ic ēow mid ʒefēan ferian wille
ofer brimstrēamas, swā ʒē bēnan sint.'
Þā in cēol stiʒon collenfyrhðe,
350 ellenrōfe. Æʒhwylcum wearð
on merefaroðe mōd ʒeblissod.

ȳð f wave, billow. ġe·swinġ n beating, surge. **on-ginnan** 3 begin.

mere-līðend m 'seafarer.' **milts** f kindness, favor. **biddan** 5 ask, request.

wuldor n glory. **aldor** m prince, leader.

dōm-weorðung f glory, honor.

blǣd m 'spirit, life.'

meotud m one who ordains; ruler.

sīð-fæt m journey. **sybb** f peace, goodwill. ġe·cȳðan W1 reveal.

holm-weard* m ocean guardian, i.e., captain.

æðele aj noble, illustrious.

þon instr of *se*, w comp. **cȳm-līċe** av splendidly. ġe·hladan 6 load.

hēah-ġe·strēon m noble treasures. **hæleð** mpl men, heroes. **sittan** 5 sit.

þēoden lord, ruler. **þrym-full** aj mighty, powerful. **wlitiġ** aj beautiful,
   fair. **reordian** W2 speak. **rīċe** aj noble, mighty.

ēċe cf 326. **hātan** 7 cf 330. **mǣre** aj renowned, glorious.

mago-þeġn m retainer, servant. **mete** m food. **syllan** W1 give.

frēfran W1 console, comfort. **fēa-sceaft** aj forlorn, helpless. **wylm** m surge.

þē = **þȳ** instr w comp. **ēað** cf 194. ȳð cf 352. ġe·þring n throng, tumult.

drohtað m condition, lot. **ā-drēogan** 2 suffer, endure.

[IV]

Ðā ofer ȳða ʒeswinʒ   Andrēas onʒann
merelīðendum   miltsa biddan
wuldres aldor,   ond þus wordum cwæð:
355 'Forʒife þē dryhten   dōmweorðunʒa,
willan in worulde   ond in wuldre blæd,
meotud manncynnes,   swā ðū mē hafast
on þyssum sīðfæte   sybbe ʒecȳðed.'
ʒesæt him þā se hālʒa   holmwearde nēah,
360 æðele be æðelum.   Æfre ic ne hȳrde
þon cȳmlicor   cēol ʒehladenne
hēahʒestrēonum.   Hæleð in sǣton,
þēodnas þrymfulle,   þeʒnas wlitiʒe.
Ðā reordode   rīce þēoden,
365 ēce ælmihtiʒ: heht his enʒel ʒān,
mǣrne maʒuþeʒn,   ond mete syllan,
frēfran fēasceafte   ofer flōdes wylm,
þæt hīe þē ēað mihton   ofer ȳða ʒeþrinʒ
drohtaþ ādrēoʒan. . . .

þinċan impers W1 w dat seem, appear. **mōd** n mind, heart.
wēron = **wǣron**. **sweġl** n sky, heaven. **brytta** m prince, lord; giver.
wuldor n glory; heaven. **waldend** m ruler, lord. **ġe·limpan 3** befall, happen.
hām m home; dwelling. **staðelian** W2 establish; make steadfast. **hell** f hell.
atol aj terrible, horrible. **scræf** n cavern, hole.
bryne-welm m surge of fire. **bīdan 1** live, remain; endure.
sār aj grevious. **sorg** f grief, affliction. **sweġl** cf 23. **lēoht** n light.
heofon m heaven. **hēah-ġe·timbrad** ppl aj high-built.
ġe·dūfan 2 dive, sink. **dēop** aj deep. **wælm/wielm** m boiling, billow (cf 27a).
niðer av down, beneath. **ness** m a steep place. **neowol** aj deep, abysmal.
grund m bottom, depth. **grēdiġ** aj hungry, covetous. **ġīfre** aj rapacious.
scyldiġ aj guilty, sinful. **weorod** n host, multitude. **for-scrīfan 1** condemn.
cleopian W2 call out, speak. **ealda** m chief, 'devil.' **hell** f place of torment.
wrecan 5 utter. **word-cwedas** mpl speech. **wēriġ** aj miserable. **reord** f
  voice. **eġesiġ*** aj dreadful. **stefn** f voice. **ðrym** m magnificence.

EXCERPT FROM *CHRIST AND SATAN*

[At the end of the Junius Manuscript (Oxford, Bodleian Library MS Junius XI) is a text to which editors generally give the title *Christ and Satan*, without clear evidence that it is at the same time a unified composition. The excerpt here tells the lament of Satan and the angels who fell with him as a result of their rebellion in heaven. The composition is highly formulaic, so much so that it gives the impression of being cobbled together with more fervor than skill: within just this excerpt one entire line repeats in **niðær under nessas   in ðone neowlan grund** (31, 90); half-lines repeat entire in **wordum and wercum** (48, 222), **ēce drihten** (239, 260), **bēman stefne** (171, 236), **habban in heofnum** (29, 43); there is simple chiastic variation in **grēdige and gīfre** (32) and **gīfre and grǣdige** (191); a formula system yields **wuldres waldend** (24), **engla waldend** (198) **sigora waldend** (217), **weoroda waldend** (187, 251), the last of these with a variant **weoroda drihten** (197); variation to accommodate alliterative requirements is clear in **ðearle gebunden** (38) and **feste gebunden** (58); and there are more. The excerpt begins immediately after mention of **engla ordfruman** 'leader of angels,' i.e., Lucifer/Satan, who is the referent of **him** in the opening line.]

I

. . . . . .

Dūhte him on mōde   þæt hit mihte swā,
þæt hīe wēron seolfe   sweʒles brytan,
wuldres waldend.   Him ðǣr wirse ʒelamp,
25   ðā hēo in helle   hām staðeledon,
ān æfter ōðrum,   in þæt atole scref,
þǣr hēo brynewelme   bīdan sceoldon
sāran sorʒe,   nāles sweʒles lēoht
habban in heofnum   hēahʒetimbrad;
30   ac ʒedūfan sceolun   in ðone dēopan wælm,
niðær under nessas   in ðone neowlan ʒrund,
ʒrēdiʒe and ʒīfre.   Ʒod āna wāt
hū hē þæt scyldiʒe werud   forscrifen hæfde.
Cleopað ðonne sē alda   ūt of helle,
35   wriceð wordcwedas   wēreʒan reorde,
eiseʒan stefne: 'Hwǣr cōm enʒla ðrym,

þēostre aj dark, gloomy.

hām m home, dwelling. þearle av severely. ġe·bindan 3 bind, fetter.

fæst aj fast, secure. fȳr-clomm* m (fire-)fetter. flōr m floor, ground. wielm
cf 30. āttor n poison. on-ǣlan W1 kindle, burn. feor av far away, remote.

æt-somne av together. sūsl n torment. þrōwian W2 suffer, undergo.

wēa m woe, affliction. wērgu* f misery. blǣd m splendor, glory.

hēah-seld n throne; lofty hall. wynn f joy, pleasure.

dryhten m lord. iū av formerly. drēam m joy, gladness.

sang m song, singing. sweġl cf 23. sēl comp aj. tīd f time, hour.

ēċa m eternal (one). æðele aj noble. stondan 6 stand; be.

hæleð m hero, warrior. hēah-seld cf 43. herian W1 praise. drihten cf 44.

word n word. weorc n deed, work. wīte n punishment, torment.

bīdan cf 27. bend m bond, fetter. hām cf 38.

ofer-hygd n pride, arrogance. wēnan W1 imagine; expect.

andswerian W2 answer. atol aj fierce, horrible. gāst m spirit.

swart aj black, dark. synfull sinful. sūsl cf 41. begrēosan* 2 be
terrified. ġe·lǣran W1 persuade, advise. lyġe m lie, deceit.

hǣlend m savior. hēran W1 obey.

āgan pret pres possess, obtain. ġe·wald n power, dominion.

heofon m heaven. eorþe f earth.

scyppend m creator. earttu = eart þū. sceaða m injurer; fiend.

fȳr-loca* m fiery enclosure. feste av firmly. ġe·bindan cf 38.

wēndes = wēndest cf 50. wuldor cf 24. woruld f world. āgan cf 55.

onwald m power, command. engel cf 36.

atol cf 26, 51. onsēon/ansīen f sight, appearance.

lēasung f lying. lȳðre av wretchedly. ġe·fēran W1 fare.

secgan W3 say, tell. sunu m son. meotod m creator; Christ.

mon-cynn n mankind. hafustu = hæfst þū. sūsl cf 41.

firen-full aj sinful, wicked. fācne aj wicked; deceitful.

aldor-ðeġn m chief, prince. reordian W2 speak.

ċearum ? cwide m saying, words. ā-firran W1 estrange from, withdraw.

drēam cf 44. be-dǣlan W1 deprive. līht/lēoht n light.

ofer-hygd cf 50. ufan av from above. for-lǣtan 7 lose, forsake.

hyht m hope, expectation. hell cf 34. flōr cf 39. beornan 3 burn.

bealo n woe, evil. blāc aj pale, livid. hweorfon 3 wander, turn.

scinna m evil spirit. for-scyppan 6 transform. sceaða cf 57.

earm aj wretched, miserable. ǣglēca m demon, fierce enemy. atol,
scref cf 26. ān-mēdla m pride, arrogance. drēogan 2 perform, take part in.

.. þe wē on heofnum   habban sceoldan?
Þis is ðēostræ hām,   ðearle ʒebunden
fæstum fȳrclommum;   flōr is on welme,
40   āttre onǣled.   Nis nū ende feor
þæt wē sceolun ætsomne   sūsel þrōwian,
wēan and wērʒu,   nālles wuldres blǣd
habban in heofnum,   hēhselda wyn.
Hwæt, wē for dryhtene iū   drēamas hefdon,
45   sonʒ on sweʒle   sēlrum tīdum,
þǣr nū ymb ðōne æcan   æðele stondað,
hæleð ymb hēhseld,   heriʒað drihten
wordum and wercum;   and ic in wīte sceal
bīdan in bendum,   and mē bættran hām
50   for oferhyʒdum   ǣfre ne wēne.'
Dā him andsweradan   atole ʒāstas,
swarte and synfulle,   sūsle beʒrorenne:
'Þū ūs ʒelǣrdæst   ðurh lyʒe ðīnne
þæt wē hēlende   hēran ne scealdon.
55   Dūhte þē ānum   þæt ðū āhtest alles ʒewald,
heofnes and eorþan,   wǣre hāliʒ ʒod,
scypend seolfa.   Nū earttu sceaðana sum,
in fȳrlocan   feste ʒebunden.
Wēndes ðū ðurh wuldor   ðæt þū woruld āhtest,
60   alra onwald,   and wē enʒlas mid ðec.
Atol is þīn onsēon!   Habbað wē alle swā
for ðīnum lēasunʒum   lȳðre ʒefēred.
Seʒdest ūs tō sōðe   þæt ðīn sunu wǣre
meotod moncynnes.   Hafustu nū māre sūsel!'
65   Swā firenfulle   fācnum wordum
heora aldorðæʒn   *on* reordadon,
on cearum cwidum.   Crist hēo āfirde,
drēamum bedēlde.   Hæfdan dryhtnes līht
for oferhyʒdum   ufan forlēton,
70   hæfdon hym tō hyhte   helle flōras,
beornende bealo.   Blāce hworfon
scinnan forscepene;   sceaðan hweorfedon,
earme æʒlēcan,   ʒeond þæt atole scref,
for ðām anmēdlan   þe hīe ǣr druʒon.

reordian cf 66. **sīð** m journey, adventure; time.

fēond m adversary; devil. **aldor** m chief, prince. **forht** aj fearful.

āgēn av again, anew. **wīte** cf 48. **worn** m a great amount. **ġe·fēlan** W1 feel.

spearcian* W2 give off sparks. **spreocan** 5 speak, say. **on-ginnan** 3 begin.

fȳr n fire. **attor** cf 40. **fæġer** aj fair, beautiful. **drēam** cf 44.

wīte cf 48. **word** cf 48. **in-drīfan*** 1 'utter.'

iū cf 44. **ængel** = **engel**.

dryhten cf 44. **dēore** aj esteemed, dear. **drēam** cf 44, 79.

miċel aj much, great. **meotod** cf 64. **menego** f multitude. **swā some**
 in like manner. **mōd** n mind, heart. **hycgan** W3 think, purpose.

tō-weorpan 3 overthrow, destroy. **wuldor** cf 24. **lēoma** m light, radiance.

bearn n child, son. **hǣlend** m saviour. **āgan** cf 55. **burh** f city, citadel.

ġe·wald cf 55. **ǣht** f possessions. **earm** cf 73. **hēap** m company, band.

hebbe = **hæbbe**. **hām** cf 38. **ġe·lǣdan** W1 lead.

wēnan cf 50. **tācen** n sign. **sutol** aj clear, manifest. **ā-sellan** W1 expel.

wærgðu f condemnation. **niðer** . . **grund** cf 31.

hæft m fetter; captivity. **hām** cf 38, 88. **ġe·ferian** W1 lead, bring.

eard m (home-) land. **ēadiġ** aj blessed, happy. **tīr** m glory, honor.

wlonc aj proud; rich. **wīn-sele** m winehall.

engel cf 36. **ðrēat** m troop, throng. **ūp-heofon** m upper heaven.

āgan cf 55. **atol** cf 51. **hām** cf 92, 88, 38.

fȳr cf 79. **on-ǣlan** W1 kindle, burn. **fāh** aj marked, 'guilty.'

ǣċe = **ēċe** av eternally. **duru** f door, gate. **draca** m dragon.

eardian W2 dwell. **hāt** aj hot. **hreðer** m breast, interior. **helpan** 3 help.

wā-līċ* aj woeful, wretched. **wīte** cf 48. **ā-fyllan** W1 fill.

nāgan = **ne āgan**. **heolstor** n place of concealment. **ġe·hȳdan** W1 hide.

neowol cf 31. **ġe·nip** n darkness. **hǣr** = **hēr**. **nǣddre** f snake, serpent.

swēġ n noise, sound. **wyrm** m serpent. **ġe·wunian** W2 inhabit, remain.

clom m bond. **feste** cf 58. **ġe·bindan** cf 38. **seondon** = **sindon**.

rēðe aj fierce. **dimm** aj dim, gloomy. **deorc** aj dark. **lȳhtan** W1 give light.

sced n shade, darkness. **scīma** m gloom, dimness. **scyppend** cf 57.

lēoht cf 28. **iū** cf 44. **ġe·wald** cf 55. **wuldor** cf 24.

atol cf 26. **ēðel** m homeland. **ġe·bīdan** 1 await, endure.

drihten cf 44. **dēman** W1 judge; proclaim.

fāh cf 96. **flōr** cf 39. **fēran** W1 go, journey.

dēofol n devil. **menego** cf 83. **dimm** cf 104. **hām** cf 38.

flyġe m flying, flight. **flyht** m flight. **þrāgum** 'from time to time.'

II

75 Eft reordade   ōðre sīðe
feonda aldor.   Wæs þā forht āʒēn,
seoððan hē ðes wītes   worn ʒefēlde.
Hē spearcade,   ðonne hē spreocan onʒān
fȳre and ātre: ne bið swelc fæʒer drēam
80 ðonne hē in wītum   wordum indrāf.
'Ic wæs iū in heofnum   hāliʒ ænʒel,
dryhtene dēore;   hefde mē drēam mid ʒode,
micelne for meotode,   and ðēos meneʒo swā some.
Þā ic in mōde   mīnum hoʒade
85 þæt ic wolde tōwerpan   wuldres lēoman,
bearn hēlendes,   āʒan mē burʒa ʒewald
eall tō æhte,   and ðēos earme hēap
þe ic hebbe tō helle   hām ʒelēdde.
Wēne þæt tācen sutol   *þā ic āseald wes on wærʒðu,*
90 niðer under nessas   in ðone neowlan ʒrund.
Nū is ēow hebbe tō hæftum   hām ʒefærde
alle of earde.   Nis hēr ēadiʒes tīr,
wloncra wīnsele,   ne worulde drēam,
ne ænʒla ðrēat,   ne wē ūpheofon
95 āʒan mōten.   Is ðes atola hām
fȳre onæled.   Ic eom fāh wið ʒod.
Æce æt helle duru   dracan eardiʒað,
hāte on reðre;   hēo ūs helpan ne maʒon.
Is ðæs wālīca hām   wītes āfylled;
100 nāʒan wē ðæs heolstres   þæt wē ūs ʒehȳdan mæʒon
in ðissum neowlan ʒenipe.   Hǣr is nēdran swǣʒ,
wyrmas ʒewunade.   Is ðis wītes clom
feste ʒebunden.   Fēond seondon rēðe,
dimme and deorce.   Ne hēr dæʒ lȳhteð
105 for scedes scīman,   sceppendes lēoht.
Iū āhte ic ʒewald   ealles wuldres,
ǣr ic mōste in ðēossum atolan   æðele ʒebīdan
hwæt mē drihten ʒod   dēman wille,
fāʒum on flōra.   Nū ic fēran cōm
110 dēofla meneʒo   tō ðissum dimman hām.
Ac ic sceal on flyʒe   and on flyhte ðrāʒum

nēosan W1 speak out.

ofer-hygd cf 50. **ord** m beginning. **on-stellan** W1 establish, institute.

wēnan cf 50. **wuldor-cyning** m king of glory.

ā-lēfan W1 grant.

ēðel cf 107. **æht** cf 87.

onwald cf 60. **āgan** cf 55. **ġe·wald** cf 55.

wuldor cf 24. **wīte** cf 48. **waldend** cf 24.

hēan aj abject, miserable. **earm** aj poor, wretched. **hweorfan** cf 71.

wadan 6 go, advance. **wræc-lāst** m exile path. **benǣman** W1 deprive of.

duguð host; glory. **be-dǣlan** cf 68. **drēam** cf 44. **āgan** cf 55.

uppe av from above.

sweġl cf 23. **brytta** cf 23.

wiht f/n creature. **wealdend** cf 24, 118. **ġe·limpan** cf 24.

wēriġ cf 35. **gāst** cf 51.

earfoðe n hardship, suffering.

fāh cf 96. **fȳr** cf 79. **fȳr-lēoma*** m fiery radiance. **stondan** cf 46.

atol cf 26, 51. **scræf** cf 26. **āttor** cf 40. **ġe·blondan** 7 mingle, mix.

lim-wæstm* m stature. **ġe·lūtian*** W2 hide. **sīd** aj wide, spacious.

sele m hall. **synn** f sin. **for-wundan** W2 wound grievously.

hāt n heat. **ċeald** n cold. **mencgan** W1 mingle.

ġe·hēran W1 hear. **helle-scealc*** subject of hell. **gnornian** W2 lament,
  bewail. **cynn** n race; people. **grund** cf 31. **mǣnan** W1 lament, mourn.

niðer, **næss** cf 31. **nacod** aj naked.

winnan 3 struggle, fight. **wyrm** cf 102. **windiġ** aj windy. **sele** cf 130.

inne-weard aj within. **atol** n terror, horror. **ġe·fyllan** W1 fill (up).

hihtlīċ aj joyous. **brūcan** 2 possess; enjoy. **burh** cf 86.

bold n house. **beorht** aj splendid. **ġe·scæft** f creation, creature.

ēage n eye. **starian** W2 look, gaze.

lēoht cf 28.

uppe cf 122.

sang cf 45. **sweġl** cf 23. **meotod** cf 64.

ēadiġ cf 92. **bearn** cf 86. **ymb-fōn** 7 encompass; grasp.

sang cf 45, 142. **sāwol** f soul.

sceððan 6 harm, injure.

nyle = **ne wille**.

hæft cf 91. **ġe·ferian** W1 carry, bring.

earda nēosan,   and ēower mā,
þe ðes oferhȳdes   ord onstaldon.
Ne ðurfon wē ðes wēnan,   þæt ūs wuldorcyninᵹ
115 æfre wille   eard ālēfan,
æðel tō æhte,   swā hē ær dyde,
ēcne onwald;   āh him alles ᵹewald,
wuldres and wīta,   waldendes sunu.
Forðon ic sceal hēan and earm   hweorfan ðȳ wīdor,
120 wadan wræclāstas,   wuldre benēmed,
duᵹuðum bedēled,   næniᵹne drēam āᵹan
uppe mid ænᵹlum,   þes ðe ic ær ᵹecwæð
þæt ic wære seolfa   swæᵹles brytta,
wihta wealdend.   Ac hit *mē* wyrse ᵹelomp.'

III

125 Swā se wēreᵹa ᵹāst   wordum sæde
his earfoðo   ealle ætsomne,
fāh in fyrnum;   fȳrlēoma stōd
ᵹeond þæt atole scræf   āttre ᵹeblonden.
'Ic eom limwæstmum   þæt ic ᵹelūtian ne mæᵹ
130 on þyssum sīdan sele,   synnum forwundod.
Hwæt, hēr hāt and ceald   hwīlum mencᵹað;
hwīlum ic ᵹehēre   hellescealcas,
ᵹnornende cynn,   ᵹrundas mænan,
niðer under næssum;   hwīlum nacode men
135 winnað ymb wyrmas.   Is þes windiᵹa sele
eall inneweard   atole ᵹefylled.
Ne mōt ic hihtlīcran   hāmes brūcan,
burᵹa ne bolda,   ne on þā beorhtan ᵹescæft
ne mōt ic æfre mā   ēaᵹum starian.
140 Is mē nū wyrsa   þæt ic wuldres lēoht
uppe mid enᵹlum   æfre cūðe,
sonᵹ on sweᵹle,   þær sunu meotodes
habbað ēadiᵹe bearn   ealle ymbfanᵹen
seolfa mid sanᵹe.   Ne ic þām sāwlum ne mōt
145 æniᵹum sceððan,
būtan þām ānum   þe hē āᵹan nyle;
þā ic mōt tō hæftum   hām ᵹeferian,

bringan W1 bring. **bold** cf 138. **biter** aj bitter; painful.

un-ġe·līċ aj unlike.

iū cf 44, 81. **ǣrror** comp av.

wlite beauty; brightness. **weorð-mynt** m glory, honor. **swēġ** cf 101.

bearm m lap, bosom.

ūtan av from without. **hebban** 6 raise up, lift.

lim n limb. **lēof** aj beloved, dear. **lof-song** m song of praise.

fāh cf 96.

ġe·wundian W2 wound. **wom** m/n stain, defect, sin. **wītes clom** cf 102.

beran 4 bear. **beornan** cf 71. **bæc** n back.

hāt cf 98. **hyht-willa*** hope of joy. **lēas** aj not having; deprived of.

feola = fela. **cwīðan** W1 lament, bewail. **firen** f sin, torment.

atol cf 26. **ǣglǣca** cf 73.

wīte cf 48. **wēriġ** cf 35. **spearca*** m spark.

þurh-drīfan 1 drive forth. **ēalā** interj ah, oh.

þrym m glory, might. **duguð** cf 121. **helm** m helmet; protection.

meotod cf 64, **miht** f might, power. **middan-eard** m earth; world.

dæġ m day. **lēoht** n light. **drēam** cf 44.

engel cf 36. **þrēat** cf 94. **ūp-heofen** cf 94.

lēas cf 158.

hand f hand. **ġe·rǣċan** W1 reach.

ēage cf 139. **lōcian** W2 look, gaze.

hūru av indeed, especially. **ēare** n ear. **ġe·hēran** cf 132.

beorht aj bright, glorious. **bēme** f trumpet. **stefn** voice, sound.

seld m hall; throne.

ā-drīfan 1 drive, expel. **ġe·wald** cf 55.

wynn cf 43. **wyrse** comp aj. **ġe·limpan** cf 24.

hiht cf 70. **ā-scēadan** 7 separate, exclude.

scīr aj bright, gleaming. **driht** f multitude, company.

ā-lǣdan W1 lead out. **lēoht** cf 28. **lāð** aj evil, hateful.

ġe·hicgan W3 consider; understand. **be-cuman** 4 come, arrive.

neowle ġe·nip cf 101. **nīð-synn*** f grievous sin. **fāh** aj stained,
spotted. **ā-weorpan** 3 cast out.

eall aj all; everything. **lēas** cf 158. **drēam** cf 44.

heofen-cyning m king of heaven. **hēran** W1 obey. **þenċan** W1 think,
intend. **cwēman** W1 please; serve. **morðer** n sin, crime; torment.

wēa cf 42. **wīte** cf 48. **wracu** f misery, retribution. **drēogan** 2
perform; bear. **be-dǣlan** cf 68. **iū-dǣd** m former deed. **fāh** cf 96.

brinȝan tō bolde   in þone biteran ȝrund.
Ealle wē syndon   unȝelīce
150 þonne þe wē iū in heofonum   hæfdon ǣrror
wlite and weorðmynt.   Ful oft wuldres [swēȝ]
brōhton tō bearme   bearn hǣlendes,
þǣr wē ymb hine ūtan   ealle hōfan,
leomu ymb lēofne,   lofsonȝa word,
155 drihtne sǣdon.   Nū ic eom dǣdum fāh,
ȝewundod mid wommum;   sceal nū þysne wītes clom
beoran beornende   in bæce mīnum,
hāt on helle,   hyhtwillan lēas.'
Þā ȝyt feola cwīðde   firna herde,
160 atol æȝlǣca,   ūt of helle,
wītum wēriȝ.   Word spearcum flēah
ǣttre ȝelīcost,   þonne hē ūt þorhdrāf:
'Ēalā drihtenes þrym!   Ēalā duȝuða helm!
Ēalā meotodes miht!   Ēalā middaneard!
165 Ēalā dæȝ lēohta!   Ēalā drēam ȝodes!
Ēalā enȝla þrēat!   Ēalā ūpheofen!
Ēalā þæt ic eam ealles lēas   ēcan drēames,
þæt ic mid handum ne mæȝ   heofon ȝerǣcan,
ne mid ēaȝum ne mōt   ūp lōcian,
170 ne hūru mid ēarum ne sceal   ǣfre ȝehēran
þǣre byrhtestan   bēman stefne!
Dæs ic wolde of selde   sunu meotodes,
drihten ādrīfan,   and āȝan mē þæs drēames ȝewald,
wuldres and wynne;   mē þǣr wyrse ȝelamp
175 þonne ic tō hihte   āȝan mōste.
Nū ic eom āscēaden   fram þǣre scīran driht,
ālǣded fram lēohte   in þone lāðan hām.
Ne mæȝ ic þæt ȝehicȝan   hū ic in ðǣm becwōm,
in þis neowle ȝenip,   *ni*ðsynnum fāh,
180 āworpen of worulde.   Wāt ic nu þā
þæt bið alles lēas   ēcan drēamas
sē ðe heofencyninȝe   hēran ne þenceð,
meotode cwēman.   Ic þæt morðer sceal,
wēan and wītu   and wrace drēoȝan,
185 ȝōda bedǣled,   iūdǣdum fāh,

ā-drīfan cf 173. **seld** cf 172.

weorod cf 33. **waldend** cf 24. **wræc-lāst** cf 120.

sorg-ċeariġ aj sad, sorrowful. **sīð** cf 75. **wīd** aj wide, broad.

hweorfan cf 71. **ġe·hēnan** W1 humble, overthrow.

andsaca m adversary, enemy. **ġingra** m follower; dependent.

ġīfre, grǣdiġ cf 32. **be-drīfan** 1 drive; pursue.

hāt cf 98. **hof** n hall. **nama** m name.

ġe·hycgan cf 178. **hæleð** cf 47.

ā-belgan 3 anger, provoke. **bearn** cf 86. **waldend** cf 24, 187.

lǣtan 7 let. **tō bysne** 'regard as an example.' **blāc** aj black, livid.

fēond m enemy; devil. **ofer-hygd** cf 50, 69. **for-weorðan** 3 perish.

niman 4 take, choose. **wynn** cf 43. **weorod** cf 33.

ġe·cȳððan W1 show, make known. **cræft** m power, skill.

mænego cf 83. **ā-drīfan** cf 173. **hæft** m captive; servant.

seld cf 172. **ġe·munan** pret pres remember, have in mind.

ċēosan 2 choose. **eard** cf 92.

nemnan W1 name, call.

beoran cf 157. **brēost** breast. **blīðe** aj happy. **ġe·þōht** m thought.

sibb f kindness. **snytero** f wisdom. **ġe·munan** cf 201.

hēah-seld cf 43. **hnīgan** 1 bow down; sink. **þenċan** cf 182.

anwalda m ruler, sovereign. **ār** f favor grace. **biddan** 5 pray for, ask.

be-hōfian W2 need. **wunian** W2 remain; dwell.

wlite cf 151. **scīnan** 1 shine.

fæġer cf 79. **folde** f earth; region.

wlitiġ aj beautiful. **wynsum** aj pleasant, fair. **wæstm** m fruit.

beorhte av brightly. **burg** cf 86. **brād** aj broad.

hyhtlīċ cf 137. **heofon-rīċe** n kingdom of heaven.

ġe·cwēme aj agreeable, pleasant. **uton** 'let us.' **ċierran** W1 turn
  (oneself). **sigor** m victory.

dēore cf 82.

hēah-setl n exalted seat, throne. **hwīt** aj white, radiant.

fēða m host, band. **ēadiġ** aj happy, blessed.

þæs ðe ic ʒeþōhte ādrīfan   drihten of selde,
weoroda waldend;   sceal nū wreclāstas
settan sorhʒceariʒ,   sīðas wīde.'

[IV]

Hwearf þā tō helle   þā hē ʒehēned wæs,
190 ʒodes andsaca;   dydon his ʒinʒran swā,
ʒīfre and ʒrǣdiʒe,   þā hiʒ ʒod bedrāf
in þæt hāte hof   þām is hel nama.
Forþan sceal ʒehycʒan   hæleða æʒhwylc
þæt hē ne ābæliʒe   bearn waldendes.
195 Lǣte him tō bysne   hū þā blācan fēond
for oferhyʒdum   ealle forwurdon.
Neoman ūs tō wynne   weoroda drihten,
[. . . .]   enʒla waldend.
Hē þæt ʒecȳdde   ðæt hē *cræft* hæfde,
200 mihta miccle,   þā hē þā mæneʒo ādrāf,
hæftas   of ðǣm hēan selde.
    ʒemunan wē   þone hālʒan drihten,
se onwald hæfð   alra ʒescefta.
Cēosan *wē ēcne* eard   *uppe* in wuldre
mid ealra cyninʒa cyninʒe,   sē is Crist ʒenemned.
205 Beoran on brēostum   blīðe ʒeþōhtas,
sibbe and snytero.   ʒemunan sōð and riht,
þonne wē tō hēhselde   hnīʒan þencað,
and þone anwaldan   āra biddan.
Þonne behōfað   sē ðe hēr wunað
210 weorulde wynnum   þæt him wlite scīne
þonne hē ōðer līf   eft ʒesēceð,
fæʒere land   þonne þēos folde sēo;
is þǣr wlitiʒ and wynsum,   wæstmas scīnað
beorhte ofer burʒum.   Þǣr is brāde lond,
215 hyhtlīcra ham   in heofonrīce,
Criste ʒecwēmra.   Uta cerran þider
þǣr hē sylfa sit,   siʒora waldend,
drihten hǣlend,   in ðǣm dēoran hām,
and ymb þæt hēhsetl   hwīte standað
220 enʒla fēðan   and ēadiʒra,

heofen-þrēat* m heavenly band. **herian** cf 47.

wordum and weorcum cf 48. **wlite** m beauty; countenance.

wuldor-cyning cf 114.

ġe·friġnan 3 learn, hear of. **fēond** cf 195. **andettan** W1 confess,
    acknowledge.

wom, witu cf 156.

ofer-hygd cf 50, 196. **ān-for-lǣtan** 7 abandon, forsake.

hraðe av quickly, straightway.

ġe·sēne aj evident. **syngian** W2 sin.

eard cf 92.

drēogan 2 perform, endure; bear. **dōm-lēas** aj inglorious. **ġe·winn** n
    struggle, strife. **wlite** cf 151. **wunian** cf 209.

hēran cf 182.

sang cf 45. **seld** cf 172.

þūsend-mǣlum av 'thousand-meal,' i.e., by thousands.

ġe·hēran cf 132. **swēġ** cf 101.

bēme, stefn cf 171. **byrht-word*** n 'Son,' 'Christ.' **ā-rīsan** arise.

ordfruma m leader; source. **æþele** cf 46.

hnīgan 1 decline, bow down. **sanct** m saint. **siġe-torht*** aj glorious
    in victory. **ġe·standan** 6 stand.

ġe·blētsian W2 bless. **bilewit** aj guileless, innocent. **hēap** m band,
    company. **dōgor** m day. **dēore** cf 82.

andfeng m guardian (?).

eorðe cf 56. **ġe·lēfan** W1 believe (in), trust.

of-þinċan W1 displease, be offence to. **þēoden** m prince, king.

stīð-mōd aj stern, resolute. **on-ginnan** 3 begin.

sprecan 5 speak.

lǣran W1 teach, show. **langsum** aj enduring. **rǣd** m advice, counsel.

miht f might, power. **ġe·lēfan** cf 244.

uta cf 216. **ofer-hycgan** W3 scorn, renounce. **helm** cf 163.

weroda waldend cf 187.

īdel aj empty, vain. **ġylp** n boasting, vaunt.

drēogan 2 bear, endure.

hāliᵹe heofenþrēatas heriᵹaðdrihten
wordum and weorcum. Heora wlite scīneð
ᵹeond ealra worulda woruld mid wuldorcyninᵹe.

V

Ðā ᵹēt ic furðor ᵹefreᵹen fēond ondetan;
225 wæs him eall ful stranᵹ [. . . . . . .]
wom and witu; hæfdon wuldorcyninᵹ
for oferhiᵹdum ānforlǣten;
cwǣdon eft hraðe ōðre worde:
'Nū is ᵹesēne þæt wē synᵹodon
uppe on earde. Sceolon nū æfre þæs
230 drēoᵹan dōmlēase ᵹewinn drihtnes mihtum.
Hwæt, wē in wuldres wlite wunian mōston
þǣr wē hālᵹan ᴣode hēran woldon,
and him sanᵹ ymb seld secᵹan sceoldon
þūsendmǣlum. Þā wē þǣr wǣron,
235 wunodon on wynnum, ᵹehērdon wuldres swēᵹ,
bēman stefne. Byrhtword ārās
enᵹla ordfruma, and tō þǣm æþelan
hnīᵹan him sanctas; siᵹetorht ārās
ēce drihten, ofer ūs ᵹestōd
240 and ᵹeblētsode bilewitne hēap
dōᵹra ᵹehwilcne, and his se dēora sunu,
ᵹāsta scyppend. ᴣod seolfa wæs
eallum andfenᵹ þe ðǣr ūp becōm,
and hine on eorðan ǣr ᵹelēfde.
245 Þā ðæs ofþūhte þæt se þēoden wæs
stranᵹ and stīðmōd. Onᵹan ic þā steppan forð
āna wið enᵹlum, and tō him eallum spræc:
"Ic can ēow lǣran lanᵹsumne rǣd,
ᵹif ᵹē willað mīnre mihte ᵹelēfan.
250 Uta oferhycᵹan helm þone micclan,
weroda waldend, āᵹan ūs þis wuldres lēoht,
eall tō æhte. Þis is īdel ᵹylp
þæt wē ǣr druᵹon ealle hwīle."

ā-drīfan cf 173.
ċeaster f city; fort; 'heaven.'
wræc-lāst cf 120. **wunian mōton** cf 231.
grim aj grim, horrible.

iorre aj angry, fierce. **ġe·weorðan** 3 become; happen.
swīð aj mighty, powerful. **menego** cf 83. **licgan** 5 lie.
lēahtor disgrace, reproach. **lyft** m air. **scacan** 5 move quickly.
flēogan 2 fly. **folde** cf 212. **fȳr** cf 79. **ymbūtan** av around, outside.
þǣh = **þēah**.

ēadiġ cf 92. **ġe·hrīnan** 1 touch.
hond cf 168. **hǣþen** aj heathen. **scealu** f throng.
grīpan 1 grasp, lay hold of. **andsaca** cf 190.
hweorfan cf 71.
unsibb enmity; discord. **on-styrian** W2 stir up.
mǣġð f race, tribe. **middan-eard** cf 164.
ġe·þolian W2 endure, bear. **biter** cf 148.
nīð m enmity, affliction. **bealo** n woe, evil. **gnornian** cf 133.
sīc aj sick at heart (?). **sorhful** aj sorrowful. **wealdan** 7 possess.
staðelian W2 establish, set up.
se ēċa cf 46.
ā-lēfan cf 115.
ēðel, tō ǣhte cf 116.
gnornian cf 133. **godes andsaca** cf 190, 268.

wrāð aj angry. **wom-cwide** m evil speech, blasphemy.

VI

'Ðā ȝewearð ūsic   þæt wē woldon swā
255 drihten ādrīfan   of þām dēoran hām,
cyninȝ of cestre.   Cūð is wīde
þæt wreclāstas   wunian mōton,
ȝrimme ȝrundas.   Ȝod seolfa him
rīce haldeð.   Hē is āna cyninȝ,
260 þe ūs eorre ȝewearð,   ēce drihten,
meotod mihtum swīð.   Sceal nū þēos meneȝo hēr
licȝan on lēahtrum,   sume on lyft scacan,
flēoȝan ofer foldan;   fȳr bið ymbūtan
on æȝhwylcum,   þæh hē uppe sēo.
265 Ne mōt hē þām sāwlum   þe ðǣr sēcað ūp,
ēadiȝe of eorþan   æfre ȝehrīnan,
ah ic be hondum mōt   hæþenre sceale
ȝrīpan tō ȝrunde,   Ȝodes andsacan.
Sume sceolon hweorfan   ȝeond hæleða land
270 and unsibbe   oft onstyrian
monna mæȝðum   ȝeond middaneard.
Ic hēr ȝeþōlian sceal   þinȝa æȝhwylces,
bitres nīðæs   beala ȝnornian,
sīc and sorhful,   þæs ic seolfa wēold,
275 þonne ic on heofonum   hām staðelode,
hwæðer ūs se ēca   æfre wille
on heofona rīce   hām ālēfan,
ēðel tō æhte,   swā hē ǣr dyde.'
Swā ȝnornedon   Ȝodes andsacan,
280 hāte on helle.   Him wæs hælend Ȝod
wrāð ȝeworden   for womcwidum.

O key of David and sceptre of the house of Israel,
who openest and none shutteth, who shuttest and
none openeth: come thou, and bring forth the captive
from the house of bondage, who sitteth in darkness
and in the shadow of death.

reccend m ruler, guide. **riht** aj just, righteous. **cyning** m king.
loca m lock, enclosure. **healdan** 7 hold, keep. **on-tȳnan** W1 reveal, open.
ēadiġ aj blessed. **ūp-weġ** m ascension. **for-wyrnan** W1 forbid, deny.
wlitiġ aj bright, fair. **wil-sīð** desired journey. **weorc** n work, deed. **dugan**
   pret pres avail, merit. **hūru** av indeed, especially. **þearf** f need, necessity.
sprecan 5 speak. **myndġian** W2 be mindful of. **ġe·scyppan** 6 create, form.

cearful aj sorrowful, care-laden. **þing** n cause, sake. **carcern** n prison.
sorgian W2 sorrow, grieve. **sunne** f sun. **wēnan** W1 expect, hope for.
līf-frēa m lord of life. **lēoht** n light, brightness. **on-tȳnan** cf 19.
mōd n spirit, heart. **mund-bora** m protector, guardian. **tȳdre** aj feeble.
ġe·wit n understanding. **tīr** m honor, glory. **be-windan** 3 encompass, wrap.
wyrðe aj worthy, deserving. **tō wuldre** 'gloriously.' **for-lǣtan** 7 forsake.
hēan-līċe av miserably, abjectly. **hweorfan** 3 turn, go.
enge aj narrow, straitened. **ēðel** m native land. **bi-scyrian** W2 deprive of,
   separate from. **secgan** W3 say, speak. **sōð** n truth. **sprecan** 5 say, speak.

EXCERPTS FROM *CHRIST I*

[The beginning of the Exeter Book (Exeter, Cathedral MS 3501, ff. 8–130) is a set of paraphrases of antiphons of Christian religious observance, the beginning of the first of them being lost. Twelve of the set have survived, and have been assigned the title *Christ I* to distinguish them from subsequent verses that are generally considered to be separate compositions (and which are commonly titled *Christ II* and *Christ III*). Two of the paraphrases are re-presented here with Latin antiphons on which they seem to have been based pre-posed to the texts. Although there are more recent, separate editions of these verses, the edition by Albert S. Cook, *The Christ of Cynewulf: A Poem in Three Parts, The Advent, The Ascension, and the Last Judgment* (Boston, 1900), remains the most generally helpful.]

> [O clavis David, et sceptrum domus Israel;
> qui aperis, et nemo claudit, claudis,
> et nemo aperit: veni, et educ vinctum
> de domo carceris, sedentem in tenebris
> et umbra mortis.]

> Ēalā þū Reccend   ond þū riht Cyninʒ,
> sē þe locan healdeð,   līf ontȳneð,
> 20 ēadʒa[n] ūpweʒas,   ōþrum forwyrneð,
> wlitiʒan wilsīþes,   ʒif his weorc ne dēaʒ.
> Hūru wē for þearfe   þās word sprecað,
> ond myndʒiað   þone þe mon ʒescōp
> þæt hē ne [.]ete   [...]ceose weorðan
> 25 cearfulra þinʒ,   þe wē in carcerne
> sittað sorʒende,   sunnan wēnað,
> hwonne ūs Līffrēa   lēoht ontȳne,
> weorðe ūssum mōde   tō mundboran,
> and þæt tȳdre ʒewitt   tīre bewinde,
> 30 ʒedō ūsic þæs wyrðe,   þe hē tō wuldre forlēt,
> þā wē hēanlīce   hweorfan sceoldan
> tō þis enʒe lond,   ēðle bescyrede.
> Forþon secʒan mæʒ   sē ðe sōð spriceð

ā-hreddan W1 deliver, save. **for-hwyrfan** 3 pervert, turn aside.
frum-cynn n race. **fīras** mpl men. **fǣmne** f maiden. **ġeong** aj young.
mæġð f virgin, maiden. **mān** n sin, evil. **lēas** aj void of. **mōdor** f mother.
ġe·ċēosan 2 choose, elect. **wer** m man. **frīgu** f embrace.
bearn n child, son. **ġe-byrd** f/n child-bearing. **brȳd** f bride. **ēacen** aj great,
    pregnant. **efen-līċ** aj like, equal. **wīf** n woman. **ġe·earnung** f 'merit'; or
    ġe-ea[c]nung f reward? conception? **dēgol** aj hidden, obscure.
dryhten m lord. **ġe·rȳne** n mystery, hidden purpose. **ġiefu** f favor, gift.
gǣst-līċ aj spiritual. **grund-scēat** m precincts of earth. **ġeond-sprūtan** 2
    overspread. **wīse** f condition, state. **in-lȳhtan** W1 enlighten, explain.
lār f doctrine, teaching. **longsum** aj enduring. **fruma** m author, lord.
hoðma m darkness, shadow. **bi-helan** 4 cloak, hide. **licgan** 5 lie.
wītga m prophet. **wōð-song** m (poetic or eloquent) song. **wealdend** m ruler.
reord f/n voice, word. **ryne** n course. **ġe·miclian** W2 enlarge, magnify.
ġe·neahhe av abundantly, earnestly. **noma** m name. **scyppend** m creator.
horsc aj wise, enlightened. **hād** m manner. **herġan** W1 praise, glorify.

> O king of peace, that wast born before all ages; come by
>   the golden gate, visit them whom thou hast redeemed,
>   and lead them back to the place whence they fell by sin.

sōð aj true. **sib-sum** aj peaceful, peaceable.

woruld f world; mankind. **þrym** m might. **wuldor-fæder** m glorious father.
ċild n child. **ā-cennan** W1 beget, bear. **cræft** m power. **meaht** f might.
eorl m 'man.' **lyft** f sky, heaven.
secg m man. **searo-þoncol** aj sagacious, shrewd. **glēaw** aj wise, shrewd.
ā-secgan W3 say, explain. **sund-būend** m dwellers-near-the-sea, 'men.'
ā-reccan W1 expound, explain. **rodor** m heaven, sky. **weard** m guardian.
frymð f beginning. **ġe·niman** 4 take. **frēo-bearn** n noble child, glorious son.
þēod f people; mankind. **cynn** n race.
ġe·friġnan 3 find out, learn. **folc** n people, nation. **fruma** m beginning.
wolcen n/m cloud, sky. **wītiġ** aj wise.
ord-fruma m creator, source. **lēoht** n day, light. **þȳstro** f/n darkness, gloom.
ġe·dǣlan W1 divide. **dryht-līċe** av in lordly manner. **dōm** m judgment.

þæt hē āhredde, þā forhwyrfed wæs,
35 frumcyn fīra. Wæs sēo fǣmne ʒeonʒ,
mæʒð mānes lēas, þe hē him tō mēder ʒecēas;
þæt wæs ʒeworden būtan weres frīʒum,
þæt þurh bearnes ʒebyrd brȳd ēacen wearð.
Nǣniʒ efenlīc þām, ǣr ne siþþan,
40 in worlde ʒewearð wīfes ʒearnunʒ;
þæt dēʒol wæs, Dryhtnes ʒerȳne.
Eal ʒiofu ʒǣstlīc ʒrundscēat ʒeondsprēot;
þǣr wīsna fela wearð inlīhted,
lāre lonʒsume, þurh līfes Fruman,
45 þe ǣr under hoðman biholen lǣʒon,
wītʒena wōðsonʒ, þā se Waldend cwōm,
sē þe reorda ʒehwæs ryne ʒemiclað
ðāra þe ʒeneahhe noman Scyppendes
þurh horscne hād herʒan willað.

. . . . . .

[O rex pacifice, tu ante saecula nate: per auream
agredere portam, redemptos tuos visita, et eos
illuc revoca unde ruerunt per culpam.]

Ēala þū sōða ond þū sibsuma,
215 ealra cyninʒa Cyninʒ Crist ælmihtiʒ,
hū þū ǣr wǣre eallum ʒeworden
worulde þrymmum mid þīnne Wuldorfæder
cild ācenned þurh his cræft ond meaht!
Nis ǣniʒ nū eorl under lyfte,
220 secʒ searoþoncol, tō þæs swīðe ʒlēaw
þe þæt āsecʒan mæʒe sundbūendum,
āreccan mid ryhte, hū þē rodera Weard
æt frymðe ʒenōm him tō Frēobearne.
Þæt wæs þāra þinʒa þe hēr þēoda cynn
225 ʒefruʒnen mid folcum, æt fruman ǣrest
ʒeworden under wolcnum, þæt wītiʒ ʒod,
līfes Ordfruma, lēoht and þȳstro
ʒedǣlde dryhtlīce, ond him wæs dōmes ʒeweald,

ġe·weald n power, rule. wīse f commandment. ā-bēodan 2 announce.
weorod n host. ealdor m lord. ā av ever. tō wīdan fēore 'for ever.'
lēoht cf 227. līxan W1 shine, gleam. ġe·fēa m joy, gladness. lifġan W3
live. cnēoris f generation, tribe. cennan W1 bear, bring forth.
sōna av soon, straightway. ġe·limpan 3 happen, come to pass. lēoma m
brightness. lēohtian W2 shine, give light. lēode f people. mæġð f nation.
torht aj bright, radiant. tungol n/m star. tīd f time, season. bī-gong m
'lapse.' settan W1 establish, ordain.
efen-eardiġende pres ptc co-dwelling. ēngan = āngan 'sole.' frēa m lord.
ōht = āwiht n anything.
snyttru f wisdom, understanding. sīd aj broad, spacious. ġe·sceaft f
creation. wealdend m ruler, lord. wyrċan W1 make, create.
horsc aj wise, enlightened. hyġe-cræftiġ aj wise.
from-cyn n origin, parentage. fīras m pl men. bearn n child, son.
sweotule av plainly, clearly. ġe·sēþan W1 show, declare. sigor m victory.
meotod m creator, lord. milts f mercy, compassion.
ār-fæst aj merciful, gracious. ȳwan W1 show, reveal, nēod f desire, zeal.
mēdren-cynn n maternal descent. cunnan pret pres know, comprehend.
ryht-ġe·rȳne n mystery. ā-reccan W1 explain, expound.
fædren-cynn n paternal descent. feor av far (comp). ō-wihte av at all.
middan-ġeard m earth, world. milde av graciously. ġe·blissian W2 bless.
hēr-cyme m advent. hǣlend m saviour.
gylden aj golden. ġeat n gate. ġēar-dagas mpl former days.
bi-lūcan 2 lock, shut in.
hēah-frēa m supreme lord. hātan 7 bid, command. on-tȳnan W1 open.
ġe·sēċan W1 seek (out), visit. gong m coming, motion.
ēað-mōd aj humble. ār f mercy, grace (gen pl). þearf n need.
ā-wyrġed pass ptc accursed. wulf m wolf. tō-stenċan W1 scatter, disperse.
dēor n beast. dǣd-scūa (?) deeds-in-darkness. ēowde n flock.
wīde av widely. tō-wrecan 5 scatter, disperse. wealdend cf 240.
blōd n blood. ġe·bycgan W1 purchase, redeem. bealo-ful aj wicked.
hȳnan W1 oppress. heardlīċe av cruelly, sorely. hæft m bondage. niman 4
take. nīod = nēod cf 245. lust m desire, longing. nerġend m protector.
biddan 5 entreat, pray. ġeorn-līċe av earnestly. brēost-ġe·hygd f/n thought
of the heart. hræd-līċe av speedily. ġe·fremman W1 do, confer. wēriġ aj
weary, wretched. wrecca m exile, outcast. wīte n torment. bona m slayer.
hell f hell. grund m bottom, abyss. hēan aj abject. ġe·drēosan 3 fall.
hond-ġe·weorc n handiwork. hæleð m hero, man. scyppend m creator.

ond þā wīsan ābēad   weoroda Ealdor:
230 'Nū sīe ʒeworden forþ   ā tō wīdan fēore
leoht, līxende ʒefēa,   lifʒendra ʒehwām
þe is cnēorissum   cende weorðen.'
Ond þā sōna ʒelomp,   þā hit swā sceolde,
lēoma lēohtade   lēoda mæʒþum,
235 torht mid tunʒlum,   æfter þon tīda bīʒonʒ;
sylfa sette   þæt þū Sunu wǣre
efeneardiʒende   mid þīnne ēnʒan Frēan
ǣrþon ōht þisses   ǣfre ʒewurde.
Þū eart sēo Snyttro   þe þās sīdan ʒesceaft
240 mid þī Waldende   worhtes ealle.
Forþon nis ǣniʒ þæs horsc,   nē þæs hyʒecræftiʒ,
þe þīn fromcyn mæʒe   fīra bearnum
sweotule ʒesēþan.   Cum nū, siʒores Weard,
Meotud moncynnes,   one þīne miltse hēr
245 ārfæst ȳwe!   Ūs is eallum nēod
þæt wē mēdrencynn   mōtan cunnan,
ryhtʒerȳno,   nū wē āreccan ne mæʒon
þæt fædrencynn   fier ōwihte.
Þū þisne middanʒeard   milde ʒeblissa
250 þurh ðīnne hērcyme,   hǣlende Crist,
ond þā ʒyldnan ʒeatu,   þe in ʒēardaʒum
ful lonʒe ǣr   bilocen stōdon,
heofona Hēahfrēa,   hāt ontȳnan,
ond ūsic þonne ʒesēce   þurh þīn sylfes ʒonʒ
255 ēaðmōd tō eorþan.   Ūs is þīnra ārna þearf!
Hafað se ārwyrʒda   wulf tōstenced,
dēor dǣdscūa,   Dryhten, þīn ēowde,
wīde tōwrecene.   Þæt ðū, Waldend, ǣr
blōde ʒebohtes,   þæt se bealofulla
260 hȳneð heardlīce,   ond him on hæft nimeð
ofer ūsse nīoda lust.   Forþon wē, Nerʒend, þē
biddað ʒeornlīce   brēostʒehyʒdum
þæt þū hrædlīce   helpe ʒefremme
wērʒum wreccan,   þæt se wītes bona
265 in helle ʒrund   hēan ʒedrēose;
ond þīn hondʒeweorc,   hǣleþa Scyppend,

ā-rīsan 1 arise. **on rihte** rightly. **cuman** 4 come.

ūp-cund aj heavenly, celestial. **æðele** aj noble, excellent. **rīċe** n kingdom.

syn-lust m sinful desire (?). **sweart** aj dark, black. **gǣst** m spirit.

for-tēon 2 lead astray. **for-tyldan** (?) 'lead astray' (?). **tīr** m glory.

won aj void of. **ermþu** = **yrmþu** f misery, suffering. **drēogan** 2 endure, undergo. **ofost-līċe** av quickly, speedily.

lēod-sceaða m enemy (of men).

helm m protector. **al-wiht** n pl all creatures. **hreddan** W1 deliver, save.

mōte ārīsan, ond on ryht cuman
tō þām ūpcundan   æþelan rīce,
þonan ūs ær þurh synlust   se swearta ӡǣst
270 fortēah ond fortylde,   þæt wē, tīres wone,
ā būtan ende   sculon ermþu drēoӡan,
būtan þū ūsic þon ofostlīcor,   ēce Drhyten,
æt þām lēodsceaþan,   lifӡende Ӡod,
Helm alwihta,   hreddan wille.

EXCERPT FROM *JUDITH*

[A metrical version of the story of Judith survives in part in a few leaves of the
Nowell Codex (BL. MS Cotton Vitellius A. xv), copied by the same hand that
transcribed the latter part of the unique text of *Beowulf*. About one-fourth of
the extant text (or one-twelfth of the estimated length of the original text) is
re-presented here—the whole of the section numbered X in the manuscript and
three lines of section XI. (The notion that sectional divisions of Anglo-Saxon
verse texts are there primarily to signify—or register—'turns' of narrative does
not stand to reason, as this excerpt illustrates.) The source of this vernacular
version of the story is a Vulgate (Latin) text of *Judith*, an apocryphal book of
the Christian bible. The meter of 'expanded lines' is not unusual, although in
this text the frequency and grouping of lines of this kind is unusual.]

X

15 Hīe ðā tō ðām symle   sittan ēodon,
    wlance tō wīnʒedrince,   ealle his wēaʒesīðas,
    bealde byrnwiʒʒende.   Þær wæron bollan stēape
    boren æfter bencum ʒelōme,
        swylce ēac būnan ond orcas
    fulle fletsittendum;   hīe þæt fæʒe þēʒon,
20 rōfe rondwiʒʒende,   þēah ðæs se rīca ne wēnde,
    eʒesful eorla dryhten.   Dā wearð Holofernus,
    ʒoldwine ʒumena,   on ʒytesālum:
    hlōh ond hlydde,   hlynede ond dynede,
    þæt mihten fīra bearn   feorran ʒehȳran,
25 hū se stīðmōda   styrmde ond ʒylede,
    mōdiʒ ond meduʒāl,   manode ʒenēahhe
    bencsittende   þæt hī ʒebærdon wel.
    Swā se inwidda   ofer ealne dæʒ
    dryhtʒuman sīne   drencte mid wīne,
30 swīðmōd sinces brytta,
        oðþæt hīe on swīman laʒon,
    oferdrencte his duʒuðe ealle,
        swylce hīe wæron dēaðe ʒesleʒene,
    āʒotene ʒōda ʒehwylces.

Swā hēt se ʒumena aldor
fylʒan fletsittendum,   oð þæt fīra bearnum
nēalǣhte niht sēo þȳstre.
     Hēt ðā nīða ʒeblonden
35 þā ēadiʒan mæʒð   ofstum fetiʒan
tō his bedreste,   bēaʒum ʒehlæste,
hrinʒum ʒehrodene.   Hīe hraðe fremedon,
anbyhtscealcas,   swā him heora ealdor bebēad,
byrnwiʒena breʒo: bearhtme stōpon
40 tō ðām ʒysterne,   þǣr hīe Iudithðe
fundon ferhðʒlēawe,   ond ðā fromlīce
lindwiʒʒende   lǣdan onʒunnon
þā torhtan mæʒð   tō træfe þām hēan,
þǣr se rīca hyne   reste on symbel,
45 nihtes inne,   nerʒende lāð,
Holofernus.   Þǣr wæs eallʒylden
flēohnet fæʒer   .. ymbe þæs folctoʒan
bed āhonʒen,   þæt se bealofulla
mihte wlītan þurh,   wiʒena baldor,
50 on æʒhwylcne   þe ðǣr inne cōm
hæleða bearna,   ond on hyne nǣniʒ
monna cynnes,   nymðe se mōdiʒa hwæne
nīðe rōfra   him þē nēar hēte
rinca tō rūne ʒeʒanʒan.
     Hīe ðā on reste ʒebrōhton
55 snūde ðā snoteran idese.
     Ēodon ðā stercedferhðe,
hæleð heora hearran cȳðan
     þæt wæs sēo hāliʒe mēowle
ʒebrōht on his burʒetelde.
     Þā wearð se brēma on mōde
blīðe, burʒa ealdor,
     þōhte ðā beorhtan idese
mid wīdle ond mid womme besmītan.
     Ne wolde þæt wuldres dēma
60 ʒeðafian, þrymmes hyrde,
     ac hē him þæs ðinʒes ʒestyrde,
dryhten, duʒeða waldend.

ʒewāt ðā se dēofulcunda,
ʒālferhð ʒumena ðrēate,
       [. . . .]
bealofull his beddes nēosan,
    þær hē sceolde his blǣd forlēosan
ǣdre binnan ānre nihte;
    hæfde ðā his ende ʒebidenne
65 on eorðan unswǣslīcne,
    swylcne hē ǣr æfter worhte,
þearlmōd ðēoden ʒumena,
    þenden hē on ðysse worulde
wunode under wolcna hrōfe.
    ʒefēol ðā wīne swā druncen
se rīca on his reste middan,
    swā hē nyste rǣda nānne
on ʒewitlocan. Wiʒʒend stōpon
70 ūt of ðām inne ofstum miclum,
weras wīnsade, þe ðone wǣrloʒan,
lāðne lēodhatan, lǣddon tō bedde
nēhstan sīðe. Þā wæs nerʒendes
    þēowen þrymful, þearle ʒemyndiʒ,
75 hū hēo þone atolan ēaðost mihte
ealdre benǣman ǣr se unsȳfra,
womfull, onwōce. ʒenam ðā wundenlocc
scyppendes mæʒð, scearpne mēce,
scūrum heardne, ond of scēaðe ābrǣd
80 swīðran folme. Onʒan ðā sweʒles weard
be naman nemnan, nerʒend ealra
woruldbūendra, ond þæt word ācwæð:
'Ic ðē, frymða ʒod ond frōfre ʒǣst,
bearn alwaldan, biddan wylle
85 miltse þīnre mē þearfendre,
    ðrȳnesse ðrym. Þearle ys mē nū ðā
heorte .. onhǣted ond hiʒe ʒeōmor,
swȳðe mid sorʒum ʒedrēfed.
    Forʒif mē, sweʒles ealdor,
siʒor ond sōðne ʒelēafan,
       þæt ic mid þys sweorde mōte

90 ʒehēawan þysne morðres bryttan.
    Ʒeunne mē mīnra ʒesynta,
þearlmōd þēoden ʒumena:
    Nāhte ic þīnre næfre
miltse þon māran þearfe.
    Ʒewrec nū, mihtiʒ dryhten,
torhtmōd tīres brytta,
    þæt mē ys torne on mōde,
hāte on hreðre mīnum.'
    Hī ðā se hēhsta dēma
95 ædre mid elne onbryrde,
    swā hē dēð ānra ʒehwylcne
hērbūendra   þe hyne him tō helpe sēceð,
mid rǣde ond mid rihte ʒelēafan.
    Þā wearð hyre rūme on mōde,
hāliʒre hyht ʒenīwod.
    Ʒenam ðā þone hǣðenan mannan
fæste be feaxe sīnum,
    tēah hyne folmum wið hyre weard
100 bysmerlīce,   ond þone bealofullan
listum ālēde, lāðne mannan,
swā hēo ðæs unlǣdan   ēaðost mihte
wel ʒewealdan.   Slōh ðā wundenlocc
þone fēondsceaðan   fāʒum mēce,
105 heteþoncolne,   þæt hēo healfne forcearf
þone swēoran him,   þæt hē on swīman læʒ,
druncen ond dolhwund.   Næs ðā dēad þā ʒȳt,
ealles orsāwle;   slōh ðā eornoste
ides ellenrōf   ōðre sīðe
110 þone hǣðenan hund,   þæt him þæt hēafod wand
forð on ðā flōre.   Læʒ se fūla lēap
ʒesne beæftan,   ʒǣst ellor hwearf
under neowelne næs   ond ðǣr ʒenyðerad wæs,
sūsle ʒesǣled   syððan æfre,
115 wyrmum bewunden,   wītum ʒebunden,
hearde ʒehǣfted   in hellebryne
æfter hinsīðe.   Ne ðearf hē hopian nō,
þȳstrum forðylmed,   þæt hē ðonan mōte

of ðām wyrmsele,   ac ðǣr wunian sceal
120 āwā tō aldre   būtan ende forð
in ðām heolstran hām,   hyhtwynna lēas.

XI

Hæfde ðā ȝefohten   foremǣrne blǣd
Iudith æt ȝūðe,   swā hyre ȝod ūðe,
sweȝles ealdor,   þe hyre siȝores onlēah.

'THE WANDERER'

['The Wanderer,' generally looked upon as the best short poem in Old English, is preserved in the Exeter Book (see Excerpts from *Christ I*). The most exhaustive edition is *The Wanderer*, ed. T. P. Dunning and A. J. Bliss (London, 1969). The text printed below may be the least-edited re-presentation of this poem. The main elements of the editing are these. The text is printed with separate lines for the metrical units ('lines') and wide space between halves of lines; line-numbering is then added. The spacing between strings of letters has been regularized—i.e., there is a blank space or there is not a blank space between words within half-lines, regardless of how much space (including no space) was left in the Exeter Book text: it is not practical to try to represent the varied spacing, especially when using modern letter shapes, even though it does seem to represent some important prosodic information recorded in the manuscript. Hyphens are added within words where the manuscript leaves space between strings of letters. Vowel length is marked. Variations in letter shapes (notably for **s** and **y**) are normalized. Minimal emendations for grammar are made in conventional ways. A very few additions are made to the pointing (the 'punctuation') of the text.

On the other hand, the punctuation is very close to that of the Exeter Book copy: it consists of points (at midline height in the MS) and majuscule or enlarged letters. There is no need for opening quotation marks to follow **Sē . . . geþōhte ... and þās word acwið** (88–91) (even though closing quotations marks would be a convenience). There is no need for the commas in modern editions when there is variation such as **āre ... metudes miltse** (1–2) or a following **þeah**-clause (2) or a concluding conditional clause such as **hycge swā hē wille** (14) or a coordination such as **cysse ond on cnēo lecge . . .** (42–3). Interrogative sentence structure is clear in a sentence beginning **hwǣr cwōm . . .** and doesn't need a question mark at its end. Not even the customary full stops ('periods') are always needed, as between the two clauses of lines 49–51, or in the middle of line 80. The pointing of the MS text is essentially a mark of separation, as lines 91–4 plainly illustrate. In many places where modern editors place a full stop—whether before a **swā**-clause (62) or before an unmarked independent clause (5)—there is no pointing in the Anglo-Saxon text.

Also, there is no glossing provided for this text, for two reasons. One is that this text has been provided with many glossaries elsewhere, some of them over-meticulous, supererogate, uncharitable, and sometimes inimical to good pedagogy and good literary interpretation. If an editor glosses a word with meaning X in one line and with meaning Y in another, insisting that the different glossing parallels the poet's intention, then one must ask how the poet, having but one word, nonetheless could signal with the same word different semantic cores in the different contexts: the contexts differ—which is a way to select from the semantic range of a word—but the word remains the same. So a modern reader of an Old English poem—to give the second reason for omitting glossing here—may be better off trying (once again) to read the poem in Old English, including reading the same word in two contexts rather than replacing it with differing glosses in two (or more) places in the text. Best returns on the effort will come from study of the MS facsimile together with the textual notes and commentary in Bernard J. Muir, *The Exeter Anthology of Old English Poetry*, 2nd ed., revised (Exeter 2000).

This long preamble to a short text is a final way of saying what has been the goal of this firstbook of Old English.]

OFT him ānhaʒa   āre ʒebīdeð
metudes miltse   þēah þe hē mōd-ceariʒ
ʒeond laʒu-lāde   lonʒe sceolde
hrēran mid hondum   hrīm-cealde sæ
5 wadan wræc-lāstas   wyrd bið ful arǣd ·
Swā cwæð eard-stapa   earfeþa ʒemyndiʒ
wrāþra wæl-sleahta   wine-mǣʒa hryre ·
Oft ic sceolde āna   ūhtna ʒehwylce
mīne ceare cwiþan · nis nū cwic-ra nán
10 þe ic him mōd-sefan   mīnne durre
sweotule asecʒan · ic tō sōþe wāt
þæt biþ in eorle   indryhten þēaw
þæt hē his ferð-locan   fæste binde
healde his hord-cofan   hycʒe swā hē wille ·
15 Ne mæʒ wēriʒ mōd   wyrde wið-stondan
ne se hrēo hyʒe   helpe ʒefremman ·
Forðon dōm-ʒeorne   drēoriʒne oft
in hyra brēost-cofan   bindað fæste ·
swā ic mōd-sefan   mīnne sceolde ·
20 oft earm-ceariʒ   ēðle bidǣled

freo-mæʒum feor   feterum sælan
siþþan ʒeara iū   ʒold-wine mī[n]ne
hrūsan heolstre biwrāh   ond ic hēan þonan
wōd winter-ceariʒ   ofer waþema ʒe-bind ·
25 sōhte sele-drēoriʒ   sinces bryttan
hwær ic feor oþþe nēah   findan meahte
þone þe in meodu-healle   [mīn] mine wisse
oþþe mec frēond-lēas[n]e   frēfran wolde
wēman mid wynnum ·   wāt sē þe cunnað
30 hū slīþen bið   sorʒ tō ʒefē-ran
þām þe him lȳt hafað   lēofra ʒeholena
Warað hine wræc-lāst   nales wunden ʒold
ferð-loca frēoriʒ   nalæs foldan blǣd ·
ʒemon hē sele-secʒas   ond sinc-þeʒe
35 hū hine on ʒeoʒuðe   his ʒold-wine
wenede tō wiste   wyn eal ʒedrēas ·
forþon wāt sē þe sceal   his wine-dryhtnes
lēofes lār-cwi-dum   lonʒe forþolian ·
Ðonne sorʒ ond slǣp   somod æt-ʒæ-dre
40 earmne ān-hoʒan   oft ʒebindað ·
þinceð him on mōde   þæt hē his mon-dryhten
clyppe ond cysse   ond on cnēo lecʒe
honda ond hēafod   swā hē hwīlum ær
in ʒeārdaʒum   ʒief-stōlas brēac ·
45 Ðonne on-wæcneð eft   wine-lēas ʒuma
ʒesihð him bi-foran   fealwe wēʒas
baþian brim-fuʒlas   brǣdan feþra
hrēosan hrīm ond snāw   haʒle ʒemenʒed ·
þonne bēoð þȳ hefiʒran   heortan benne
50 sāre æfter swǣsne ·   sorʒ bið ʒe-nīwad
þonne māʒa ʒemynd   mōd ʒeond-hweor-feð;
ʒrēteð ʒlīw-stafum   ʒeorne ʒeond-scēawað
secʒa ʒe-seldan [·]   swimmað eft on weʒ
flēo-tendra ferð   nō þær fela brinʒeð
55 cūðra cwide-ʒiedda [·]   cearo bið ʒe-nīwad
þām þe sendan sceal   swīþe ʒeneahhe
ofer waþe-ma ʒebind   wēriʒne sefan ·
For-þon ic ʒe-þencan ne mæʒ   ʒeond þās woruld

for hwan mōd-sefa   mīn ne ʒesweor-ce
60 þonne ic eorla līf   eal ʒeond-þence
hū hī fǣr-līce   flet ofʒēafon
mōdʒe maʒu-þeʒnas   swā þes middan-ʒeard
ealra dōʒra ʒehwām   drēoseð ond fealleþ ·
forþon ne mæʒ weorþan wīs   wer ǣr he āʒe
65 wintra dǣl in woruld-rīce   wita sceal ʒe-þyldiʒ ·
Ne sceal nō tō hāt-heort   ne tō hrædwyrde ·
ne tō wāc wiʒa   ne tō wanhȳdiʒ ·
ne tō forht · ne tō fæʒen · ne tō feoh-ʒīfre ·
ne nǣfre ʒielpes tō ʒeorn   ǣr hē ʒeare cun-ne ·
70 beorn sceal ʒebīdan   þonne hē bēot spriceð
oþþæt collen-ferð   cunne ʒearwe
hwider hreþra ʒehyʒd   hweor-fan wille ·
Onʒietan sceal ʒlēaw hæle   hū ʒæstlīc bið ·
þonne ealre þisse worulde wela   wēste stondeð ·
75 swā nū missenlīce   ʒeond þisne middan-ʒeard
winde biwāune   weallas ston-daþ
hrīme bihrorene   hrȳðʒe þā ederas
w-ōriað þā wīn-salo   waldend licʒað
drēame bidrorene   duʒuþ eal ʒe-cronʒ
80 wlonc bi wealle   sume wīʒ fornom
ferede in forð-weʒe   sum-ne fuʒel oþbær
ofer hēanne holm   sumne se hāra wulf
dēaðe ʒedǣlde   sumne drēoriʒ-hlēor
in eorð-scræfe   eorl ʒehȳdde
85 ȳþde swā þisne eard-ʒeard   ælda scyppend
oþþæt burʒ-wara   breahtma lēase
eald enta ʒeweorc   īdlu stōdon ·
Sē þonne þisne weal-steal   wīse ʒeþōhte
ond þis deorce līf   dēope ʒeond-þenceð
90 frōd in ferðe   feor oft ʒemon
wæl-sleahta worn   ond þās word acwið ·
hwǣr cwōm mearʒ · hwǣr cwōm maʒo ·
     hwǣr cwōm māþþum-ʒyfa ·
hwǣr cwōm symbla ʒesetu · hwǣr sin-don sele-drēamas ·
ēalā beorht bune · ēalā byrn-wiʒa ·
95 ēalā þēodnes þrym   hū sēo þrāʒ ʒewāt

ʒenāp under niht-helm   swā hēo nō wære ·
Stondeð nū on lāste   lēofre duʒuþe
weal wundrum hēah   wyrmlīcum fāh ·
eorlas fornōman   asca þrȳ-þe
100 wæpen wæl-ʒīfru   wyrd sēo mære
ond þās stān-hleoþu   stor-mas cnyssað
hrīð hrēosende   hrūsan bindeð
wintres wōma   þonne won cymeð
nīpeð niht-scua   norþan onsendeð
105 hrēo hæʒl-fare   hæleþum on andan ·
eall is earfoðlīc   eorþan rīce
onwendeð wyrda ʒe-sceaft   weoruld under heofonum ·
hēr bið feoh læne · hēr bið frēond læne ·
hēr bið mon læne · hēr bið mæʒ læne
110 eal þis eorþan ʒesteal   īdel weorþeð ·
Swā cwæð snottor on mōde
    ʒesæt him sundor æt rūne [·]
til biþ sē þe his trēowe ʒehealdeþ
    ne sceal næfre his torn tō rycene
beorn of his brēostum acȳþan
    nem-þe hē ær þā bōte cunne
eorl mid elne ʒefremman [·]
    wēl bið þām þe him āre sēceð
115 frōfre tō fæder on heofonum
    þær ūs eal sēo fæstnunʒ stondeð:-:₇

INDEX OF TERMS AND TOPICS

The purpose of this index is to help with basic look-up of terms that need to be understood as an aid to learning Old English. Not every mention of every item is indexed, 'case' being the most conspicuous example.